Naturalizations of Foreign Protestants

IN THE

American and West Indian Colonies

(Pursuant to Statute 13 George II, c. 7).

I0146195

EDITED BY

M. S. GIUSEPPI, F.S.A.,

ASSISTANT SECRETARY OF THE HUGUENOT SOCIETY OF LONDON.

Southern Historical Press, Inc.
Greenville, South Carolina

This volume was reproduced
from a personal copy located in
the Publishers private library

Please direct all correspondence and book orders to:
SOUTHERN HISTORICAL PRESS, Inc.
PO Box 1267
Greenville, SC   29602-1267

Originally printed: London, England 1921
ISBN #978-1-63914-114-2
Printed in the United States of America

Introduction.

THE present volume contains all the returns sent from the Colonies to the Lords Commissioners for Trade and Plantations in pursuance of the Act 13 George II, c. 7 (' An Act for Naturalizing such foreign Protestants and others therein mentioned, as are settled, or shall settle, in any of his Majesty's Colonies in America '), which have been found amongst the records of those Commissioners now classified with the records of the Colonial Office preserved at the Public Record Office.

The general principles of the law regulating naturalizations in the English Plantations and Colonies have already been explained by Dr. Shaw in the Introduction he wrote to *Letters of Denization and Acts of Naturalization of Aliens in England and Ireland, 1603—1700*, issued by this Society in 1911.* Therein the provisions of this Act of 13 Geo. II are set out and its special importance in the history of our Colonial Naturalization law is emphasised. Briefly, it may be said that the effect of the Act was the same as that designed by the short-lived Act of 7 Anne, c. 5 for England, namely, to provide a simpler mechanism for naturalizing the great numbers of religious refugees than was already provided by cumbrous and doubtless expensive private Acts of the various Colonial Assemblies, by giving those qualified by a seven years residence in any colony, with a few limitations, the rights of natural-born subjects of Great Britain upon their taking the prescribed oaths before the Chief Judge or other Judge of the colony wherein they had resided. Special provision was made for an Affirmation in place of the oaths to be made by Quakers, and both Quakers and Jews were exempted from the obligation of receiving the Sacrament of the Lord's Supper within three months of their taking the oaths or making affirmation. For every naturalization under this Act a payment of two shillings and no more was to be made.

In the present introduction no attempt will be made to set out the history of the various immigrations of religious refugees into the American colonies. The best part of the material for that history necessarily does not exist in this country. All that can be attempted here is to explain the machinery of the Act 13 Geo. II so far as is necessary for an understanding of the returns made under it which are here printed; to draw such general deductions as are permissible from these returns as to the alien settlements in America; and to point out any reasons there may be against their acceptance as a complete record of those settlements for the period they cover.

Firstly, therefore, very clear and full directions for the registration of every naturalization under the Act both in the Colony and in England were contained in its provisions. The

* Huguenot Soc. Publ., XVIII, pp. xxvii—xxxii.

Judge before whom the oaths or affirmation were taken was to make a due and proper entry thereof in a book to be kept for the purpose under a penalty of ten pounds for every omission. Similarly every Secretary of a Colony, wherein the naturalization took place, was to enter the same in a special book upon notification from the Judge under the like penalty. Further, he was required under a penalty of £50 to transmit to the Office of the Commissioners for Trade and Plantations in London or Westminster at the end of every year, to be computed from 1 June 1740, a true and perfect list of the names of all in his Colony who had entitled themselves to the benefit of the Act in that year. The lists so transmitted were to be regularly entered by the said Commissioners in a book or books to be kept for that purpose in their Office fo public view and inspection.

It is, as already stated, the records of the naturalizations under the Act formerly preserved at the Board of Trade which form the matter of the present volume. Two of the entry books prescribed in the last direction are now in existence.* In all probability no more were ever kept, for the second is obviously unfinished. These books were transcribed by the late Mrs. Shaw with the intention, as stated in the Introduction already referred to, of being included in the volume of Denizations and Naturalizations for the period between 1701 and 1800 upon which her husband is at present engaged for the Society. It happened, however, that when the proof sheets of his transcript were ready for correction, Dr. Shaw owing to the pressure of other work occasioned by the War, was unable to attend sufficiently at the Public Record Office to examine them with the original entry books. The present editor therefore undertook this task, but on going into the matter with Dr. Shaw found not only that the original returns by the Colonial Secretaries from which the entry books were compiled were in existence but that they extended in the case of some colonies to later years than appear to have been entered in the books. These later lists would have so extended Dr. Shaw's volume that on his suggestion and with the approval of the Council it was decided to print them in a separate volume.

For a fuller understanding of the contents of the following pages and the steps here taken to render the record as complete as possible a brief explanation is necessary of the archive system of the Commissioners of Trade and Plantations, who until the year 1782 represented jointly with the Secretary of State the central administrative authority over the Colonies. Their records divide themselves into the three broad classes usual to all administrative bodies, namely (a) original correspondence including all letters, reports, papers, etc., sent in to the Board; (b) entry books and registers including copies of letters sent out by the Board, minutes of its proceedings, copies or entries of returns such as those in the present volume and registers of papers received and the like; and (c) miscellanea including papers of personal interest, accounts, drafts, etc.

Almost from their first appointment in 1695 the Commissioners were methodical in the filing of the letters and reports they received. These were sorted under the several colonies or provinces, save that in the case of those provinces which had been granted by the Crown to proprietors, e.g. Pennsylvania Maryland, the New Jerseys, the papers were bundled together under the general title: 'Proprieties.' Under each colony the bundles, arranged in chronological order and long since bound up as volumes, were distinguished by

* C.O. 324, Nos. 55, 56.

a letter of the alphabet and the papers in them by this letter and a consecutive number. Reference to these papers was made from the registers of them which are still preserved. Shortly afterwards references to the entry books of the out-letters were added in these registers, and finally to the Journals or Minute Books of the Board. By means of the general catalogue of the records now preserved at the Public Record Office and classified as belonging to the Colonial Office * the references in these registers can almost invariably be readily identified.

It will be seen that in the lists which have been printed here from the two entry books already described the writer was careful to give the bundle letter and the number of the original which he copied. In all cases those originals have been found and examined with the copy as entered in the books. Variations from the copy in these originals and all particulars in them which were not copied out are shown in parentheses. As these originals are the actual lists sent over by the secretaries in the various colonies they represent a stage in the process nearer to the first entry in the colonial court and are consequently of greater authority than the entry books.

As to the lists which were not copied into these books the registers of correspondence have been carefully gone through to the year 1782 when the Board ceased to exist and every reference in them to a list of naturalizations under the Act of George II has been looked up and the list copied and printed, so that, as far as the Board's papers are concerned, it is hoped that the present volume contains a complete record of all naturalizations under the Act.

We have next to consider the evidence of the lists as to the alien settlements in the American colonies during the eighteenth century. In the first place, it will be noted that not even in each colony were the returns made out uniformly. The Act required nothing more than a list of the names to be sent to the Commissioners in London, although entry had to be made in the Court where the naturalization took place and in the Office of the Secretary of the particular colony of the certificate, and the names of the two credible witnesses to it, of the administration of the Sacrament within three months before the taking of the oaths, which was necessary in the case of all persons save Quakers and Jews naturalized in pursuance of the Act. Only in the case of New York did the Colonial Secretary think fit occasionally to include the names of these witnesses in his returns to the Board of Trade (pp. 31—33 below).

Usually indeed the New York lists far exceed those from the other colonies in the detailed particulars furnished. Not only did the Secretary give the place of residence of the alien but also sometimes his exact religious denomination and his occupation. From no other colony was the latter information supplied.+ The colonial residence is given generally, though not invariably, in the Pennsylvania lists. Only in the few returns from Virginia is the valuable information of the alien's country of origin given.

In the matter of religious denominations it is generally only possible from these lists to make a distinction between Protestants (other than Quakers and Moravians), Quakers, Moravians and Jews. Quakers under the Act of 1740 were the only persons specifically exempted from taking the oaths, and it was doubtless because it was found that the Act did

---

* P.R.O. Lists and Indexes. No. XXXVI (1911).

+ For the trades, etc., represented see the Index of Subjects.

not cover the case of the Moravians, who had the like conscientious scruples as to the taking of an oath, that the later Act of 20 George II c. 44 (1747) was passed extending the benefits of the original Act to all foreign Protestants who had such scruples. Moravians first appear in the Pennsylvania lists in 1750, and although subsequently they are classed with the Quakers as affirmers they can as a rule be readily distinguished from them by the fact that they were not similarly exempted from taking the Sacrament, the date of taking which is, with the exception of the period between 1756 and 1760, inserted in the lists from this colony.

The numbers of the aliens in the several colonies naturalized under the Act of 1740 and their religious denominations so far as they can be deduced from the lists are set out in the following table :—

	Jamaica, 1740—1750.	Maryland, 1743—1753.	Massachusetts, 1743.	New York, 1740—1770.	Pennsylvania, 1740—1772.	South Carolina, 1741—1748.	Virginia, 1743—1746.	Total.
Protestants (not denominated) ...	9	127	I	43	4247	23	23	4473
Dutch Reformed	—	—	—	46	—	—	—	46
Church of England	—	—	—	13	—	—	—	13
French	—	—	—	27	—	—	—	27
German Reformed Church	—	—	—	19	—	—	—	19
German Evangelical Church ...	—	—	—	1	—	—	—	1
Lutherans	—	—	—	134	—	—	—	134
Moravians	—	—	—	—	75	—	—	75
Quakers, etc.	—	—	—	1	2074	—	—	2075
Unitas Fratrum	—	—	—	5	—	—	—	5
Jews	152	—	—	35	16	I	—	204
Total	161	127	I	324	6412	24	23	7072

From the above table it will be seen that from the provinces of New York and Pennsylvania only were any returns of naturalizations under the Act received by the Board up to within a few years of the outbreak of the revolt. Moreover, not far short of eight-ninths of the total number we have belong to a single colony, Pennsylvania. An examination of the lists from this colony reveals the further fact that considerably more than a third of the total of 6,412 naturalizations, 2,658 to be exact, were effected at the sessions of the Supreme Court held between 24 September and 26 October 1765. No explanation of this fact can at present be offered. After 1765 the Pennsylvania naturalizations dwindle rapidly, and number 247 only for the seven years 1766 to 1772.

Both in New York and Pennsylvania, however, aliens resident in other provinces were occasionally naturalized. In 1753 one member of the Dutch Reformed Church living in New Jersey and in 1763 a Jew living in Rhode Island were naturalized in the New York

Court. In Pennsylvania the number of residents of other provinces naturalized between 1760 and 1772 and included in the above total of 6412 is as follows :—

	Protestants.	Quakers.
Maryland	8	29
New Jersey	11	16
North Carolina	1	—
Virginia	1	1

Although the nationality of the aliens in Pennsylvania is not stated it is sufficiently obvious from their names that they were very largely Germans. This is further borne out by the German town names they appear to have given to some of their settlements. Germantown, adjoining Philadelphia, was no doubt mainly populated by them, and in addition we have such place names as Franconia, Frankfort, Weisenberg, two Hanovers, two Strasburgs, two Manheims and apparently no less than five Heidlebergs. The large immigrations of Germans into the colony during the eighteenth century were evidently exercising the mind of the provincial legislative, for in January 1749–50 an Act was passed ' for prohibiting the Importation of Germans and other Passengers in too great numbers in any one Vessel.'* This was evidently dictated by reasons of health for the Act speaks of the mortality and disease that had been already caused by the overcrowding of vessels and prescribes a certain cubic space to be allowed to each passenger in every ship bound for the ports of the province. A supplemental Act was passed by the same legislative in 1765 insisting upon the provision of a surgeon and medicine chest in each ship and prescribing means of disinfection.†

In New York where we have generally more precise religious denominations stated the immigrants appear to have been largely Lutherans, but we find a certain number of members of the Dutch Reformed Church and a few of the French Churches. Jews, evidently of German origin, are found both there and in Pennsylvania, but the largest number of members of this race belongs to Jamaica where they appear to have been mainly of Spanish descent. From Jamaica alone of the West Indian islands were any returns of naturalization under the Act received by the Commissioners.

Finally, the question remains how far the returns of naturalization sent from the various colonies to the Board of Trade and Plantations in obedience to the Act of 1740 enable one to judge the probable character and numbers of the alien immigrants in America during the period for which the Act was in force. Here two considerations must be taken into account.

In the first place, from six only of the thirteen American colonies and from one only of the West Indian islands do returns appear ever to have been sent to the Commissioners. Was the Act never put into force in the remaining colonies or islands, or were their secretaries remiss in the performance of the duty it laid upon them to send over every year a complete list of the naturalizations effected in their respective colonies in accordance with its provisions?

* C.O. 5. 1243.   † C.O. 5. 1250 (No. 69).

The complete answer to these questions could only be found in the existence in the archives of the present States of lists of naturalizations under the Act of which no copy is to be found amongst the Board of Trade's own records. Whether this is the case we have not at present the means of knowing. We may be tolerably certain from the fact that, in all cases where the receipt by the Board of such a list is recorded in its register, the actual list is now forthcoming that the lists now extant among the records are all that it ever received. At the same time, although we cannot claim that our search has been exhaustive, we have not succeeded in finding any evidence that in the case of the non-transmission of the yearly list by the secretary in the colony, steps were ever taken by the Board to enforce the penalty imposed by the Act. That a secretary might sometimes allow several years to elapse before sending over his lists we have an instance in the following letter from Pennsylvania, but it does not here appear that the secretary's ultimate compliance with his duty was the result of any representation from the Commissioners in London.

Philadelphia, 27 April, 1763.

Sir,

It was my duty as Secretary of this Province to have transmitted to you at the end of every year the Lists of all Foreigners naturalized under the late Act of Parliament made in their favour, but the various matters which continually occurred in war time occupied my mind so much that I forgot this branch of my duty, and I hope this will be received as a good Apology for my neglect.

Herewith you will receive complete Lists of all Foreigners who have taken the Benefits of the Act for naturalizing foreign Protestants since my last, namely, since the month of September in the year 1753 to September 1761.

I have only to acquaint you that Mr. Joseph Shippon [sic], who is the present Secretary in my place, will very punctually send you the Lists after that time.

I have the Honour to be
Sir,
Your most obedient humble Servant,
RICHARD PETERS.

The Secretary of the Board of Trade.

[Holograph : endorsed :] Proprieties. Letter from Mr. Peters, Secretary of Pennsylvania, to Mr. Pownall, dated 27 April, 1763, inclosing Lists of Persons naturalized from 1753 to 1761. Read July 6, 1763. 10 Papers.*

So far as Mr. Shippen is concerned his lists appear to have been sent over regularly each year, usually in duplicate and occasionally in triplicate.

The second consideration we have to bear in mind in attempting to deduce any estimate of the numbers of the alien population in the various American colonies from these lists is that naturalization under the Act of 1740 did not entirely supersede the earlier mode of naturalization by the Colonial Governors when the terms of their commissions empowered

* C.O. 5. 1276 (X. 40).

them to confer such benefit or more usually by Act of the respective legislative bodies approved by the Governors.

Complete lists of all persons naturalized in the different colonies by Acts of their respective Assemblies, although most useful, would appear to be impossible of attainment from the collections of those Acts which now exist amongst the Colonial Office records. For the earlier years of the eighteenth century the collections are imperfect. ·Sufficient, however, now remains to enable us to draw some general deductions as to the nature of those Acts and to form some idea how far they continued in vogue after the year 1740.

In each colony the form of the Naturalization Act seems to have become stereotyped at an early date, but this form and the benefits conferred by the Acts varied considerably as between colony and colony.

In New York, for instance, naturalization as granted by Act of Assembly was unqualified. The persons named in each Act were declared 'to be naturalized to all intents, constructions and purposes whatsoever, and from henceforth and at all time hereafter shall be intituled to have and enjoy all rights and liberties, privileges and advantages, which his Majesty's natural-born subjects in this Colony have and enjoy, or ought to have and enjoy, as fully to all intents and purposes whatsoever, as if all and every of them had been born in this Colony.' They were only required to take the Oaths appointed by law and subscribe the Test and Abjuration Oath in a court of record in the colony within a twelvemonth of the passing of the Act and to pay certain fees amounting in all to 19s. to the Speaker of the Assembly and the Judge and Clerk of the Court.

Whether because the privileges thus conferred were considered to be superior to those obtainable under the British Act of 1740 or for some other reason, it is clear that for many years after the passing of the latter, there were aliens in the Colony of New York who thought it preferable to pay the additional fees in order to be naturalized by Act of the Colonial Assembly. In 1761 170 were so naturalized under two several Acts, in 1762 78.[*] There were 23 in 1763, 15 in 1764, 12 in 1765, 15 in 1766, 39 in 1768, 31 in 1769, 43 in 1770, 51 in 1771, 19 in 1772 and 94 in 1773 all included in Acts of Assembly.[†]

In Pennsylvania on the other hand, where the 1740 Act was made such full use of, we find, as we might expect, but few instances of naturalization by Acts of the Provincial Assembly. Subsequent to 1740 no private Naturalization Act of this Colony exists in the collection at the Public Record Office until 1763 when six persons were naturalized under one Act.[‡] Thenceforward until 1773, a period for which the collection is apparently complete there are five such Acts only, namely one each in 1765 (three persons),[§] 1766 (four persons),[||] 1771 (one),[**] 1772 (one)[††] and 1773 (six).[‡‡] All these persons are described as Protestants,·and what is of especial value their occupations and places of origin are stated. Nearly all came from German states, thus bearing out the inference to be drawn from our lists, but one, a minister of religion, was a Swede and two were Danes.

The Pennsylvania Naturalization Acts are all in the same form and bear such titles as

---

* C.O. 5. 1168 and 1169.   †C.O. 5. 1167—1179 *passim*. The 31 names in the letter of 1769 (S.s. 79, printed on p. 39) belong to a New York Naturalization Act of that year and have not been included in the totals shown in the above table.   ‡ C.O. 5. 1249 (36).   § C.O. 5. 1250 (65). || C.O. 5. 1251 (85).   ** C.O. 5. 1253 (179).   †† C.O. 5. 1254 (207).   ‡‡ Ibid. (227).

'An Act the better to enable the Persons therein named to hold lands, and to invest them with the privileges of natural-born subjects of this Province.' No exceptions from these privileges are mentioned but the persons named are, after taking the oaths and declarations directed by Acts of Parliament made for securing the King's person and government and for preventing the dangers which may happen by Popish Recusants, declared to be deemed freely and fully able to trade, etc., freight and transport all goods and merchandize not prohibited by law to be imported or exported, as if they had been natural liege people of the King of Great Britain born in the Province; they were also to be able to hold and enjoy all manner of lands, tenements, hereditaments, and real and personal estate acquired by purchase or gift, to sue in all manner of actions and to enjoy all the rights, liberties, etc., belonging to his Majesty's natural subjects born within the Province.

The fact that the Statute of 13 George II did not cover the case of the Moravians was early felt in Pennsylvania and met by an **Act of** Assembly passed on 3 February 1742-3 'for naturalizing such Foreign Protestants as are settled or shall settle within this Province who, not being of the People called Quakers, do conscientiously refuse the taking of any Oath.'* This declared that all such persons should, on conforming to the Act 13 George II, be deemed to be the King's natural-born subjects of the Province. This anticipated by several years the later Act of the British Parliament of 1747, and it is rather surprising that it was not found to be *ultra vires* by the home Government. Moravians were not specially distinguished in the Pennsylvania lists until 1750, but it is probable that they were included in the preceding years amongst the Quakers as affirmers.

The case of the two provinces of New Jersey, East and West, is in singular contrast to that of Pennsylvania, for we have not a single list of naturalizations under the Act of 1740 effected in their courts, although, as we have seen, residents of New Jersey were naturalized in the Court of Philadelphia. Possibly the Board of Trade's practice of combining the Proprieties, to which both New Jersey and Pennsylvania belonged, in a joint administration was held to render a naturalization effected in any of these provinces equally valid in the others. On the other hand objection may have been taken in New Jersey to the fact that there was nothing in the Act of 13 George II to make anyone naturalized under it ineligible to be of the King's Council or of the General Assembly of the Colony or to hold any post or office of trust within it, for in all the private Naturalization Acts of that Colony, and there are many, there is a clause excluding the grantees from such benefits.

This question of the eligibility of persons naturalized under the 1740 Act to become members of a Colonial Assembly crops up in another form in Maryland. Maryland was another of the Proprieties, but in this case, as we have seen, we have actual lists of naturalizations in conformity with the Act down to the year 1753, although subsequently all the naturalizations of residents of the colony by the same means that we know of were effected in Pennsylvania. The fact, however, that it is not possible to identify the Mr. Hagar mentioned in the following letter in any of the lists raises the question whether there may not have continued to be naturalizations in the Maryland Court of which no lists were sent to the Board.†

* C.O. 5. 1242.
† There are a Philip Hager and a John Haagar in 1765, but both were then resident in Pennsylvania.

That no opposition was generally raised in this colony to the eligibility of naturalized aliens sitting in its Assembly may be concluded from the unqualified benefits conferred on such persons who were naturalized by Act of that Assembly.* Nevertheless the Assembly, as will be seen by the letter, which is quoted below, had passed an Act to render any person disabled by the laws of England from sitting in Parliament ineligible for election to the Assembly. As the Act 13 George II had declared that all persons naturalized under it were not to be qualified to sit in the Parliaments of Great Britain or Ireland, this Act of the Maryland Assembly would have similarly debarred those persons from serving in that Assembly. Accordingly, to remedy this defect an Act was passed in the Assembly at Annapolis in 1771 which on reference to the Board of Trade was evidently held by its law officer to be invalid.† The following extract from a letter of the Lieutenant Governor of the Colony dealing with this matter contains several points of interest affecting the character and status of the foreign settlers in America :—

Annapolis, 29th January, 1773.

My Lord,

I am to acknowledge the Honor of your Lordship's Letter of the 4th November 1772 (No. 1).   *   *   *   *   *   *   *   *   *

I shou'd be extremely Sorry if the Explanation I am to give your Lordship of the Motive for passing the Act Cap. 1, shou'd not prove satisfactory ; for I can venture to assure your Lordship that this Act was not intended to contravene the Statute in any degree, and that the People, in whose Favor it was passed, have the Merit of being must usefull subjects. In Consequence of the Encouragement given by Statute a great Number of German Emigrants have settled in North America, particularly in Pensylvania, and the frontier County of Maryland. They are generally an industrious, laborious People.—Many of them have acquired a considerable share of property.—Their Improvement of a Wilderness into well stock'd Plantations, the Example and beneficial Effects of their extraordinary Industry have raised, in no small Degree, a spirit of Emulation among the other Inhabitants. That they are a most usefull People, and merit the publick **Regard** is acknowledged by all who are acquainted with them.

It happened that one Mr. Hagar, a German who had been Naturalized according to the Statute, was elected one of the Burgesses to serve in Assembly for the frontier County.— When the Assembly met, it became a Question whether he was eligible or not, and it was determined in the Negative by a Majority of one only, as your Lordship will observe on having Recourse to the transmitted Copy of the Votes and Proceedings, p. 9. 10.

It was understood that, if the Limitation or Proviso in the 13 of George 2nd Cap. 7. had been omitted, by the general Purview of the Act Mr. Hagar would have been eligible, and that the Limitation or Proviso " that no Person, who shall become a natural born Subject of this Kingdom by Virtue of this Act shall be of the Privy Council or a Member of either

---

* For the general form of the Maryland Naturalization Acts see the ' Act for Naturalization of Thomas Harvey of Calvert County [a Frenchman] and his Children,' C.O. 5. 736, p. 42.

† For the provisions of this Act see C.O. 5. 738, ' An Act for vesting in such foreign Protestants as are now naturalized, or shall be hereafter naturalized in this Province, all the Rights and Privileges of Natural-born Subjects.'

House of Parliament or capable of taking, having, discharging or enjoying any Office or Place of Trust within the Kingdoms of Great Britain or Ireland, civil or military, or of having, accepting or taking any Grant from the Crown of any Lands, Tenements or Heredita-ments within the Kingdoms of Great Britain or Ireland." I say, My Lord, that this Limitation or Proviso alone did not extend to disqualify Mr. Hagar to be a Member of the Maryland Assembly; but an Act of Assembly having provided that no Person, Disabled by the Laws of England from sitting in Parliament, should be elected to serve in Assembly, the Question arose on the Proviso in the Statute, and the Reference of the Act of Assembly to the Laws of England conjunctly, and though a Majority of the Lower House of Assembly thought Mr. Hagar on the Question to be ineligible, yet the Act Cap. 1. unanimously passed for the very purpose that a Person in his Situation might in future be chosen a Member of the Assembly, and your Lordship will perceive on turning to p. 53. 54. that Mr. Hagar was re-elected. Such, My Lord, was my motive for passing the Act Cap. 1. And permit me to assure your Lordship if I had entertained any Suspicion that this Act impugned in any Degree the Statute, I would have dissented to it avowedly on that very ground.

In Pensylvania Foreigners naturalized may be chosen Members of the Assembly, and there is Reason to apprehend that if they shou'd not have (since the point has been stirred) the same Privelege in Maryland, it would be a great disadvantage to this Colony, especially as (notwithstanding they maintain their Ministers by Contribution) they are equally taxed with others to support the established Clergy; a Charge to which they are not liable in Pensylvania, where there is no such Establishment.

The effect of this Act is meerly local, the Design of it was in no Degree to set aside the Limitation contained in the Statute, and the pervisions of it are allmost necessary on account of the Privelege enjoyed by Foreigners naturalized in Pensylvania. On these Considerations I hope for your Lordship's most favourable Construction. *　　*　　*　　*

[*Signed* :] Robt. Eden.

[*Endorsed* :] Letter from Lt. Govr. Eden to the Earl of Dartmouth, dated Jan'ry 29, 1773 [&c.]
Read Decr. 20, 1773.*

The following letter on the subject from the Board's law officer in London, though of later date than the Lieutenant Governor's letter, had doubtless determined the Commissioners' attitude many months before the receipt of the letter :—

To the Right Honourable the Lords Commissioners for Trade and Plantations.

May it please your Lordships. In humble Obedience to your Lordships' Commands Signified to me by Mr. Pownall, I have perused and considered Twenty Nine Acts passed by the Governor and Assembly of the Province of Maryland in the Year 1771. Intitled

*　　*　　*　　*　　*　　*　　*　　*　　*

And I am humbly of opinion that the said Acts are well founded on the Powers of Legislature granted by the Royal Charter of his Majesty King Charles the first.

*C.O. 5. 1278 (Z. 51). The long interval of time between the date of the letter and its production before the Board is remarkable.

I have also perused and considered another Act passed in the same Year 1771 Intitled, " An Act for vesting in such foreign Protestants as are now Naturalized or shall be hereafter Naturalized in this Province, all the rights and privileges of Natural Born Subjects."

And am humbly of opinion that the same is altogether void, inasmuch as it can have no Effect, unless it be construed to be a Repeal of the Sixth Section of the Statute of the 13th of his late Majesty Cap. 7, by which Construction it becomes repugnant to the Laws of this Realm. 9 Febry., 1773.   [*Signed :*] R. JACKSON.

[*Endorsed :*] Rece'd   ⎫
              Read   Febr'y 11⎭ 1773.*

Before, however, the Lieutenant Governor's letter had been read to the Board on 20 Dec. 1773 the Statute 13 George III. c. 25 had been passed. This declared that all persons who had been naturalized in conformity with the Act of 13 Geo. II and another of Geo. III should be capable of holding any office or place of trust, either civil or military, and taking and holding any grant of lands, etc., from the Crown, though they were still to be debarred from holding such offices and lands within the Kingdoms of Great Britain and Ireland.

There is one American Colony which we know from other sources to have been largely populated in the eighteenth century by religious refugees from Europe but of which we have no record in the following returns. This was the new Colony of Georgia founded by royal charter of 9 June 1732. Here the Acts of the Colony are equally silent on the question of naturalization, possibly because under the terms of the charter the question did not arise. A clause in the charter expressly declared that it should be lawful for the Trustees for the establishment of the Colony 'to transport into the said Province of Georgia to be there settled all such and so many of our loving subjects *or any foreigners that are willing to become our subjects and live under our Allegiance in the said Colony,* as shall willingly go to inhabit and reside there. A further clause declared that all persons born in Georgia were to enjoy the liberties of free denizens within any of the dominions of the Crown.

From the considerations that have been adduced it will be seen that the evidence furnished by the lists that we now print is insufficient to enable us to form any correct or full estimate of the numbers and character of the alien immigrations into the American colonies during the eighteenth century. Yet the lists have a value, apart from that attaching to the genealogical interest in the many names which they contain, in that they constitute the whole source to be found in our own country of our information as to the effect of one particular Act of Parliament for bringing the subjects of those immigrations within the pale of their fellow colonists of British birth. To fellows of the Huguenot Society they have the further interest of showing to some extent how as late as the eighteenth century religious persecution was still tending to drive out of Europe the followers of the Reformation.

                                                    M. S. GIUSEPPI.

28 Feb., 1921.

* C.O. 5. 1278 (Z. 40).

Naturalizations of Foreign Protestants in the American and West Indian Colonies.

(Pursuant to Statute 13 George II.)

[Note.—The following lists have been transcribed, so far as they extend, from the two Entry Books formerly belonging to the Board of Trade and Plantations, and known as 'Plantations General, 59 and 60,' but now referred to as **C.O. 324,** 55 and 56 respectively. The lists have been checked in all cases with the original certificates sent to the Board by the Secretaries for the respective Colonies, and important variations and additions in these are shown in parentheses. For the Colonies of Virginia, New York and Pennsylvania (including Maryland and New Jersey) later certificates than were copied into these Entry Books exist, and these have been transcribed from the papers amongst the original correspondence of the Board now classed with the Colonial Office records preserved at the Public Record Office.]

C.O. 324-55.

A list of persons that have intituled themselves to the Benefit of the Act (13 *Geo. II*) for Naturalizing such Foreign Protestants and others therein mentioned as are settled or shall settle in any of His Majesty's Colonies in America.

BARBADOS [*no entry*].

ANTIGUA [*no entry*].

NEVIS [*no entry*].

ST. CHRISTOPHER [*no entry*].

MONTSERRAT [*no entry*].

JAMAICA.

W. 34 (1 June, 1740, to   Tuesday, the 25th day of November, 1740.
   1 June, 1741).   Persons professing the Jewish Religion.
         Jacob Mendes Gutteres.
         Benjamin Bravo.
         Abraham Ribiero.
         Moses Lopes Heneriques (Henriques).
         Jacob Pinto Brandon.
         David Bravo.
         Isaac Fuertado (Feurtado).
         Moses Martins.
         Del. Mz. Da Costa.
         Isaac Ramalho.
         Moses Cohen Delara.
         Aaron Lamera.

b

JAMAICA.

Thursday, the 26th day of February, 1740[-1].
Persons professing the Jewish Religion.

ELIAS FERNANDES CORCHE.
MOSES ALVARES CORCHE.
ARON DIAS FERNANDES.
JACOB DE LA PENHA.
JACOB GUTTERES HENRIQUES.
SOLOMON MENDES.
JACOB LYON.
DAVID TORRES.
HENRIQ' ISRAEL.
ISAAC HENRIQUES CAMPOS.
DAVID SALOM.
JACOB DA SILVA.
ABM. LAGUNA.
JACOB FERNANDES MESQUITTA.
BENJN. RODRIQUES GABRIEL.
JOSEPH ABRATHAR.
DANIEL DOVALLE.
ISAAC HENRIQUES SEQUIRA.
ISL. DE LA PENHA.
MOSES RODRIQUES.
ISAAC FERNANDES PRLL.
ISAAC DA SILVA HENRIQUES.
RAPL. MENDES.

Tuesday, the 2nd day of March, 1740[-1].
RACHAELL CARDOSA ....
    a person professing the Christian Religion.

W. 44 (1 June, 1740, to
1 June, 1741. Addi-   Tuesday, the 26th day of May, 1741.
tional list).   Persons professing the Jewish Religion.
ABRAHAM HENRIQUES SEQUIRA.
SOLOMON CURIEL.
ABRAHAM LOPEZ HENRIQUES.
JACOB LOPEZ DE CRASTO.

W. 53 (1 June, 1741, to   Tuesday, the 25th day of August, 1741.
1 June, 1742).   Persons professing the Jewish Religion.
ISAAC NUNEZ DA COSTA.
DANIEL ALVES FERNANDES.
ISAAC LOPES PRETTE.
PHINELIAS MATTOS.
ISAAC DEVALLE.
JACOB NUNEZ DA COSTA.

Tuesday, the 24th day of November, 1741.
JACOB BRANDON.
JOSEPH SOARES.
MENASHE RIBAS.
LEAH SOARES.
REBECCA PENNEA,

Wednesday, the 24th day of February, 1741[-2].
MOSES ALVARES.

Wednesday, the 26th day of May, 1742.
DAVID MENDEZ.
JOSHUA GOMEZ SILVA.

Wednesday, the 26th day of May, 1742.
Persons professing the Christian Religion.
JOSEPH LAVOU.
LEWIS FORTUNE.

W. 61 (1 June, 1742, to   Persons professing the Jewish Religion.
1 June, 1743).   Wednesday, the 1st day of September, 1742.
RODRIQUES MOEDA.

Wednesday, the 1st day of December, 1742.
DANIEL DA SILVA.
DANIEL CARDOZO.

Wednesday, the 23rd day of February, 1742[-3].
JACOB PEREIRA MENDES.
ESTHER PEREIRA MENDES.
ESTER DA COSTA ALVARINGA.
LEAH RAMALHO.
RACHAEL ALVARINGA.
RACHAEL DA COSTA ALVARINGA.
SARAH SANCHES.
MOSES LADESMA.
ISAAC GOMES SILVA.

Tuesday, the 31st day of May, 1743.
ABRAHAM NUNEZ DA COSTA.
LEAH MARTINS.
SARAH CARDOZO.
LEAH CARDOZO.
RACHAEL OROIBO FURTADO.
SARAH NUNEZ.
RACHAEL HENRIQUES.
MOSES ALVARES CORREA.
JACOB LAGUNA, Junr.
MOSES LEVY.
ISAAC HENRIQUES CUNA.

Tuesday, the 31st day of May, 1743.
Persons professing the Christian Religion.
FRANCIS LINTON.

W. 76 (1 June, 1743, to   Persons professing the Jewish Religion
1 June, 1744).   Tuesday, the 30th day of August, 1743.
MOSES NUNEZ DA COSTA.
ISAAC CAMPOS ALMEYDA.
JACOB LOPES (LOPEZ) HENRIQUES.
HANAH LOPES (LOPEZ) RIZ.

JAMAICA.

Tuesday, the 29th day of November, 1743.
ISAAC MENDES CUNHA.
DAVID FERNANDES.
JOSEPH ALVARES CORCHO.
JACOB CORDOSO.
RACHAEL (RACHEL) CORDOSO.
JOSHUA NUNEZ.
ABIGAIL MENDES.

Tuesday, the 28th day of February, 1743[-4].
SIME MENDES.
REBECCA LAGUNA.
SARAH LOPES HENRIQUES.
RACHAEL (RACHEL) LOPES HENRIQUES.
HENRY LEVY.
REINA TORRES.
ABRAHAM DOVALL SALDANA.

Friday, the 1st day of June, 1744.
DAVID VALENTIA.
ABIGALL VALENTIA.

W. 102 (1 June, 1744, to Tuesday, the 27th day of November, 1744.
1 June, 1745). Persons professing the Jewish Religion.
DAVID DA SILVA FLES.

Thursday, the 6th Day of December, 1744.
Persons professing the Christian Religion.
PETER FREDRICK CALAME.

Tuesday, the 26th day of February, 1744[-5].
Persons professing the Jewish Religion.
JACOB NUNES HENRIQUES.
ABRM. ROIZ CARDOZO.
ABIGAIL FERNANDEZ.
ABRAM DE CAMPOS, Senr.

W. 123 (1 June, 1745, to Tuesday, the 27th day of August, 1745.
1 June, 1746). Persons professing the Jewish Religion.
MOSES NUNES HENRIQUES.
ESTHER LOPES PEREIRA.
JUDITH OROBIO FURTADO.
RICE VEGA.
RACHEL HENRIQUES.
ESTHER SALOM.
ISAAC RODRIQUES MIRANDA.
ELIAS LAZARES.
ESTHER PINTO BRANDON.
RICA CAMPOS ALMEYDA.

Thursday, the 5th day of September, 1745.
Person professing the Christian Religion.
MATHEW (MATTHEW) CROE.

November Court.
None.

Persons professing the Jewish Religion.
Thursday, the 27th day of February, 1745[-6].
SOLOMAN ABRAHAMS.

Thursday, the 27th day of May, 1746.
MOSES AQUILAR.
SOLOMON SALDANA.

W. 140 (1 June, 1746, to Persons professing the Jewish Religion.
   1 June, 1747).   Tuesday, the 26th day of August, 1746.
ABRAHAM SANCHES.
MOSES RODERIQUES.
BENJAMIN SANCHES.
GABRIEL MENDES.
MOSES PERA. DA COSTA.
RACHEL FERNANDES PEREIRA.
ESTHER MENDES.
JUDICA DA SILVA.
RICA DA SILVA.
RACHEL MENDES.
JUDITH MENDES.
ESTHER MENDES.

Wednesday, the 26th day of November, 1746.
RACHEL LOPEZ DEPAIS.

Tuesday, the 24th day of February, 1746[-7].
ABRAHAM SURZEDAS.
RACHAEL SARZEDAS.

May Court.
None.

X. 26 (1 June, 1747, to Persons professing the Jewish Religion.
   1 Sept., 1748).   Tuesday, the 23rd day of February, 1747[-8].
REBECCA NUNEZ VIZEA.
ESTER HENRIQUES FURTADO.

May Court.
None.

Wednesday, the 31st day of August, 1748.
ABRAHAM PEREIRA MENDES.

X. 54 (1 Sept., 1748, to November Court.
   1 Aug., 1749).   None.

JAMAICA.

Persons professing the Jewish Religion.
(February Court.)
BEN. DIAS FERNANDES.
SAMLL. PRA. MENDES.
DANIEL LOPES BARRIOS.
DAVID NUNIS (NUNES) TROIS.
ABRAHAM CAVILLE.

May Court.
None.

X. 62 (1 June, 1749, to   August Court.
1 June, 1750.)   None.

Tuesday, the 28th day of November, 1749.
Persons professing the Christian Religion.
PETER ROUSE.

Persons professing the Jewish Religion.
ESTER NUNES TROIS.
JUDITH HENRIQUES CAMPOS.
ESTER DIAS FERNANDES.
RACHEL HENRIQUES CUNTRA.

Tuesday, the 27th day of February, 1749[-50].
ABRAHAM OF BENJAMIN PERSIRA (PEREIRA) MENDES
JACOB NUNES DE LARA.
DANIEL ABUQUERQUES.
MOSES MESQUITTA, Senr.
JOSHUA ABOAB.

Tuesday, the 29th day of May, 1750.
ALEXANDER NATHANE.

X. 76 (1 June, 1750, to   August Court.
1 June, 1751).   Persons professing the Jewish Religion.
None.

Wednesday, the 28th day of November, 1750.
ABIGAIL LOPEZ.
MOSES DIAS FERNANDES.
ISAAC HENRIQUEZ FURTADO.

Tuesday, the 26th day of February, 1750.
ISAAC RODRIQUES NUNES.
JACOB MENDES SEIXAS.

Persons professing the Christian Religion.
ANTHOYNE LACOURT.
JAQUES BERANGER.

May Court, 1751.
None.

BAHAMAS [*no entry*].

BERMUDA [*no entry*].

GEORGIA [*no entry*].

SOUTH CAROLINA.

(South Carolina, Secretary's Office, 13 February, 1741[-2].

A List of Persons who have taken the benefit of the late Act of Parliament to Naturalize themselves by Certificates from Benjamin Whitaker, Esqr., Chief Justice of the Province, sworn before him in Court of General Sessions of the Peace and Recorded in this Office as followes :)

G. 67.

DANIEL BOURZET, Certificate Recorded January 20th, 1741[-2].
DAVID CHRISTINA, Certificate Recorded January 20th, 1741[-2].
PETER CALVET, Certificate Recorded January 22nd, 1741[-2].
FRANCIS DALGAS, Certificate Recorded January 20th, 1741[-2].
PETER DELMÈTRE, Certificate Recorded January 26th, 1741[-2].
FRANCIS GUISHARD, Certificate Recorded January 20th, 1741[-2].
JOSEPH TOBIAS, a Jew, Certificate Recorded December 11th, 1741.
JAMES VOLOUX, Certificate Recorded January 20th, 1741[-2].
MATTHEW VANALL, Certificate Recorded, January 20th, 1741[-2].

(All which are Recorded in this Office in Book E. E.—J. HAMMERTON, Secretary.)

Persons' Names.	Time when Naturalized.
DAVID CHRISTINA.	October 24th, 1741.
JEAN PRIRIE BREZ.	October 24th, 1741.
GABRIEL GUIGNARD.	October 24th, 1741.
JOHN ERNEST POYAS.	October 24th, 1741.
JEAN LEWIS POYAS.	October 24th, 1741.
DANIEL BOURGET.	October 24th, 1741.
FRANCIS GUICHARDE.	November 12th, 1741.
MATHIEU VANALL.	November 12th, 1741.
FRANCIS HIS X MARK DALGAS.	November 12th, 1741.
JAQUES VOULOUX.	November 12th, 1741.
PR. COLVET.	November 12th, 1741.
PIERRE DELMESTRE.	November 12th, 1741.
FREDERICK GRIMKEE.	February 8th, 1742-3.
PETER BOUQUET.	August 14th, 1744.
FRANCOIS VARAMBAUGH.	August 14th, 1744.
MARK ANTHONY BESSILLEU.	August 14th, 1744.
DANIEL CHOPARD.	August 14th, 1744.
DANIEL FAYSSOUX.	October 18th, 1744.
JEAN RODOLPH LE GRAND.	October 18th, 1744.
JOHN MARTINI.	May 12th, 1748.
AD. LOYER.	May 12th, 1748.
FREDERICK HOLZENDORF.	May 12th, 1748.
JOHN PAUL GRIMKEE.	May 12th, 1748.

I. 38.

(Secretary's Office in Charlestown, South Carolina. Certified by William George Freeman, Department Secretary.)

NORTH CAROLINA [*no entry*].

VIRGINIA.

Persons Naturalized.	When Naturalized.
V. 37. JAMES MARYE, a Frenchman.	April 26th, 1743. [This date is not given in the original certificate, dated 1 June, 1743, of Thomas Nelson, junr., Department Secretary.]
V. 43.* PETER STEPHAN, a German, (a native of Hidelburgh on the River Mayne, in the Empire of Germany, who hath resided for the space of seven years and more in that part of Orange County designed to be called Frederick).	October 21st, 1743.
V. 48.* JAMES PORTEUS, a Swede (of the County of Orange, a native of the City of Stockholm, in the Kingdom of Sweden).	May 2nd, 1744.

VIRGINIA.

[*The following Certificates for this Colony were not entered into the Entry Book.*]

(C.O. 5, 1326.)

V. 86. Pursuant to the Directions of the Act of Parliament you receive the inclosed Certificates of Foreigners naturalized in this Colony which are registered in my Office at Williamsburgh. I am [&c.] THOS. NELSON, Virginia.

[*Addressed*] THOS. HILL, Esq., Secretary to the Lords Commissioners of Trade and Plantations.

[*Endorsed*] Received July 3 } 1746.
Read   do.

[*Enclosures*] (1) Virginia. At a General Court held at the Capitol, October 15, 1745,

JACOB MANSBOIL
LAWRENCE GRAYS
THOMAS WEELAND
MATTHEW GESLER
CONRAD BROIL
CHRISTOPHER UHL
MARTIN WALK

Natives of the Dukedom of Wirtemberg in Germany, who have resided in this Colony upwards of seven years last past and have not been absent out of the same the space of two months at any one time, came into Court between 9 and 12 in the forenoon, produced Certificates of their having received the Sacrament, and took and subscribed the Oaths appointed, [&c.]

[*Signed*] BEN. WALLER, Cl. Cur.

Registered in the Secretary's Office of Virginia by Ben. Waller, Cl. Sec. Off.

(2) Virginia. At a General Court held at the Capitol October 28, 1745:
WILLIAM RICKLEY, a native of the Canton of Berne, in Swisserland.
[*Similar Certificate to the foregoing, signed and registered as above.*]

V. 87. Two further Certificates transmitted with the foregoing letter of Mr. Nelson :—
(1) General Court at the Capitol, October 19, 1745 :

TOBIAS WILHOID
JOHN WILHOID

}Natives of the Electorate of Mentz, in Germany.

* (Both certificates signed by Benjamin Waller, Cl. Cur.)

(2) Virginia. General Court held at the Capitol October 23, 1745 :
JACOB CHRISTMAN, a native of the city of Worms, in Germany.
[*Both Certificates similar to the foregoing and similarly signed and registered.*]

V. 106. Four Certificates endorsed ' Certificates of Foreign Protestants Naturalized in the Colony of Virginia, between yᵉ 20th of October, 1744, and yᵉ 19th of April, 1746. Registered in the Secretary's Office of Virginia, by Ben. Waller, Cl. Cur. and Secretary. Transmitted by him to the Secretary of this Board. Received Aug. 10th. Read Do. yᵉ 20th, 1747.'

(1) General Court, October 20, 1744 :
JOHN PAUL VOGT, a native of Frankfort in Germany.
ANDREW VOGT, a native of Carlsbad
JOHN BUM GARDNER, a native of Risenbach, in Sweden.

(2) General Court, April 17, 1745 :
PHILIP LUNG, a native of Sarprigkn, in Germany,
NICHOLAS LUNG, a native of Wigsden, in Germany.
(Both Quakers—affirmed.)

(3) General Court, April 19, 1745 :
ZACHARIAH BLANKENBEEKER   Natives of Nieuberg, in the Bishoprick of
JOHN THOMAS   Spire.
HENRY AHLER, a native of Wirtenberg, in Germany.
JOHN ZIMMERMAN, a native of Saltzfeld in Germany.

(4) General Court, April 19, 1746 :
PETER FLESHMAN, a native of Germany.

[*All Certificates similar in form to the previous ones and signed and registered by Ben. Waller.*]

C.O. 324-55 (*continued*).

MARYLAND.

Between the 1st of June 1742 and the 1st of June 1743.

V. 4.   ZACHARIAH SPENCER.
             TITUR LONEY.
             PHINEAS ALFERINO.
             JOHN HOUSE.
             PHILIP KINCE.
             MATTHEW REISLIN.
             PETER HAROUT.
             CONRAD KEMP.

(Certified under seal of Provincial Court of Maryland by William Ghiselin, Clerk, Secretary's Office and Provincial Court.)

Between the 1st of June 1743 and the 1st of June 1744, viz.,
October Term 1743.

V. 11.   JACOB FAUZS.
             MARTIN KIJSMÜLLER.
             JOHN VERDRISS (VERDRESS).
             VALENTINE VERDRIS.
             GEORGE SCHWEINHART.
             PETER MIDDLECAVE.
             MICHAEL WILL.
             DAVID YOUNG.
             MARK PICKLER.

MARYLAND.

Jacob Shrier.
Martin Whisther.
Martin Shope.
Christopher Geston (Getson) Tanner.
John Hend.
Gesper Mier.
Isaac Miller.
Conjuist Gash.
David Harriott.
Mateas Ambrose.
George Scheildler.
John George Huzel.
Andrew Shriver.
Lutwick Shriver.
Conrad Echard.
George Shriver.
John Shrier.
Nicholas Shrier.
Jaed Knave.
Adam Stall.
Jacob Stern.
Jacob Staley.
Henry Boughtall.
Godfrey Gash.

(Certified under Seal of Provincial Court of Maryland by Richard
Burdus, Clerk, Secretary's Office and Provincial Court.)

April Term, 1746.

V. 37.   George Gump.

(This is repeated in V. 60 which is described as a Duplicate, a note
stating that the originals had not been received.
Similarly certified by the same.)

(Persons Naturalized between 1 June, 1746, and 1 June, 1747.)
V. 60.   Christian Kemp.
Gilbert Kemp.
Peter Hoofman.

October Term, 1747.

Jacob Stull.
George French.
Jacob Miller.
Isaac Simmons.
Joseph Vulgemat.
Jacob Rorrer.
Henry Avey.
Andrew Hobre.
Felta Gratt.
Martin Keisner.
Ludowick Miller.
Jonathan Isagar.
Nicholas Wrightnomer.

October Term, 1748.
V. 64. HENDRICK SIEX.

Frederick County April Assizes, 1749.
HENRY ROADES.
CHRISTOPHER STABLE.
ADAM SPAUGHT.
LAWRENCE GREEGER.
JACOB WALLER.
LEONARD MASSER.
GEORGE SMITH.
CONRAD HOLLINGSMITH.
PHILIP KNABELT.
JOHN MILLER.
TITTRICK MASSONER.
JOHN GEORGE SMITH.
JACOB AMBROSE.
GODFRET MUNG.
GEORGE GOATS.
PETER APPLE.
GEORGE MICHAEL GESSERON.
GEORGE CLEM.
JACOB SMITH.
GEORGE SOLDENER.
HENRY SMITH.
FREDERICK WILHYDE.
NICHOLAS WHELSALE.
FREDERICK UNSELD.
MARTIN WELSELD, Senr. [Senr. omitted in orig.]
MARTIN WELSELD, Junr.
JACOB VERTREESE.
JACOB FRANK.
GEORGE CUNCE BETINY.
JOHN SIMON KERN.
VALENTINE USELMAN.
MICHAEL ROMAR.
FREDERICK VERTREESE.
JOHN MICHAEL HAFNER.
FREDERICK HAFNER.
THOMAS SLIGH.
JACOB SLIGH.
HENRY SIN.
BARTHOLOMEW MONTS (MOONTS).
DAVID DELATER.
MICHAEL THOMAS.
HENRY TORDINE.
JOHN YOUNG.
MARTIN ADAM.
RODOLPH KELLER.
JOHN NAPH.
JOHN WYMER.
BARNARD YOUNG.
PETER YOUNG.

[NOTE.—The following names are at the end of V. 131, which is a duplicate list of all Naturalizations in Maryland under the Act of 13 *Geo. II* from October 1742.* It should be noted there are certain discrepancies, not only in the spelling of the names, but also in the dates of the Naturalizations between this list and those preceding for the same province.]

April Term, 1750.

FEITERS HARTWAY.
DANIEL BARNETS.

September Term, 1750.

PETER MYER.

September Term, 1751.

FREDERICK KEMP.
JOHN HOOFMAN.
CARL BERNITZ.
ANGEL ISRAELLO.
GEORGE HARTMAN.
MICHAEL MEYERER.
CONNERAH SHMITH.
JOHN SEMMER.

September Term, 1752.

VALENTINE MIER.
JACOB CLONT.
HENDRICK CUIKES.

April Term, 1753.

HENRY REIDENHAUR (REIDENAUR).
PETER REIDENHAUR (REIDENAUR).
MATTHIAS REIDENHAUR (REIDENAUR).
CONRAD HAGMAYER.
CASPARUS WINTENORTH (WINTENOTH).

* This general list was sent by covering letter of Edm. Jenings, dated 5th Sept., 1753, 'lest a miscarriage may have happened to some of the lists formerly returned.' (V. 130.)

PENNSYLVANIA.

Persons Naturalized in 1740 and 1741.

(Supreme Court at Philadelphia, held 10 and 11 April, 1741.)

Persons' Names.	Of what County.	Time of taking the Sacrament.
JOHAN PHILIP BEHM.	Philadelphia County.	April 11th, 1741.
HENRICK WARNER.	Philadelphia County.	April 11th, 1741.
SEBASTIAN GRAAFF.	Philadelphia County.	February 10th, 1740.
JOHAN DEDRICK YOUNGMAN.	Philadelphia County.	April 11th, 1741.
GEORGE HONIG.	Lancaster County.	April 10th.
FEIGHT GEORGER.	Philadelphia County.	April 7th.
JOHN GEORGE MERSTALLER.	Bucks County.	April 2nd.
JOHAN DEDRICK BUCHERT.	Philadelphia County.	April 11th.
GEORGE JACOB SPINGLER.	Philadelphia County.	February 4th, 1740.
PAUL LINSENBEKLER.	Philadelphia County.	April 7th, 1741.
ANDREAS OVERBECK.	Philadelphia County.	April 5th, 1741.
CHRISTOPHER SMITH.	Philadelphia County.	April 5th, 1741.
HENRY RUMFELDT.	Bucks. County.	April 2nd.
JOHANNES SHAFER.	Philadelphia County.	April 7th.
THEOWALD BAWM.	Philadelphia County.	February 4th, 1740.
HENRICK DEVALD.	Philadelphia County.	April 11th, 1741.
CONRAD NIEDERMARDT.	Chester County.	March 29th.
ADAM EICHELY.	Philadelphia County.	April 11th.
FRANCIS ROOS.	Philadelphia County.	April 5th
JOHANNES KASTNER.	Lancaster County.	April 11th.
CHRISTIAN LEAMAN.	Philadelphia County.	April 5th.
JOHAN ADAM SCHROCHER.	Philadelphia County.	April 2nd.
CHARLES HUNTER.	Philadelphia County.	February 5th, 1740.
VALENTINE BERNDHEISELL.	Philadelphia County.	April 11th, 1741.
UBRICK STEPHAN.	Philadelphia County.	April 5th.
JACOB FRYE.	Philadelphia County.	April 7th, 1741.
JACOB MILLER.	Philadelphia County.	March 31st.
HANS MICHAEL CRUMRYNE.	Philadelphia County.	April 9th.
JOHANNES NEIHAWSEN.	Philadelphia County.	April 11th.
STEPHEN BRECHT.	Lancaster County.	April 11th.
JOHN JOST HECK.	Lancaster County.	April 11th.

T. 50.

PENNSYLVANIA.

(Philadelphia, May 7th, 1741 :
  The foregoing is a true and perfect List taken from the Original Certificate under the Hands of Thomas Græme and Thomas Griffiths, Esqs., remaining in my Office.

PAT. BAIRD, Secretary.

Supreme Court at Philadelphia, 25, 26 and 27 Sept., 1740.)

Persons' Names.	Of what County.	Time of taking the Sacrament.
PETER KOCK.	Philadelphia City.	August 10th, 1740.
JOHN MASON.	Philadelphia City.	September 23rd.
GUSTAVUS HESSELIUS.	Philadelphia City.	September 23rd.
FREDERICK SMITH.	Philadelphia City.	September 23rd.
ANDREW REINBERG.	Philadelphia County.	September 23rd.
JACOB HOFFMAN.	Philadelphia County.	September 22nd, 1740.
JOHN GEORGE MYER.	Philadelphia County.	September 22nd, 1740.
JACOB BYAR.	Bucks. County.	June 29th.
MICHAEL FERSLER.	Bucks. County.	September 21st.
JACOB SERVER.	Bucks. County.	September 22nd.
JOANNES BARTHOL. REIGER, Lutheran Minister.	Lancaster County.	September 19th.
JOHN WILLIAM STRAUBE.	Philadelphia County.	September 21st.
JACOB ARENT.	Philadelphia County.	September 22nd.
ANDREAS BERNHARD.	Philadelphia County.	June 29th.
JACOB ARWOGAUST.	Bucks. County.	June 29th.
OSWALD WALT.	Philadelphia County.	June 29th.
LEONARD MELIHAR.	Philadelphia County.	September 22nd.
ADAM KITTLER.	Philadelphia County.	August 3rd.
GEORGE BERGSTRASER.	Bucks. County.	September 22nd, 1740.
GEORGE HENRY HARTSLE.	Bucks. County.	September 22nd, 1740.
JOHN FREY.	Bucks. County.	September 22nd, 1740.
GEORGE BECK.	Philadelphia County.	September 25th.
CHRISTOPHER ANKENBRAND.	Philadelphia County.	September 25th.
JOHN RODEY.	Bucks. County.	September 22nd.
BLESSIUS BYAR.	Philadelphia City.	September 22nd.
JOHN WENDELL BRECHBILL.	Philadelphia City.	September 7th.
BARTHOLOMEUS HORNBERGHER.	Bucks. County.	September 11th.
PETER RULE.	Bucks. County.	September 22nd.
PETER GRUBER.	Bucks. County.	September 11th.
GEORGE HARTSELL.	Bucks. County.	September 22nd.
DEDRICK RUDEY.	Bucks. County.	September 22nd.
PHILIP HENRICK SELLER.	Bucks. County.	September 22nd.
JOSEPH PENKICK.	Philadelphia County.	September 25th.
GEORGE REIGER.	Philadelphia County.	July 15th.
CASPAR SIMON.	Philadelphia County.	July 29th.
URIAH HUMBLE, Junr.	Bucks. County.	September 25th.
ANDREW TRUMBOLE.	Philadelphia County.	June 29th.
JOHN GEORGE KEPLER.	Philadelphia County.	September 1st.
HANS BERNARD KEPLER.	Philadelphia County.	July 29th.
MICHAEL SEBASTIAN.	Philadelphia County.	September 1st.
HIERONIMUS HANS.	Philadelphia County.	September 25th.
HENRICK HANS.	Philadelphia County.	September 1st.
GEORGE ROUP.	Bucks. County	July 22nd.
MATHIAS OTTO.	Philadelphia County.	September 1st.
VALENTINE GEYGAR.	Philadelphia County.	September 25th.
PETER ROUP.	Bucks. County.	July 22nd.

PENNSYLVANIA.

Persons Naturalized in 1740.

Persons' Names.	Of what County.	Time of taking the Sacrament
JOHN LERICK.	Bucks. County.	July 22nd, 1740.
ELIAS HASELL.	Bucks. County.	July 22nd, 1740.
JACOB KEEFER.	Bucks. County.	July 22nd, 1740.
MATHIAS PENDER.	Philadelphia County.	September 25th.
JOHN FREDERICK RICHARD.	Philadelphia County.	September 25th.
BALTHAZAR SAILOR.	Philadelphia County.	September 1st.
JACOB WALTER.	Philadelphia County.	September 7th.
MARTIN HUMBLE.	Bucks. County.	September 25th.
PETER RITTER.	Philadelphia County.	September 1st.
BARTHOLOMEW MAUL.	Philadelphia County.	September 23rd.
JOHN VOGLER.	Philadelphia County.	September 23rd.
MATHEUS NEES.	Philadelphia County.	September 21st.
JOHN PHILIP STREITER,	Bucks. County.	September 21st.
Lutheran Minister.		
HENRICK RITTER.	Bucks. County.	September 11th.
HENRY SCHLEYDORN.	Philadelphia City.	August 3rd.
MATHIAS SCHUTZ.	Philadelphia City.	July 30th.
MATHIAS SCHUTZ, Junr.	Philadelphia City.	August 3rd.
JOHN LEONARD STONE.	Philadelphia County.	July 6th.
ADAM REDER.	Philadelphia County.	September 22nd.
VALENTINE KEELER.	Philadelphia County.	September 22nd.
LEONARD KNOPP.	Bucks. County.	September 22nd.
HENRICK PETERS.	Philadelphia County.	September 22nd.
NICHOLAS COOB, Junr.	Philadelphia County.	September 25th.
HENRY MATHISON.	Philadelphia City.	July 27th.
JOHN MICHAEL DILL.	Philadelphia City.	July 26th.
GEORGE ALLBRIGHT.	Philadelphia City.	August 3rd, 1740.
FEELIX FESLER.	Philadelphia City.	September 23rd.
JACOB UTTREY.	Philadelphia City.	September 7th.

Quakers.

At a Court held the 25th, 26th and 27th of September, 1740.

	Persons' Names.	Of what County.
T. 50.	JOHN CRESSMAN.	Philadelphia County.
	HENRY OTT.	Bucks. County.
	JOHN GEORGE VANLAOR.	Chester County.
	BENJAMIN ROSSENBERGH.	Philadelphia County.
	ISAAC MILLER.	Philadelphia County.
	CHRISTIAN SNIDER.	Philadelphia County.
	LODOWICK HARNONG.	Philadelphia County.
	JOHN VANFOSSEN.	Philadelphia County.
	JOHN SHELLIBERGER.	Philadelphia County.
	CHRISTOPHER TREWBEY.	Bucks. County.
	MATHIAS NICE.	Philadelphia County.
	CHRISTIAN STOWFER.	Philadelphia County.
	HENRY STETTLER.	Philadelphia County.
	DEWALD NICE.	Bucks. County.
	PHILIP REDIVAL.	Philadelphia County.
	JOHN HUNTER.	Philadelphia County.

PENNSYLVANIA.

Persons' Names.	Of what County.
MICHAEL RYER.	Philadelphia County.
GERRART SHRAGER.	Philadelphia County.
GOSSEN SHRAGER, Junr.	Philadelphia County.
ANDREW FISHER.	Philadelphia County.
MICHAEL WRITTER.	Philadelphia County.
ISAAC GRALL.	Philadelphia County.
GEORGE WOOD.	Philadelphia County.
JOHANNES SNIDER.	Philadelphia County.
NICHOLAS WALLBER.	Bucks. County.
BARTHOLOMEW WRITTER.	Philadelphia County.
DANIEL WARLEY.	Philadelphia County.
ANTHONY HUNTER.	Philadelphia County.
JACOB PETERS.	Philadelphia County.
PETER PETERS.	Philadelphia County.
VALENTINE KEELER.	Philadelphia County.
HENRY GROTHOUSE.	Lancaster County.
JOHN PHILIP SHELLIG.	Philadelphia County.
JACOB HUBER.	Lancaster County.
HENRICK HERMELL.	Philadelphia County.
JACOB COLLMAN.	Philadelphia County.
ABRAHAM SAILER.	Philadelphia County.
ANTHONY GILBERT.	Philadelphia County.
JACOB NAGLEE.	Philadelphia County.
ABRAHAM KINTZING.	Philadelphia City.
GEORGE HAWS.	Philadelphia County.
GEORGE SHORN.	Philadelphia County.
DANIEL BERNDALLER.	Philadelphia County.
HERMAN GOTSHALL.	Philadelphia County.
BLASIUS DANIEL MACKINET.	Philadelphia County.
CASPAR OTT.	Bucks. County.
ALEXANDER DIBBIN DURFER.	Bucks. County.
JOHN GROOTHOUSE.	Philadelphia County.
JACOB SOUTER.	Philadelphia County.
MARTIN WIGHTMAN.	Lancaster County.
GEORGE BENSELL.	Philadelphia County.
CHARLES BENSELL.	Philadelphia County.
NICHOLAS RABINE.	Philadelphia County.
PHILIP SHARP.	Philadelphia County.
VALENTINE SHADAIRE.	Philadelphia County.
ADAM LEBERGER.	Philadelphia County.
JOHN GULL.	Philadelphia County.
CASPAR FEIGHT.	Philadelphia County.
PAUL WYKERLINE.	Philadelphia County.
JOHN OMSTADT.	Philadelphia County.
PETER SNIDER.	Bucks. County.
GARRET RATTENHAWSEN.	Philadelphia County.
JOHN BARTHOLOMEW.	Philadelphia County.
JOHN WOOD.	Philadelphia County.
MARK MINSER.	Philadelphia County.
JOHN GEORGE HOFFMAN.	Philadelphia County.
BERNARD WOOLFINGER.	Philadelphia County.
BALTES REZER.	Philadelphia County.

Persons' Names.	Of what County.
GEORGE CROSSMAN.	Philadelphia County.
JOHN GEORGE LITTLE JOHN.	Bucks. County.
HENRY BARD.	Philadelphia County.
CASPAR WISTAR.	Philadelphia City.
JOSEPH SMITH.	Philadelphia County.
JOHN HEISER.	Philadelphia County.
JOHN RUSH.	Philadelphia County.
THOMAS MYER.	Philadelphia City.
JOHN WISTAR.	Philadelphia City.
ARENT HASSERT.	Philadelphia City.
DAVID DESHLER.	Philadelphia City.

(Philadelphia, May 7th, 1740:

The foregoing is a true List taken from the Original Certificate under the Hand of Jeremiah Langborne, Esq., in my Office by   PAT. BAIRD, Secretary.)

([*Covering letter with T. 63*] Sir,—I was honoured with your Letter of the 11th of August last, acknowledging the receipt of mine of May 7th preceding, with the Lists of Foreigners naturalized here; and am glad that the manner in which those Lists were transmitted proved satisfactory to their Lordships.

I now have the Honour to transmit herewith lists of such Foreigners as have taken the Benefit of the Naturalization Act in this Province within this year last past; and am [&c.]
Philadª, April 24th, 1742.   PATRICK BAIRD.
Thomas Hill, Esq.

Supreme Court held at Philadelphia, 24 Sept., 1741.)

Persons Naturalized in 1741.

	Persons' Names.	Of what County.	Time of taking the Sacrament.
T. 63.	JOHN CASPAR STOEVER.	Lancaster County.	September 20th, 1741.
	CONRAD SHARFF.	Lancaster County.	September 13th, 1741.
	NATHANIEL LYTNER.	Lancaster County.	September 20th, 1741.
	MICHAEL RHYNE.	Lancaster County.	September 20th, 1741.
	ELIAS LANG.	Philadelphia County.	August 30th, 1741.
	MARTIN REYER.	Philadelphia County.	August 30th, 1741.
	BARTLE COOKER.	Philadelphia County.	August 30th, 1741.
	PETER BALSBACH.	Lancaster County.	September 22nd, 1741.
	JOHANNES GORNER.	Lancaster County.	September 13th, 1741.
	LAWRENCE LAWFER.	Philadelphia County.	August 30th, 1741.
	PHILIP REID.	Philadelphia County.	August 30th, 1741.
	GEORGE WELLKER.	Philadelphia County.	August 30th, 1741.
	HANS ADAM MAYRER.	Philadelphia County.	August 23rd, 1741.
	BENEDICT STRAUM.	Philadelphia County.	August 30th, 1741.
	JOHANNES DUNCKELL.	Philadelphia County.	September 16th, 1741.
	ULRICK SHERER.	Philadelphia County.	September 15th, 1741.
	HANS GEORGE KAPPLE.	Philadelphia County.	September 24th, 1741.
	MICHAEL REEDER.	Philadelphia County.	August 30th, 1741.
	HENRICK HOOVER.	Philadelphia County.	September 21st, 1741.
	HENRICK GOLLMAN.	Philadelphia County.	August 30th, 1741.
	JOHANNES TRICKTENHENGST.	Philadelphia County.	September 16th, 1741.
	PETER BEYSELL.	Philadelphia County.	August 23rd, 1741.

c

PENNSYLVANIA.

Persons' Names.	Of what County.	Time of taking the Sacrament.
JACOB FREDERICK REIGER.	Lancaster County.	Sep. 30th (13th), 1741.
GEORGE ZIMMERMAN.	Philadelphia County.	August 30th, 1741.
HENRICK KLEIN.	Lancaster County.	August 13th, 1741.
JOHN BISHOP.	Lancaster County.	September 24th, 1741.
PHILIP EMMERT.	Philadelphia County.	August 16th, 1741.
GEORGE PALTSGRAAFF.	Philadelphia County.	August 16th, 1741.
JACOB KRAUS.	Philadelphia County.	September 16th, 1741.

Persons Naturalized in 1742.
(Supreme Court held 10 April, 1742.)

Persons' Names.	Of what County.	Time of taking the Sacrament.
CHRISTIAN MARKLING.	Philadelphia County.	March 23rd, 1741.
NICHOLAS KERN.	Bucks. County.	March 9th, 1741.
PETER TRACHSELL.	Bucks. County.	March 9th, 1741.
PETER TRACHSELL, Junr.	Bucks. County.	March 9th, 1741.
ABRAHAM WOTRING.	Bucks. County.	February 20th, 1741.

[*Secretary's Certificate in similar form to foregoing dated Philadelphia, April 24, 1742.*]

Persons Naturalized in 1742 and 1743.
(Supreme Court at Philadelphia, 24 Sept., 1742.)

V. 5.

Persons' Names.	Of what County.	Time of taking the Sacrament.
PETER ULRICK.	Philadelphia County.	September 19th, 1742.
FREDERICK ANTES.	Philadelphia County.	September 12th, 1742.
JOHAN PETER WALLBER.	Bucks. County.	September 5th, 1742.

(Supreme Court at Philadelphia, 11, 12 and 13 April, 1743.)

HANS ADAM OX.	Philadelphia County.	January 25th, 1742.
LEONARD OX.	Philadelphia County.	April 3rd, 1743.
JOHAN MICHAEL WEICHELL.	Philadelphia County.	April 3rd, 1743.
JOHN BROWN.	Philadelphia County.	April 3rd, 1743.
MICHAEL KNOLL.	Philadelphia County.	April 10th, 1743.
MICHAEL KALB.	Philadelphia County.	April 10th, 1743.
SIMON BELZENER.	Philadelphia County.	April 10th, 1743.
GEORGE HILIG.	Philadelphia County.	February 12th, 1742.
JOHAN MARTIN DERR.	Philadelphia County.	April 3rd, 1743.
JACOB KEITZ MILLER.	Lancaster County.	April 3rd, 1743.
LEONARD BUCK.	Philadelphia County.	April 3rd, 1743.
WENDEL SWEGGER.	Lancaster County.	April 3rd, 1743.
MICHAEL RANCK.	Lancaster County.	April 3rd, 1743.
MICHAEL BRUBAGH.	Lancaster County.	April 3rd, 1743.
JOHN DEWED DARFER.	Lancaster County.	April 3rd, 1743.
JOHN SMOSE.	Lancaster County.	April 3rd, 1743.
JACOB KELLER.	Lancaster County.	April 3rd, 1743.
ADAM MILLER.	Lancaster County.	April 3rd, 1743.
GEORGE SAILER.	Philadelphia County.	April 5th, 1743.
NICHOLAS STEYLER.	Bucks. County.	April 5th, 1743.
PETER WALBER.	Bucks. County.	April 4th, 1743.
HANS GEORGE OVERBECK,	Philadelphia County.	April 3rd, 1743.
ADAM STUMP,	Lancaster County.	April 3rd, 1743.

Persons' Names.	Of what County.	Time of taking the Sacrament.
HENRICK MOYER.	Lancaster County.	April 3rd, 1743.
LEONARD CROW.	Lancaster County.	April 5th, 1743.
JACOB KOUGH.	Philadelphia County.	February 3rd, 1742.
JOHN DEANY.	Philadelphia County.	April 9th, 1743.
GEORGE MOYER.	Philadelphia County.	April 4th, 1743.
ANDREAS MAAS.	Bucks. County.	April 9th, 1743.
PHILIP STIOR.	Lancaster County.	April 3rd, 1743.
DAVID BEEHLER.	Lancaster County.	April 3rd, 1743.
LEONARD MILLER.	Lancaster County.	April 3rd, 1743.
JACOB WISE.	Lancaster County.	April 3rd, 1743.
JACOB WISE, JUNR.	Lancaster County.	April 3rd, 1743.
JOHN BERGER.	Lancaster County.	April 3rd, 1743.
SEBASTIAN REYER.	Lancaster County.	April 3rd, 1743.
MICHAEL HEINTZ.	Philadelphia County.	April 4th, 1743.
MICHAEL HEINTZ, Junr.	Philadelphia County.	April 4th, 1743.
ANTHONY HEINTZ.	Bucks. County.	April 4th, 1743.
PETER CUNRADT.	Philadelphia County.	January 25th, 1742.
JACOB MAWRER.	Philadelphia County.	April 3rd, 1743.
FREDERICK MAURER.	Philadelphia County.	April 3rd, 1743.
CONRAD TEMPLEMAN.	Lancaster County.	April 4th, 1743.
MATTHIAS RINGER.	Philadelphia County.	April 9th, 1743.
GEORGE STULTZ.	Philadelphia County.	April 4th, 1743.
JOHAN PETER KOOGHER.	Lancaster County.	April 3rd, 1743.
BERNHART RENN.	Philadelphia County.	April 10th, 1743.
PETER HEYBEY.	Philadelphia County.	April 3rd, 1743.
HENRY CHRIST.	Philadelphia County.	April 3rd, 1743.
LAWRENCE BAST.	Philadelphia County.	April 3rd, 1743.
ULRICK BURKHALTER.	Bucks. County.	April 4th, 1743.
CONRAD BORDER.	Philadelphia County.	April 5th, 1743.
JOHN NICHOLAS MERTZ.	Philadelphia County.	April 5th, 1743.
MICHAEL HOFFMAN.	Bucks. County.	April 5th, 1743.
HENRY CIRCLE.	Philadelphia County.	April 4th, 1743.
MICHAEL KRAPS.	Philadelphia County.	April 10th, 1743.
HENRY KRAPS.	Philadelphia County.	April 10th, 1743.
SIMON KRAPS.	Philadelphia County.	April 10th, 1743.
JOHANNES MIEKENDURFFER.	Bucks County.	April 3rd, 1743.
JACOB FELLMAN.	Philadelphia County.	April 3rd, 1743.
JOHN GEO. EVENSIDELL.	Philadelphia County.	April 4th, 1743.

Quakers.

V. 5.

Persons' Names.	Of what County.
JOHN CIMMERMAN or CARPENTER.	Lancaster County.
JOHN BOUCHER.	Lancaster County.
JOHN WILLIAM CROX.	Philadelphia County.
HENRY OTTMAN.	Philadelphia County.
HENRY WET STONE.	Philadelphia County.
NICHOLAS HARMANY.	Philadelphia County.
CONRAD FISHER.	Philadelphia County.
JOSEPH ALBRIGHT.	Bucks. County.
ABRAHAM ASHMAN.	Philadelphia County.
GEORGE KELCKNER.	Philadelphia County.

NATURALIZATIONS

PENNSYLVANIA.

Persons' Names.	Of what County.
HENRICK REEZER.	Lancaster County.
WILLIAM REEZER.	Lancaster County.
ULRICK REEZER.	Bucks. County.
JOHANNES RYME (KYME).	Philadelphia County.
JOHAN GEO. STONEMAN.	Philadelphia County.
JOHN STINEMAN.	Philadelphia County.
FEDERICK FANDY.	Germantown.
VALENTINE GREASMORE.	Philadelphia County.
JACOB SHAID.	Bucks. County.
JOHN LESHER.	Philadelphia County
MATHIAS BECK.	Philadelphia County.
WILLIAM SPECK.	Philadelphia County
MICHAEL KELCKNOR.	Philadelphia County
INGLE PETER.	Philadelphia County
ABRAHAM PETER.	Philadelphia County.
GABRIEL BOUYER.	Philadelphia County.
PETER RODERMILL.	Philadelphia County.
CHRISTIAN STUMP.	Lancaster County.
MICHAEL NETT.	Lancaster County.
MICHAEL NETT, Junr.	Lancaster County.
ELIAS WAGONER.	Philadelphia County.
GABRIEL ISEBERGER.	Philadelphia County.
FLORIAN BOOBINGER.	Philadelphia County.
GEORGE ADAM WIDENER.	Philadelphia County.
DAVID WISER.	Philadelphia County.
SEBASTIAN CIMMERMAN.	Philadelphia County.
DANIEL LEIVAN.	Philadelphia County.
JOHN PERDO.	Philadelphia County.
PHILIP FAUST.	Philadelphia County.
SEBASTIAN WAGONAR.	Chester County.
DEDRICK BIDLEMAN.	Philadelphia County.
JACOB KARST.	Philadelphia City.
SEBASTIAN DERR.	Bucks. County.
PHILIP SCHMYER.	Bucks. County.
PHILIP BEYER.	Philadelphia County.
JOHN LYNE.	Lancaster County.
REINARD VOGDES.	Philadelphia County.
CHRISTOPHER WEIFER.	Philadelphia County.
WILLIAM GREANMORE.	Philadelphia County.
GEORGE CASPER SLEHER.	Philadelphia County.
ABRAHAM BARTOLET.	Philadelphia County.
JOHN BARTLET, Junr.	Philadelphia County.
JACOB VETTER.	Philadelphia County.
CHRISTIAN BROWER.	Chester County.
PETER BRECKER.	Lancaster County.
ADAM WIDENAR.	Philadelphia County.
JOHN WIDTNER.	Philadelphia County.
JOHN GEO. WIDTNER.	Philadelphia County.
MICHAEL SPOONE.	Philadelphia County.
MARTIN KINDIG.	Lancaster County.
JOHN KINDIG.	Lancaster County.
WILLIAM POTT.	Lancaster County.

Persons' Names.	Of what County.
ABRAHAM SHELLY.	Bucks. County.
LAWRENCE SLAYMAKER.	Lancaster County.
JACOB GRAFF.	Lancaster County.
CHRISTIAN KINTZING.	Philadelphia County.
JOHANNES BALDT (BABELT).	Philadelphia County.
JACOB BALDT.	Philadelphia County.
RUDOLPH MAROLFF.	Philadelphia County.
CHARLES KRES.	Philadelphia County.
SEBASTIAN MILLER.	Philadelphia County.
CHRISTIAN TAPPAN.	Lancaster County.
EMANUEL SASSAMANHAWS.	Philadelphia County.
JOHANNES LEDDRAUGH.	Philadelphia County.
GEORGE BEIGHLEY.	Philadelphia County.
JACOB TATWAITER (TATWAILER).	Bucks. County.
ANDREAS LEDDRAUGH.	Philadelphia County.
PETER DUNCKLEBERRY.	Philadelphia County.
JOHN LINGENFELTER.	Lancaster County.
JACOB WISE.	Philadelphia County.
JACOB KALCKLOESER.	Germantown, Philadelphia County.
IMANUEL KALCKLOESER.	Germantown, Philadelphia County.
ABRAHAM BRYDER.	Bucks. County.
JACOB WISLAR.	Philadelphia County.
JACOB MAST.	Lancaster County.
JOHN ACCRE. .	Philadelphia County.
JOHN ADAMS.	Philadelphia County.
CHRISTIAN ALLEBAUGH.	Philadelphia County.
COLLEE HEFFLEFINGER.	Philadelphia County.
CASPAR BOWMAN.	Philadelphia County.
DANIEL STOUFFER.	Philadelphia County.
VALENTINE KRATZ.	Philadelphia County.
PETER BEIDLER.	Philadelphia County.
JACOB BUCKWALTER.	Philadelphia County.
ULRICK BEIDLER.	Philadelphia County.
ISAAC MEYER.	Philadelphia County.
JOHANNES BROWER.	Chester County.
ULRICK SCHERER.	Philadelphia County.
JACOB CLEMENS.	Philadelphia County.
HANS MEYER.	Philadelphia County.
ANDREAS SWARTZ.	Philadelphia County.
LAWRENCE CORNELIUS.	Philadelphia County.
HENRY HEFFLEFINGER.	Philadelphia County.
NICHOLAS UPLINGER.	Philadelphia County.
NICHOLAS HADLEMAN(HALDEMAN).	Chester County.
NICHOLAS HADLEMAN(HALDEMAN) Junr.	Philadelphia County.
CHRISTIAN BEIDLER.	Philadelphia County.
ABRAHAM FLURY.	Philadelphia County.
JOHN BEYLE.	Philadelphia County.
JACOB BUSSART.	Chester County.
PETER ASH.	Chester County.
HENRY RUDHT.	Philadelphia County.
JOHANNES BRAND.	Philadelphia County.
JACOB LANTES.	Philadelphia County.
JACOB (JOHANNES) BEKNER.	Philadelphia County.

PENNSYLVANIA.

Persons' Names.	Of what County.
Johannes Swing.	Philadelphia County.
Jacob Krop.	Philadelphia County.
Jacob Graffe.	Philadelphia County.
Hans Wyerman.	Philadelphia County.
Hans Wyerman, Junr.	Philadelphia County.
Jacob Wyerman.	Philadelphia County.
Jacob Greder.	Philadelphia County.
Christian Haldeman.	Philadelphia County.
Henry Rosyberger.	Philadelphia County.
Jacob Oberholser.	Philadelphia County.
Jacob Oberholser, Junr.	Philadelphia County.
Jacob Winer.	Philadelphia County.
Jacob Engars.	Chester County.
Johannes Engars.	Chester County.
Jost Engar.	Chester County.
Jacob Landes, Junr.	Philadelphia County.
Michael Driftain (Dirstein).	Bucks. County.
Conrad Stemm.	Philadelphia County.
Abraham Myer (Meyer).	Philadelphia County.
Julius Kassle.	Philadelphia County.
Johannes Kassle.	Philadelphia County.
Hans Ulrick Burgher.	Philadelphia County.
Jacob Shoemaker.	Philadelphia County.
Jacob Hogman.	Philadelphia County.
Samuel Mosleman.	Philadelphia County.
Jacob Hefflefinger.	Philadelphia County.
Philip Hough.	Philadelphia County.
Jacob Bach.	Chester County.
Jacob Landes.	Philadelphia County.
Jacob Sable Kool.	Bucks. County.
Jacob Overholster.	Philadelphia County
Henry Overholster.	Philadelphia County.
John Bower.	Philadelphia County.
Samuel Bower.	Philadelphia County.
Henry Dentlinger.	Philadelphia County.
Julius Julius.	Philadelphia County.
Christian Meyer.	Philadelphia County.
John Henry Schynder.	Philadelphia County.
Abraham Meyer.	Philadelphia County.
Peter Shelbert.	Philadelphia County.
Johannes Stump.	Lancaster County.
Christian Meyer, Junr.	Philadelphia County.
Hans Reiff.	Philadelphia County.
Jacob Sessenning.	Lancaster County.
Francis Ladshower.	Philadelphia County.
Peter Mell.	Philadelphia County.
Johannes Steiner.	Chester County.
John Clemens.	Philadelphia County.
Federick Allderfer.	Philadelphia County.
Hans Ulrick Stober.	Philadelphia County.
Martin Greter.	Philadelphia County.
John Kiem.	Philadelphia County.

Of what County.	Persons' Names.
NICHOLAS ENGLEHART.	Philadelphia County.
HENRY WENGER.	Philadelphia County.
GEORGE REEZER.	Chester County.
CHRISTIAN CRALL.	Bucks. County.
JACOB HUNTSBERGER.	Philadelphia County.
FREDERICK STYNER.	Philadelphia County.
ANDREAS HOFFMAN.	Chester County.
ANTHONY NOBLE.	Philadelphia City (paintor [*sic*]).
PETER SWARTZ.	Philadelphia County.
JOHANNES MAK.	Germantown, Philadelphia County.
ANDREAS BUZZARD.	Philadelphia County.
CHRISTIAN BRANDIMAN.	Philadelphia County.
JOHANNES SEIGLER.	Philadelphia County.
PETER BINGAMON.	Philadelphia County.
CHRISTOPHER RHEINWALD.	Philadelphia County.
VALENTINE BAKER.	Lancaster County.
MICHAEL KRIDER.	Philadelphia County.
GEORGE DRESHER.	Philadelphia County.
CHRISTOPHER DRESHER.	Philadelphia County.
GEORGE KRIBELL.	Philadelphia County.
GEORGE HEIDRICK.	Philadelphia County.
ABRAHAM HEDRICK (HEIDRICK).	Philadelphia County.
HANS HUBNER.	Philadelphia County.
CHRISTOPHER MOLL.	Philadelphia County.
LEONARD HENDRICKS.	Philadelphia County.
PAUL HENDRICKS.	Philadelphia County.
WENDELL WIAND.	Philadelphia County.
CASPAR KRIBELL.	Philadelphia County.
DAVID SEIBT.	Philadelphia County.
JOHANNES HEANES.	Philadelphia County.
JOST SHINGLER.	Philadelphia County.
CHRISTOPHER WEIGNER.	Philadelphia County.
CHRISTIAN LEHMAN.	Germantown, Philadelphia County.
JOHN LEHMAN.	Germantown, Philadelphia County.
CHRISTOPHER YEAKELL.	Philadelphia County.
ABRAHAM YAKELL.	Philadelphia County.
BALTHAZAR HEIDRICK.	Philadelphia County.
JOHN HUBENER, Junr.	Philadelphia County.
ABRAHAM YAKELL.	Philadelphia County.
CHRISTOPHER YAKELL.	Philadelphia County.
JOHN YAKELL.	Bucks. County.
BALTHAZAR YAKELL.	Bucks. County.
DAVID MESSHTER.	Philadelphia County.
GEORGE SCHULTZ.	Philadelphia County.
BALTHAZAR KAUS.	Bucks. County.
WILLIAM SMITH.	Philadelphia County.
MARTIN HILDEBIDLE.	Philadelphia County.
JOHN GEO. WAMBELDT.	Bucks. County.
ANDREW HAWK.	Philadelphia County.
JACOB LEVAN.	Philadelphia County.
CUNRAD HENNINGER.	Philadelphia County.
GEORGE SCHOLTZ, Junr.	Philadelphia County.
MELCHIOR SCHOLTZ.	Philadelphia County.
CHRISTOPHER SCHOLTZ.	Philadelphia County.

PENNSYLVANIA.

Persons' Names.	Of what County.
JOHN MOCK.	Philadelphia County.
MELCHIOR WEIGNER (WIEGNER).	Philadelphia County.
ABRAHAM BEYER, Junr.	Philadelphia County.
HANS WEIGNER.	Philadelphia County.
CHRISTOPHER NOYMAN.	Philadelphia County.
WILLIAM CARICIS.	Philadelphia County.
NICHOLAS MORITZ.	Philadelphia County.
HERMAN JUNGHEN.	Philadelphia County.
HENRY LUKEN BEELL.	Philadelphia County.
HENRY GRUBB.	Philadelphia County.
CONRAD GRUBB.	Philadelphia County.
MICHAEL KUNTZ.	Philadelphia County.
JOHN HALLMAN.	Philadelphia County.
FREDERICK (FEDERICK) BAKER.	Philadelphia County.
JOHANNES SHINHOLSER.	Chester County.
JACOB SHWARTZ.	Bucks. County.
CHRISTOPHER BASTIAN.	Philadelphia County.
LODEWICK ENGLEHART.	Philadelphia County.
DEWALD KEMP.	Philadelphia County.
JOHANNES QUARTSTILWAG.	Bucks. County.
PETER FEDEROFF (FEDEROLFF).	Philadelphia County.
PAUL BRANNER.	Philadelphia County.

(A true copy from the Records of the Supream Court of Pennsylvania :
Certified by John Ross, Proton' Let this be delivered to the Secretary of the Province of Pennsylvania that an Entry thereof may by him be made, pursuant to the Tenor of the Act of Parliament in such case lately made and provided. JOHN KINSEY.)

(Supreme Court at Philadelphia, 24, 26 and 27 Sept., 1743.)

	Persons' Names.	Of what County.	Time of taking the Sacrament.
V. 28.	JOHN CONRAD RADD	Philadelphia County.	September 11th, 1743.
	JOHN JACOB RATHE.	Philadelphia County.	September 11th, 1743.
	MICHAEL BETTLEY.	Lancaster County.	September 18th, 1743.
	MATHIAS HIGNER.	Philadelphia County.	September 18th, 1743.
	MICHAEL HANINGER	Philadelphia County.	September 18th, 1743.
	JOHANNES SCHREYCK.	Lancaster County.	July 3rd, 1743.
	MELCHER INGEL.	Lancaster County.	August 21st, 1743.
	JACOB MYER.	Bucks. County.	September 18th, 1743.
	ADAM HILL.	Philadelphia County.	August 21st, 1743.
	GOTLIFF HILL.	Lancaster County.	September 21st, 1743.
	HENRY ACKER.	Bucks. County.	September 16th, 1743.
	MICHAEL MOLL.	Philadelphia County.	September 18th, 1743.
	BERNARD HUBBLEY.	Lancaster County.	September 18th, 1743.
	JACOB SMITH.	Philadelphia County.	September 18th, 1743.
	BURCHARD HOFFMAN.	Philadelphia County.	September 11th, 1743.
	GETTY GRIMM.	Bucks. County.	September 19th, 1743.
	CHRISTOPHER EXLINE.	Philadelphia County.	May 25th, 1743.
	MELCHIOR SUSHOLT.	Philadelphia County.	September 11th, 1743.
	CHRISTOPHER STADLER.	Bucks. County.	September 16th, 1743.
	PHILIP JACOB ACKRE.	Bucks. County.	September 19th, 1743.

Persons' Names.	Of what County.	Time of taking the Sacrament.
GEORGE STANINGAR.	Bucks. County.	September 19th, 1743.
HENRY RICKE.	Bucks. County.	September 19th, 1743.
JOHN LICHTENWALLNER.	Bucks. County.	September 19th, 1743.
JACOB SNEFFLE.	Lancaster County.	September 18th, 1743.
CASPER SHAFFNER.	Lancaster County.	Taken in the presence of John Hanneberger and Jacob Koontz as by their Depositions appear.
PETER KNOPPLE.	Lancaster County.	Taken as the above two.
HANS JACOB KUNTZ.	Lancaster County.	} Taken by them as the
JOHN HANNIBERGER.	Lancaster County.	} Depositions of Peter Knopple and Casper Shaffner appear.

Quakers.

	Persons' Names.	Of what County.
V. 28.	HENRY KENDRICK.	Lancaster County.
	JACOB BOYER.	Lancaster County.
	RUDOLPH STONER.	Lancaster County.
	ANDREW MUSSEMAN.	Lancaster County.
	JACOB HARNEST.	Lancaster County.
	JOHN BYER.	Lancaster County.
	SAMUEL BYER.	Lancaster County.
	ABRAHAM SMITH.	Lancaster County.
	ULRICK HOOVER.	Lancaster County.
	JACOB BESLER.	Philadelphia County.
	JACOB HOOVER.	Lancaster County.
	JOHN KINGRY.	Lancaster County.
	RUDOLPH BEHME.	Lancaster County.
	JACOB RHORA.	Lancaster County.
	JOHN RHORA.	Lancaster County.
	ANDREW ACKRE.	Bucks. County.
	PHILIP GAVY.	Bucks. County.
	PETER LEMAN.	Lancaster County.
	JOHN MEEM.	Philadelphia County.
	GEORGE SPINGLER.	Philadelphia County.
	HENRY LEBART.	Lancaster County.
	MARTIN SCHULTZ.	Lancaster County.
	CHRISTIAN HOOVER.	Lancaster County.
	HANS MUSSLE.	Lancaster County.

(Said Supreme Court, 10, 11 and 12 April, 1744.)

	Persons' Names.	Of what County.	Time of taking the Sacrament.
V. 28.	PHILIP SWICKACK.	Lancaster County.	March 23rd, 1743-4.
	GEORGE THOMAS SOWDER.	Lancaster County.	April 8th, 1744.
	JOHN WOLFERSPARGER.	Lancaster County.	April 1st. 1744.
	GEORGE WATERMAN.	Lancaster County.	February 26th, 1743.
	JOHN SHEFFER.	Lancaster County.	March 25th, 1744.
	PHILIP SCHATZ.	Lancaster County.	February 26th, 1743.
	HENRY SAUNDER.	Lancaster County.	April 6th, 1744.
	WYRICK PENCE.	Lancaster County.	April 6th, 1744.
	JACOB HOUGH.	Lancaster County.	March 26th, 1744.
	GEORGE HOUGH.	Lancaster County.	March 26th, 1744.
	SAMUEL HOUGH.	Lancaster County.	March 26th, 1744.

PENNSYLVANIA.

Persons' Names.	Of what County.	Time of taking the Sacrament.
RUDOLPH DRAUGH.	Lancaster County.	March 25th, 1744.
GEORGE SWOPE.	Lancaster County.	April 1st, 1744.
CHRISTIAN CROLL.	Lancaster County.	March 18th, 1743-4.
LODOVICK WILLANGER.	Philadelphia County.	March 25th, 1744.
GEORGE CROANER.	Bucks. County.	March 25th, 1744.
JOHN RICHARD.	Philadelphia County.	March 25th, 1744.
ADAM SIMON KICHN.	Lancaster County.	April 8th, 1744.
BALTZER STEEVER.	Bucks. County.	March 25th, 1744.
CHRISTIAN STAMBAUGH.	Bucks. County.	March 25th, 1744.
LEONARD HARMAN.	Philadelphia County.	April 1st, 1744.
CRONOMUS HICKMAN.	Lancaster County.	April 8th, 1744.
VALENTINE UNRUW.	Lancaster County.	April 2nd, 1744.
JOHN RYALL.	Lancaster County.	April 2nd, 1744.
JACOB WILHELM.	Lancaster County.	April 2nd, 1744.
ELIAS MYER.	Lancaster County.	March 25th, 1744.
MATHIAS BETTLEY.	Lancaster County.	March 25th, 1744.
GEORGE VAFFENBERGER.	Lancaster County.	March 25th, 1744.
PETER BERNHARD.	Philadelphia County.	April 1st, 1744.
NICHOLAS CARVER.	Chester County.	April 5th, 1744.
JOHN CAMBREE.	Philadelphia County.	April 1st, 1744.
PETER GARDNER.	Lancaster County.	April 11th, 1744.
GEORGE AMMOND.	Lancaster County.	April 11th, 1744.

Quakers.

	Persons' Names.	Of what County.
V. 28.	PETER BUNN.	Philadelphia County.
	JOHN FREDERICK.	Philadelphia County.
	JOHN MILLER.	Lancaster County.
	ULRICK LYPE.	Lancaster County.
	HENRY ABERLEE.	Lancaster County.
	HANS SHOWNOWER.	Lancaster County.
	JOHN HARTMAN.	Philadelphia County.
	PETER GOOD.	Lancaster County.
	JOHN FALTZ.	Lancaster County.
	CONRAD WEISER.	Lancaster County.
	OSWALD HASTADDER.	Lancaster County.
	JOHN HASTADDER.	Lancaster County.
	JOSEPH CRELL.	Philadelphia City.

(Said Supreme Court, 24 and 25 Sept., 1744.)

	Persons' Names.	Of what County.	Time of taking the Sacrament.
V. 28.	JOHN GEORGE GRAFF.	Lancaster County.	September 5th, 1744.
	JOHN DAVID SICKLE.	Philadelphia County.	September 24th ,1744.
	GODFREY BROWN.	Lancaster County.	August 22nd, 1744.
	JOHN PHILIP DE BERTHOLT.	Philadelphia County.	September 24th, 1744.
	ANDREW WOLF.	Philadelphia County.	September 16th, 1744.
	HENRY MILLER.	Philadelphia County.	September 24th, 1744.
	JOHN MICHAEL HEYTER.	Philadelphia County.	September 24th, 1744.

Quakers.

Persons' Names.	Of what County.
V. 28.	
CHRISTIAN RODARMARLE.	Philadelphia County.
DANIEL LODOWICK.	Philadelphia County.
PAUL RODARMARLE.	Philadelphia County.
JACOB HOFMAN.	Philadelphia County.
PETER LOBACK.	Philadelphia County.
LEONARD HULSTER.	Lancaster County.
VALENTINE FREEMAN.	Lancaster County.
ANDREW STRICKLER.	Lancaster County.
ANDREW ELLIOTT.	Lancaster County.
JOHN JOHNSTON.	Lancaster County.
HANS GARBER.	Lancaster County.
MICHAEL GARBER.	Lancaster County.
MICHAEL BRECHTH.	Lancaster County.

(Said Supreme Court, 10 and 11 April, 1745.)

Persons' Names.	Of what County.	Time of taking the Sacrament.
V. 28.		
JACOB HEAGY.	Lancaster County.	April 8th, 1745.
BALTHAZAR SEES.	Lancaster County.	January 1st, 1744.
DAVID KERGER.	Philadelphia County.	April 10th, 1745.
MATHIAS VENRICK.	Lancaster County.	December 25th, 1744.

Quakers.

Persons' Names.	Of what County.
V. 28.	
WILLIAM MYE.	Philadelphia County.
ULRICK STOUPHER.	Lancaster County.
RUDOLPH SALVER.	Bucks. County.
MATHIAS WINDLE.	Philadelphia County.
BENJAMIN BOUCHER.	Lancaster County.
CASPER CREESERMER.	Philadelphia County.
GEORGE RITER.	Philadelphia County.
NICHOLAS EYES.	Philadelphia County.

(Quakers—continued.

Said Supreme Court, 24 Sept., 1745.)

ABRAHAM HARTRAMPFF.	Philadelphia County.
GEORGE WIGNER.	Philadelphia County.
ABRAHAM WIGNER.	Philadelphia County.
MELCHIOR MAYSTER.	Philadelphia County.
GEORGE HOFFMAN.	Philadelphia County.
CHRISTOPHER KRIBEL.	Philadelphia County.
GEORGE REINWALT.	Philadelphia County.
CHRISTOPHER SEIBR [sic].	Philadelphia County.
CHRISTOPHER HIBNER.	Philadelphia County.
DAVID HIBNER.	Philadelphia County.
MICHAEL SCHAIRER.	Lancaster County.
JONENS JONER.	Lancaster County.
CHRISTIAN GEMELIN.	Philadelphia County.
PHILIP SHAFFER.	Lancaster County.
MICHAEL BROOKS.	Lancaster County.
DAVID SHEWBERT [sic].	Philadelphia County.
JACOB BEIDLEMAN.	Bucks. County.

PENNSYLVANIA.

(Said Supreme Court, 24 Sept., 1745.)

[NOTE.—This is marked 'Duplicate," with note 'Original not Received,' but see above,
V. 28.]

Of what County.	Persons' Names.
V. 47.	ABRAHAM HARTRAMFF.	Philadelphia County.
	GEORGE WIGNER.	Philadelphia County.
	ABRAHAM WIGNER.	Philadelphia County.
	MELCHIOR MAYSTER.	Philadelphia County.
	GEORGE HOFFMAN.	Philadelphia County.
	CHRISTOPHER KRIBEL.	Philadelphia County.
	GEORGE REINWALT.	Philadelphia County.
	CHRISTOPHER SEIBT [sic].	Philadelphia County.
	CHRISTOPHER HIBNER.	Philadelphia County.
	DAVID HIBNER.	Philadelphia County.
	MICHAEL SCHAIRER.	Lancaster County.
	JONENS JONER.	Lancaster County.
	CHRISTIAN GEMELIN.	Philadelphia County.
	PHILIP SHAFFER.	Lancaster County.
	MICHAEL BROOKS.	Lancaster County.
	DAVID SHUBERT [sic].	Philadelphia County.
	JACOB BEIDLEMAN.	Bucks County.

(Said Supreme Court, 10 and 11 April, 1746.)

	Persons' Names.	Of what County.	Time of taking the Sacrament.
V. 47.	VALENTINE URICH.	Lancaster County.	February 2nd, 1745.
	MARTIN KALDER.	Lancaster County.	February 2nd, 1745
	JOHN LODWICK SEIPEL.	Philadelphia City.	April 4th, 1746.
	JACOB MAAG.	Philadelphia City.	April 4th, 1746.
	JACOB WEINE.	Philadelphia City.	April 4th, 1746.
	MICHAEL LUTZ.	Bucks. County.	February 2nd, 1745.
	GEORGE RUCH.	Bucks. County.	February 2nd, 1745.
	MICHAEL RUCH.	Bucks. County.	February 2nd, 1745.
	Revd. Mr. JOHN JUSTICE JACOB BERGESTOCK.	Bucks. County.	February 2nd, 1745.

Quakers.

	Persons' Names.	Of what County.
V. 4.	JACOB REISER.	Lancaster County.
	JOHN KEIDER.	Philadelphia County.
	JOHN SCHLICHTER.	Philadelphia County.
	ABRAHAM RIFE.	Philadelphia County.
	JACOB RUCK.	Philadelphia County.

(Said Supreme Court, 24 Sept., 1746.)

	Persons' Names.	Of what County.	Time of taking the Sacrament.
V. 48.	JOHANNES RUDOLPH.	Philadelphia County.	July 27th, 1746.
	GEORGE HORNE.	Philadelphia County.	September 14th, 1746.
	LEONARD NUTZ.	Lancaster County.	September 21st, 1746.
	SIMON SHIRMAN.	Lancaster County.	September 21st, 1746.
	JOHANNES MAYER.	Lancaster County.	August 31st, 1746.
	JOHANNES HABERLING.	Lancaster County.	September 14th, 1746.

Quakers.

Persons' Names.	Of what County.
V. 48.	MICHAEL MESINGER.	Philadelphia County.
	JACOB MEILY.	Lancaster County.
	PETER FOLK.	Lancaster County.
	JOHN SNIEVLY.	Lancaster County.
	HENRY HEILMAN.	Philadelphia County.
	VALENTINE HEYSER.	Philadelphia County.

(Said Supreme Court, 10, 11, 13 and 14 April, 1747.)

	Persons' Names.	Of what County.	Time of taking the Sacrament.
V 48.	JOHAN DANIEL BOUTON.	Philadelphia City.	February 1st, 1746.
	ELIAS STRICKER.	Philadelphia County.	February 1st, 1746.
	JOHN STRICKER.	Philadelphia City.	February 1st, 1746.
	MICHAEL ROIS (REIS).	Lancaster County.	March 8th, 1746.
	JOHANNES WOLFERT.	Lancaster County.	March 8th, 1746.
	CHRISTIAN MYER.	Lancaster County.	March 8th, 1746.
	GEORGE BROSIUS.	Lancaster County.	March 8th, 1746.
	JACOB HOFFMAN.	Lancaster County.	March 8th, 1746.
	ADAM MORGAN.	Philadelphia County.	April 5th, 1747.
	GEORGE KERN.	Philadelphia County.	March 30th, 1747.
	Revd. Mr. TOBIAS WAGENAR.	Philadelphia County.	March 25th, 1747.
	GEORGE KOCHER.	Philadelphia County.	January 18th, 1746
	JOHN CHRISTOPHER CUN.	Philadelphia County.	March 28th, 1747.
	LEONARD REIBER.	Philadelphia County.	March 28th, 1747.
	PHILIP MANN.	Philadelphia County.	March 28th, 1747.
	JOHN PHILIP DOLD.	Philadelphia County.	April 5th, 1747.
	JACOB MULLER.	Philadelphia County.	April 5th, 1747.
	GODFRIED HARLACHER.	Philadelphia County.	April 5th, 1747.
	GEORGE DANNEHAUER.	Philadelphia County.	April 5th, 1747.
	ADAM HINTON.	Philadelphia County.	April 5th, 1747.
	PAUL GEISEL.	Philadelphia County.	April 12th, 1747.
	MICHAEL EGE.	Philadelphia County.	April 12th, 1747.
	CHRISTOPHER LOIST.	Philadelphia County.	March 25th, 1747.

Person's Name.	Of what County.
MOSES HEYMAN, a Jew.	Philadelphia County

Quakers.

Persons' Names.	Of what County.
V. 48.	LUDWIG PLUM.	Philadelphia County.
	PETER BRETT (PRETT).	Lancaster County.
	NICHOLAS CRON.	Philadelphia County.
	DANIEL WOMELSDORFF.	Philadelphia County.
	ELIAS BUDLEMAN (BEIDLEMAN)	Bucks. County.
	CHRISTOPHER CROFFERN.	Lancaster County.
	JOHN DROUT.	Philadelphia County.
	VALENTINE LIER.	Lancaster County.
	HERICK ROTTER.	Bucks. County.
	JOHANNES EGENTER (EIGENTER).	Bucks. County.
	DOMINICUS GASSNER.	Philadelphia County.
	CONRAD WEIGNAR.	Philadelphia County.
	NICHOLAS KROFT.	Philadelphia County.
	JOHN HOUSOM.	Lancaster County.

[NOTE.—The returns V. 47 and V. 48 are duplicated in V. 57, which, however, contains later ones (*see below*).]

[*The Certificates for Pennsylvania are continued below on p. 41.*]

NEW YORK.

Persons Naturalized between the 1st of June, 1740, and the 1st of June, 1741.

Protestants.	Jews.
Gg. 68. PHILIP MILLER.	DAVID GOMEZ.
JOHANNES MILLER.	MORDECAI GOMEZ.
JOHANNES CHRIST.	DANIEL GOMEZ.
FREDERICK SENSIBACK.	JACOB TERRO, Junr.
JOHN CHRIST SENSIBACK.	SAMUEL LEVY.
HIERONIMUS VELDEN.	SAMUEL MYERS COHEN.
ZACHARIA BECKER.	ABRAHAM MYERS COHEN.
MARTINUS SNIDER.	ABRAHAM ISAACS.
COENRADT RIGHTMEYRE.	ISAAC LEVY.
MARTINUS MARCKELL.	SOLOMON MYERS.
STEPHEN DE LANCEY.	JOSEPH SIMSON.
JAMES FAVIERE.	SOLOMON BARES.
MARIE BRINGIER.	DAVID HUY.
JEAN EMAU.	ABRM. RODRIGUES DE RIVERES.
JOHN ROG.	DANLL. RODRIGUES VINERA.
JOHN AUBOYNEAU.	MOSES LOPEZ.
	JUDAH HAYES.
	LEVY SAMUEL.
	SOLOMON HART, Junr.

(Certified by Geo. Jos. Moore, Deputy Secy.)

Names of the Persons Naturalized.	Their Religious Profession.	The Month and Year.
Gg. 81.		
MOSES GOMBAULD.	Dutch Reformed.	July 28th, 1741.
DANIEL BONTECOU.	French Church.	July 31st, 1741.
JAMES BUVELOT.	French Church.	July 31st, 1741.
JOHANNES KURTS.	French Church.	October 20th, 1741.
SAMUEL GILLOT.	Lutheran.	October 21st, 1741.
JONAS SPACH.	French Reformed.	October 21st, 1741.
GEORGE JACOB SORNBERGER.	French Reformed.	October 23rd, 1741.
JOHANNES WEBER.	Lutheran.	October 23rd, 1741.
CHRISTOPHER SNEIDER.	Lutheran.	October 23rd, 1741.
ADAM BETSER.	Lutheran.	October 23rd, 1741.
ISAAC NUNES HENRIQUES.	Lutheran.	October 23rd, 1741.
ABRAHAM DE LEAS.	Jew.	October 23rd, 1741.
CHARLOTTE BOUYER FAVIERES.	Jew.	April 27th, 1742.
WILLIAM LAWRENCE.	French Church.	October 25th, 1742.

(Certified by the same.)

G. 97. (The 3rd, 4th and 5th columns are taken from the original certificate and have not been copied in the Entry Book.)

Names of Persons Naturalized.	Religion.	Their Temporal Profession and Place of Abode,	Ministers Certifying Receiving the Sacrament.	The Names of the Witnesses to the Certificate.	The Day and Year.
MOSES LEVY.	Jew.	City of New York, Merchant.			April 19th, 1743.
JOHANNES HUNTZIGER.	Lutheran.	Dutches County, Blacksmith.	Michael Christian Knell.	John Phafen. Laurens Van Boskerch.	April 25th, 1743.
JOHN JACOB OEL.	Lutheran.	County of Albany, Clerk.	Henry Barclay.	Jacob Glen. Jacob H. Tenlyck.	July 28th, 1743.
LAWRENTZ DIEL.	Lutheran.	Dutches County, Yeoman.	Michael Christian Knell.	E. Christian Hoyer. Henderick Beringer.	October 19th, 1743.
JOHAN PETER GERNREICK.	Lutheran.	Same County, Yeoman.	Michael Christian Knell.	Johan Valentine Scheffer. Andries Wiederwax.	October 24th, 1743.

(Certified by the same.)

Gg. 118. (The 3rd column is given only in the original certificate.)

Names of Persons Naturalized.	Their Religious Profession.	Their Temporal Profession and Place of Abode.	The Month and Year.
GEORGE PETERSON.	Lutheran.	Of the City of New York, Sugar Boiler.	April 17th, 1744.
JONAS MOLECK.	Lutheran.	Of same place, Baker.	April 23rd, 1744.
HENRICK HATER [sic].	Dutch Reformed.	Of same place, Carman.	August 7th, 1744.
CASPARUS SCHULTZ.	Lutheran.	Of Dutches County, Farmer.	October 17th, 1744.
JOHANNES PETER KLYN.	Lutheran.	Of same County, Farmer.	October 17th, 1744.
JOHANNES STAATS.	Lutheran.	Of same County, Farmer.	October 17th, 1744.
HENDRICK DIETER.	Lutheran.	Of same County, Farmer.	October 17th, 1744.
CHRISTOPHELL FRITZ.	Lutheran.	Of same County, Farmer.	October 17th, 1744.
ANDREW WEYS.	Lutheran.	Of same County, Carpenter.	October 18th, 1744.

Certified by the same.

NEW YORK.

Gg. 161.

Names of the Persons Naturalized.	Their Religious Profession.	The Month and Year.
GEORGE PETERSON,	Lutheran.	April 17th, 1744.
JONAS MOLECK.	Lutheran.	April 23rd, 1744.
HENRICK HEDER [sic].	Dutch Reformed.	August 7th, 1744.
CASPARUS SCHULTZ.	Lutheran.	October 17th, 1744.
JOHANNES PETER KLYN.	Lutheran.	October 17th, 1744.
JOHANNES STAATS.	Lutheran.	October 17th, 1744.
HENDRICK DIETER.	Lutheran.	October 17th, 1744.
CHRISTOPHER FRITZ.	Lutheran.	October 17th, 1744.
ANDREW WEYS.	Lutheran.	October 18th, 1744.
WILLIAM VAN DALSEM.	Lutheran.	August 1st, 1745.

(Certified by Jno. Catherwood, Secretary.)

[This with the variation noted and the addition of Van Dalsem, whose temporal profession is not here given, is a duplicate of Gg. 118. Weys, however, is bracketed with the preceding persons from Schultz downwards as 'Farmers,' and the original Certificate has the following two additional columns immediately preceding the final one :—

Minister Certifying Receiving the Sacrament.		The Names of the Witnesses to the Certificate.
(Peterson) (Moleck)	} Mich Christn Knoll.	Charles Beekmann, Johan David Wolf. Hans Pfeffer, Henrick Behr.
(Heder)	G. D. Bois.	Abraham Lott, Johannes Lott.
(Schultz) (Klyn)		Johannis Snue, Teunis Snyder. Johannes Snue, Frederick Beringer.
(Staats)	G. M. Weiss.	The same.
(Dieter)		The same.
(Fritz)		Johannis Snue, Teunis Snyder.
(Weys)	Mich Christn Knoll.	Johannis Snyder, Christian Haver.
(Dalsem).	Johs Ritzema.	Elbert Haring, Ahasuerus Turck.]

Gg. 213.

(The 3rd column is given only in the original certificate.)

Names of the Persons Naturalized.	Their Religious Profession.	Their Temporal Profession and Place of Abode,	The Month and Year.
WILLIAM VAN DALSEN.	Lutheran.	Of the City of New York, School Master.	August 1st, 1745.
JOHN MICHEL WILL.	Lutheran.	Of the same City, Cordwainer.	October 31st, 1745.
JOHN GEORGE DEBELE.	Lutheran.	Of the same City, Gardiner.	October 31st, 1745.
ISAAC SEIXAS.	Jew.	Of the same City, Merchant.	November 4th, 1745.
ANDREAS REBER.	Lutheran.	Of the same City, Shop Keeper.	November 5th, 1745.
CASPARUS HERTZ.	Lutheran.	Of the same City, Cartman.	April 17th, 1746.
ERICH CHRISTIAN HOYER.	Lutheran.	Of the same City, School Master.	July 29th, 1746.
EMUS HELMS.	Church of England.	Of the same City, Marriner.	August 4th, 1746.
JACOB RODRIQUES REVERA.	Jew.	Of the same City, Merchant.	January 21st, 1746.
HANS JACOB HUBER.	Dutch Reformed.	Of the same City, Yeoman.	April 23rd, 1747.
CHRISTOPHER MEYER.	Lutheran.	Of the same City, Cartman.	July 30th, 1747.

(Certified by Geo. Banyar, D. Secy.)

Hh. 22. *(The 3rd, 4th and 5th columns of this and the following are given only in the original certificates.)*

Names of Persons Naturalized.	Their Religious Profession.	Their Temporal Profession and Place of Abode.	Ministers Certifying Receiving the Sacrament.	The Names of the Witnesses to the Certificates.	The Month and Year.
JOHAN TEUNIS SINSEBACK.	Dutch Ref.	Of Ulster County, Yeoman.	Geo. Wills Mancius.	Daniel Schneider, Johannes Schneider.	Oct. 20th, 1747.
DANIEL SCHNEIDER.	Dutch Ref.	Of the same County, Yeoman.	Do.	Johan Teunis Sinseback, Johannes Schneider.	Oct. 20th, 1747.
JOHANNES KOOL.	Dutch Ref.	Of the City of New York, Cordwainer.	G. D. Bois.	William Crelus, Christian Stouber.	Oct. 23rd, 1747.
ANDRIES MICHELL.	Dutch Ref.	Of the same City, Labourer	} I. Ritzema.	Johannes Myer, Daniel Smith.	Apr. 21st, 1748.
DANIEL SMITH.	Dutch Ref. Do.	Of the same City, Tallow Chandler.		Johannes Ooueback, Andries Michell.	Apr. 21st, 1748.
ISAAC HAYS.	Jew.				Apr. 26th, 1748.
CHRISTOPHER GODLIEB CREUTZ	Lutheran.	Of the same City, Baker.	Michl Christn Knoll.	Henricus Schriffer, Casparus Hertz.	Aug. 1st, 1748.
MOSES BENJAMIN FRANKS	Jew.	Of the same City.		Henry Heder, William Laurens.	Oct. 18th, 1748.
ANTHONY STEENBAGH.	Dutch Ref.	Of the same City, Baker.	G. D. Bois.		Oct. 19th, 1748.
JOHN ANDREW HERING.	Lutheran.	Of the same City, Weaver.	M. C. Knoll.	Charles Beekman, Junr, John Michael Wille.	Oct. 25th, 1748.

(Certified by Geo. Banyar, D. Secy.)

Hh. 70.

Names of Persons Naturalized.	Their Religious Profession.	Their Temporal Profession and Place of Abode.	Ministers Certifying Receiving the Sacrament.	The Names of the Witnesses to the Certificates.	The Month and Year.
JOHN LEWIS.	Ch. of Eng.	Of the City of New York, Marriner.	Henry Barclay.	Coenradt Ten Eyck, Abrahm Ten Eyck.	Jan. 18th, 1748.
JOHN HENRY GOETSCHIUS.	Dutch Ref.	Of Hackinsack in New Jersey, Minister of the Gospel.	U. Van Sinderen.	Abrahm Lott, Barent Vandewater.	Jan. 19th, 1748.
JOHN MAURITZIUS GOETSCHIUS	Dutch Ref.	Of the same place, Chirurgeon.	Jno Henricus Goetschius,	Abrahm Lott, Barent Vandewater.	Jan. 19th, 1748.
DAVID PYPER.	Lutheran.	Of the City of New York, Taylor	M. Christian Knoll.	Johan George Windlinger, Valente Lambert.	Apr. 18th, 1749.
GOTTFRIED GISELBRECHT	Lutheran.	Of Dutches County, Physician.	M. Christian Knoll.	Casper Hertz, Henricus Scheffer.	Apr. 24th, 1749.
MATHEW BOWMAN.	Lutheran.	Of the City of New York, Yeoman.	M. Christian Knoll.	Leendert Riegeler, John Michael Will.	July 28th, 1749.

(Certified by Geo. Banyar, D. Secy.)

NEW YORK.

Hh. 142. *(The 3rd column in this and the following is given only in the original certificates.)*

Jacob Tenni.	New York City.	Cartman.	October 17th, 1749.
Daniel Speder.	New York City.	Cartman.	October 18th, 1749.
Henderick Sneyder.	New York City.	Cartman.	April 17th, 1750.
Jacob Melsiger (Metsiger).	New York City.	Yeoman.	April 17th, 1750.
Johannes Zuerigher.	New York City.	Yeoman.	April 17th, 1750.
Bernard Kynlander.	Westchester County.	Tanner.	April 21st, 1750.
John Shoals.	New York City.	Marriner.	April, July 31st, [sic: April not in orig].
Mattys Knecht.	New York City.	Mason.	August 1st, 1750.
Philip Schaff.	New York City.	Brass Founder.	August 1st, 1750.
Jacob Grim.	New York City.	Feltmaker.	August 1st, 1750.
Johan Adam (Mildenbergen).	Albany County.	Husbandman.	August 2nd, 1750.
Johan Peter Sax.	New York City.	Farmer.	August 2nd, 1750.
Elizabeth Axson.	New York City.	Widow.	October 18th, 1750.
Henderick Witeman.	Ulster County.	Brass Button Maker.	October 18th, 1750.
Nicholas Melsbach.	Ulster County.	Farmer.	October 18th, 1750.
Hans Ulrich Binder.	Ulster County.	Husbandman.	October 18th, 1750.
Christian Rokkenfelder.	Ulster County.	Blacksmith.	October 18th, 1750.
Phillipus Sensebach.	Dutches County.	Farmer.	October 18th, 1750.
William Cyffer.	Dutches County.	Farmer.	October 18th, 1750.
Johannes Schurri.	Dutches County.	Blacksmith.	October 18th, 1750.
William Smith.	New York City.	Butcher.	October 18th, 1750.
John Ute.	New York City.	Butcher.	October 18th, 1750.
Jacob Steinbrinner.	New York City.	Blacksmith.	October 18th, 1750.
Johann Henrich Bush.	Ullster County.	Blacksmith.	October 22nd, 1750.

(Certified by Geo. Banyar, D. Secy.)

Ii. 52.

Henry van den Ham.	Church of England.	Of the City of New York, Vintner.	January 15th, 1750.
Christopher Jacobi.	Lutheran.	Of Germantown in the Prov. of Pennsylvania, Stocking Weaver.	Jan. 15th, 1705 [sic.]. (1750 in original.)
John Fred Oosterman.	Lutheran.	Of the City of New York, Labourer.	April 10th, 1751.
James Heroy.	Church of England.	Of the said City, Cartman.	January 21st, 1752.
Charles Heroy.	Church of England.	Of Westchester County, Weaver.	January 21st, 1752.
Josiah Crane.	Church of England.	Of the City of New York, Merchant.	April 21st, 1752.
Jacob Boshart.	Dutch Reformed.	Of the said City, Stone Cutter.	April 21st, 1752.
William Brown.	Dutch Reformed.	Of Schoharyin in Co. of Albany, Wheelwright.	July 29th, 1752.
Johann Jacob Werth.	Dutch Reformed.	Do. Doctor of Physick.	July 29th, 1752.
Johan Willem Ditz.	Dutch Reformed.	Do. Shoemaker.	July 29th, 1752.
Johannes Jacob Graaf.	Dutch Reformed.	Of King's County, Farmer.	July 29th, 1752.
Hans George Ranck.	Dutch Reformed.	Of Ulster County, Shoemaker.	July 29th, 1752.
Lawrence Alsdorf.	Dutch Reformed.	Of Ulster County, Farmer.	July 29th, 1752.
Hans George Niets.	Dutch Reformed.	Of Ulster County, Farmer.	July 29th, 1752.

(Certified by Geo. Banyar, D. Secy.)

[*The following Certificates for this Province were not entered into the Entry Book.*]

C.O. 5 1070.

O.o. 62.

List of Persons Naturalized pursuant to Stat. 13 Geo. II, from 17 Jan., 1753, to 20 Oct., 1758.

Names of the Persons Naturalized.	Their Religious Profession.	Their Temporal Profession and Place of Abode.	Month.	Year.
TUNIS RISLER.	Dutch reformed.	City of New York, Baker.	17 Jan.	1753.
JACOB FUNCK.	Lutheran.	City of New York, Baker.	17 Oct.	1753.
JOHANNES MICHAEL SAX.	Lutheran.	City of New York, Baker.	17 Oct.	1753.
PETER MELSBACK.	Dutch reformed.	Ulster County, Farmer.	17 Oct.	1753.
BENJAMIN MINEMA.	Dutch reformed.	Dutchess County, Clerk.	24 Oct.	1753.
GERARDUS HAAGHORT.	Dutch reformed.	Essex County, in the Province of New Jersey, Clerk.	24 Oct.	1753.
JEREMIAH BEAUDOVIN.	French Protestant.	City of New York, Staymaker.	17 Jan.	1754.
JOHN VELDTMAN.	Church of England.	Richmond County, Farmer.	31 July	1754.
LODOWICK ROOS.	——	——	31 July	1754.
WILLIAM RHINELANDER.	Church of England.	City of New York, Yeoman.	31 July	1754.
MOSES CLEMENT.	Church of England.	City of New York, Cabinet Maker.	16 April	1755
BALTHAZAR WINTHROP.	Lutheran.	City of New York, Mariner.	23 Oct.	1755.
MATHIAS SMITH.	——	——	24 Oct.	1755.
CASPER CASPER.	——	——	24 Oct.	1755.
CHRISTOPHER SMITH.	——		24 Oct.	1755.
ELIAS FRITZ.	Lutheran.	City of New York, Yeoman.	21 April	1757.
JACOB FRY.	Church of England.	West Chester County, Yeoman.	24 Oct.	1757.
JOHN HENDRICK BROWN.	Dutch reformed.	City of New York, Baker.	25 July	1758.
ISAAC ADOLPHUS.	Jew.	City of New York, Trader.	27 July	1758.
GODFRIED STREIT.	Lutheran.	City of New York, Cordwainer.	20 Oct.	1758.

Examined with the Record in the Secretary's Office of New York, By

[*Signed*] GEO. BANYAR, D. Sec'ry.

NEW YORK

C.O. 5 1070.

O.o.63.

List of Persons Naturalized pursuant to Stat. 13 Geo. II, from 16 Jan., 1759, to 21 Oct., 1761.

Names of the Persons Naturalized	Their Religious Profession.	Their Temporal Profession and Place of Abode.	Month.	Year.
HYAM MYERS.	Jew.	City of New York, Butcher.	16 Jan.	1759.
MANUEL MYERS.	Jew.	City of New York, Trader.	16 Jan.	1759.
HENRY RITTER.	Lutheran.	City of New York, Cordwainer.	19 Apr.	1759.
MICHAEL RITTER.	Lutheran.	City of New York, Taylor.	19 Apr.	1759.
JOHN GOODPERLET.	Lutheran.	City of New York, Taylor.	19 Apr.	1759.
ANDREW FREDERICK.	Lutheran.	City of New York, Baker.	17 Apr.	1760.
JOHN PAINTER.	Lutheran.	City of New York, Shopkeeper.	31 July	1760.
JOHN GEORGE LORILLAND.	French Protestant.	City of New York, Yeoman.	27 Oct.	1760.
MATHEW HOYER.	Lutheran.	City of New York, Baker.	28 Oct.	1760.
GEORGE MICHAEL KEYSER.	Lutheran.	City of New York, Labourer.	21 Jan.	1761.
DAVID HENRY MELLOW.	Lutheran.	City of New York, Mariner.	21 Jan.	1761.
JAMES BLANCHARD.	French Protestant.	City of New York, Cooper.	22 Apr.	1761.
JOHN PETER CHAPPELLE.	French Protestant.	City of New York, Labourer.	22 Apr.	1761.
MATHEW MORRELL.	French Protestant.	City of New York, Labourer.	22 Apr.	1761.
JOHN HENRY TIERS.	French Protestant.	City of New York, Labourer.	22 Apr.	1761.
JACOB EPPLY.	Lutheran.	City of New York, Carman.	22 Apr.	1761.
ANDREW LADNER.	Lutheran.	City of New York, Baker.	22 Apr.	1761.
BENJAMIN LINDER.	Lutheran.	Do., Practitioner in Physick.	29 July	1761.
JOHN MULLER.	Lutheran.	City of New York, Labourer.	29 July	1761.
BERNARD GANS.	Reformed German Church.	City of New York, Vintner.	29 July	1761.
JACOB HEITZ.	Lutheran.	City of New York, Carman.	29 July	1761.
CORNELIUS KUYPER.	Unitas Fratrum.	City of New York, House Painter.	29 July	1761.
JOHN CHRISTOPHER ARMPRIESTER.	Reformed German Church.	City of New York, Inholder.	21 Oct.	1761.
PHILIP WILL.	Reformed German Church.	City of New York, Pewterer.	21 Oct.	1761.
HENRY WILL.	Reformed German Church.	City of New York, Pewterer.	21 Oct.	1761.
JOHN PHILIP SPIES.	Reformed German Church.	City of New York, Cordwainer.	21 Oct.	1761.
JOHN REMMY.	Reformed German Church.	City of New York, Potter.	21 Oct.	1761.
GEORGE LEONARD.	Lutheran.	City of New York, Butcher.	21 Oct.	1761.
JACOB RISLAR.	Lutheran.	City of New York, Tallow Chandler.	21 Oct.	1761.
BLAZEY MOORE.	Lutheran.	City of New York, Inholder.	21 Oct.	1761.
JOHANNES PETRUS ROKHEFFELLER.	Reformed Dutch Church.	County of Albany, Farmer.	21 Oct.	1761.
SIMON ROKHEFFELLER.	Reformed Dutch Church.	County of Albany, Farmer.	21 Oct.	1761.
JOHN MULLEDALLER.	Reformed German Church.	City of New York, Cordwainer.	21 Oct.	1761.

New York, 8th January, 1762. Examined with the Record in the Secretary's Office, By

[*Signed*] GEO. BANYAR, D. Sec'ry.

C.O. 5 1071. P. p. 28 (bound up between P. p. 66 and 67).

List of Persons Naturalized pursuant to Stat. 13 Geo. II, from 21 Jan., 1762, to 27 Oct., 1763.

Names of the Persons Naturalized.	Their Religious Profession.	Their Temporal Profession and Place of Abode.		Month and Year.
DANIEL TIERS.	French Protestant.	City of New York,	Labourer.	21 Jan. 1762.
MATHEW TIERS.	Do.	Do.	Blacksmith.	21 Jan. 1762.
MAGDALEN TIERS.	Do.	Do.	Spinster.	21 Jan. 1762.
CHRISTOPHER TOBIAS.	Quaker.	Queen's County,	Yeoman.	23 Jan. 1762.
JOHN HESS.	Lutheran.	City of New York,	Tallow Chandler.	21 Apr. 1762.
DAVID RITMAN.	Do.	Do.	Carpenter.	21 Apr. 1762.
WENDEL BOOS.	Do.	Do.	Baker.	21 Apr. 1762.
CHRISTIAN PONTIUS.	Do.	Do.	Taylor.	21 Apr. 1762.
ANDREAS REGLER.	Do.	Do.	Butcher.	21 Apr. 1762.
ALEXANDER OXBURY.	Church of England.	Do.	Cordwainer.	21 Apr. 1762.
NICHOLAS CROOB.	Lutheran.	Do.	Do.	21 Apr. 1762.
PETER VALLADE.	French Protestant.	Do.	Merchant.	21 Apr. 1762.
PETER LOUILLARD.	Do.	Do.	Stocking Weaver.	21 Apr. 1762.
JOHN PETER TETARD.	Do.	Do.	Clerk.	21 Apr. 1762.
JOHN CARLE.	Do.	Do.	Do.	21 Apr. 1762.
PETER ROUGEON.	Do.	Do.	Ship Carpenter.	21 Apr. 1762.
JOSEPH ANTHONY.	Do.	West Chester County,	Merchant.	22 Apr. 1762.
ABRAHAM ANDREWS.	Jew.	City of New York,	Shopkeeper.	22 Apr. 1762.
JOHANNES PANET.	Dutch reformed.	Do.	Gentleman.	29 July 1762.
PETER DURAND.	French Protestant.	Do.	Taylor.	29 July 1762.
ANDREW HABENER.	Lutheran.	Do.	Cordwainer.	29 July 1762.
MICHAEL GRESS.	Do.	Do.	Sadler.	29 July 1762.
FREDERICK RANZIER.	Do.	Do.	Cooper.	29 July, 1762.
JOHN GASNER.	Do.	Do.	Glazier.	29 July, 1762.
JACOB HOERTSE.	Do.	Do.	Mason.	29 July, 1762.
VALENTINE RHINEHART.	Do.	Do.	Inholder.	29 July, 1762.
FREDERICK DEETZ.	Do.	Do.	Taylor.	29 July, 1762.
GEORGE WORKHARD.	Do.	Do.	Baker.	21 Oct. 1762.
JACOB MULLER.	Dutch reformed.	Manor of Cortlandt,	Farmer.	29 Oct. 1762.
OTHO PARISIEN.	French Protestant.	City of New York,	Silversmith.	18 Jan. 1763.
EGYDIUS WONDERLY.	Lutheran.	Do.	Joiner.	20 Apr. 1763.
MICHAEL RITMAN.	Do.	Do.	Weaver.	20 Apr. 1763.
FREDERICK RUGER.	Do.	Do.	Carman.	20 Apr. 1763.
JOHN GEORGE CROSSKOP.	Do.	Do.	Baker.	20 Apr. 1763.
TOBIAS LERVER.	Do.	Orange County,	Husbandman.	20 Apr. 1763.
JOHN MANNEL.	Do.	Do.	Do.	20 Apr. 1763.
CHRISTIAN FROLICK.	Unitas Fratrum.	City of New York,	Sugar Baker	21 Apr. 1763.
ISAAC ELIZER.	Jew.	Rhode Island,	Merchant.	23 July 1763.
FREDERICK SIGISMD. LENTZ.	Lutheran.	City of New York,	Gentleman.	18 Oct. 1763.
JOHN VOGEL.	Do.	Do.	Vintner.	19 Oct. 1763.
CONRADT BARNES.	Do.	Do.	Hatter.	19 Oct. 1763.
ADAM MULLER.	Dutch reformed.	Manor of Cortlandt,	Farmer.	19 Oct. 1763.
ANDRIES MULLER.	Do.	Do.	Do.	19 Oct. 1763.
JURIAN VOSS.	Do.	Do.	Do.	19 Oct. 1763.
PETER SWARTZ.	Do.	Do.	Do.	19 Oct. 1763.
LEVY HART.	Jew.	Colony of New York,	Merchant	27 Oct. 1763.
JONAS SOLOMONS.	Do.	Do.	Do.	27 Oct. 1763.

Secretary's Office, New York, 28th March, 1764. Examined with the Record in this Office, By

[*Signed*] GEO. BANYAR, D. Sec'ry.

[NOTE.—According to the Board of Trade Register, Q.q. 17 should be a List of Persons Naturalized in the Province of New York. No date is given, and the number is missing from the volume of original correspondence. There appears, however, to be no hiatus between the preceding and the following lists.]

NATURALIZATIONS

NEW YORK.
C.O. 5 1072. Q.q. 63.

List of Persons Naturalized pursuant to Stat. 13 Geo. II, from 18 Jan., 1764, to 22 Jan., 1766.

Names of the Persons Naturalized.	Their Religious Profession.	Their Temporal Profession and Place of Abode.		Time when Naturalized.
NICHOLAS TOULON.	French Protestant.	Westchester County, Mariner.		18 Jan. 1764.
NAPTHALY HART MEYERS.	Jew.	City of New York, Merchant.		27 Apr. 1764.
JOHN GEORGE.	Dutch reformed.	Orange County, Farmer.		31 July, 1764.
WILLIAM BELL.	Do.	Do.	Cooper.	17 Oct. 1764.
JOHN STREBELL.	Lutheran.	Abany[sic] County, Farmer.		26 Oct. 1764.
JACOB BLATTNER.	Do.	Do.	Miller & Mill-wright.	23 Apr. 1765.
JACOB HENDERER.	Do.	Do.	Cordwainer.	23 Apr. 1765.
DAVID WOLHAUPTER.	Do.	City of New York, Turner.		23 Apr. 1765.
JACOB KLINCK.	Do.	Do.	Carman.	13 Apr. 1765.
DANIEL FUETER.	Unitas Fratrum.	Do.	Silversmith.	31 July, 1765.
NICHOLAS KILMAN.	Lutheran.	Do.	Innholder.	2 Aug. 1765.
Revd. JOHN CASPAR FRYENMOET.	Dutch reformed.	Albany County, Minister of the Gospel.		15 Oct. 1765.
JOHN THYS KOUS.	Do.	Dutches Do., Farmer.		15 Oct. 1765.
JOHAN PETER ROSE.	Do.	Albany Do., Shoemaker.		15 Oct. 1765.
MICHAEL HARTESTEIM.	Lutheran.	City of New York, Labourer.		15 Oct. 1765.
GEORGE FACH.	Do.	Do.	Baker.	15 Oct. 1765.
REYNOLD LODZ.	French Protestant.	Queen's County, Gardiner.		15 Oct. 1765.
JOHN MULLER.	Reformed German Church.	City of New York, Doctor of Physick.		15 Oct. 1765.
JOHN KLINE.	Do.	Do.	Baker.	15 Oct. 1765.
DAVID-GARTNER.	Do.	Do.	Taylor.	15 Oct. 1765.
FREDERIC SCHONNERET.	Lutheran.	Do.	Shopkeeper.	18 Oct. 1765.
ALEXANDER FINK, Jun.	Do.	Do.	Butcher.	18 Oct. 1765.
JACOB OTT.	Do.	Do.	Do.	18 Oct. 1765.
HENRY FACH.	Do.	Do.	Shoemaker.	18 Oct. 1765.
GEORGE LUCAM.	Do.	Do.	Butcher.	18 Oct. 1765.
MARTIN MENOLD.	Do.	Do.	Shoemaker.	18 Oct. 1765.
WILHELM LEONHARD.	Reformed German Church.	Do.	Baker.	21 Oct. 1765.
MICHAEL KOPP.	Do.	Do.	Cooper.	21 Oct. 1765.
HENRICH HORNEFFER.	Do.	Do.	Baker.	21 Oct. 1765.
HENRICK OERTLY.	Do.	Do.	Yeoman.	21 Oct. 1765.
JOHN FISCHER.	Lutheran.	Do.	Tanner.	21 Oct. 1765.
HENRY ZIMMERMAN.	Do.	Do.	Carpenter.	21 Oct. 1765.
LUDEWIG CAMMERDINGER.	Do.	Do	Taylor.	21 Oct. 1765.
JOHN KLEIN.	Do.	Do.	Nail Smith.	21 Oct. 1765.
PHILIP EKERT.	Do.	Do.	Carpenter.	21 Oct. 1765.
CHRISTOPH SCHEL.	Do.	Do.	Cartman.	21 Oct. 1765.
GODFRIED BRUGMAN.	Do.	Do.	Mason.	21 Oct. 1765.
GEORGE KLEIN.	Do.	Do.	Baker.	21 Oct. 1765.
PETER POYSHERT.	Do.	Do.	Placksmith.	21 Oct. 1765.
DAVID GOBEL.	Do.	Do.	Baker.	21 Oct. 1765.
MICHAEL WEBER.	Do.	Do.	Shoemaker.	21 Oct. 1765.
PHILIP MANNHARD.	Do.	Do.	House Carpenter.	23 Oct. 1765.
MATHEW SCHENERHINGER.	Do.	Do.	Hatter.	23 Oct. 1765.
MARTIN EGLE.	Do.	Do.	Carpenter.	23 Oct. 1765.
JOHN HERBERT.	Do.	Do	Butcher.	23 Oct. 1765.
PETER STUBARARE.	Do.	Do.	Stocking Weaver.	23 Oct. 1765.
JOHN DANIEL WIEDERSHEIN.	Do.	Do.	Butcher.	23 Oct. 1765.
DANIEL VOSHEE.	Do.	Do.	Tobacco Cutter.	23 Oct. 1765.
JOSEPH JESURUM PINTO.	Jew.	Do.	Minister of the Jewish Congregn.	22 Jan. 1766.

Secretary's Office, New York, 3rd February, 1766. Examined with the Record in this Office.
By me [Signed] GEO. BANYAR, D. Sec'ry.

C.O. 5. 1073. R.r. 30.

List of Persons Naturalized pursuant to Stat. 13 Geo. II, from 21 April, 1767, to 20 Jan., 1768.

Names of the Persons Naturalized.	Their Religiou ∞ Profession.	Their Temporal Profession and Place of Abode.	Time when Naturalized.
JOHN ALBERT WEYGAND.	Lutheran.	City of New York, Minister of the Gospel.	21 Apr. 1767.
WILLIAM BRITT.	Reformed Protestant Dutch Church.	County of Westchester, Farmer	24 Apr. 1767.
JOHN ENTERS.	Do.	Do.	Ditto.
HENRY DETLOFF.	Lutheran.	City of New York, Cartman.	Ditto.
GEORGE STUBER.	Do.	Do. Taylor.	Ditto.
GEORGE MAN.	Do.	Orange County, Farmer.	Ditto.
JANE DE JONCOURT.	Church of England.	City of New York, Widow.	20 Jan. 1768.

Secretary's Office, New York, 18 February, 1768. Examined with the Record in this Office, By
[*Signed*] GEO. BANYAR, D. Sec'ry.

C.O. 5. 1074. S.s. 59.

List of Persons Natu⌐ ..zed pursuant to Stat. 13 Geo. II, from 20 April, 1768, to 18 Jan., 1769.

Names of Persons Naturalized.	Their Religious Profession.	Their Temporal Profession and Place of Abode.	Time when Naturalized.
JOHN DEALING.	Unitas Fratrum.	City of New York, Shopkeeper.	20 April 1768.
LAWRENCE KILBRUNN.	Do.	Do. Merchant.	Do.
CHRISTOPHER JOHNSON.	Lutheran.	Do. Tavernkeeper.	Do.
BARENT SMITH.	Reformed Protestant Dutch Church.	Do. Taylor.	27 July 1768.
JOHN JOUCH.	Lutheran.	Do. Shingle Shaver.	18 Oct. 1768.
CARL LUNEMAN.	Do.	Do. Carpenter.	Do.
JOHN PETER LORENTZ.	Reformed Protestant Dutch Church.	Dutches County, Yeoman.	22 Oct. 1768.
JOHN DE VOYELLES.	Church of England.	Orange County, Gentleman.	18 Jan. 1769.

Secretary's Office, New York, 1 February, 1769. Examined with the Record in this Office, By
[*Signed*] GEO. BANYAR, D. Sec'ry.

S.s. 79.

To the Right Honourable the Lords Commissioners for Trade and Plantations.

May it please your Lordships. In humble obedience to your Lordships' commands, signified to me by Mr. Pownall, I have perused and considered an Act passed by the Assembly of his Majesty's Colony of New York in May 1769, Intituled, An Act for Naturalizing Garret Schotler, John Brunckhorst, John Samler, Michael Srum, Joseph Steirer, Daniel Duchemin, Adrian De Ronde, Matheus De Ronde, John Cherbacker, Jachen Christian Schaltz, Johan Jacob Stapell, Philip Oswald, John Sticklen, William Cline, Coenrad Wolfe, George Powers, Michael Hennegor, Anthony Apple, Francis Ortman, John Hill, Anthony Dodine, John Michael Richers, Daniel Sleght, Pierre Eugene Du Simitiere, Jacob Moses, John Brooks, Jubaliste Dupuy, Honore Marsequie, Louis Faugeres, Charles Freidenbergh, and George Woolrice.

And I am humbly of opinion that the same is proper in point of Law, which is humbl⌐ submitted by, my Lords, your Lordships' most obedient most humble servant. [*Signed*]
22nd June, 1770.   R. JACKSON.

[*Endorsed* :]   Received June 24 ⎫
                  Read July 2   ⎭ 1770.

NATURALIZATIONS

NEW YORK.

C.O. 5. 1075. T.t. 4.

List of Persons Natural — pursuant to Stat. 13 Geo. II, from 18 April, 1769, to the end of April Term, 1770.

Names of Persons Naturalized.	Their Religious Profession.	Their Temporal Profession and Place of Abode.		Time when Naturalized.
DAVID GRIM.	German Evangelical Church.	City of New York, Vintner.		18 Apr. 1769.
JOHN HEERBENK.	German Reformed Congregation.	Do.	Tanner.	20 Apr. 1769.
HENRY ROSSEL.	Do.	Do.	Do.	Do.
ANSTON APPEL.	Do.	Do.	Baker.	Do.
JOHN HILL.	Do.	Do.	Labourer.	Do.
PETER CHAPPELLE, Jun.	French Protestant.	Do.	Stocking Weaver.	Do.
DANIEL TIER.	Do.	Do.	Cartman.	Do.
JOHN RIES.	Lutheran.	Outward of Do., Farmer.		Do.
LUDEWYK KRAUSKOP.	Do.	Do.	Do.	Do.
ADAM ALL.	Do.	City of New York, Yeoman.		19 Apr. 1769.
DIETRICK HEYER.	Do.	Do.	Sugar Boyler.	Do.
JACOB MOORE.	Do.	Outward of Do., Farmer.		20 Apr. 1769.
JOHN FAGH.	Do.	City of New York, Cartman.		Do.
GEORGE DEYBERTSYER.	Do.	Do.	Chimneysweeper.	Do.
HENDRICK SNYDER.	Reformed Protestant Dutch Church.	Orange County, Farmer.		21 Apr. 1769.
CHRISTOPHER BELL.	Do.	Do.	Do.	Do.
HARMANUS TRUMPER.	Do.	Do.	Do.	Do.
EDWARD WILLIAM KIERS.	Do.	Do.	Merchant.	25 July 1769.
FREDERICK BREYTIGAM.	Lutheran.	City of New York, Baker.		26 July 1769.
JOHN RANDEKER.	Do.	Do.	Cartman.	Do.
JOHN WESTERMEYER.	Do.	Do.	Baker.	Do.
CHRISTIAN WILL.	German Reformed Congregation.	Do.	Pewterer.	18 Oct. 1769.
JONATHAN ECKART.	Lutheran.	Do.	Trader.	Do.

Secretary's Office, New York, 2 July, 1770. Examined with the Record in this Office, By

[*Signed*] GEO. BANYAR, D. Sec'ry.

C. O. 324. 55 (continued).

CONNECTICUT [no entry].

RHODE ISLAND [no entry].

MASSACHUSETS.

NICOLAS BUDD, October 10th 1743.

NEW HAMPSHIRE [no entry].

PENNSYLVANIA.

(Supreme Court at Philadelphia, 25 Sept., 1747.)

	Persons' Names.	Of what County.	Time of taking the Sacrament
V. 57.	JACOB VANDERWEIGHT.	Philadelphia County.	June 29th, 1747.
	PETER SPYCKER.	Philadelphia County.	August 23rd, 1747.
	JOHN GEORGE CRYSMAN.	Philadelphia County.	August 23rd, 1747.
	GEORGE POGER.	Philadelphia County.	August 23rd, 1747.
	PETER HOLTZETTER.	Philadelphia County.	August 23rd, 1747.

Quakers.

	Persons' Names.	Of what County.
V. 57.	CHRISTOPHER HIGHMAGER.	Bucks. County.
	CHRISTIAN SENSENIG.	Lancaster County.
	ADAM STOUT.	Philadelphia County.
	HENRICK WYERMAN.	Bucks. County.
	JOHN LOB.	Bucks. County.
	CHRISTIAN SOUDER.	Philadelphia County.

(Said Supreme Council, 13 and 15 April, 1748.)

	Persons' Names.	Of what County.	Time of taking the Sacrament.
V. 57.	JACOB NÜSS.	Philadelphia County.	April 9th, 1748.
	GEORGE MILL.	Philadelphia County.	April 10th, 1748.
	PETER SOMIJ.	Lancaster County.	April 10th, 1748.
	JOHANNES LEHMENN.	Philadelphia County.	April 10th, 1748.
	GEORGE EMANN.	Philadelphia County.	April 10th, 1748.
	MICHAEL YOACHUM.	Philadelphia County.	April 10th, 1748.
	HENRY RAMSAUR.	Philadelphia County.	April 10th, 1748.
	GEORGE NOLL.	Lancaster County.	April 11th, 1748.
	JACOB HAUK.	Bucks County.	April 3rd, 1748.
	PHILIP BALSHAZAR CRÖESMAN.	Philadelphia County.	March 13th, 1747.
	ADAM CLAMPFERR.	Philadelphia City.	April 10th, 1748.
	WILLIAM CLAMPFERR.	Philadelphia City.	April 10th, 1748.
	MATTHIAS LAMBERT.	Lancaster County.	April 10th, 1748.
	WENDAL NEFT.	Philadelphia County.	April 10th, 1748.
	MICHAEL DURR.	Philadelphia County.	April 10th, 1748.
	(CHRISTOPER KRAUS.	Philadelphia County.	Who conscientiously scruples to take an Oath.)

PENNSYLVANIA.

(Said Supreme Court, 26 Sept., 1748.)

Persons' Names.	Of what County.	Time of taking the Sacrament.
V. 91. MICHAEL BECKER.	Philadelphia County. (Lives in the Northern Libertys of the City of Philadelphia.)	September 18th, 1748.
ANTHONY NEWHOUSE.	Philadelphia County.	September 18th, 1748.
JOHANNES EBLER.	Lancaster County.	July 22nd, 1748.
JOHAN PETER FRAXEL.	Bucks. County.	September 5th, 1748.
MAGDALEN ANSPACHEN, wife of PETER ANSPACHEN.	Lancaster County.	July 22nd, 1748.
JACOB GEARI.	Philadelphia County.	September 4th, 1748.
CAPER HOLTZ HOUSEN.	Bucks. County.	September 5th, 1748.
MARGARET REIS, wife of MICHAEL REIS.	Lancaster County.	September 22nd, 1748.
ANNA MARIA NAEFEN, wife of MICHAEL NAEFEN.	Lancaster County.	July 22nd, 1748.
ANDREW MILLER.	Lancaster County.	September 22nd, 1748.

Quakers.

Persons' Names.	Of what County.
MELCHIOR HARTRAMFF.	Philadelphia County.
JACOB YONER.	Lancaster County.
JOHN BUCKS.	Lancaster County.

(Said Supreme Court, 11 April, 1749.)

Persons' Names.	Of what County.	Time of taking the Sacrament.
V. 92. MICHAEL NEES	Lancaster County.	March 25th, 1749.
HENDRICK HEILIG.	Philadelphia County.	March 26th, 1749.
HENRY SHELLENBERG.	Philadelphia County.	March 25th, 1749.
WILLIAM LABAER.	Bucks. County.	March 25th, 1749.
CONRAD TIMBERMAN.	Philadelphia County.	March 18th, 1749.
ANNA DORETHEA KEIZ.	Bucks. County.	March 26th, 1749.
MATTHIAS REEL.	Bucks. County.	March 25th, 1749.
DANIEL HISTER.	Philadelphia County.	March 25th, 1749.
MICHAEL HILLEGAS.	Philadelphia County.	March 26th, 1749.
GEORGE SHIVE.	Philadelphia County.	March 25th, 1749.
PETER SCHOLL.	Bucks. County.	March 25th, 1749.
MICHAEL RITTER.	Philadelphia County.	March 25th, 1749.
LAWRENCE DEHR.	Philadelphia County.	March 25th, 1749.
ANDREW BOYER.	Philadelphia County.	March 25th, 1749.
ABRAHAM FAUST.	Bucks. County.	March 25th, 1749.
HENRICK YOUNG.	Philadelphia County.	March 25th, 1749.
NICHOLAS RUSH (RAUSH).	Philadelphia County.	March 25th, 1749.
JOHN GAUFRES.	Philadelphia County.	March 25th, 1749.
ADAM MILLER.	Philadelphia County.	March 25th, 1749.
JOHN GEORGE ROTT.	Bucks. County.	March 25th, 1749.
MICHAEL SMALL.	Lancaster County.	March 25th, 1749.
JOHN JACOB FOX.	Philadelphia County.	March 31st, 1749.
JOHN WIDMAN.	Lancaster County.	March 25th, 1749.
CONRAD SCHNEIDER.	Philadelphia County.	March 25th, 1749.
NICHOLAS ICKS.	Philadelphia County.	March 26th, 1749.
JOHN STONE.	Lancaster County.	March 25th, 1749.
ADAM MOSER.	Lancaster County.	March 25th, 1749.
DAVID STRIPE.	Bucks. County.	March 25th, 1749.

Quakers.

Persons' Names.	Of what County.
FELIX BRUNNER.	Bucks. County.
MICHAEL KELLER.	Bucks. County.
JACOB DUBES.	Bucks. County.
JOHN HUBER.	Bucks. County.
CHRISTIAN WILLOWER.	Bucks. County.
JACOB WETZELL.	Bucks. County.
PETER ETTER.	Philadelphia County.
JACOB FRANK.	Philadelphia County.
DANIEL ETTER.	Philadelphia County.
THOMAS HAIL.	Philadelphia County.
ANDREW GODSHALL.	Philadelphia County.
JOHN GROUT.	Philadelphia County.
HENRY BOWMAN.	Lancaster County.
CASPER SHERICK.	Lancaster County.

(Said Supreme Court, 25 and 26 Sept., and 4 Oct., 1749.)

	Persons' Names.	Of what County.	Time of taking the Sacrament.
V. 94.	VOLENTINE STOBER.	Lancaster County.	August 27th, 1749.
	HENRY MOTS.	Lancaster County.	September 27th, 1749.
			(Corrected to 17.)
	PETER BAKER.	Lancaster County.	August 27th, 1749.
	SOLOMON LIBKEP.	Bucks County.	September 17th, 1749.
	JOHN DETHRICK HELD.	Philadelphia County.	August 6th, 1749.
	JOHN GROSE.	Philadelphia County.	August 6th, 1749.
	JOHN WILLIAM FISHER	Lancaster County.	September 30th, 1749.
	PHILIP FILCHMIR.	Lancaster County.	September 30th, 1749.
	FRANCIS CREEK.	Lancaster County.	September 30th, 1749.
	CHRISTOPHER ORISH.	Lancaster County.	September 17th, 1749.
	CONRAD FRICK.	Philadelphia County	September 3rd, 1749.
	JOHN SIGISMUND HANELY.	Lancaster County.	September 19th, 1749.
	ANDREW CREUTZER.	Lancaster County.	September 30th, 1749.
	MICHAEL MILLER.	Lancaster County.	September 30th, 1749.
	MICHAEL AXER.	Lancaster County.	September 30th, 1749.
	LOODWICK CORNMAN.	Lancaster County.	September 30th, 1749.
	GODFRET REORHER.	Lancaster County.	September 30th, 1749.
	ADAM LINN.	York County.	August 27th, 1749.

Persons' Names.	Of what County.
JOSEPH SIMON, a Jew.	Lancaster County and Bor'.

Quakers.

JOHN CHRISTOPHER HEEBNER.	Philadelphia County.
MELCHIOR CREEBLE.	Philadelphia County.
CHRISTOPHER WAGNER.	Philadelphia County.
CASPER SEIBT.	Philadelphia County.
CHRISTOPHER HOFFMAN	Philadelphia County.
(HOFFMANN).	

(Said Supreme Court, 12 April, 1750.)

	Persons' Names.	Of what County.	Time of taking the Sacrament.
V. 95.	ANDREW MILLER.	Philadelphia County.	April 8th, 1750
	DIETHERIC RAMSAUR.	Philadelphia County.	March 25th, 1750.
	ADAM WARTHAM.	Philadelphia County.	April 8th, 1750.

Quakers.

Persons' Names.	Of what County.
ADAM DRULLINGER.	Bucks. County.
JACOB BRUA.	Lancaster County.
JOHN STONER.	Chester County.
MARTIN BECHTEL.	Philadelphia County.
CHRISTIAN BLIM.	Philadelphia County.
PETER ENGLE.	Chester County.
CHRISTIAN CROUP.	Lancaster County.
CHRISTIAN PERRY.	Chester County.
ANDREW HEIT.	Chester County.
RODERICK SMITH.	Chester County.

Persons' Names.	Of what County.	Time of taking the Sacrament.
JACOB WEISS, a moravian.	Philadelphia Co. & City.	April 1st, 1750.

Quakers [&c.].

Persons' Names.	Of what County.
JOSEPH SHERICK.	Lancaster County.
MICHAEL SWOOPE.	York County.
JACOB SHANTZ.	Philadelphia County.
HENRY BEAR.	Chester County.
BENJAMIN WIDMER.	Lancaster County (a Protestant who conscientiously scruples to take an Oath).

(Said Supreme Court, 25 Sept., 1750.)

[The names of the Townships in this and the following list (V. 100) are given in the original Certificates only.]

	Persons' Names.	Of what Township.	Of what County.	Time of taking the Sacrament.
V. 99.	PETER PENER.	Hatfield.	Philadelphia.	September 9th, 1750.
	FREDERICK WAMBOLD.	Towamensin.	Philadelphia.	August 26th, 1750.
	GEORGE WINTER.	Alsace.	Philadelphia.	August 5th, 1750.
	ADAM RIFEL.	Alsace.	Philadelphia.	September 16th, 1750.
	MICHAEL HAUK.	North Wales.	Philadelphia.	July 3rd, 1750.
	PHILIP SHRIENER.	Manheim.	Lancaster.	September 21st, 1750.
	LEONARD BILLMYER.	Manheim.	Lancaster.	September 21st, 1750.
	JOHN VALENTINE SHREINER.	Manheim.	Lancaster.	August 18th, 1750.
	JACOB BILLMYER.	York.	York.	September 2nd, 1750.
	JACOB FACKLER.	York.	York.	September 2nd, 1750.
	HERMAN BOTT.	York.	York.	September 2nd, 1750.
	CHRISTOPHER TRENCLE.	Lancaster.	Lancaster.	August 5th, 1750.
	NICHOLAS HAVENER.	Talpahaken.	Lancaster.	September 16th, 1750.
	PETER GEBHART.	Talpahaken.	Lancaster.	September 16th, 1750.

Quakers [&c.].

Persons' Names.	Of what Township.	Of what County.
DAVID NITCHMAN, a moravian.	Bethlem.	Bucks; took the Sacrament Aug. 27th, 1751 (as certified by the Bishop of the Unitas Fratrum), at Bethlehem.
RUTHOL LAP.	Hatfield.	Philadelphia.
MELCHIOR HEAVENOR.	Frederick.	Philadelphia.
JOHN CHRISTY.	Lancaster.	Lancaster.
JOHN FURREY.	Hempfield.	Lancaster.
ULRICK SHULLEBERG.	Hempfield.	Lancaster.
HENRY STRICKLER.	Hempfield.	Lancaster.
BOSTIAN HAUPT.	Skippack.	Philadelphia.
HENRY SNIDER.	Dunegall.	Lancaster.

(Said Supreme Court, 11 April, 1751.)

Persons' Names.	Of what Township.	Of what County.	Time of taking the Sacrament.
V. 100. STEPHEN CONRAD.	Tulpahocken.	Lancaster.	April 7th, 1751.
JOHN GEORGE KEHL.	Tulpahocken.	Lancaster.	April 7th, 1751.
MARIA URSULA KELM.	Tulpahocken.	Lancaster.	April 7th, 1751.
MATHIAS SMITH.	Tulpahocken.	Lancaster.	April 7th, 1751.
NICHOLAS BITTELL.	New Providence.	Philadelphia.	April 7th, 1751.
GEORGE KLEPPINGER.	North Wales.	Philadelphia.	April 7th, 1751.
JONAS KOHLER.	Moyamensin.	Philadelphia.	April 7th, 1751.
JACOB RIEDY.	Marlborough.	Philadelphia.	April 7th, 1751.
HENRY REID.	Upper Sulford.	Philadelphia.	April 7th, 1751.
JOHN FISHER.	Upper Sulford.	Philadelphia.	April 7th, 1751.
BARNARD ZOWMAN.	Helm.	York.	March 24th, 1750.
JOSEPH SOLOMON.	Lancaster	Lancaster.	A Jew sworn on the Old Testament only.
BARNARD LAUBERS WEILER.	Philadelphia.	Philadelphia.	April 8th, 1751.
BERNARD HOLSINGER.	York.	York.	March 24th, 1750.
MARTIN BOWER.	Manchester.	York.	March 24th, 1750.
CONRAD SHUTZ.	Lower Merion.	Philadelphia.	April 7th, 1751.
HENRY SHUTZ.	Springfield.	Philadelphia.	April 7th, 1751.
JACOB WHIGTMAN.	Frederick.	Philadelphia.	April 7th, 1751.
CONRAD KEEHMLE.	Northern Liberties of Philadelphia.	Philadelphia.	April 10th, 1751.
MATHIAS BUSH, a Jew.	Philadelphia City	Philadelphia.	Sworn on the Old Testament only.
ADAM WEBER.	Philadelphia City	Philadelphia.	April 7th, 1751.
CHARLES EWALD.	Philadelphia City	Philadelphia.	April 7th, 1751.
JOHN FREDERICK VIGERA.	Philadelphia City	Philadelphia.	April 7th, 1751.
JACOB ROAR.	Chaising.	Bucks.	April 7th, 1751.

Quakers [&c.].

Persons' Names.	Of what Township.	Of what County.
LEONARD SING.	Towamensin.	Philadelphia.
ULRICK PENINGER.	Sulford.	Philadelphia.
JOHN ROWTROCK.	Upper Sacham.	Bucks.
JACOB STOUT.	Rock Hill.	Bucks.
CHRISTIAN KOPLIN.	New Providence.	Philadelphia.
MICHAEL HOVERSTICHT.	Conestogo.	Lancaster.
JACOB RUBLEY.	Conestogo.	Lancaster.
PHILIP HERKER.	Marlborough.	Philadelphia.
GEORGE SLIPPLEAR.	Strasburg.	Lancaster.
WILLIAM YOUNG.	Philadelphia City.	Philadelphia.
MARTIN BOELER, a moravian, (took the Sacrament "some weeks before " the 8th Day of April, 1751, the Day of the Date of the Certificate of the Revd. Mr. Christian Rauch, as 'tis expressed in the said Certificate).	Warwick.	Lancaster.

PENNSYLVANIA.

V. 120. (Supreme Court at Philadelphia, 25 Sept., 1751.)

Foreigners' Names.	Of what Township.	Of what County.	Sacrament when taken.
PHILIP CUNIUS.	Upper Hanover.	Philadelphia.	Sept. 22nd, 1751.
DAVID MÜLLER.	Lower Milford.	Bucks.	Sept. 20th, 1751.
GEORGE PRY.	Marlborough.	Philadelphia.	Sept. 20th, 1751.
GEORGE LEIDICK.	Frederick.	Philadelphia.	Sept. 22nd, 1751.
JOHN NICHOLAS SEYDEL.	New Providence.	Philadelphia.	Sept. 1st, 1751.
EVA BARBARA HOLSTEIN.	Heidleberg.	Lancaster.	Sept. 15th, 1751.
ANDREW GROFF.	Bethel.	Lancaster.	Sept. 15th, 1751.
MARTIN KAPP.	Heidleberg.	Lancaster.	Sept. 15th, 1751.
EVA MARGARETTA KAP(P).	Heidleberg.	Lancaster.	Sept. 15th, 1751.
CHRISTIAN MILLER.	Heidleberg.	Lancaster.	Sept. 15th, 1751.
EVA MARIA MILLER.	Heidleberg.	Lancaster.	Sept. 15th, 1751.
GEORGE EMMERT.	Bethel.	Lancaster.	Sept. 15th, 1751.
EVA MARIA EMMERT.	Bethel.	Lancaster.	Sept. 15th, 1751.
PETER WERNER.	Heidleberg.	Lancaster.	Sept. 15th, 1751.
PHILIP HAUTZ.	Bethel.	Lancaster.	Sept. 22nd, 1751.
PHILIP LAWRENCE HAUTZ.	Bethel.	Lancaster.	Sept. 22nd, 1751.
JOHN SIEBLE.	Bethel.	Lancaster.	Sept. 22nd, 1751.
DANIEL HOUY.	Bethel.	Lancaster.	Sept. 14th, 1751.
GEORGE LAROW.	East Caln.	Chester.	Aug. 18th, 1751.
JONAS LAROW.	Pextang.	Lancaster.	July 19th, 1751.
PETER PISEL.	Marlborough.	Philadelphia.	Sept. 15th, 1751.
GEORGE SLACKER.	Upper Hanover.	Philadelphia.	Sept. 22nd, 1751.
GEORGE LECHNER.	Tulpyhoccon.	Lancaster.	Sept. 15th, 1751.
GEORGE DOLLINGER.	Tulpyhoccon.	Lancaster.	Sept. 15th, 1751.
JACOB KATTERMAN.	Tulpyhoccon.	Lancaster.	Sept. 15th, 1751.
FRANCIS WENERY.	Tulpyhoccon.	Lancaster.	Sept. 22nd, 1751.
PETER LAUCKS.	Tulpyhoccon.	Lancaster.	Sept. 22nd, 1751.
JOHN TRAUTMAN.	Tulpyhoccon.	Lancaster.	Sept. 22nd, 1751.
JOHN IMEL.	Tulpyhoccon.	Lancaster.	Sept. 15th, 1751.
SIMON CARLL.	Tulpyhoccon.	Lancaster.	Sept. 15th, 1751.
GEORGE HOFFMAN.	Makonsey.	Bucks.	Sept. 3rd, 1751.
JACOB WART.	Makonsey.	Bucks.	Sept. 22nd, 1751.
JOHN GEORGE LECHNER.	Hempfield.	Lancaster.	Sept. 15th, 1751.
MICHAEL EBERT.	Manchester.	York.	Sept. 1st, 1751.
MARTIN EBERT.	Manchester.	York.	Sept. 1st, 1751.
BALTHAZAR KNOERTZER.	Dover.	York.	Sept. 1st, 1751.
MARTIN WATZ.	Lancaster.	Lancaster.	Sept. 1st, 1751.
ULRICK NESLEY.	Springfield.	Philadelphia.	Aug. 3rd, 1751.
JOHN PETER SPEIHT.	New Hanover.	Philadelphia.	Sept. 22nd, 1751.
HENRY KELLER.	Chaising.	Bucks.	Sept. 24th, 1751.

Quakers [&c.].

Foreigners' Names.	Of what Township.	Of what County.
VOLENTINE STICKLE.	Oley.	Philadelphia.
CONRAD BOP.	Colebrookdale.	Philadelphia.
GEORGE WOOLFORD.	Cocolico.	Lancaster.
PETER SIMERMAN.	Cocolico.	Lancaster.
JACOB MACHLEN.	Colebrookdale.	Philadelphia.
JEREMIAH JACKLE.	Germantown.	Philadelphia.
GEORGE GRAFF.	Lancaster.	Lancaster.
KILLEAN WICE.	Germantown.	Philadelphia.
MELCHIOR MENG.	Germantown.	Philadelphia.

V. 120.   (Said Supreme Court, 11 April, 1752.)

Foreigners' Names.	Of what Township.	Of what County.	Sacrament when taken.
MARTIN EISENHAVER.	Bethel.	Lancaster.	March 29th, 1752.
PETER EISENHAVER.	Bethel.	Lancaster.	March 29th, 1752.
ELIZABETH EISENHAVER.	Bethel.	Lancaster.	March 29th, 1752.
JOHN GEO. GROF.	Bethel.	Lancaster.	April 4th, 1752.
JEREMIAH TRACSLER.	Mocconsey.	Bucks.	March 29th, 1752.
HENRY OAL.	Heidleberg.	Bucks.	March 29th, 1752.
ELIAS BONDER.	Heidleberg.	Bucks.	March 29th, 1752.
JOHN SHORT.	Egypt.	Bucks.	March 29th, 1752.
PETER WOODRING.	Egypt.	Bucks.	March 29th, 1752.
HENRY WALTER.	Cocolico.	Lancaster.	March 29th, 1752.
WILLIAM HAWKER (HAUKER).	Cocolico.	Lancaster.	March 29th, 1752.
THOMAS DORMER.	Cordwainer of the City of Philadelphia.		March 29th, 1752.

Quakers.

Affirmers' Names.	Of what Township	Of what County.
CORNELIUS LANE.	Manheim.	Lancaster.
PETER LANE.	Manheim.	York.
BOLSER SPANGLER.	York.	York.
HENRY EVERLI.	Bethel.	Lancaster.
JOHN ADAM SCHAW(S).	Skippack.	Philadelphia.

(Said Supreme Court, 25 Sept., 1752.)

Foreigners' Names.	Of what Township.	Of what County.	Sacrament when taken.
JACOB FOLMAR.	Tulpyhoccon.	Berks.	Aug. 16th, 1752.
FREDERICK HERTJOG.	Upper Salford.	Philadelphia.	Sept. 20th, 1752.
SOLOMON HEIM-BONN.	Of the City of Philadelphia.		Jews sworn on the
MICHAEL ISRAEL.	Of the City of Philadelphia.		Old Testament only.

Quakers [&c.].

Affirmers' Names.	Of what Township.	Of what County.
GEO. NICH. MAYER.	Philadelphia City.	Philadelphia
ANDREW WINT.	Upper Saucon.	Northampton
PAUL ANTHONY.	Upper Hanover.	Philadelphia
FREDERICK BAKER.	Philadelphia City.	Philadelphia

(Said Supreme Court, 10 April, 1753.)

Foreigners' Names.	Of what Township.	Of what County.	Sacrament when taken.
PETER SMIDT.	Cocolico.	Lancaster.	April 8th, 1753.
MICHAEL HOOBLEY.	Lancaster Town.	Lancaster.	Feb. 14th, 1753.
PETER BACKER.	Providence.	Philadelphia.	April 8th, 1753.

Quakers [&c.].

Affirmers' Names.	Of what Township.	Of what County.
LEWIS CLOTS.	Upper Milford.	Northampton.
PETER MILLER, Junr.	Philadelphia City.	Philadelphia.
ADAM REDD.	Newberry.	York.
JOHN EGGMAN.	Strasburg.	Lancaster.

PENNSYLVANIA.

Affirmers' Names.	Of what Township.	Of what County.
MARCUS FORNEY.	Manheim.	York.
CONRAD PRICE.	Oley.	Berks.
HENRY KONN.	Hallam.	York.
CHRISTIAN HOOBER.	Hempfield.	Lancaster.
JOHN SHULTZ.	Hallam.	York.
LEONARD FESSLER.	Earl.	Lancaster.
GEORGE WERFIELD.	Bart.	Lancaster.
MELCHIOR WERFIELD.	Bart.	Lancaster.
JACOB EHRENHART.	Salisbury.	Northampton.
JOHN KNAWS (KNAUS).	Upper Milford.	Northampton.
ADAM SHULER.	Upper Milford.	Northampton.
MARTIN STUTSMAN.	Cowisseoppen.	Berks.
PETER SITES.	Bart.	Lancaster.
FRANCIS RUTTER.	Exeter.	Berks.
GEORGE RUTTER.	Exeter.	Berks.
RUDOLPH HECKELER.	Exeter.	Berks.
SEBASTIAN HENRY KNAUSS.	Salisbury.	Northampton.
JOHN WAGNER.	Oley.	Berks.
JOHN FRANCKLEBERGER.	Paradise.	York.
ANTHONY DESHLER.	Philadelphia City.	Philadelphia.
FREDERICK ROMIG.	Maccungy.	Northampton.
CONRAD KEARSNER.	Windsor.	Berks.

(Supreme Court at Philadelphia, 24 Sept., 1753.)

X 41.

Jurors' Names.	Township.	County.	Sacrament when taken.
GEORGE ESTHERLY.	Franconia.	Philadelphia.	Sept. 16th, 1753.
MARTIN BUMBARGER.	Lancaster.	Lancaster.	Aug. 26th, 1753.
JACOB ORNDT.	Rockhill.	Bucks.	Sept. 9th, 1753.
HENRY BUMBARGER (BUMBERGER).	Rockhill.	Bucks.	Sept. 9th, 1753.
JOHN MARTIN.	Upper Dublin.	Philadelphia.	Aug. 20th, 1753.
PETER GEERHART.	Franconia.	Philadelphia.	Sept. 9th, 1753.
JACOB LYDIE.	Franconia.	Philadelphia.	Sept. 16th, 1753.
BERNARD KOUNTZER.	Franconia.	Philadelphia.	Sept. 16th, 1753.
BENJAMIN SPYKER.	Lancaster.	Lancaster.	Aug. 26th, 1753.
HENRY TOOPES.	Bethel.	Lancaster.	Sept. 16th, 1753.
HENRY GLYN.	New Hanover.	Philadelphia.	Sept. 22nd 1753.
MICHAEL DORRERER			
(DODDERERER).Colebrookdale.		Berks.	Sept. 22nd 1753.
MICHAEL FORTNEE.	Lancaster.	Lancaster.	Sept. 22nd 1753.
GEORGE MEELZER (MEELZGER).	Lancaster.	Lancaster.	Sept. 2nd. 1753.
ABRAM HOOBLER.	Bethel.	Lancaster.	Sept. 16th, 1753.
JACOB EICHHOLTZ.	Lancaster.	Lancaster.	Sept. 2nd. 1753.
JOHN MICHAEL BYERLY.	Lancaster.	Lancaster.	Sept. 2nd. 1753.
LUDWICK LAUMAN.	Lancaster.	Lancaster.	Sept. 2nd. 1753.
MICHAEL GROSS.	Lancaster.	Lancaster.	Sept. 19th, 1753.
VALENTINE CRUG (KRUG).	Lancaster.	Lancaster.	Sept. 2nd. 1753.
JOHN BARR.	Lancaster.	Lancaster.	Aug. 26th, 1753.

Quakers.

Affirmers' Names.	Township.	Of what County.
BENEDICT ESTLEMAN.	Conestogo.	Lancaster.
MICHAEL HESS.	Conestogo.	Lancaster.
JOHANNES THOMAS.	Lancaster.	Lancaster.
JACOB MARKLEY.	Perquiomen.	Philadelphia.
JACOB ROSS.	Philadelphia City.	Philadelphia.
GERRARD BRENOR.	Manor.	Lancaster.
MICHAEL SHAVER.	Tolpohockon.	Berks.
PETER SHAVER.	Tolpehocken.	Berks.
FREDERICK SHAVER.	Tolpohocken.	Berks.
JOHN REESER.	Maiden Creek.	Berks.
JOHN YERB.	Warwick.	Lancaster.
MELKER WAGGONER.	Worcester.	Philadelphia.
DANIEL KEPOTZ.	Conestogo.	Lancaster.
WENDAL (WENDALL) WHOLE.	Earl.	Lancaster.
JOHN BOWMAN.	Strasburgh.	Lancaster.
JACOB YERB.	Warwick.	Lancaster.
ISAAC WHOLE.	Earl.	Lancaster.

(Supreme Court at Philadelphia, 10 April, 1754.)

Foreigners' Names.	Township.	County.	Sacrament when taken.
VALENTINE NUNGASSER.	Upper Salford.	Philadelphia.	March 31st, 1754.
CHARLES SWARTZ.	Lower Salford.	Philadelphia.	March 31st, 1754.
DANIEL KOKERT.	Lower Saucon.	Northampton.	April 7th, 1754.
MICHAEL WILHELM.	Williamstown.	Northampton.	April 10th, 1754.
JACOB MILLER.	Hereford.	Berks.	April 10th, 1754.
JACOB DECK.	Williamstown.	Northampton.	April 7th, 1754.
CASPER RITTER.	Upper Milford.	Northampton.	April 10th, 1754.
JACOB PFISTER.	Philadelphia.	Philadelphia.	April 14th, 1754.
MARTIN GATTER.	Philadelphia.	Philadelphia.	April 14th, 1754.
MATHIAS CLEINE.	Philadelphia.	Philadelphia.	April 14th, 1754.
GEORGE JACOB YOUNG.	Moyamensick.	Philadelphia.	April 14th, 1754.
JOHANNES NEGLEE.	Moyamensick. (Philadelphia.)	Philadelphia.	April 14th, 1754.
JACOB WHITMAN.	Passyunck.	Philadelphia.	April 14th, 1754.
JOHN CUBBER.	Cressom.	Philadelphia.	April 14th, 1754.
CHRISTOPHER GALLER.	Philadelphia.	Philadelphia.	April 14th, 1754.
GEORGE HOFFMAN.	Germantown.	Philadelphia.	April 14th, 1754.
JACOB SWENKEE.	Cressom.	Philadelphia.	April 14th, 1754.
HENRY MAAG.	Moyamensick.	Philadelphia.	April 14th, 1754.

Quakers.

Foreigners' Names.	County.	Township.
ANDREW BOYER.	Heidleburgh.	Berks.
JOHN SARVER.	Heidleburgh.	Berks.
ERNAST SIGSMOND SEYDLE.	Alsace.	Berks.
DAVID ELY.	Richmond.	Berks.
PHILIP EPRIGHT.	Earl.	Lancaster.
URICK (ULRICK) HOOY.	Maiden Creek.	Berks.
MICHAEL DAISER.	Earl.	Lancaster.
LEONARD STONE.	Earl.	Lancaster.
LEONARD MILLER.	Earl.	Lancaster.
JACOB KERN.	Reading.	Berks.
JOHN GONKLE.	Berry.	Lancaster.
CHRISTIAN NEEGLE.	Lower Saucon.	Northampton.
DANIEL REMICH.	Lower Saucon.	Northampton.

PENNSYLVANIA.

(Supreme Court at Philadelphia, 24 Sept., 1754.)

Foreigners' Names.	Township.	County.	Sacrament when taken.
CHRISTOPHER SHIBLER.	Philadelphia.	Philadelphia.	Sept. 22nd, 1754.
ARNST KURTS.	Philadelphia.	Philadelphia.	Sept. 22nd, 1754.
JOHN (JOSEPH *struck through*, JN⁰ *written over*) BARNED.	Perquiomen.	Philadelphia.	Sept. 11th, 1754.
CARL RYAR.	Providence.	Philadelphia.	Sept. 22nd, 1754.
MICHAEL SIMON.	Philadelphia (Cresson).	Philadelphia.	Sept. 22nd, 1754.
NICHOLAS SWINGLE.	Heidleburgh.	Lancaster.	Sept. 23rd, 1754.
ADAM WILRICK.	Lebanon.	Lancaster.	Sept. 8th, 1754.
ELIAS DETRICK.	Easton.	Northampton.	Sept. 1st, 1754.
GEORGE BUTTON.	Philadelphia.	Philadelphia.	Sept. 22nd, 1754.
ANDREAS OHL.	Marlborough.	Philadelphia.	Aug. 25th, 1754.
DANIEL KRANINGER.	Cresson.	Philadelphia.	Sept. 22nd, 1754.
HENRY MUHLENBURGH.	Providence.	Philadelphia.	Sept. 15th, 1754.
JOHN CHRISTOPHER HARTWICK.	Philadelphia.	Philadelphia.	Sept. 15th, 1754.

Quakers.

Foreigners' Names.	Township.	County.
JOHN WAGLE.	Easton.	Northampton.
HENRY LANE.	Manheim.	Lancaster.
HENRY SHANK.	Strasburg.	Lancaster.

(Supreme Court at Philadelphia, 10 April, 1755.)

Foreigners' Names.	Township.	County.	Sacrament when taken.
DAVID GUSY (? GIESY).	Upper Salford.	Northampton.	March 30th, 1755.
FRANCIS ROTH.	Salisbury (Salsbury).	Northampton.	March 30th, 1755.
ADAM BLANK.	Salisbury (Salsbury).	Northampton.	March 30th, 1755.
JACOB TIMANUS.	Upper Dublin.	Philadelphia.	March 30th, 1755.
VALENTINE PUFF.	Upper Dublin.	Philadelphia.	March 30th, 1755.
MARTIN BOGER.	Long Swamp.	Berks.	March 30th, 1755.
JOHANNES FORER.	Tulpehoccon.	Berks.	March 30th, 1755.
JOHN BOYER.	Heidleburgh.	Berks.	March 30(29)th, 1755.
PHILIP FENTERMAKER.	Long Swamp.	Berks.	March 23rd, 1755.
JACOB GIRARDIN.	Long Swamp.	Berks.	March 23rd, 1755.
SAMUEL BURGER.	Long Swamp.	Berks.	March 23rd, 1755.
CHRISTIAN RUTH.	Maccungy.	Northampton.	March 23rd, 1755.
FREDERICK KELWIG.	Long Swamp.	Berks.	March 23rd, 1755.
DEWALD CARNE.	Long Swamp.	Berks.	March 23rd, 1755.
JOSEPH BURREY.	Long Swamp.	Berks.	March 23rd, 1755.
JOHN HISS.	Berks.	Berks.	March 30th, 1755.
BUDOLPH BERGER.	Maxatawny.	Berks.	March 23rd, 1755.
MICHAEL KNABB (KNAB).	Oley.	Berks.	March 30th, 1755.
CHRISTIAN DOLL.	Perquiomen.	Philadelphia.	April 6th, 1755.
GEORGE STOLNAKER.	Upper Milford.	Northampton.	March 30th, 1755.
JOHN ORDT.	Upper Milford.	Northampton.	March 30th, 1755.
NICHOLAS SWINGLE.	Tulpehoccon.	Berks.	March 30th, 1755.
PETER GEORGE.	Bockhill (Rockhill).	Bucks.	Feb. 26th, 1755.
ADAM DOWNEY.	Hilltown.	Bucks.	March 30th, 1755.
CHRISTIAN KERN.	Rockhill.	Bucks.	March 30th, 1755.

Foreigners' Names	Township.	County.	Sacrament when taken.
GODFREY KNOUS.	Whitehall.	Northampton.	March 31st, 1755.
FREDERICK NIGHAT.	Whitehall.	Northampton.	April 3rd, 1755.
NICHOLAS SWINGTE.	Bockhill (Rockhill).	Bucks.	Jan. 26, 1755.
GEORGE STOUT.	Salsbury.	Northampton.	March 30th, 1755.
ADAM LISTS.	Tulpehoccon.	Berks.	March 30th, 1755.
MICHAEL FLORAS.	Upper Milford.	Northampton.	April 8th, 1755.
JOHN DEITER.	Heidleburgh.	Berks.	March 29th, 1755.
ADAM DESHLER.	Whitehall.	Northampton.	March 31st, 1755.
H. B. FRANKS.	Yorktown.	York.	A Jew.
PETER KITTLE (? HITTLE).	Upper Milford	Northampton.	April 8th, 1755.
ADAM HEAVELY.	Whitehall.	Northampton.	March 31st, 1755.
LAWRENCE GOOD.	Whitehall.	Northampton.	March 31st, 1755.
GEORGE JACOB KERN (KARN).	Whitehall.	Northampton.	April 3rd, 1755.
HENRY WILHELM.	Upper Milford.	Northampton.	April 8th, 1755.
ISAAC DALEP.	Upper Milford.	Northampton.	April 8th, 1755.

Quakers.

Foreigners' Names.	Township.	County.
JOST VALLERT (VOLLERT).	Salsbury.	Northampton
HENRY CHRIST.	Maxatawny.	Berks.
FRANCIS YOST.	Alsace.	Berks.
ELIAS ROTTER.	Robeson.	Berks.
CHRISTIAN HELLER.	Upper Milford.	Northampton.
MICHAEL KYPER.	Upper Milford.	Northampton.
MICHAEL SMITH.	Upper Milford.	Northampton.
GEORGE HEISLER.	Germantown.	Philadelphia.
CHRISTOPHER BEENIVOLT (BEENIVALT).	Worcester.	Philadelphia.
MARTIN BRAND.	Philadelphia.	Philadelphia.
JOHN ETTER.	Donegall.	Lancaster.
DAVID NEWMAN.	North Wales.	Philadelphia.
CHRISTOPHER HEBENER.	Frederick.	Philadelphia.
GEORGE ANDREWS.	Towamensing.	Philadelphia.
GEORGE KREEBEL.	Towamensing.	Philadelphia.
DAVID BARRINGER.	Upper Milford.	Northampton.
MATTHIAS BUMGARDNER (BUMBGARDNER).	Donegall.	Lancaster.
VALENTINE WESTHOFFER.	Cocolico.	Lancaster.
GEORGE HENDERICK.	Lebannon (Lebannan).	Lancaster.
CHRISTIAN VANDASHANT (VANLASHANT).	Germantown.	Philadelphia.
WILLIAM BAKER.	Philadelphia City.	Philadelphia.

(Supreme Court at Philadelphia, 24 Sept., 1755.)

Jurors' Names.	Township.	County.	Sacrament when taken.
HENRY LORAH.	Frankonay (Frankoney)	Philadelphia.	Sept. 21st, 1755.
REINHOLT ABENDSHEN.	Berks.	Berks.	Aug. 31st, 1755.
GRAFT HINER (? KINER).	Alsace.	Berks.	Sept. 21st, 1755.
FREDERICK CRESSMAN.	Northampton.	Philadelphia.	Sept. 24th, 1755.
ABRAHAM ORNT.	Frankonay (Frankoney)	Philadelphia.	Sept. 21st, 1755.

NATURALIZATIONS

PENNSYLVANIA.

Jurors' Names.	Township.	County.	Sacrament when taken.
JACOB GRAFF.	Philadelphia City.	Philadelphia.	Sept. 14th, 1755.
ALBRIGHT STRAUS.	Barn.	Berks.	Aug. 24th, 1755.
JACOB CRYSLER.	Philadelphia City.	Philadelphia.	Sept. 14th, 1755.
CHRISTR. DICKENSHAT.	Upper Salford.	Philadelphia.	Aug. 31st, 1755.
GEORGE SWINEHART.	Cole Brook.	Berks.	Sept. 14th, 1755.
HENRY NEWKIRK.			Sept. 14th, 1755.
MICHAEL SWINEHART.	Douglass.	Philadelphia.	Sept. 14th, 1755.
LUDWICK PICKLE.	Douglass.	Philadelphia.	Sept. 14th, 1755.
CHRISTR NEWMAN.	New Hanover.	Philadelphia.	Sept. 22nd, 1755.
NICHOLAS YOST.	Alsace.	Berks.	Sept. 21st, 1755.
ANDREW SMITH.	Hanover.	Philadelphia.	Sept. 22nd, 1755.
JOHN SPYKER.	Lebanon (Lebanan).	Lancaster.	Sept. 16th, 1755.
GEO. SWANK.	Perquiomen.	Philadelphia.	Sept. 23rd, 1755.
MATHIAS KEELER.	Douglass.	Philadelphia.	Sept. 22nd, 1755.
VALENTINE GERBER.	Reading.	Lancaster.	Sept. 21st, 1755.
CONRADT BEAM.	Cole Brook (Colebrook).	Berks.	Sept. 8th, 1755.
NICHOLAS SWANK.	Norrington.	Philadelphia.	Sept. 24th, 1755.
CONRADT SPEECH.	Hanover.	Philadelphia.	Sept. 22nd, 1755.
JOHN GATES.	Upper Salford.	Philadelphia.	Aug. 31st, 1755.
PHILIP YOST.	Limerick.	Philadelphia.	Sept. 22nd, 1755.
JOHN SHNUKE.	Lebannon.	Lancaster.	Aug. 31st, 1755.
NICHOLAS MARTIN.	Heidleburgh.	Lancaster.	Sept. 21st, 1755.
CASPER GORE.	Bethel.	Lancaster.	Aug. 5th, 1755.
PHILIP GEPHART.	Tulpehoccon.	Berks.	July 27th, 1755.
HENRY SHEWEN.	Berks.	Berks.	July 27th, 1755.
SEBASTIAN STAIN.	Bethel.	Lancaster.	July 27th, 1755.

Quakers.

Affirmers' Names	Township.	County.
PHILIP LINGHEAR.	Lancaster.	Lancaster.
ANDREW BOYER.	Worcester.	Philadelphia.
JOHN BUCKAUS.	Germantown.	Philadelphia.
SAMUEL FILBERT.	Barn.	Berks.
STEPHEN BERNARD.	Maiden Creek.	Berks.
PETER HYSLER.	Germantown.	Philadelphia.
TOBIAS BEKLE.	Heidleburgh.	Lancaster.
YOST OLEWINE.	Upper Milford.	Bucks.
JACOB KEEN.	Heidleburgh.	Berks.
FREDERICK GERHART.	Heidleburgh.	Berks.
PETER OUFENSANBERGER.	Earl.	Lancaster.
DAVID BREACK.	Earl.	Lancaster.
JOHN GOTLECK.	Barn.	Lancaster.
LAZARUS WINGER.	Heidleburgh.	Berks.
JOHN MEYER.	Heidleburgh.	Berks.
JACOB MILLER.	Barn.	Berks.
GEORGE STUMP.	Franconia.	Philadelphia.
JACOB GREATER.	Heidleburgh.	Berks.
HENRY STAR.	Heidleburgh.	Berks.
PETER KNOP.	Heidleburgh.	Berks.
IACOB WHISTLER.	Manor.	Lancaster.

Affirmers' Names.	Township.	County.
DANIEL HECKEDOWN.	Lebanon.	Lancaster.
GERHART ETTER.	Lebanon.	Lancaster.
JOHN HERGARATER.	Maxatawny.	Berks.
VALENTINE GROSS.	Hempfield.	Lancaster.
DANIEL BURNEMAN.	Upper Hanover.	Philadelphia.
CHRISTN. FRY.	Hamfield.	Lancaster.
PETER REESAKER.	Warwick.	Lancaster.
CHRISTIAN PALMAR.	Hamfield.	Lancaster.
HENRY SMITH.	Lebanon.	Lancaster.
FREDERICK KEYSELL.	Warwick.	Lancaster.
VALENTINE MILLER.	Manor.	Lancaster.
CHRISTIAN RICHEOP.	Providence.	Philadelphia.
GEORGE LESTS.	Heidleburgh.	Lancaster.

(Supreme Court at Philadelphia, 10 April, 1756.)

Quakers.

Foreigners' Names.	Township.	County.
RUDOLPH HONAKER.	Rockhill.	Bucks.
JACOB MINER.	Easton.	Easton.
MARTIN WEYBREYTHE.	Manheim.	Lancaster.
HENRY SCHWEITZER.	Manheim.	Lancaster.

(Supreme Court at Philadelphia, 24 Sept., 1756.)

Foreigners' Names.

PHILIP BROWN.
GEORGE LINTZ.
JOHN PHILIP HEIST.

Quakers.

HENRY MEYER.
GEORGE TELP.
JOHN WILLIAMS.

(Supreme Court at Philadelphia), 10 April, 1757.

Foreigners' (Jurors') Names.

JACOB EHRENZELLER.
JACOB HEAUKE.
JOHN NICHOLAS HEIST.
JOHN SEIDEL.
GEORGE KENTZ.
ANDREW NAPPINGER.
GOLIFFE SEIGLE.
ADAM FALKER.
JACOB DOWDLE.
GEORGE ARNSTMEYER.
CONRAD BAPP.
JOHN CONRAD SCHWEIGHAUSER.
DAVID SHAFFER.
CHRISTOPHER HANS MAN (MANN).
PHILIP PEAL.

PENNSYLVANIA.

Affirmers' Names.

PETER EVERLY.
TETERICH MARSHAL (MARSHALL).
ADOLPH MEYER.
JACOB EVERLY.
ULRICK STALEY.

(Supreme Court at Philadelphia), 24 Sept., 1757.

Jurors' Names.

MICHAEL THEIS.
MICHAEL HOFFMAN.
MARTIN LETTERMAN.
RUDOLPH OBERLING.
PETER KNIGHT.
ANTONY LERCH.

Affirmers' Names.

JOHN COOK.
JOHN DEDEIR.
HENRY LESHIER.
JOHN WEAVER.
CASPER DUMERNIELT.
DAVID DUMERNIELT.
LEWIS CASLER (CASLAR).

(Supreme Court at Philadelphia), 10 April, 1758.

Jurors' Names.

ANTHONY FORREST (FOREST).
ADAM SPAAN.
GABRIEL RIECHER.
ALEXANDER SHEFFER.
WILLIAM PAWMAN (? BAWMAN).
GEORGE SPRECKER.
MARTIN TOMY.
CATHERINA COCH (KOCH).
BALTZER ERLACH.
JOHN UNFERSAHT.
JOHN FREDERICK ROHR.
JOSEPH HISTER (HISLER).
JACOB ISAAC.
VALENTINE SHALLOS.

(Supreme Court at Philadelphia), 25 Sept., 1758.

Jurors' Names.

ABRAHAM BROSIS.
NICHOLAS SYSINGER.
HENRY HAUN.
MARTIN KAUST.
AUDONES EUGEL.
(ISAAC YOUNG.)
PETER RUPP.

Jurors' Names.

HENRY REITMEYER.
GEORGE SHULTZ.
HENRY DEACANHALL (DEACANHALT).
CHRISTIAN ORENDOLF.
ADAM SLIGER (SLEGER).
EVERHART MARTIN.
ANTONY DERDER.
MICHAEL KAUBLE.
CONRAD BEM.
JOHN ADAM MILLER.
JOHN GEORGE REES.
GEORGE KAST.
GEORGE FREDK. BYER.
MICHAEL PARTIUS.

(Supreme Court at Philadelphia), 10 April, 1759.

Jurors' Names.

PAUL BAILLET (BAILLIET).
MICHAEL SPIEGLE.
MICHAEL NEWHART.
MICHAL KARCHER.
ANDREW BRECHEL.
CHRISTIAN HERNER.
CATHERINA KOUFMAN.
JOHN EGLE.
NEGRO FRY.

Affirmers' Names.

STOPHEL HANLEY.
STOPHEL HAIMSEL.
CHRISTIAN FERNSTERMAKER.
JOHN BENNER.
BASTIAN BENNER.
GREGORIUS MAISTER.
PETER KEEHLINE.
GEO. SCHLOSSER.
ULRICK HANSBERGER.
BALTZER YEAGLE.
JOHN BEETELL.
MARTIN KARCHER.
BENEDICT KAYMAN.

(Supreme Court at Philadelphia), 24 Sept., 1759.

Jurors' Names.

GEORGE LOUTZ.
NICHOLAS BOYER.
JACOB SHAREN.
PETER FEATHER.
JACOB YAIGER.
PETER HAAS.
GEORGE GEISLER.
LODOVICK TILLINGER.

PENNSYLVANIA.

Jurors' Names.

MARTIN HECKRENDOM (HECKENDOM).
JOHN BISHOP.
JOHN MOLL.
JACOB BEGTOL.
HENRY HERNER (KERNER).
DURST FISTER.
ADAM KOOKERT.
NICHOLAS FRANCIS.
MICHAEL FLEESE.
JOHN GEO. MYERLEY (MYERLY).
DAVID MYERLY.
HENRY RADEBACK.
JNO. NICH. ENSMINGER.
JNO. NICH. HENNICKE.
JOHN ALBUGHT HACKENMILLAR (HACKENMILLER).
JOHN SNEIDER.
JACOB HOOKART.
CHRISTIAN LAUGHBAUGH.

Affirmers' Names.

HIERONIMUS HENNIG.
MICHAEL LODWICK.
JOHN POTT.
LODOWICK IMBLER.
CASPER MANTZ.
PHILIP GREENVALT (GREENWALT).
GEORGE YOKE.
ABRAHAM IMMOBERSTAKE.
PETER SHITZ.
FREDERICK MAYNARD.
CONRAD WEAVER.
ADAM GOOS.
JOHN TITMORE.
MICHAEL DIFFIDERFER.
JOHN TAYLOR.
CHRISTIAN STRIBELY.
BASTIAN LEVAN.

(Supreme Court at Philadelphia), 10 April, 1760.

Jurors' Names.

RUDOPH (RUDOLPH) BRENEISEN.
MICHAEL REUTER.
GERRAHRT HIBSHMAN.
JOHANNES HERNST (ERNST).
JOHN PHILIP BURKHARD.
JOHN GEO. STONE.
FREDERICK WORTH (WIRTH).
HENRY STEEL.
LORENZE MARQUETAND.
WILLIAM BUSH.
JOHN NICHOLAS JOBB (JOB).

Jurors' Names.
LEONARD MAY.
JOHN GEORGE SNEIDER.
MICHAEL OHL.
JOHN CASPER GRAFFE.
HENRY GICKERT.
ADAM BOONE.
FREDERICK FROM.
MATHIAS WEAVER.
HENRY SAUER.
JACOB BARGE.
CHRISTOPHER GRAFFE.
PETER DICK.
HENRY BRUNNER.
PETER DEAL.
PETER PARIS.
ABRAHAM WILD.
EMANL. FREDK. WECKERLE.
JACOB COHLER (KOHLER).
MICHAEL SCHLONECKER.
MICHAEL SCHLONECKER, Junr.
GEBHART BERTHOLD.
JOHN WILLIAM HOFFMAN.
CONRAD BROWNE.
DIER BAUER.
MARTIN KIND.
JOSEPH WELSHANCE.
MARTIN DANNER.
GEORGE MICHAEL KAM.
JOHN GITTENGER.
JOHN SHULTZ.
NICHOLAS KINTZER.
JACOB DUNDER.
GEORGE WOLF.
JACOB BRICKER.
JOHN HOY.
ADAM STRICKER.
PETER KOKER.
HENRY PROCTER.
ADAM HAMBRIGHT.
CONRAD HYSSLEY.
LEONARD LEIGHNER.
LEONARD ABEL.
CHRISTIAN MILHEIM.
GEORGE CHRISTIAN SINN.
MICHAEL KARLE.
FREDERICK GETWICKS.
NICHOLAS BEDINGER.
MARTIN ICLEBERGER.
PETER RAP (RAPP).
MICHAEL KUHNS.
JOHN WOLF.
JNO. JACOB SHOEMAKER.
HENRICK WOLF.
WINEBERT TSHOUDER.

PENNSYLVANIA.

Jurors' Names.

JACOB WILHELM.
ANNA CATH. WILHELM.
FREDK. NUNGESSER.
JACOB GROTZ.
MATHIAS KERN.
PETRIEM WEILAND.
MICHAEL KLEIN.
CHRIST. HENRY REINHOLD.
JOHN MICHAEL AMWEG.
MARTIN BURKHOLDER.
MARTIN DRESBACK.
LEONARD MAYER.
FREDERICK MAYER.
MATHIAS KELCHNER.
PETER ULER.
PHILIP TEIGLER (ZEIGLER).
PHILIP ENTLER.
GEORGE DERR.
LUCAS ROUS.
WILLIAM KOCK.
GEO. BURKHARD.
WILLM. SHIMEL (SHIMELL).
JOHN BEEBER.
MICHAEL THIRNESE (KIRNISE).
PETER HAUS.
NICHOLAS MAYER.
HARMAN MOHR.
MARIA CATHA. ALBRIGHT.
GEORGE MAYER.
CONRAD AMMA.
JACOB TEIGLER (ZEIGLER).
NICHS. WOLFHART.
JOHN BEISSER.
JACOB DICTRICK.
NICHOLAS KERNER.
LAWRENCE REESE.
PHILIP DICK.
ADAM PROBST.
JOHN SAWTER.
GODFRIED BOCKRIES (BOCKUIS).
LODOWICK SANNER.
GEORGE BUSH.
ANDREAS SHEFFER.
CHRIST. GRUBBER.
PHILIP MEETH.
JOHN GEORGE EPPELY.
PAUL REISER.
MARTIN FISCHER.
CHRIST. REENHART UHL.
ULRICK TOLLINGER (ZOLLINGER).
JACOB MAAG.
JACOB HAGY.
JOHN HENRY KATZ.

Jurors' Names.

WILLIAM KAINS.
MELCHIOR SMITH.
MICHAEL RADEBACK.
MARTIN BECKER.
HENRY KIK.
PETER BUKER (BUGER).
CHRISTIAN CASSEL.
HENRY WILLM. STEIGLE.
DAVID DUCKENER.
HENRY YOUNG.
GEORGE BECKER.
HENRY SOUTER.

Quakers.

Affirmers' Names.

RUDOLPH NAGLEE.
JOHN GURR (GUR).
ADAM CUTWALTZ.
GEORGE HARTMAN.
FREDERICK SHOUS.
CONRAD STREIBER.
GEORGE FREDERICK (FREDRICK).
JACOB PECK.
JOHN NICHOL (NICHOLL).
JACOB RICH.
GEORGE WELLER.
GEORGE STROTZ (? SHOTZ).
CHRISTIAN SLEIGHTY.
WILLIAM PUTT.
FREDERICK POST.
LEONARD BIDDLEMAN.
JOHN BITTING.
ELIAS HAMMELL.
JACOB GROVE.
FRANCIS MICHL. BISHOP.
JACOB STOVE.

(Supreme Court at Philadelphia, 24 Sept., 1760.)

Jurors' Names.	Township.	County.	Sacrament when taken.
JOHN ECKERT.	Heidleburg.	Berks.	Sept. 18th, 1760.
JOHN FOCKS.	City of Philadelphia.	Philadelphia.	Sept. 7th, 1760.
MARTIN ALSTAT.	Exeter.	Berks.	Sept. 7th, 1760.
MICHAEL FEITHORN.	Reading.	Berks.	Sept. 14th, 1760.
ADAM EPLER.	Reading.	Berks.	Aug. 10th, 1760.
NICHOLAS ALSTAL.	Exeter.	Berks.	Sept. 7th, 1760.
JOHN CUNNUIS.	Harford.	Berks.	Sept. 7th, 1760.
PHILIP FAASS.	Frederick.	Philadelphia.	Sept. 21st, 1760.
PETER BUKER.	Earl.	Lancaster.	Sept. 21st, 1760.
PHILIP RUNK.	Earl.	Lancaster.	Sept. 21st, 1760.
CASPAR YOST.	Earl.	Lancaster.	Sept. 21st, 1760.
JOHN BNOWBRAKER.	Earl.	Lancaster.	Sept. 21st, 1760.
HENRY WOOLSKULL.	Earl.	Lancaster.	Sept. 21st, 1760.

PENNSYLVANIA.

Jurors' Names.	Township.	County.	Sacrament when taken.
WILLIAM GIGIR.	Hanover.	Philadelphia.	Sept. 7th, 1760.
CHRISTOPHER WAGMAN.	Lebanon.	Lancaster.	Aug. 17th, 1760.
ABRAHAM SHERPER.	Reading.	Berks.	Aug. 10th, 1760.
CONRAD MARK.	Warwick.	Lancaster.	Sept. 14th, 1760.
CHRISTIAN HOLLENJER.	Warwick.	Lancaster.	Sept. 14th, 1760.
MELCHIOR HAFFA.	Greenwich.	Berkshire.	Sept. 14th, 1760.
PHILIP ERPFF.	Heildeburg.	Lancaster.	Sept. 21st, 1760.
CHRISTOPHER WEIDMAN.	Cocolico.	Lancaster.	July 6th, 1760.
LAWRENCE HOUSHOLDER.	Cocolico.	Lancaster.	July 6th, 1760.
MICHAEL KRAUS.	Greenwich.	Berks.	Sept. 14th, 1760.
PETER FISHER.	Exeter.	Berks.	Sept. 7th, 1760.
PAUL DURST.	Exeter.	Berks.	Sept. 7th, 1760.
CONRAD KELLER.	Exeter.	Berks.	Sept. 7th, 1760.
JNO. FRED. HANDSHUH.	Philadelphia.	Philadelphia.	Sept. 21st, 1760.
FREDERICK YAISSER.	Lancaster.	Lancaster.	Aug. 31st, 1760.
MICHL. KELKNER.	Richmond.	Berks.	Sept. 14th, 1760.
MICHAEL ZIESTER.	Reading.	Berks.	Sept. 21st, 1760.
FREDERICK SPIEGLE.	Maccungy.	Northampton.	Sept. 6th, 1760.
GEORGE NUTZ.	Richmond.	Berks.	Sept. 14th, 1760.
GEORGE SHUHNTZ.	Colebrookdale.	Berks.	Sept. 21st, 1760.
JACOB SHUHNTZ.	Colebrookdale.	Berks.	Sept. 21st, 1760.
WILLIAM FIGEL.	Maccungy.	Northampton.	Sept. 6th, 1760.
MATTHIAS BURGHER.	Lancaster.	Lancaster.	Aug. 31st, 1760.
JACOB BOYER.	Exeter.	Berks.	Sept. 7th, 1760.
MATHIAS DETER.	Exeter.	Berks.	Sept. 7th, 1760.
GEORGE HOYLE.	Elizabeth.	Lancaster.	July 6th, 1760.
FREDERICK WALKICH.	Amity.	Berks.	Sept. 14th, 1760.
JOHN GEORGE MEYER.	Philadelphia.	Philadelphia.	Sept. 7th, 1760.
JACOB LOESER.	Lancaster.	Lancaster.	Aug. 31st, 1760.
DANIEL RUDY.	Manheim.	Lancaster.	Aug. 31st, 1760.
MARTIN SHRIENER (? SHAIENER).	Manheim.	Lancaster.	Aug. 31st, 1760.
MARTIN VENTHEUSE (? VENTHEUSEL).	Lancaster.	Lancaster.	Aug. 31st, 1760.
JOHN NICHOLAS KURTZ.	Philadelphia.	Philadelphia.	Sept. 21st, 1760.
CONRAD BONNER.	Philadelphia.	Philadelphia.	Sept. 7th, 1760.
GEORGE SONN.	York.	York.	July 1st, 1760.
JOHN SHMECK.	Alsace.	Berks.	July 20th, 1760.
JOHN GEO. FITLER.	Philadelphia.	Philadelphia.	Sept. 7th, 1760.
NICHOLAS SHUBERT.	Eastor (Easton)	Northampton.	Sept. 21st, 1760.
JACOB BECKER.	Northern Liberties.	Philadelphia.	Sept. 21st, 1760.
CHARLES HESSLIN.	Richmond.	Berks.	Sept. 14th, 1760.
GEORGE VOLICK (VOLIK).	Richmond.	Berks.	Sept. 14th, 1760.
MARTIN OFFNER.	Lancaster.	Lancaster.	Aug. 24th, 1760.
PHILIP MOSER.	Philadelphia.	Philadelphia.	Sept. 21st, 1760.
FŒLIX HUZLIMAN.	Philadelphia.	Philadelphia.	Sept. 21st, 1760.
HENRY ARNT.	Philadelphia.	Philadelphia.	Sept. 21st, 1760.
THOMAS SEHLEY.	Frederick.	Frederick in Maryland.	July 22nd, 1760.
GEORGE HACKER.	Cocolico.	Lancaster.	July 6th, 1760.
GEORGE WHITMAN.	Cocolico.	Lancaster.	July 6th, 1760.
GEORGE REIGER.	Richmond.	Berks.	Sept. 14th, 1760.
WENDAL BUKER.	Philadelphia.	Philadelphia.	Sept. 21st, 1760.
BARNABY BUKER.	Philadelphia.	Philadelphia.	Sept 21st, 1760.

Jurors' Names.	Township.	County.	Sacrament when taken.
JNO. NICHOLAS HANDWIRK.	Heidleburgh.	Northampton.	Aug. 31st, 1760.
CONRAD BEEN.	Hartford.	Berks.	Aug. 14th, 1760.
CONRAD GILBERT.	Douglass.	Philadelphia.	Sept. 23rd, 1760.
BERNARD GILBERT.	Douglass.	Philadelphia.	Sept. 23rd, 1760.
LUDWICK HERRING.	Douglass.	Philadelphia.	Sept. 23rd, 1760.
CHRISTOPHER HIENKLE.	Douglass.	Philadelphia.	Sept. 23rd, 1760.
DANL. NYER.	Douglass.	Philadelphia.	Sept. 23rd, 1760.
JACOB CAWER (CARVER).	City of Philadelphia.	Philadelphia.	Sept. 7th, 1760.
ANDREAS KIEKELINE.	Hilltown.	Bucks.	Sept. 20th, 1760.
JACOB REES.	Rockhill.	Bucks.	Sept. 7th, 1760.
JOHN WALKER.	Marlborough.	Philadelphia.	Sept. 21st, 1760.

Affirmers' Names.	Township.	County.
FREDERICK LIENBACK.	Oley.	Berks.
JOHN LIENBACK.	Oley.	Berks.
HENRY LIENBACK.	Oley.	Berks.
JOHN KILLIS.	Towamensing.	Philadelphia.
MICHAEL HOFMAN.	Gwinedth.	Philadelphia.
JOHN KELLER.	Salisbury.	Northampton.
STEPHEN DYSHER.	Richmond.	Berks.
JACOB TRIBBLEBESS.	Richmond.	Berks.
CONRAD MANISMIT.	Maxatawny.	Berks.
JACOB WHITMORE.	Strasburgh.	Lancaster.
JACOB HOYLE.	Warwick.	Lancaster.
CHRISTIAN GOOD.	Hempfield.	Lancaster.
LEONARD CLINE.	Lancaster.	Lancaster.
DETRICK COQUELIN.	Cocolico.	Lancaster.
JOHN COQUELIN.	Cocolico.	Lancaster.
VALENTINE BOWMAN.	Elizabeth.	Lancaster.
FREDERICK WAIDLE.	Lancaster.	Lancaster.
SEBASTIAN KELLER.	Elizabeth.	Lancaster.
JOHN TENDLER.	Cocolico.	Lancaster.
JOHN STOKEY.	Elizabeth.	Lancaster.
PETER LITTLE.	Germany.	York.
GEORGE SCHWANTZ.	Lancaster.	Lancaster.
HENRY YUNKEN.	Springfield.	Philadelphia.

(Supreme Court at Philadelphia), 10 (and 11) April, 1761.

Foreigners' Names.	Township.	County.	Sacrament when taken.
MATTHIAS LEOPALD.	City of Philadelphia.	Philadelphia.	March 22nd, 1761.
JNO. FREDERICK HAGNER.	City of Philadelphia.	Philadelphia.	March 22nd, 1761.
WILLIAM STRAINER.	City of Philadelphia.	Philadelphia.	March 22nd, 1761.
JNO. GEORGE LAIB.	City of Philadelphia.	Philadelphia.	March 22nd, 1761.
JNO. JACOB RHODE.	City of Philadelphia.	Philadelphia.	March 22nd, 1761.
JNO. WEISMAN.	City of Philadelphia.	Philadelphia.	March 22nd, 1761.
MATTHIAS SMITH.	Tulpohockon.	Philadelphia (Berks).	March 22nd, 1761.
PETER GOTTSHALL.	Hempfield.	Lancaster.	April 4th, 1761.
GEORGE FRED. BAISH.	Lancaster.	Lancaster.	April 4th, 1761.
JOHN APPLEMAN.	Paradice.	York.	March 22nd, 1761.
CONRAD WEINS.	Earl.	Lancaster.	March 22nd, 1761.
JACOB GRAFF, Junr.	City of Philadelphia.	Philadelphia.	March 22nd, 1761.
SEBASTIAN MUFFLER.	City of Philadelphia.	Philadelphia.	March 22nd, 1761.
ANDREAS HOLSBAUM.	Earl.	Lancaster.	March 22nd, 1761.

PENNSYLVANIA.

Foreigners' Names.	Township.	County.	Sacrament when taken.
GEORGE WEBER.	Cocolico.	Lancaster.	March 22nd, 1761.
DAVID SCHURCK.	Earl.	Lancaster.	March 22nd, 1761.
PHILIP RHODE.	Earl.	Lancaster.	March 22nd, 1761.
GEORGE WERNS.	Earl.	Lancaster.	March 22nd, 1761.
GERHARD KAFROTH.	Cocolico.	Lancaster.	March 22nd (24th), 176
JACOB DUMMIN.	Earl.	Lancaster.	March 22nd (24th), 176
HENRY FEDDER.	Cocolico.	Lancaster.	March 22nd (24th), 176
GEORGE YUND.	Earl.	Lancaster.	March 23rd, 1761.
JOHANNES SCHNEIDER.	Bern.	Berks.	March 22nd, 1761.
DAVID LAW.	Orange County in North Carolina.		March 22nd, 1761.
JOHANNES HOFFMAN.	Bern.	Berks.	March 22nd, 1761.
ULRICK BADMAKER.	Bern.	Berks.	March 22nd, 1761.
JNO. ANDREW MISSERSMITH.	City of Philadelphia.	Philadelphia.	March 22nd, 1761.
HENRY KEPPELL (KEPPELE).	City of Philadelphia.	Philadelphia.	March 22nd, 1761.
JNO. ANDREW RHOR.	City of Philadelphia.	Philadelphia.	Feb. 22nd, 1761.
HERMAN WEBER.	Bern.	Berks.	April 1st, 1761.
JACOB STEEN.	Bern.	Berks.	April 1st, 1761.
CONRAD SCHNEIDER.	Bern.	Berks.	April 1st, 1761.
HERMAN RICK.	Bern.	Berks.	March 22nd, 1761.
GEORGE WAGGONER.	Bern.	Berks.	April 1st, 1761.
WILKELM LEIMEISTER.	Bern.	Berks.	March 22nd, 1761.
CHRISTIAN HOFFMAN.	Bern.	Berks.	March 22nd, 1761.
JNO. ALTHOUSE.	Bern.	Berks.	April 1st, 1761.
PETER RUTH.	Cumru.	Berks.	March 15th, 1761.
JACOB BORDNER.	Tulpohockon.	Berks.	April 7th, 1761.
VALENTINE MAYER.	Tulpohockon.	Berks.	April 7th, 1761.
GEO. WOLF.	Tulpohockon.	Berks.	April 7th, 1761.
GEORGE CANTER.	Tulpohockon	Berks.	April 7th, 1761.
CHRISTIAN BOOK.	Lancaster.	Lancaster.	March 22nd, 1761.
ABRAHAM RIBLET.	Lancaster.	Lancaster.	March 22nd, 1761.
JOHN BENTZ.	Mannor.	Lancaster.	March 22nd, 1761.
WILLIAM HEADRICK.	Bern.	Berks.	March 22nd, 1761.
YOST HEADRICK (HEDRICK).	Bern.	Berks.	March 22nd, 1761.
MARTIN ERNHOLD.	Tulpohockon.	Berks.	March 22nd, 1761.
BERNARD SHERTELE.	Bern.	Berks.	March 22nd, 1761.
YOST SHOEMAKER.	Bern.	Berks.	March 22nd, 1761.
VALENTINE MOGLE.	Bern.	Berks.	March 29th, 1761.
LUDWICK SAMAN.	Bern.	Berks.	March 29th, 1761.
EBERHARD GUSHWIND.	Bern.	Berks.	March 29th, 1761.
ULRICK BAGENTOSS.	Bern.	Berks.	April 1st, 1761.
HENRY GRUBER.	Heidleburg.	Berks.	March 22nd, 1761.
MICHAEL SHOWER.	Heidleburg.	Berks.	March 22nd, 1761
HERMAN HASSINGRO.	Oley.	Berks.	April 5th, 1761.
JACOB WAGNER.	Bern.	Berks.	April 5th, 1761.
CHRISTOPHER WAGNER.	Bern.	Berks.	April 5th, 1761.
JACOB LANCISCUS.	Alsace.	Berks.	April 5th, 1761.
RUDOLPH GERHART.	Alsace.	Berks.	April 5th, 1761.
JACOB YOUNG.	Exeter.	Berks.	April 5th, 1761.
VICTOR SPIESS.	Alsace.	Berks.	April 5th, 1761.
PHILIP REEZER.	Alsace.	Berks.	April 5th, 1761.

Foreigners' Names.	Township.	County.	Sacrament when taken.
PHILIP LOWDINBACH.	Exeter.	Berks.	April 5th, 1761.
GEORGE YOH.	Exeter.	Berks.	April 5th, 1761.
CHRISTIAN WEEKS.	Exeter.	Berks.	April 5th, 1761.
CONRAD KELLER.	Alsace.	Berks.	April 5th, 1761.
ADAM GERHART.	Alsace.	Berks.	April 5th, 1761.
JACOB WYLER.	Exeter.	Berks.	April 5th, 1761.
YOST WAGNER.	Ruscomb.	Berks.	April 5th, 1761.
JOHN SHOCK.	Bern.	Berks.	March 29th, 1761.
NICHOLAS FINGER.	Earl.	Lancaster.	April 3rd, 1761.
JACOB STUKE.	Philadelphia.	Philadelphia.	March 22nd, 1761.
JNO. ENGLE BROWN.	Cumru.	Berks.	March 22nd, 1761.
CHRISTOPHER SCHAUB.	Cocolico.	Lancaster.	April 1st, 1761.
PETER FRANKHOUSER.	Brecknock.	Lancaster.	April 1st, 1761.
JNO. RYSWICK.	Upper Milford.	Northampton.	March 22nd, 1761.
CHRISTOPHER KEISER.	Tulpehockon.	Berks.	March 22nd, 1761.
JNO. WURMAN.	Bedminster.	Bucks.	March 28th, 1761.
FRED. TACKSES.	Heidleburg.	Berks.	March 22nd, 1761.
REINHART ROREBACK.	Cumru.	Berks.	March 22nd, 1761.
NICHOLAS MARRITT.	Warwick.	Lancaster.	March 19th, 1761.
MARTIN SPIEKLER.	Warwick.	Lancaster.	March 19th, 1761.
HENRY DEHOFF.	Warwick.	Lancaster.	March 19(29)th, 1761.
LUDWICK BEEKER.	Hempfield.	Lancaster.	March 19th, 1761.
PETER GUDELIUS.	Rapho.	Lancaster.	March 29th, 1761.
JACOB RAN.	Exeter.	Berks.	April 6th, 1761.
LEONARD HOEKGENUG.	Exeter.	Berks.	April 7th, 1761.
BERNARD FEATHER.	Warwick.	Lancaster.	March 22nd, 1761.
GEORGE REINER.	Upper Milford.	Northampton.	March 29th, 1761.
ANTHONY LAMBRIGHT.	Heidleburg.	Berks.	April 1st, 1761.
MATTHIAS STOUT.	Heidleburg.	Berks.	March 22nd, 1761.
VALENTINE SCHNEIDER.	Cocolico.	Lancaster.	March 22nd, 1761.
PHILIP STOBER.	Brecknock.	Lancaster.	March 22nd, 1761.
CASPER MESNER.	Brecknock.	Lancaster.	March 22nd, 1761.
CHRISTIAN MESNER.	Brecknock.	Lancaster.	March 22nd, 1761.
GEORGE WEAVER.	Earl.	Lancaster.	March 29th, 1761.
MATTHEW MEYER.	Philadelphia.	Philadelphia.	March 22nd, 1761.
PAUL KOBER.	Philadelphia.	Philadelphia.	Feb. 22nd, 1761.
CHRISTIAN RUTH.	Bern.	Berks.	April 1st, 1761.
NICHOLAS KLEE.	Bern.	Berks.	March 22nd, 1761.
GEORGE METTLER.	Bern.	Berks.	April 7th, 1761.
SEBASTIAN CRIME.	Bern.	Berks.	April (March) 29th, 1761.
JACOB CRIME.	Bern.	Berks.	April (March) 29th, 1761.
JOHN YOST.	Frederick.	Philadelphia.	April (March) 28th, 1761.
JACOB GICKERT.	Tulpohockon.	Berks.	April 3rd, 1761.
PETER FITZER.	Heidleberg.	Berks.	March 22nd, 1761.
SAML. KUTH.	Reading.	Berks.	April 6th, 1761.
GEORGE BICK.	York.	York.	March 22nd, 1761.
JACOB SCHNEIDER.	York.	York.	March 22nd, 1761.
JACOB BOTT.	York.	York.	April 5th, 1761.
MICHAEL RUTH.	Heidelburgh.	Berks.	March 15th, 1761.
JOHN BULLMAN.	Heidleburg.	Berks.	March 15th, 1761.
PHILIP ADAM SHERMAN.	Heidleburg.	Berks.	March 15th, 1761.
JACOB RUTH.	Heidleburg.	Berks.	March 15th, 1761.
JOHN HEHART.	Heidleburg.	Berks.	March 15th, 1761.

PENNSYLVANIA.

Jurors' Names.	Township.	County.	Sacrament when taken.
MICHAEL MILLER.	Heidleburg.	Berks.	March 15th, 1761.
MICHAEL TRAXALL.	Whitehall.	Northampton.	March 22nd, 1761.
JNO. CHRISTOPHER SPINGLER.	Reading.	Berks.	April 7th, 1761.
JOHN METTAVER (METTAUER).	Cocolico.	Lancaster.	March 22nd, 1761.
HENRY REECH.	Cocolico.	Lancaster.	March 22nd, 1761.
HENRY HANSE.	Warwick.	Lancaster.	March 19th, 1761.
MATTHIAS HOFFER.	Warwick.	Lancaster.	Feb. 15th, 1761.
MICHAEL WOLF.	Warwick.	Lancaster.	March 19th, 1761.
ADAM KEENER.	Warwick.	Lancaster.	Feb. 15th, 1761.
WILLIAM SPOTZ.	Heidleburg.	Lancaster.	April 7th, 1761.
JOHN BERNARD FRANK.	Earl.	Lancaster.	March 29th, 1761.
CONRAD FARSNAUGHT.	Earl.	Lancaster.	March 22nd, 1761.
MARTIN SCHWENK.	Upper Milford.	Northampton.	March 23rd, 1761.
JACOB SMITH.	Upper Milford.	Northampton.	March 23rd, 1761.
GEORGE PFOTEZER.	Warwick.	Lancaster.	Feb. 8th, 1761.
SAML. WOLFF.	Warwick.	Lancaster.	Feb. 8th, 1761.
DANIEL HUBER.	Warwick.	Lancaster.	Feb. 8th, 1761.
JACOB MILLER.	Warwick.	Lancaster.	Feb. 8th, 1761.
CHRISTOPR. REEM.	Lancaster.	Lancaster.	March 22nd, 1761
PHILIP SENG.	Lancaster.	Lancaster.	March 22nd, 1761.
PHILIP DENNIUS.	Lebannon.	Lancaster.	April 7th, 1761.
JOHN BONNETT.	Lebannon.	Lancaster.	April 7th, 1761.
PETER WOLFF.	Lebannon.	Lancaster.	April 7th, 1761.
NICHS. SCHREINER.	Philadelphia.	Philadelphia.	April 9th, 1761.
NICHS. GAMPERT.	Philadelphia.	Philadelphia.	April 9(8)th, 1761.
JOHN MOHN.	Cumru.	Berks.	March 15th, 1761.
WILLIAM ERMET.	Reading.	Berks.	March 22nd, 1761.
NICHS. SCHAPPART.	Reading.	Berks.	March 22nd, 1761.
WILLIAM MARKS.	Reading.	Berks.	March 22nd, 1761.
GEORGE WEIDNER.	Maiden Creek.	Berks.	April 7th, 1761.
BATIZER MYERLY.	Reading.	Berks.	March 22nd, 1761.
HENRY GEIGER.	Heidleburgh.	Northampton.	March 23rd, 1761.
MARTIN GINGINGER.	Maccungy.	Northampton.	March 22nd, 1761.
PHILIP HENRY RAPP.	Germantown.	Philadelphia.	March 22nd, 1761.
PETER HERR.	Whitehall.	Northampton.	March 22nd, 1761.
ANDREAS HERTZ.	Salisbury.	Northampton.	March 22nd, 1761.
MELCHER DEBLER.	Tulpohockon.	Berks.	March 22nd, 1761.
GEORGE HAFFNER.	Blocklem.	Berks.	April 8th, 1761.
ABRAHAM KEEFER.	Richmond.	Berks.	March 6th, 1761.
HENRY SWASS.	Richmond.	Berks.	March 6th, 1761.
GEORGE SHEFFER.	Richmond.	Berks.	March 6th, 1761.
MICHAEL CLINE.	Lower Milford.	Bucks.	March 22nd, 1761.
CASPAR NYPE.	Alsace.	Bucks.	March 6th, 1761.
MARTIN CRAFFT.	Reading.	Berks.	March 22nd, 1761.
JOHN BEBBER.	Maxatawny.	Berks.	April 6(5)th, 1761.
DEWALD BEBBER.	Richmond.	Berks.	April 6(5)th, 1761.
ULRICK HARTMAN.	Worcester.	Philadelphia.	March 23rd, 1761.
RUDOLPH KIDWILER.	Lower Milford.	Bucks.	April 5th, 1761.
CHARLES WITZ.	Frankford and New Hanover.	Philadelphia.	March 22nd, 1761.
JACOB LIBEGUT.	Frankford and New Hanover.	Philadelphia.	March 22nd, 1761.

Jurors' Names.	Township.	County.	Sacrament when taken.
MICHAEL BRAND.	Frankford and New Hanover.	Philadelphia.	March 22nd, 1761.
MELCHIOR SHENVEE (SHEENER).	New Hanover.	Philadelphia.	April 1st, 1761.
LUDWICK SHIEK.	New Hanover.	Philadelphia.	April 1st, 1761.
PETER HOWG.	Frederick.	Philadelphia.	March 28th, 1761.
MARTIN YORGER.	New Hanover.	Philadelphia.	April 1st, 1761.
PHILIP ADAM DIETER (DIELER).	Earl.	Lancaster.	March 29th, 1761.
JOHN SMIDT.	New Providence.	Philadelphia.	March 23rd, 1761.
CHRISTIAN SITZMAN.	Lower Milford.	Bucks.	March 23rd, 1761.
ABRAHAM HAUSER.	White Marsh.	Philadelphia.	March 23rd, 1761.
JOHN GREENWALT.	White Marsh.	Philadelphia.	March 22nd, 1761.
PETER BURKHOLDER.	Whitehall.	Northampton.	March 22nd, 1761.
JACOB RUMMAN.	Upper Dublin.	Philadelphia.	March 23rd, 1761.
DAVID DESHLER.	Whitehall.	Northampton.	March 15th, 1761.
GEORGE HENRY JOSEPH.	Rockhill.	Bucks.	March 22nd, 1761.
CASPAR SLATTER.	Upper Dublin.	Bucks.	March 23rd, 1761.
GEORGE SHOUB.	Horsham.	Philadelphia.	March 23rd, 1761.
JACOB KOPP.	Upper Dublin.	Philadelphia.	March 15th, 1761.
JACOB SCHYCK.	Upper Dublin.	Philadelphia.	March 15th, 1761.
MICHAEL HORLACTIOR (? HORLACHER).	Lower Milford.	Bucks.	April 9th, 1761.
BLESS WEIBER.	Montgomery	Philadelphia.	March 22nd, 1761.
PHILIP BEHM.	Marlsborough.	Philadelphia.	April 16th, 1761.
WIGAND PANNIBECKER.	Upper Hannover.	Philadelphia.	March 15th, 1761.
JNO. NICHS. YOUNG.	Upper Hannover.	Philadelphia.	March 22nd, 1761.
LUDWICK ZEIGLER.	Mannor.	Lancaster.	March 22nd, 1761.
MELCHIOR BARR.	Maccungy.	Northampton.	March 23rd, 1761.
ULRICK SPINNER.	Lower Milford.	Bucks.	March 22nd, 1761.
HENRY SWARTZ.	Heidleberg.	Berks.	March 22nd, 1761.
MICHL. HARTMAN DILLO.	Upper Milford.	Northampton.	March 22nd, 1761.
CHRISTR. GOODMAN.	Upper Milford.	Northampton.	March 25th, 1761.
GEORGE SHAMBACK.	Lower Salford.	Philadelphia.	March 28th, 1761.
DANIEL ROTT.	Whitehall.	Northampton.	March 15th, 1761.
DANIEL TRAXELL.	Whitehall.	Northampton.	March 15th, 1761.
CHRISTIAN BIRKENBEIEL.	Passyunk.	Philadelphia.	March 22nd, 1761.
PHILIP SPEAR.	Worcester.	Philadelphia.	March 23rd, 1761.
HENRY WOLFF.	Cumru.	Berks.	March 22nd, 1761.
ANDREAS BOYER.	Upper Milford.	Northampton.	April 6th, 1761.
GEO. KERSHNER.	Saucon.	Northampton.	April 6th, 1761.
GEO. REINHARD.	Saucon.	Northampton.	April 6th, 1761.
ABRAM DANNEHOWER.	Saucon.	Northampton.	April 6th, 1761.
FREDERICK SHEFFER.	Saucon (Maccungy).	Northampton.	April 6(8)th, 1761.
HENRY HUBER.	Lower Milford.	Bucks.	March 22nd, 1761.
JOHN WASPIE.	Philadelphia.	Philadelphia.	March 22nd, 1761.
JOHN JACOB MILLER.	Upper Hannover.	Philadelphia.	March 22nd, 1761.
FRANCIS WESTGO.	Upper Milford.	Northampton.	March 23rd, 1761.
NICHS. ROTTENBERGER.	Upper Milford.	Northampton.	March 23rd, 1761.
ADAM BERGER.	Bethel.	Lancaster.	March 22nd, 1761.
CHRISTR. BARR.	Whitehall.	Northampton.	March 22nd, 1761.
HENRY BRUNNER.	Upper Saucon.	Northampton.	April 6th, 1761.
JACOB ENGLE.	Douglass.	Philadelphia.	March 22nd, 1761.
ANDREW HONNETTA.	Douglass.	Philadelphia.	April 1st, 1761.
HENRY FETTER.	Salisbury.	Northampton.	March 22nd, 1761.
ANDREW ERDMAN.	Upper Saucon.	Northampton.	April 6th, 1761.

f

PENNSYLVANIA.

Jurors' Names.	Township.	County.	Sacrament when taken.
MICHAEL SIEDER.	Upper Saucon.	Northampton.	April 6th, 1761.
BALTZER BOYLE.	Upper Saucon.	Northampton.	April 6th, 1761.
HENRY EKELL.	Bedminster.	Bucks.	April 8th, 1761.
GEO. SCHELLMEIR.	North Wales.	Philadelphia.	March 15th, 1761.
MICHL. PUTTS.	Springfield.	Bucks.	April 5th, 1761.
CHRIST. SHUKES.	Springfield.	Bucks.	April 5th, 1761.
NICHS. WIERPACK.	Springfield.	Bucks.	April 5th, 1761.
JACOB OVERPECK (OVERPEEK).	Springfield.	Bucks.	April 5th, 1761.
CHRISTIAN DÜY.	Germantown.	Philadelphia.	March 22nd, 1761.
MATTHIAS FOLTZ.	Lower Merrion.	Philadelphia.	March 22nd, 1761.
CHRISTIAN SCHNEIDER.	Lower Merrion.	Philadelphia.	March 22nd, 1761.
HENRY REES.	Upper Milford.	Northampton.	March 23rd, 1761.
JACOB SEIDER.	Cumru.	Berks.	March 22nd, 1761.
JOHN GROCE.	Reading.	Berks.	March 22nd, 1761.
VALENTINE STIENMETZ.	Saucon.	Northampton.	April 6th, 1761.
CHRISTIAN DONNACRE.	Philadelphia.	Philadelphia.	Feb. 22nd, 1761.
JNO. REMIGUIS SPIEGLE.	Philadelphia.	Philadelphia.	March 22nd, 1761.
LEONARD FREELY.	Germantown.	Philadelphia.	March 22nd, 1761.
JNO. PETER WITBERGER.	Philadelphia.	Philadelphia.	April 10th, 1761.
GEORGE ADAM GAAH.	Philadelphia.	Philadelphia.	March 22nd, 1761.
GEORGE KEEMER.	Germantown.	Philadelphia.	March 22nd, 1761.
JOHN HABERACKER.	Reading.	Berks.	April 7th, 1761.
NICHOLAS SHILFER (SHITFER).	Heidleburg.	Berks.	March 15th, 1761.
JNO. NICHOLAS PRAXELL.	Whitehall.	Northampton.	March 22nd, 1761.
JNO. SCHNEIDER.	Whitehall.	Northampton.	March 22nd, 1761.
ULRICK FLICKINGER.	Whitehall.	Northampton.	March 22nd, 1761.
PHILIP UPP.	Brecknock.	Lancaster.	March 29th, 1761.
DURST THOMAS (THOMA).	Heidleburg.	Lancaster.	April 7th, 1761.
GEORGE HOLER.	Heidleburg.	Lancaster.	April 7th, 1761.
FRED. WOLFESBERGER.	Heidleburg.	Lancaster.	April 7th, 1761.
JOHN MEYER.	Heidleburg.	Lancaster.	April 7th, 1761.
MARTIN HETFELSINGER.	Heidleburg.	Lancaster.	April 7th, 1761.
JACOB DUI.	Heidleburg.	Lancaster.	April 7th, 1761.
ADAM BOLLMAN.	Heidleburg.	Lancaster.	April 7th, 1761.
YOST HOFFMAN.	Heidleburg.	Lancaster.	April 7th, 1761.
PETER LAMB.	Heidleburg.	Berks.	March 15th, 1761.
ADAM HICKMAN.	Alsace.	Berks.	March 22nd, 1761.
JOHN ADAM SCHNEIDER.	Hanover.	Philadelphia.	April 6th, 1761.
YOST STERBACK.	Helm.	York.	April 5th, 1761.
JACOB YOST.	Whitpain.	Philadelphia.	March 22nd, 1761.
SAMUEL SEGER.	Whitehall.	Northampton.	April 5th, 1761.
CHRISTIAN SEGER.	Whitehall.	Northampton.	April 5th, 1761.
CHRISTIAN BERGER.	Bern.	Berks.	April 1st, 1761.
LAWRENCE KEHNLY.	Maccungy.	Northampton.	April 5th, 1761.
NICHOLAS LONG.	Tulpohockon.	Berks.	April 7th, 1761.
JOHN RAEBER.	Bern.	Berks.	April 1st, 1761.
JACOB HUBLER.	Tulpohockon.	Berks.	April 7th, 1761.
JOHN SCHOP.	Tulpohockon.	Berks.	April 7th, 1761.
ADAM HUEY.	Easton.	Northampton.	April 5th, 1761.
TOBIAS RETTER.	Heidleburg.	Lancaster.	March 29th, 1761.
GEO. SCHWINGLE.	Tulpohockon.	Lancaster.	April 5th, 1761.
ABRAHAM NETF.	Tulpohockon.	Lancaster.	April 5th, 1761.

Jurors' Names.	Township.	County.	Sacrament when taken.
Jacob Netf.	Tulpohockon.	Lancaster.	April 5th, 1761.
Henry Moke.	Warwick.	Lancaster.	March 30th, 1761.
Andreas Mohr.	Heidleburg.	Lancaster.	March 29th, 1761.
Caspar Ipa.	Heidleburg.	Lancaster.	March 29th, 1761.
John Matthias Albert.	Heidleburg.	Lancaster.	March 29th, 1761.
Nicholas Hess.	Philadelphia.	Philadelphia.	March 22nd, 1761.
Jacob Eyler.	Philadelphia.	Philadelphia.	March 22nd, 1761.
Christopher Steigh.	Mannor.	Lancaster.	March 22nd, 1761.
Henry Shenck.	Mannor.	Lancaster.	March 22nd, 1761.
William Moy.	Bern.	Berks.	March 22nd, 1761.
John Endres.	Cocolico.	Lancaster.	April 3rd, 1761.
Michael Hentzell.	Bern.	Berks.	March 22nd, 1761.
Conrad Ernst.	Heidleberg.	Berks.	March 22nd, 1761.
Michael Oberly.	Earl.	Lancaster.	March 23rd, 1761.
Nicholas Lesher.	Cocolico.	Lancaster.	April 1st, 1761.
Jacob Kuhl.	Heidleburg.	Berks.	March 22nd, 1761.
Nicholas Holder, Senr.	Bern.	Berks.	March 22nd, 1761.
Nicholas Holder, Junr.	Bern.	Berks.	March 22nd, 1761.
John Henry Cline.	Philadelphia.	Philadelphia.	March 22nd, 1761.
Jacob Genslin.	Germantown.	Philadelphia.	March 22nd, 1761.
Martin Noll.	Philadelphia.	Philadelphia.	March 22nd, 1761.
John Waldschmith.	Cocolico.	Lancaster.	March 22nd, 1761.
Jacob Dick.	Alsace.	Berks.	April 7th, 1761.
George Diehl.	Alsace.	Berks.	April 7th, 1761.
David Rein.	Alsace.	Berks.	April 7th, 1761.
Adam Wagner.	Alsace.	Berks.	April 7th, 1761.
Jacob Bucher.	Alsace.	Berks.	April 7th, 1761.
William Miller.	Alsace.	Berks.	April 7th, 1761.
Wolfgang Hackner.	Alsace.	Berks.	April 7th, 1761.
Fred. Goodhart.	Alsace.	Berks.	April 7th, 1761.
Julius Kerper.	Alsace.	Berks.	April 7th, 1761.
Jacob Librook.	Alsace.	Berks.	April 7th, 1761.
Christr. Gotshall.	Alsace.	Berks.	April 7th, 1761.
Gabriel Schopp.	Alsace.	Berks.	April 7th, 1761.
Christr. Smith.	Alsace.	Berks.	April 7th, 1761.
George Rehm.	Alsace.	Berks.	April 7th, 1761.
Michael Fetter.	Alsace.	Berks.	April 7th, 1761.
Valentine Hemalbarger.	Tulpohockon.	Berks.	March 22nd, 1761.
Catherina Schuen.	Bethel.	Berks.	April 6th, 1761.
Yost Tobie.	Bern.	Berks.	March 29th, 1761.
Jacob Hoffman.	Bern.	Berks.	March 29th, 1761.
Martin Kersener.	Bern.	Berks.	April 1st, 1761.
Adam Stumm.	Bern.	Berks.	April 1st, 1761.
Caspar Lerk.	Heidleburg.	Berks.	April 1st, 1761.
Michael Geissleman.	Strasburg.	York.	April 1st, 1761.
Daniel Dehl.	Codorus.	York.	April 1st, 1761.
John Glaidy.	York.	York.	April 5th, 1761.
Sebastian Stohler.	Donegal.	Lancaster.	March 29th, 1761.
John Feltman.	Lancaster.	Lancaster.	March 22nd, 1761.
Daniel Dewald.	York.	York.	March 22nd, 1761.
Jacob Wagner.	York.	York.	March 22nd, 1761.
John Jacob Ottinger.	Manchester.	York.	March 22nd, 1761.
John Herick Cline.	York.	York.	March 22nd, 1761.
Francis Noll.	Manheim.	York.	March 22nd, 1761.

NATURALIZATIONS

PENNSYLVANIA.

Jurors' Name.	Township.	County.	Sacrament when taken.
GEORGE NEISS.	Manchester.	York.	March 22nd, 1761.
JACOB RUDISILLY.	Manchester.	York.	March 22nd, 1761.
MICHL. WOMMER.	Bern.	Berks.	April 5th, 1761.
JOHN WOLF.	Manchester.	York.	April 5th, 1761.
GEORGE GERRNANT.	Bern.	Berks.	March 22nd, 1761.
JOHN ZINN.	Dover.	York.	March 22nd, 1761.
JACOB MEYER.	Dover.	York.	March 22nd, 1761.
PETER OBB.	Dover.	York.	March 22nd, 1761.
PETER STREEHER.	Dover.	York.	April 5th, 1761.
JACOB EPLER.	Bern.	Berks.	April 3rd, 1761.
PETER HARBINE.	Bern.	Berks.	April 3rd, 1761.
PHILIP MAHOMER.	Bern.	Berks.	April 3rd, 1761.
CHIRSTIAN ALBRIGHT.	Bern.	Berks.	April 3rd, 1761.
JOHN FAUST.	Bern.	Berks.	April 3rd, 1761.
GEORGE RESSLER.	Bern.	Berks.	April 3rd, 1761.
DANIEL ZACHARISS.	Bern.	Berks.	April 3rd, 1761.
JOHN MICHL. WOMER.	Bern.	Berks.	April 3rd, 1761.
VALENTINE EPLER.	Bern.	Berks.	April 3rd, 1761.
JACOB ALBRIGHT.	Bern.	Berks.	April 3rd, 1761.
CHRISTIAN OLDHOUSE.	Bern.	Berks.	April 3rd, 1761.
GEORGE GRAFFT.	York.	York.	March 22nd, 1761.
CONRAD GENTZLER.	York.	York.	March 22nd, 1761.
HENRY BOTT.	York.	York.	March 22nd, 1761.
RYNHARD BOTTS.	York.	York.	March 22nd, 1761.
JOHN RUNKETT.	Bern.	Berks.	March 22nd, 1761.
MICHAEL KEISER.	Heidleburg.	Berks.	March 22nd, 1761.
HENRY SPOHN.	Heidleburg.	Berks.	March 22nd, 1761.
HENRY ZANK.	Lancaster.	Lancaster.	March 22nd, 1761.
MARTIN POTTIKER.	Heidleburg.	Berks.	March 22nd, 1761.
PHILIP BREITENBACK.	Heidleburg.	Lancaster.	April 5th, 1761.
WILLIAM STOY.	Lancaster.	Lancaster.	March 22nd, 1761.
JACOB GRIM.	Bern.	Berks.	March 29th, 1761.
GEORGE GANSELL.	Bern.	Berks.	March 22nd, 1761.
HENRY SPEECHER.	York.	York.	March 22nd, 1761.
JOHN KUSTER.	Heidleburg.	Lancaster.	March 22nd, 1761.
MICHL. SPINGLER.	Heidleburg.	Lancaster.	March 22nd, 1761.
NICHOLAS TREBER.	Manheim.	Lancaster.	March 26th, 1761.
JOHN TREBER.	Manheim.	Lancaster.	March 26th, 1761.
HENRY DERR.	Maiden Creek.	Berks.	April 7th, 1761.
JOHN HURAND.	Maiden Creek.	Berks.	April 7th, 1761.
JOHN SHOTTER.	Earl.	Lancaster.	April 3rd, 1761.
MICHAEL DENY.	Pikeland.	Chester.	March 15th, 1761.
MICHAEL SIFERT.	Vincent.	Chester.	March 15th, 1761.
MICHAEL STOUT.	Bern.	Berks.	April 1st, 1761.
JNO. JACOB RABBOLD.	Reading.	Berks.	April 6th, 1761.
MATTHIAS DORNBACK.	Bern.	Berks.	March 29th, 1761.
SEBASTIAN RHUTT.	Bern.	Berks.	March 29th, 1761.
HENRY SANGER.	Reading.	Berks.	April 6th, 1761.
MARTIN BAYER.		Berks.	April 5th, 1761.
FREDERICK KERN.	Upper Milford.	Northampton.	March 22nd, 1761.
JOHN MADE.	Bern.	Berks.	March 29th, 1761.
NICHOLAS RUNKETT.	Bern.	Berks.	March 29th, 1761.

Jurors' Names.	Township.	County.	Sacrament when taken.
GEORGE ENGLEHARD.	Cumru.	Berks.	April 7th, 1761.
MARTIN MORE.	Bern.	Berks.	March 29th, 1761.
JACOB HECK.	Bern.	Berks.	April 1st, 1761.

Quakers [&c.].

Foreigners' Names.	Township.	County.	If Moravian Sacrament when taken.
JACOB SEIGERIST.	York.	York.	
LUDWICK MOHLER.	Earl.	Lancaster.	
MARTIN FUNK.	Cocolico.	Lancaster.	
RUDY BOLLINGER.	Cocolico.	Lancaster.	
PETER HEFFLEY.	Cocolico.	Lancaster.	
JOHN BOWMAN.	Cocolico.	Lancaster.	
JACOB MARTIN.	Cocolico.	Lancaster.	
JOHN SENZEMAN.	Cocolico.	Lancaster.	
JACOB KELLER.	Cocolico.	Lancaster.	
VALENTINE HOFFMAN.	Lancaster.	Lancaster.	
PETER DENNY.	Lancaster.	Lancaster.	
DETRICK FANNERSTICK.	Cocolico.	Lancaster.	
CONRAD BOLTHOUSE.	Cocolico.	Lancaster.	
ANDREW GEAR.	Earl.	Lancaster.	
PAUL GEAR.	Earl.	Lancaster.	
JOHN FEEGLY.	Rapho.	Lancaster.	
JOHN BOUGHER.	Cocolico.	Lancaster.	
MARTIN STOVER.	Manor (Mannor).	Lancaster.	
VALENTINE YOUNG.	Upper Saucon.	Northampton.	
JOHN CHRISTR. HAYNE.	Lancaster.	Lancaster.	
HENRY MOHLER.	Cocolico.	Lancaster.	
GEORGE BLESSKENNER.	Cocolico.	Lancaster.	
GEORGE KELLER.	Cocolico.	Lancaster.	
JACOB MOHLER.	Cocolico.	Lancaster.	
JOHN MATHER.	Cocolico.	Lancaster.	
CHRISTIAN BRENZER.	Elizabeth.	Lancaster.	
PETER BROOKER.	Heidleburg.	Berks.	
VALENTINE HOFF.	Oley.	Berks.	
JACOB STONMETZ.	Northern Liberties.	Philadelphia.	
JOHN LOREY.	Amity.	Berks.	
PETER BRYELL.	Oley.	Berks.	
MICHAEL ANDREAS.	Cocolico.	Lancaster.	
JACOB REEZER.	Bern.	Berks.	
PHILIP REEZER.	Bern.	Berks.	
ADAM SPITTELMYER.	Alsace.	Berks.	
PETER WYLAND.	Warwick.	Lancaster.	
JOHN FEISSER.	York.	York.	March 21st, 1761.
FRANTZ LUDWICK BEROT.	York.	York.	March 21st, 1761.
GEORGE IGLEFRITZ.	Dover.	York.	March 21st, 1761.
JOHN BEITZELL.	Dover.	York.	March 21st, 1761.
BEMHART HEWRISON.	Dover.	York.	March 21st, 1761.
JOHN FISHILL.	York.	York.	March 21st, 1761.
GEORGE HOLLER.	Helm.	York.	
WILLIAM REEL.	York.	York.	
WILLIAM WOITZ.	Cocolico.	Lancaster.	
JOHN HOVER.	Manheim.	Lancaster.	
CHRISTIAN HARTMAN.	Manheim.	Lancaster.	

NATURALIZATIONS

PENNSYLVANIA.

Foreigners' Names.	Township.	County.	If Moravian Sacrament when taken
JOHANNES PETER.	Philadelphia.	Philadelphia.	
WILDER LAUDERMELIGH.	Heidleburg.	Lancaster.	
JACOB MILLNER.	Cocolico.	Lancaster.	
CONRAD RUSH.	Germantown.	Philadelphia.	
JNO. MAUYER.	Upper Milford.	Northampton.	
VALENTINE YOUNG.	Oley.	Berks.	
ADAM YOUNG.	Exeter.	Berks.	
MICHAEL SMALL.	Philadelphia.	Philadelphia.	
LAZARUS WEIDNER.	Oley.	Berks.	
DICHUS WEIDNER.	Oley.	Berks.	
PHILIP WEINNIMER.	Philadelphia.	Philadelphia.	
LAWRENCE REMICH.	Worcester.	Philadelphia.	
JOHN ADAM KITTERING.	Derry.	Lancaster.	March 19th, 1761.
PHILIP TRAPP.	Upper Saucon.	Northampton.	
PETER TYSE.	Upper Saucon.	Northampton.	
HANS KELLER.	Heidleburg.	Berks.	
JACOB LANNIUS.	Helm.	York.	March 21st, 1761.
PETER HUBER.	Warwick.	Lancaster.	March 20th, 1761.
JACOB SHANTZ.	Warwick.	Lancaster.	March 20th, 1761.
JACOB SHIRTZER.	Warwick.	Lancaster.	March 20th, 1761.
JOHN RUPE.	Cocolico.	Lancaster.	
JOHN WINGHER.	Cocolico.	Lancaster.	
JOSEPH WINGHER.	Cocolico.	Lancaster.	
FRANCIS SCHUNCK.	Providence.	Philadelphia.	
CHRISTIAN KINSEY.	Alsace.	Berks.	
ADAM SWARTZBACK.	Alsace.	Berks.	
ANTHONY HAMSHAW.	Oley.	Berks.	
JOHN GROVE.	Reading.	York.	
JACOB SHEFFER.	Maxatawny.	Berks.	
JACOB LEWIS.	Upper Saucon.	Northampton.	
CHRISTIAN ESS.	Lebannon.	Lancaster.	
PETER HERPLE.	Oley.	Berks.	
PHILIP CRATZER.	Upper Milford.	Northampton.	
ANDREAS GEIRING.	Salisbury.	Northampton.	April 3rd, 1761.
CONRAD MILLER.	Richmond.	Berks.	
BALTZER REEM.	Richmond.	Berks.	
PETER BEEL.	Richmond.	Berks.	
HENRY LOWMAN.	Cocolico.	Lancaster.	
ABRAHAM PAUL.	Cocolico.	Lancaster.	
JOHN SNEEBLY.	Bethel.	Lancaster.	
NICHOLAS HUBER.	Lebanon.	Lancaster.	
ANDREAS IZENHEART.	Maccungy.	Northampton.	
CHARLES SHALLY.	Lebanon.	Lancaster.	
JOHN APPLE.	Lower Saucon.	Northampton.	
HENRY ALSHOUSE.	Easton.	Northampton.	
ABRAHAM BERLIN.	Easton.	Northampton.	
FREDERICK SAIGER.		Lancaster.	
JOHN STAILY.	Bethel.	Lancaster.	
MARTIN APPLE.	Lower Saucon.	Northampton.	
BERNARD BARE.	Upper Milford.	Northampton.	
MELCHOR KNEPLY.	Upper Saucon.	Northampton.	
CHRISTIAN HOFFERT.	Whitpain.	Philadelphia.	

Foreigners' Names.	Township.	County.	
HENRY BUSH.	Easton.	Northampton.	
HENRY WEAVER.	Upper Saucon.	Northampton.	
GREGORIUS SHULTZ.	Maccungy.	Northampton.	
ANDREAS WARNER.	Towamensing.	Philadelphia.	
JOHN KNAGY.	Bethel.	Lancaster.	
JOHN VANLASHY.	Carnarvon.	Lancaster.	
LEONARD ECKSTINE.	Germantown.	Philadelphia.	
ELIAS REED.	Maiden-Creek.	Berks.	
HENRY SLEIGHTER.	Franconia.	Philadelphia.	
GEORGE FREDERICK.	Upper Salford.	Philadelphia.	
CHRISTOPHER WAGGONER.	Lower Saucon.	Northampton.	
CRALLUIS LARCH.	Lower Saucon.	Northampton.	
JOHN MELCHER.	Lower Saucon.	Northampton.	
MOSES TRABLE.	Montgomery.	Philadelphia.	
JOHN KING.	Towamensing.	Philadelphia.	
GEORGE STARNHER.	Germantown.	Philadelphia.	
JACOB CHRISTIAN GLEIM.	Germantown.	Philadelphia.	
MICHAEL STILES.	Germantown.	Philadelphia.	

C. O. 324. 56.

A List of persons that have intitled themselves to the benefit of the Act (13th Geo. 2^d) intitled "An Act for Naturalizing such foreign Protestants and others therein mentioned as are settled or that shall settle in any of His Majesty's Colonies in America."

PENNSYLVANIA.

Proprieties Bundle, X. 41, Sept. 24th, 1761.

(Supreme Court, Philadelphia, 24 and 25 Sept., 1761.)

Foreigners' Names.	Township.	County.	Sacrament when taken.
ALBRIGHT KOCHLER.	Conestogo.	Lancaster.	July 26th, 1761.
FREDERICK ZEEGLE.	Conestogo.	Lancaster.	July 26th, 1761.
ABRAHAM WEIDMAN.	Lebanon.	Lancaster.	Sept. 13th, 1761.
GEORGE MILLER.	Lebanon.	Lancaster.	Sept. 13th, 1761.
JACOB SCHWAUB.	Lebanon.	Lancaster.	Sept. 13th, 1761.
MARTIN EICHOLD.	Heidleburg.	Lancaster.	Sept. 13th, 1761.
CHRISTIAN BECHTEL.	Tulpeho(c)kon.	Berks.	Aug. 17th, 1761.
JACOB LENHERR (LEHNHERR).	Warwick.	Lancaster.	Sept. 13th, 1761.
JACOB ENCK.	Warwick.	Lancaster.	Sept. 13th, 1761.
ADAM JACOBS.	Warwick.	Lancaster.	Sept. 13th, 1761.
GEORGE MICHAEL WEISS.	Cocolico.	Lancaster.	Sept. 13th, 1761.
JACOB BULLINGER.	Cocolico.	Lancaster.	Sept. 13th, 1761.
JOHN BUTTSER.	Earl.	Lancaster.	Sept. 20th, 1761.
THOMAS KURR.	Tulpehockon.	Berks.	Aug. 17th, 1761.
JACOB KIDLER.	Reading.	Berks.	Sept. 16th, 1761.
JOHN PHILIP SCHMID.	Reading.	Berks.	Sept. 16th, 1761.
JOHN HENRY GOSTLER.	Reading.	Berks.	Sept. 16th, 1761.
JNO. HENRICK BYERLO.	Reading.	Berks.	Sept. 16th, 1761.
MICHAEL LUIB.	Cumrey.	Berks.	Sept. 13th, 1761.
NICHOLAS GOUGHER.	Tulpehockon.	Berks.	Sept. 13th, 1761.
ABRAHAM RAIGUEL.	Lebanon.	Lancaster.	Sept. 13th, 1761.
JOHN MILLER.	Lebanon.	Lancaster.	Sept. 13th, 1761.

PENNSYLVANIA.

Foreigners' Names.	Township.	County.	Sacrament when taken.
JACOB GRAFF.	Lebanon.	Lancaster.	Sept. 13th, 1761.
HENRY GAEBLE.	Reading.	Berks.	Sept. 18th, 1761.
WILHELM ERHMAN.	Reading.	Berks.	Sept. 18th, 1761.
JOSEPH BERRITT.	Reading.	Berks.	Sept. 18th, 1761.
GEORGE ERNST MAURER.	Reading.	Berks.	Sept. 18th, 1761.
ERHARD ROST.	Reading.	Berks.	Sept. 18th, 1761.
PHILIP SAILER.	Reading.	Berks.	Sept. 18th, 1761.
PETER KNOBB.	Oley.	Berks.	Sept. 20th, 1761.
HENRY NEWKIRETS (? NEWKIRCH).	Oley.	Berks.	Sept. 20th, 1761.
CHRISTR. SMITH.	Philadelphia.	Philadelphia.	Sept. 20th, 1761.
CONRAD BAB.	Alsace.	Berks.	Sept. 14th, 1761.
GEORGE NEISS.	Alsace.	Berks.	Sept. 14th, 1761.
MICHAEL GLOSSER.	Alsace.	Berks.	Sept. 14th, 1761.
ADAM APPEL.	Alsace.	Berks.	Sept. 14th, 1761.
JACOB MIKELY.	Whiteland.	Northampton.	Aug. 9th, 1761.
JACOB HOTTENSTYN.	Manheim.	Lancaster.	Sept. 20th, 1761.
NICHS. WINEGARDNER.	Lancaster.	Lancaster.	Sept. (Aug.) 23rd, 1761
WILLIAM GRAFFE.	Reading.	Berks.	Sept. 18th, 1761.
TOBIAS HELSEL.	Paradise.	York.	Aug. 30th, 1761.
JACOB SHOEMAKER.	Lampeter.	Lancaster.	Sept. 20th, 1761.
FREDERICK SHINGLE.	Lampeter.	Lancaster.	Aug. 23rd, 1761.
PHILIP UMBORNE.	Lebanon (Lampeter).	Lancaster.	Aug. 23rd, 1761.
JACOB SHAFFNER.	Lebanon.	Lancaster.	Aug. 23rd, 1761.
JOHN HUBER.	Lebanon.	Lancaster.	Aug. 23rd, 1761.
DIEDERICK MARTIN.	Oley.	Berks.	Sept. 20th, 1761.
SEBASTIAN MORGAN.	Gomery.	Berks.	Sept. 18th, 1761.
JOHN MAURICE ROW.	Lancaster.	Lancaster.	Aug. 23rd, 1761.
CHRISTR. BRYTENHART.	Lancaster.	Lancaster.	Aug. 23rd, 1761.
NICHS. MESSER SMITH.	Lancaster.	Lancaster.	Aug. 23rd, 1761.
CHARLES SNYDER.	Lancaster.	Lancaster.	Aug. 23rd, 1761.
CHRISTR. KNEERENSHIELD.	Lancaster.	Lancaster.	Aug. 23rd, 1761.
FREDERICK MARTIN.	Elizabeth.	Lancaster.	Sept. 13th, 1761.
MARTIN SCHUDY.	Elizabeth.	Lancaster.	Sept. 13th, 1761.
CHRISTIAN WALLBORN.	Heidleburg.	Lancaster.	Sept. 13th, 1761.
MARTIN BATTORFF.	Heidleburg.	Lancaster.	Sept. 13th, 1761.
SEBASTIAN KROWSER.	Reading.	Berks.	Sept. 16th, 1761.
CONRAD BROWN.	Reading.	Berks.	Sept. 16th, 1761.
SAMUEL SHULTZ.	Reading.	Berks.	Sept. 16th, 1761.
PHILIP WEISS.	Reading.	Berks.	Sept. 16th, 1761.
JACOB WILD.	Lancaster.	Lancaster.	Sept. 20th, 1761.
ADAM BOTT.	York.	York.	Aug. 30th, 1761.
PETER SCHAUB.	Cocolico.	Lancaster.	Sept. 6th, 1761.
PETER FEESER.	Cocolico.	Lancaster.	Sept. 6th, 1761.
ADAM KRILL.	Cocolico.	Lancaster.	Sept. 6th, 1761.
NICHOLAS WEINHOLD.	Cocolico.	Lancaster.	Sept. 6th, 1761.
MARCUS EGLE.	Cocolico.	Lancaster.	Sept. 6th, 1761.
GEORGE HOTT.	Brecknock.	Lancaster.	Sept. 6th, 1761.
WILLIAM OLDHOUSE.	Sarancony (Torancony).	Philadelphia.	Sept. 13th, 1761.
JOHN HENRY KRAUSS.	Philadelphia.	Philadelphia.	Sept. 20th, 1761.
FRANCE BROSMAN.	Heidleburg.	Lancaster.	Sept. 13th, 1761.

Foreigners' Names.	Township.	County.	Sacrament when taken.
AUGUSTINE WIDDER.	Strasburg.	Lancaster.	Sept. 20th, 1761.
CHARLES MILLER.	Strasburg.	Lancaster.	Sept. 20th, 1761.
MICHAEL SENGHAAS.	Lebanon.	Lancaster.	Sept. 20th, 1761.
RUDOLPH FRY.	Hanover.	Lancaster.	Sept. 14th, 1761.
FRED. DRIESH.	Lancaster.	Lancaster.	Aug. 23rd, 1761.
ADAM KOWSMAN.	Lancaster.	Lancaster.	Aug. 23rd, 1761.
HENRY KLIEN.	Lebanon.	Lancaster.	Aug. 23rd, 1761.
JOHANNES KOCK.	Reading.	Berks.	Sept. 6th, 1761.
MICHAEL KOCK.	Reading.	Berks.	Sept. 6th, 1761.
MARTIN YOUNG.	Reading.	Berks.	Sept. 6th, 1761.
JNO. PETER KLINGER.	Reading.	Berks.	Sept. 6th, 1761.
MARTIN EGE.	Reading.	Berks.	Sept. 6th, 1761.
JOHN DENGLER.	Reading.	Berks.	Sept. 6th, 1761.
ANDREAS SALZGEBER.	Heidleburg.	Lancaster.	Aug. 2nd, 1761.
MATHIAS STREEHER.	Lebanon.	Lancaster.	Aug. 30th, 1761.
MATHIAS STREEHER, Junr.	Lebanon.	Lancaster.	Sept. 6th, 1761.
PHILIP JACOB ZINN.	Dover.	York.	Sept. 15th, 1761.
MICHAEL BENTZ.	Earl.	Lancaster.	Aug. 30th, 1761.
JACOB FRY.	Brecknock.	Lancaster.	Aug. 23rd, 1761.
JNO. ADAM HAUSHALLER.	Cumru.	Berks.	Sept. 6th, 1761.
NICHOLAS GOWER.	Cumru.	Berks.	Sept. 6th, 1761.
JOHN GODLIN BRYNINGER.	Cumru.	Berks.	Sept. 6th, 1761.
HENRY SCHLABACK.	Brecknock.	Lancaster.	Sept. 6th, 1761.
LUDWICK WOLFART.	Earl.	Lancaster.	Sept. 20th, 1761.
PHILIP MAURER.	Earl.	Lancaster.	Sept. 20th, 1761.
MICHAEL FISCHER.	Alsace.	Berks.	Sept. 20th, 1761.
JOHN CASPAR YAGER.	Philadelphia.	Philadelphia.	Sept. 20th, 1761.
JOHN SWITZER.	Reading.	Berks.	Sept. 6th, 1761.
JOHN HENRY RADIN.	Lebanon.	Lancaster.	July 26th, 1761.
GEORGE MARKS.	Reading.	Berks.	Sept. 6th, 1761.
CHRISTR. EMBIG.	Lebanon.	Lancaster.	July 26th, 1761.
HENRY RINCEL.	Lebanon.	Lancaster.	July 26th, 1761.
GEORGE SCHUPP.	Brecknock.	Lancaster.	Sept. 13th, 1761.
MARTIN YOCK.	Earl.	Lancaster.	Aug. 30th, 1761.
JNO. MARTIN BRININGER (BRYNINGER).	Cumru.	Berks.	Sept. 6th, 1761.
PHILIP SULZBACK.	Northern Liberties.	Philadelphia.	Sept. 20th, 1761.
GEORGE HEIST.	Reading.	Berks.	Sept. 6th, 1761.
DETRICK SHEFFER.	Rockland.	Berks.	Sept. 20th, 1761.
PETER REHM, Senr.	Heidleburg.	Lancaster.	Sept. 13th, 1761.
PETER REHM, Junr.	Heidleburg.	Lancaster.	Sept. 13th, 1761.
GEORGE SCHUFFER.	Rockland.	Berks.	Sept. 20th, 1761.
GEORGE MEESS.	Heidleburg.	Lancaster.	Sept. 13th, 1761.
ADAM ECKART.	Philadelphia.	Philadelphia.	Sept. 20th, 1761.
MICHL. BOHR.	Lebanon.	Lancaster.	Aug. 30th, 1761.
WILLIAM STEHR.	Lebanon.	Lancaster.	Aug. 30th, 1761.
TILLMAN SHITZ.	Warwick.	Lancaster.	Sept. 13th, 1761.
GEORGE REINHARD.	Elizabeth.	Lancaster.	Sept. 13th, 1761.
JOHN WOLFERSBERGER.	Heidleburg.	Lancaster.	Sept. 13th, 1761.
JOHN FUTWIELER.	Heidleburg.	Lancaster.	Sept. 13th, 1761.
MICHAEL RUSH. Senr.	Reading.	Berks.	Sept. 6th, 1761.
MICHAEL RUSH, Junr.	Reading.	Berks.	Sept. 6th, 1761.
ANASTASIUS UHLER.	Lebanon.	Lancaster.	Aug. 30th, 1761.
WENDAL HOYL.	Bethel.	Lancaster.	Aug. 30th, 1761.

PENNSYLVANIA.

Foreigners' Names.	Township.	County.	Sacrament when taken.
ADAM HALLMAN.	Lebanon.	Lancaster.	Sept. 13th, 1761.
LUDWICK MOHN.	Cumru.	Berks.	Sept. 18th, 1761.
JOHN NEWCOMER.	Alsace.	Berks.	Sept. 18th, 1761.
CHS. LUDWICK MECKLINBURGH.	Philadelphia.	Philadelphia.	Sept. 20th, 1761.
CHRISTR. CURFESS.	Philadelphia.	Philadelphia.	Sept. 20th, 1761.
GEORGE HEFFT.	Brecknock.	Lancaster.	Sept. 6th, 1761.
ABRAHAM KERN.	Brecknock.	Lancaster.	Sept. 6th, 1761.
JOHN SOUDER (SNIDER).	Reading.	Berks.	Sept. 6th, 1761.
HENRY KITNER.	Bern.	Berks.	Sept. 13th, 1761.
PHILIP STAFFER.	Brecknock.	Lancaster.	Sept. 6th, 1761.
GEORGE STRAAL.	Bern.	Berks.	Sept. 13th, 1761.
WENDAL KOEMER.	Marlboro.	Philadelphia.	Sept. 16th, 1761.
MICHAEL GROWL.	Cumru.	Berks.	Sept. 21st, 1761.
LAWRENCE BITTER.	Lebanon.	Lancaster.	Sept. 30th, 1761.
JOHN DEETZ.	Lebanon.	Lancaster.	Sept. 30th, 1761.
LENHART (LEHNHART) RUBBERT.	Reading.	Berks.	Sept. 18th, 1761.
JOHN PHILIP KLINGER.	Reading.	Berks.	Sept. 18th (6th), 1761.
ALEXANDER KLINGER.	Reading.	Berks.	Sept. 18th (6th), 1761.
MATTHIAS KINNELIN.	Reading.	Berks.	Sept. 18th (6th), 1761.
JNO. GEORGE EISINBEISS.	Reading.	Berks.	Sept. 18th (6th), 1761.
GEORGE STRADLER.	Douglass.	Berks.	Sept. 13th, 1761.
JNO. MARTIN FRITZ.	Amity.	Berks.	Sept. 13th, 1761.
JOHN GEORGE HAFNER.	Passyunck.	Philadelphia.	Sept. 20th, 1761.
GEORGE RIESS.	Northern Liberties.	Philadelphia.	Sept. 20th, 1761.
ANDREW CAMMEREL.	Warwick.	Lancaster.	Aug. 23rd, 1761.
CHRISTIAN GYGER.	Warwick.	Lancaster.	Aug. 23rd, 1761.
JOHN SHRYBER.	Manheim.	Lancaster.	Aug. 23rd, 1761.
JOHN KEISLER.	Rapho.	Lancaster.	Aug. 30th, 1761.
HENRY MAYER.	Rapho.	Lancaster.	Aug. 30th, 1761.
MICHAEL FOLEMIR.	Cumru.	Berks.	Sept. 6th, 1761.
PHILIP WACKS.	Alsace.	Berks.	Sept. 13th (18th), 1761.
JACOB YOACHAM.	Providence.	Philadelphia.	Sept. 20th, 1761.
GEORGE GAYER.	Warwick.	Lancaster.	Sept. 13th, 1761.
CHRISTOPHER BOYER.	Reading.	Berks.	Sept. 6th, 1761.
GEORGE HOFFER.	Cocolico.	Lancaster.	Sept. 20th, 1761.
ADAM NEW.	Derry.	Lancaster.	Aug. 2nd, 1761.
NICHOLAS NEW.	Lebanon.	Lancaster.	Aug. 30th, 1761.
CONRAD ROSE.	Oley.	Berks.	Sept. 20th, 1761.
JOHN ELBERTH (EBERTH).	Bern.	Berks.	Sept. 21st, 1761.
ANDREW EBBERT.	Reading.	Berks.	Sept. 18th, 1761.
VALENTINE VOGT.	Douglass.	Philadelphia.	Sept. 16th, 1761.
VALENTINE PROPST.	Albany.	Berks.	Sept. 20th, 1761.
NICHOLAS SCHWEIGER.	Maxatawney.	Berks.	Sept. 20th, 1761.
GEORGE BEEBER.	Maxatawney.	Berks.	Sept. 20th, 1761.
GEORGE KUTZ.	Maxatawney.	Berks.	Sept. 20th, 1761.
GEORGE SELL.	Maxatawney.	Berks.	Sept. 20th, 1761.
HENRY ALSBACK.	Cumru.	Berks.	Sept. 16th, 1761.
PETER KNORR.	Cumru.	Berks.	Sept. 16th, 1761.
NICHOLAS YOST.	Cumru.	Berks.	Sept. 16th, 1761.
JNO. ADAM NEIDIG.	Cumru.	Berks.	Sept. 16th, 1761.
FREDERICK CASEMIR MILLER.	Reading.	Berks.	Sept. 16th, 1761.
NICHS. HEIDSHU.	Alsace.	Berks.	Sept. 16th, 1761.

Foreigners' Names.	Township.	County.	Sacrament when taken.
MICHAEL HESSLER.	Alsace.	Berks.	Sept. 16th, 1761.
GEORGE HOFFMAN.	Alsace.	Berks.	Sept. 16th, 1761.
PHILIP SPRING.	Alsace.	Berks.	Sept. 16th, 1761.
CONRAD GLINDER.	Alsace.	Berks.	Sept. 16th, 1761.
CASPAR SNEBLE.	Bethel.	Berks.	Sept. 13th, 1761.
LUDWICK SCHUI.	Bethel.	Lancaster.	Sept. 13th, 1761.
CONRAD WOLFHART.	Heidleburg.	Lancaster.	Aug. 16th, 1761.
JOHN GUNCKET (GUNCKEL).	Bethel.	Berks.	Sept. 20th, 1761.
CONRAD HART.	Cumru.	Berks.	Sept. 6th, 1761.
FREDERICK BARLET.	Reading.	Berks.	Sept. 6th, 1761.
JOHN MARKS RININGER.	Upper Salford.	Philadelphia.	Sept. 6th, 1761.
CONRAD STEER.	Rockhill.	Bucks.	Aug. 16th, 1761.
MARTIN SHABEEKER.	Rockhill.	Bucks.	Aug. 16th, 1761.
MICHAEL YOH.	Skippack.	Philadelphia.	Aug. 16th, 1761.
HENRY GITTELMAN.	Upper Salford.	Philadelphia.	Sept. 6th, 1761.
JOHN JOSEPH ROTH.	Upper Salford.	Philadelphia.	Aug. 16th, 1761.
PHILIP WENTZ.	Upper Salford.	Philadelphia.	Sept. 6th, 1761.
HENRY HEIST.	Marlboro.	Philadelphia.	Aug. 13th, 1761.
MICH. GRATZ.	Marlboro.	Philadelphia.	Aug. 13th, 1761.
JOHN RIESS.	Maccungy.	Northampton.	Sept. 13th, 1761.
LAWRENCE FICKS.	Reading.	Berks.	Sept. 6th, 1761.
ABRAHAM SHRIENER.	Rockhill.	Bucks.	Sept. 13th, 1761.
HENRICK ENGEL.	Douglass.	Philadelphia.	Sept. 20th, 1761.
CHRISTIAN SNEEDER.	Earl.	Lancaster.	Sept. 21st, 1761.
THOMAS YERGER.	Hanover.	Philadelphia.	Sept. 13th, 1761.
VALENTINE SHERER.	New Providence.	Philadelphia.	Sept. 20th, 1761.
ANDREW YERGER.	New Hanover.	Philadelphia.	Sept. 13th, 1761.
JNO. RUEF SNYDER.	Amity.	Berks.	Sept. 20th, 1761.
MARTIN BOWER.	Rockhill.	Bucks.	Aug. 30th, 1761.
GEORGE GILBERT.	Colebrookdale.	Berks.	Sept. 21st, 1761.
JACOB GIEGER.	New Hanover.	Philadelphia.	Sept. 13th, 1761.
LEONARD IMMEL.	York.	York.	Aug. 30th, 1761.
FREDERICK KRELMER (KREIMER).	Greenwich.	Berks.	Sept. 13th, 1761.
JACOB DIETRICK.	Greenwich.	Berks.	Sept. 13th, 1761.
GEORGE WALDHAWER.	Brecknock.	Lancaster.	Aug. 23rd, 1761.
CHRISTOR. WALDHAWER.	Brecknock.	Lancaster.	Aug. 23rd, 1761.
FREDERICK GLASS.	Earl.	Lancaster.	Aug. 30th, 1761.
MICHAEL PROPST.	Albany (Abany sic.).	Berks.	Sept. 24th, 1761.
JOHN KEISTLER.	Albany (Abany sic.).	Berks.	Sept. 24th, 1761.
SIMON FREESE.	Albany (Abany sic.).	Berks.	Sept. 24th, 1761.
JACOB HOGABUGH (HOGGABUGH).	Albany (Abany sic.).	Berks.	Sept. 24th, 1761.
JACOB DREESS.	Albany (Abany sic.).	Berks.	Sept. 24th, 1761.
CHARLES KACHLIN.	Hilltown.	Bucks.	Aug. 30th, 1761.
CONRAD STIGHTER.	Reading.	Berks.	Sept. 6th, 1761.
JACOB KIEMIL.	Weisemburgh.	Northampton.	Sept. 13th, 1761.
GEORGE MICHAEL KOLB.	New Hanover.	Philadelphia.	Sept. 20th, 1761.
ADAM KECK (KOCH).	Entemir.	Cumberland.	Sept. 24th, 1761.
NICHOLAS SWARTZ.	Long Swamp.	Berks.	Sept.13th, 1761.
GEORGE EBERHARD.	Philadelphia.	Philadelphia.	Sept. 22nd, 1761.
JACOB ROTH.	Philadelphia.	Philadelphia.	Sept. 22nd, 1761.
DANIEL EBERHARD.	Passyunk.	Philadelphia.	Sept. 24th, 1761.
JNO. CHRIST. (FRED.) WOLFF.	Philadelphia.	Philadelphia.	Sept. 20th, 1761.
JNO. DANL. MAYLANDER.	Philadelphia.	Philadelphia.	Sept. 20th, 1761.
GEO. CHR. REINHOLD.	Philadelphia.	Philadelphia.	July 5th, 1761.

NATURALIZATIONS

PENNSYLVANIA.

Foreigners' Names.	Township.	County.	Sacrament when taken.
JEREMIAH BARR.	Bern.	Berks.	Sept. 6th, 1761.
CASPAR FILLING.	Elizabeth.	Lancaster.	Aug. 16th, 1761.
JOHN BOWSE.	Douglas.	Berks (Bucks).	Sept. 20th, 1761.
PETER MECOMER.	Heidleberg.	Northampton.	Sept. 13th, 1761.
GEO. ADAM HEILMAN.	Vincent.	Chester.	Sept. 20th, 1761.
GEO. CHR. EBBERLY.	Philadelphia.	Philadelphia.	July 5th, 1761.
JNO. JACOB BINDER.	Philadelphia.	Philadelphia.	Sept. 20th, 1761.
JNO. FRED. UHLAND.	Philadelphia.	Philadelphia.	Sept. 20th, 1761.

Quakers [&c.].

Foreigners' Names.	Township.	County.	Moravians Sacrament when taken.
JOHN GRUBER.	Derby.	Chester.	
JACOB ROHRER.	Cocolico.	Lancaster.	
MICHL. BOWER.	Warren.	York.	
WILLM. REASER (REESER).	Reading.	Berks.	
JOHN MILEY.	Cocolico.	Lancaster.	
NICHS. SURFACE.	Cocolico.	Lancaster.	
HENRY BRUNNER.	Warwick.	Lancaster.	
ULRICK SUPINGER.	Cocolico.	Lancaster.	
CHRISTOPHER SULLINGER.	Cocolico.	Lancaster.	
CHRISTIAN UPLINGER.	Warwick.	Lancaster.	
JACOB LIDERT.	Warwick.	Lancaster.	
ULRICK WEETMORE.	Rapho.	Lancaster.	
JOHN BENDER.	Warwick.	Lancaster.	Aug. 29th, 1761.
FRED. RAUTFORIN.	Conestogo.	Lancaster.	
CATH. LEVEN, *formerly* QUINMORE (QUIMORE).	Oley.	Berks.	
CHRISTIAN BRUNESTROTTZ.	Cocolico.	Lancaster.	
JACOB FOUTZ.	Strasburgh.	Lancaster.	
EMANUEL BROLLIER.	Cocolico.	Lancaster.	
JOHN CLINNEYENNY.	Cumru.	Berks.	
PETER ASSUM.	Lancaster.	Lancaster.	
ABRAHAM SMOUDTZ.	Lebannon.	Lancaster.	
GEORGE BRENDEL.	Heidleburg.	Berks.	Sept. 6th, 1761.
SIMON AIGLER.	Heidleburg.	Berks.	Sept. 6th, 1761.
MICH. LOWER.	Heidleburg.	Berks.	Sept. 6th, 1761.
JOHN BENTZ.	Manchester.	York.	
JOHN MOYER.	Upper Saucon.	Northampton.	
JACOB DOBLER.	Bethlehem.	Lancaster.	
GEORGE SYSINGER.	Oley.	Berks.	
BERNARD ROPOST (? PROPOST).	Alsace.	Berks.	
MARTIN BOUHER.	Warwick.	Lancaster.	
GEORGE SCHWEETER.	Earl.	Lancaster.	
BARTHOLW. SEGUIST (SEGRIST).	Earl.	Lancaster.	
JOHN CARVIR.	Cumru.	Berks.	
CHRISTIAN SUKE.	Cumru.	Berks.	
JOSEPH MISHLER.	Cumru.	Berks.	
JACOB MISHLER.	Cumru.	Berks.	
ADAM RICKABACKER.	Alsace.	Berks.	
PHILIP BRENDLO (BRENDLE).	Cocolico.	Lancaster.	
JOHN RUBY	Brecknock.	Lancaster.	

Foreigners' Names.	Township.	County.	If Moravian. Sacrament when taken.
PHILIP ECKERT.	Leacock.	Lancaster.	
JOHN SHUTTZ (SHULTZ).	Lebanon.	Lancaster.	Sept. 13th, 1761.
CONRAD SWARTZ.	Lancaster.	Lancaster.	
GEORGE MILEY.	Warren.	York.	
JOHN STOUFFER.	Warwick.	Lancaster.	
CHRISTR. WILKER (WILLHER).	Warwick.	Lancaster.	
BARBARA RITTER.	Albany.	Berks.	
DANIEL BOIN.	Bethel.	Lancaster.	Sept. 10th, 1761.
BIRNHARD FABER.	Bethel.	Lancaster.	Sept. 10th, 1761.
JACOB SPICKLER (SPIKLER).	Bethel.	Lancaster.	
ADAM FABER.	Bethel.	Lancaster.	
PHILIP BAKE.	Bethel.	Lancaster.	
JACOB GOOTZ.	Maxatawny.	Berks.	
JOHN NEWCOMAT.	Hempfield.	Lancaster.	
MATTHIAS SEIDLER.	Lancaster.	Lancaster.	
JOHN BEIDLER.	Providence.	Philadelphia.	
JACOB SPEEDLER.	Cocolico.	Lancaster.	
JOHN MARCKLE (MARKLE).	Cocolico.	Lancaster.	
DORST THOMAS.	Lebanon.	Lancaster.	
ABRAHM. BOMPER.	Bethlehem.	Northampton.	Aug. 29th, 1761.
ANDREAS SCHOUTE.	Bethlehem.	Northampton.	Aug. 29th, 1761.
JOHN LISHER.	Bethlehem.	Northampton.	Aug. 29th, 1761.
FREDK. BUCKLE (BACKLE).	Bethlehem.	Northampton.	Aug. 29th, 1761.
ANDREAS WEBER.	Bethlehem.	Northampton.	Aug. 29th, 1761.
FRANCIS GROVE.	Chanceford.	York.	
JOHN AMEND.	Windsor.	Berks (York).	
FREDERICK HOOVE.	Oley.	Berks.	
ANTHONY SNIDER.	Lancaster.	Lancaster.	
BARBARA RITTER.	Albany.	Berks.	
PETER GANTER.	Lancaster.	Lancaster.	June 27th, 1761.
DAVID TRESSLER.	Lancaster.	Lancaster.	Aug. 22nd, 1761.
BERNARD RODEBECK.	Lancaster.	Lancaster.	Aug. 22nd, 1761.
MARTIN PFATTAGER.	Heidleburg.	Berks.	
JOHN MARTIN.	Upper Hanover.	Philadelphia.	
JACOB HOCKNOWER (KOCHNOWER).	Conestogo.	Lancaster.	
VALENTINE ECKBERT.	Alsace.	Berks.	
GEORGE TRONE.	Manheim.	Yorks.	
HENRY BOWMAN.	Manheim.	Yorks.	
PHILIP HENRY DAHNE.	Lancaster.	Lancaster.	Aug. 29th, 1761.
JOHN HICKMAN.	Strasburg.	Lancaster.	
MATHIAS BYSHER.	Manchester.	York.	
PHILIP BUSHUNG.	Lampeter.	Lancaster.	
ADAM DEASISBACK.	Leacock.	Lancaster.	
JACOB ROWLAND (ROWLOND).	Earl.	Lancaster.	
JOHN CHRISTN. GUTEYAHR.	Warwick.	Lancaster.	Aug. 29th, 1761.
ANDREW HOOVER.	Frederick County in Maryland.		
JACOB KOCKANOWER.	Manheim.	Lancaster.	
ABRAHAM KURTZ.	Earl.	Lancaster.	
CHRISTIAN SMOKER.	Earl.	Lancaster.	
CHRISTIAN ROHRBACK.	Cocolico.	Lancaster.	
JACOB KEENTZLY.	Mountjoy.	Lancaster.	Sept. 6th, 1761.
JOHN HECKENDORN.	York.	York.	Sept. 9th, 1761.
JACOB VIEST.	Paradice.	York.	

PENNSYLVANIA.

Foreigners' Names.	Township.	County.	Moravian Sacrament when taken.
JOHN FISHEL.	Manchester.	Lancaster.	
LUDWICK SHALLY.	Lebanon.	Lancaster.	
VALENTINE KALLER.	Lebanon.	Lancaster.	
JOHN MATEZER.	Oley.	Berks.	
JACOB EARLEY.	Amity.	Berks.	
JOHN KEEVER.	Bethel.	Hunterdon, New Jersey.	
HENRY BAKER.	New Hanover.	Philadelphia.	

[The following certificates for this Colony have not been entered into the Entry Book.]

C. O. 5. 1276.

X. 51.

Supreme Court held at Philadelphia, 10 and 12 April, 1762.

Foreigners' Names	Township.	County.	Sacrament, when taken.
CHRISTIAN MOY.	New Hanover.	Philadelphia.	9 April, 1762.
WERNER WEITZEL.	Cumru.	Berks.	21 March, 1762.
DANIEL MASSERLY.	Dover.	York.	21 March, 1762.
JOHN NICHOLAS KING.	Dover.	York.	21 March, 1762.
LUDWICK DAVID RIPPELL.	Dover.	York.	21 March, 1762.
JOHN PETER WOLFFE.	Dover.	York.	21 March, 1762.
JOHN LEONARD SHEDORON.	Dover.	York.	21 March, 1762.
MICHAEL ZINSER.	City of Philadelphia.	Philadelphia.	14 March, 1762.
JOHN PETER GOODLING.	Dover.	York.	21 March, 1762.
JOHN NICHOLAS SCHRAM.	Dover.	York.	21 March, 1762.
JOHN WOLFF.	Dover.	York.	21 March, 1762.
JOHN BACKENSTOOSE.	Lancaster.	Lancaster.	21 February, 1762.
PETER LENT.	Winchester.	York.	8 April, 1762.
FREDERICK WEITZELL.	Cumru.	Berks.	4 April, 1762.
PETER BEER, Senior.	Lancaster.	Lancaster.	21 February, 1762.
BARNET WOLF.	Lancaster.	Lancaster.	21 February, 1762.
FREDERICK YOUSE.	York.	York.	4 April, 1762.
JOHN FOCKLER.	York.	York.	4 April, 1762.
ANDREW BUDESILL.	York.	York.	4 April, 1762.
LUDWICK MAYER.	York.	York.	4 April, 1762.
MICHAEL SOMMER.	York.	York.	4 April, 1762.
WENDALL LAUMEISTER.	York.	York.	4 April, 1762.
CONRAD MAUL.	Manheim.	York.	7 March, 1762.
YOST WAGGONER.	Manheim.	York.	4 March, 1762.
PHILIP GRABER.	Manchester.	York.	4 March, 1762.
PHILIP HOSS.	Manchester.	York.	4 March, 1762.
HENRY GRABER.	Manchester.	York.	4 March, 1762.
ADAM ROPPERT.	Manchester.	York.	4 March, 1762.
BALTZER SHAFER.	Lancaster.	Lancaster.	21 February, 1762.
PETER RIEGHTER.	Lancaster.	Lancaster.	21 February, 1762.
JOHN HUBER.	Germany.	York.	4 April, 1762.
JOHN SHAUMAN.	Germany.	York.	4 April, 1762.
GEORGE SPANSEILER.	Germany.	York.	4 April, 1762.
JOHN SHORON.	Germany.	York.	4 April, 1762.
LUDWICK MILLER.	Germany.	York.	4 April, 1762.
ANDREAS FUCKS.	Reading.	Berks.	4 April, 1762.

Foreigners' Names.	Township.	County.	Sacrament when taken.
JACOB DEEM.	Cumru.	Berks.	4 April, 1762.
JOHN SWARTZHOWFT.	Bern.	Berks.	4 April, 1762.
ANDREAS SHABER.	Reading.	Berks.	4 April, 1762.
JACOB KUNTZ.	Albany.	Berks.	4 April, 1762.
GEORGE BURKHARD.	Lancaster.	Lancaster.	21 February, 1762.
VALENTINE WEBER.	Lancaster.	Lancaster.	21 February, 1762.
JOHN DOLL.	Lancaster.	Lancaster.	21 February, 1762.
JOHN GRAFF.	Mannor.	Lancaster.	21 February, 1762.
HENRY BOTT.	Mannor.	Lancaster.	21 February, 1762.
PHILIP MILLER.	Manchester.	York.	4 April, 1762.
MICHAEL LONG.	Manchester.	York.	4 April, 1762.
JOHN GEORGE SPAHR.	Dover.	York.	4 April, 1762.
JOHN CASPAR MARGBERG.	Lancaster.	Lancaster.	21 February, 1762.
JOHN HOOFNAIGLE.	Lancaster.	Lancaster.	21 February, 1762.
ABRAHAM CAUBAL.	Lancaster.	Lancaster.	21 February, 1762.
ADAM LE ROY.	Lancaster.	Lancaster.	21 February, 1762.
HENRY BERGEY.	Whitehall.	Northampton.	4 April, 1762.
JACOB MOOR.	Salsburg.	Northampton.	4 April, 1762.
JACOB PETRE.	Windsor.	Bucks.	4 April, 1762.
JOHN WIRMLEY.	Lancaster.	Lancaster.	7 March, 1762.
JACOB KROWTER.	Heidleburg.	Lancaster.	4 April, 1762.
LAWRENCE SHRUNCK.	Heidleburg.	Berks.	1 April, 1762.
VALENTINE BAREMGARTNER.	Heidleburg.	Berks.	1 April, 1762.
PETER RETI.	Heidleburg.	Berks.	1 April, 1762.
VALENTINE KAYSER.	Heidleburg.	Berks.	1 April, 1762.
UTI RITSCHART.	Heidleburg.	Berks.	1 April, 1762.
BALTZER ZERCH.	Heidleburg.	Berks.	1 April, 1762.
DETRICK SOLE.	Heidleburg.	Berks.	4 April, 1762.
HENRY SOLE.	Heidleburg.	Berks.	4 April, 1762.
HENRY FRY.	Heidleburg.	Berks.	4 April, 1762.
JOHN BAST.	Maxatawny.	Berks.	4 April, 1762.
GEORGE SIBBERT.	Rockland.	Berks.	4 April, 1762.
JOHN WESNER.	Albany.	Berks.	4 April, 1762.
ADAM HAWKER.	Cocolico.	Lancaster.	4 April, 1762.
ADAM OBERLY.	Cocolico.	Lancaster.	4 April, 1762.
CHARLES SCHAID.	Elizabeth.	Lancaster.	4 April, 1762.
JACOB SCHNEIZER.	Cocolico.	Lancaster.	4 April, 1762.
PHILIP HOFFMAN.	Warwick.	Lancaster.	4 April, 1762.
MICHAEL DEWALD.	Windsor.	Berks.	4 April, 1762.
GERHARD WILL.	Windsor.	Berks.	4 April, 1762.
ANDREW HAGEBUCK.	Albany.	Berks.	4 April, 1762.
GEORGE KISHTLER.	Albany.	Berks.	4 April, 1762.
PHILIP MILLER.	Linden.	Northampton.	4 April, 1762.
HENRY LEASE.	Maiden Creek.	Berks.	5 April, 1762.
HENRY SCHEIZER.	Windsor	Berks.	5 April, 1762.
PHILIP HENZEL.	Windsor.	Berks.	5 April, 1762
BASTIAN KREICHER.	Windsor.	Berks.	5 April, 1762.
ADAM LUKEMBIEL.	Windsor.	Berks.	5 April, 1762.
JOST KREICHER.	Windsor.	Berks.	5 April, 1762.
CASPAR SMIT.	Windsor.	Berks.	5 April, 1762.
DAVID ALSPACH.	Windsor.	Berks.	5 April, 1762.
DAVID BRENNING.	Windsor.	Berks.	5 April, 1762.
JOHN FRAUNVELTER.	Maiden Creek.	Berks.	5 April, 1762.
FREDERICK BLATT.	Maiden Creek.	Berks.	5 April, 1762.

PENNSYLVANIA.

Foreigners' Names.	Township.	County.	Sacrament when taken.
Frederick Lease.	Roscombe Manor.	Berks.	5 April, 1762.
Hieronimus Proback.	Leacock.	Lancaster.	28 March, 1762.
Christian Grow.	Leacock.	Lancaster.	28 March, 1762.
John Schnabeli.	Tulpehocken.	Berks.	21 March, 1762.
Paul Lingel.	Heidleberg.	Berks.	21 March, 1762.
John Pontius.	Tulpehocken.	Berks.	21 March, 1762.
Michael Powser.	Tulpehocken.	Berks.	4 April, 1762.
Caspar Hinckel.	Tulpehocken.	Berks.	4 April, 1762.
Valentine Urledick.	Reading.	Berks.	4 April, 1762.
John Christr. Neidlin.	Reading.	Berks.	4 April, 1762.
Frederick Wm. Frick.	Reading.	Berks.	4 April, 1762.
Werner Stam.	Bern.	Berks.	1 April, 1762.
Adam Sontag.	Bern.	Berks.	1 April, 1762.
Jacob Fox.	Bern.	Berks.	4 April, 1762.
Jacob Stough.	Heidleberg.	Berks.	4 April, 1762.
George Christian.	Tulpehockon.	Berks.	4 April, 1762.
Martin Cronmiller.	York.	York.	4 April, 1762.
Peter Pens.	Dover.	York.	4 April, 1762.
Philip Mayer.	Tulpehockon.	Berks.	21 March, 1762.
Detrick Mayer.	Manchester.	York.	21 March, 1762.
Andrew Schaub.	Cocolico.	Lancaster.	9 April, 1762.
Hans Ulrick Angst.	Worcester.	Philadelphia.	9 April, 1762.
Henrick Conrad.	Worcester.	Philadelphia.	9 April, 1762.
Joseph Dinshirtz.	Heidleberg.	Lancaster.	7 March, 1762.
Jacob Wertz.	Antrim.	Cumberland.	10 April, 1762.
Leonard Sable.	Manchester.	York.	10 April, 1762.
John Wolf.	Limerick.	Philadelphia.	10 April, 1762.
Adam Protzman.	Skippack.	Philadelphia.	10 April, 1762.
John Michl. Shubert.	Philadelphia.	Philadelphia.	14 March, 1762.
Melchior Hay.	Williams.	Northampton.	4 April, 1762.
Jacob Prutzman.	Williams.	Northampton.	4 April, 1762.
Geo. Thos. Heymberger.	Philadelphia.	Philadelphia.	10 April, 1762.
Herman Hatchy.	Upper Dublin.	Philadelphia.	9 April, 1762.
Daniel Reinhard.	Upper Dublin.	Philadelphia.	9 April, 1762.
Jacob Gobler.	Upper Dublin.	Philadelphia.	9 April, 1762.
John Ederick.	Whitemarsh.	Philadelphia.	9 April, 1762.
George Troutman.	Tulpehocken.	Lancaster.	21 February, 1762.
John George Beck.	Philadelphia.	Philadelphia.	14 March, 1762.
John George Sauter.	Philadelphia.	Philadelphia.	14 March, 1762.
John George Kugler.	Passyunck.	Philadelphia.	14 March, 1762.
Geo. Adam Rockeberger.	Philadelphia.	Philadelphia.	14 March, 1762.
Geo. Adam Pfister.	Philadelphia.	Philadelphia.	14 March, 1762.
Gallus Sleighter.	Philadelphia.	Philadelphia.	10 April, 1762.
John Christian Lœser.	Upper Dublin.	Philadelphia.	11 April, 1762.
George Snœring.	Philadelphia.	Philadelphia.	11 April, 1762.
Henry Krips.	Southwark.	Philadelphia.	11 April, 1762.
George Ludwick Meyer.	Lancaster.	Lancaster.	17 March, 1762.
Paul Weilzel.	Lancaster.	Lancaster.	21 February, 1762.
Geo. Ernst Lindenberger.	Philadelphia.	Philadelphia.	11 April, 1762.
John George Heirness.	Philadelphia.	Philadelphia.	11 April, 1762.
William Staddleman.	Lower Merion.	Philadelphia.	11 April, 1762.
Jacob Korr.	Whitpain.	Philadelphia.	11 April, 1762.
Baltzer Spitznagle.	Whitpain.	Philadelphia.	11 April, 1762.

Foreigners' Names.	Township.	County.	Sacrament when taken.
BALTZER WEIG.	Gwinedth.	Philadelphia.	11 April, 1762.
BARBARA HEHL.	Philadelphia.	Philadelphia.	14 March, 1762.
JACOB HILTZHEIMER.	Philadelphia.	Philadelphia.	29 March, 1762.
JOHN ODENHEIMER.	Philadelphia.	Philadelphia.	29 March, 1762.

Quakers and other Protestants who scruple to take an Oath.

JACOB ECKER.	Cocolico.	Lancaster.	
JOHN FRANCIS REINEIR.	Cocolico.	Lancaster.	
NICHOLAS BURKHART.	Philadeplhia.	Philadelphia.	
ADAM CAMEL.	Philadelphia.	Philadelphia.	
ANDREW GELLINGER.	Lancaster.	Lancaster.	
HENRY WERT.	Manheim.	York.	
JACOB BLECK.	Of Frederick County in Maryland.		
JOHN KRŒMER.	Manor.	Lancaster.	3 Apr., 1762.
FREDERICK WEISEL.	Springfield.	Bucks.	
JOHN ARTZ.	Heidleburg.	Berks.	
JOHN CRUSH.	Lancaster.	Lancaster.	
GEORGE EVERLY.	Lancaster.	Lancaster.	
PETER MUMMA.	Hempfield.	Lancaster.	
GEORGE HOOFNEY.	Manheim.	Lancaster.	
JACOB STONER.	Leacock.	Lancaster.	
MARTIN WISNER.	Exeter.	Berks.	
ROSIND KIRSTEN.	Oley.	Berks.	
HENRY ULIUS.	Dover.	York.	
CHRISR. MASTER.	Hartford.	Berks.	
PHILIP BOYER.	New Providence.	Philadelphia.	
NATHANIEL SEIDEL.	Bethlehem.	Northampton.	13 Mar., 1762.
NICHS. HENRY EBERHARDT.	Warwick.	Lancaster.	13 Mar., 1762.
MATHIAS WEISS.	Bethlehem.	Northampton.	13 Mar., 1762.
JACOB SLAMBACK.	Manheim.	York.	
ANTHONY KREBER.	Manheim.	York.	
MARTIN KRYDER.	Germantown.	Philadelphia.	
CONRAD RŒSILIE.	Lower Saucon.	Northampton.	
CASPAR WENK.	Maxatawny.	Berks.	
JACOB FRY.	Lower Saucon.	Northampton.	
VALENTINE ERTEL.	Dover.	York.	
CONRAD DETRY.	Franconia.	Philadelphia.	
JOHN RODE.	Byberry.	Philadelphia.	
FREDERICK FETZER.	Mannor of Moreland.	Philadelphia.	
TOBIAS WEBER.	Passyunk.	Philadelphia.	
JOHN SUMER.	Mannor of Moreland.	Philadelphia.	
GEORGE PICCUS.	Germantown.	Philadelphia.	

List certified by JOSEPH SHIPPEN, Jr., Secretary. Philadelphia, 16 Nov., 1763.

X. 52.

(Supreme Court held at Philadelphia, 24 Sept., 1762.)

MARTIN SCHNEIDER.	Earl.	Lancaster.	19 Sept., 1762.
JOHN HOMSHIR.	Lebannon.	Lancaster.	12 Sept., 1762.
PETER OLINGER.	Lebannon.	Lancaster.	8 Aug., 1762.
JACOB HACKER.	Lebannon.	Lancaster.	8 Aug., 1762.
GEORGE GLASSBENNER.	Lebannon.	Lancaster.	8 Aug., 1762.
GEORGE MICHL, BALMIR.	Lebannon.	Lancaster.	8 Aug., 1762

PENNSYLVANIA.

Foreigners' Names.	Township.	County.	Sacrament when taken.
GEORGE HOUSEHOLDER.	Lebannon.	Lancaster.	8 Aug., 1762.
PETER SHAAFF.	Lebannon.	Lancaster.	12 Sept., 1762.
LUDWICK LAY.	Lancaster.	Lancaster.	12 Sept., 1762.
JOHN PETER CUGNET.	Lancaster.	Lancaster.	12 Sept., 1762.
CASPER SENGHAAS.	Lebanon.	Lancaster.	29 Aug., 1762.
GEORGE EHLER.	Lancaster.	Lancaster.	22 Aug., 1762.
JOHN KANN.	Lancaster.	Lancaster.	12 Sept., 1762.
BENJAMIN MOSES CLAVA.	a Jew.		
GEORGE PETRI.	Cocolico.	Lancaster.	16 Sept., 1762.
PHILIP BECHTOE.	Cocolico.	Lancaster.	16 Sept., 1762.
SIMON WISHONG.	Brecknock.	Lancaster.	16 Sept., 1762.
PETER LEDERMAN.	Heidelburg.	Lancaster.	21 Sept., 1762.
MARTIN ENGLEBRIGHT.	York.	York.	20 Sept., 1762.
PAUL GYER.	York.	York.	20 Sept., 1762.
NICHOLAS OTT.	York.	York.	20 Sept., 1762.
SIMON LAIBELL.	Heidleburg.	Lancaster.	1 Aug., 1762.
JOHN WALL.	York.	York.	19 Sept., 1762.
MICHAEL WELSH.	York.	York.	19 Sept., 1762.
GODFRIED KENIG.	York.	York.	19 Sept., 1762.
JACOB PHILIP KENIG.	York.	York.	19 Sept., 1762.
CHRISTR. RODERMILL.	Codorus.	York.	29 July, 1762.
MICHL. WEBER.	Heidleburg.	Lancaster.	1 Aug., 1762.
PETER SCHAIN.	Colebrookdale.	Berks.	19 Sept., 1762.
GEORGE ELLINGER.	Lebannon.	Lancaster.	8 Aug., 1762.
JOHN COMFORT.	Helm.	York.	19 Sept., 1762.
HENRY SMITH.	Helm.	York.	19 Sept., 1762.
HENRY BAUN.	Helm.	York.	19 Sept., 1762.
ANDREW COMFORT.	Helm.	York.	19 Sept., 1762.
JNO. HURBACH.	Helm.	York.	19 Sept., 1762.
JACOB STENEE.	Helm.	York.	19 Sept., 1762.
JOHN MELFORD.	Coventry.	Chester.	19 Sept., 1762.
CASPER MELFORD.	Coventry.	Chester.	19 Sept., 1762.
JOHN KLINE.	Bern.	Berks.	12 Sept., 1762.
CHRISTR. SCHWEETZER.	Cocolico.	Lancaster.	16 Sept., 1762.
ANDREW CLINE.	Lancaster.	Lancaster.	22 Aug., 1762.
RUDOLPH SPENGLER.	Paradise.	York.	19 Sept., 1762.
JACOB STAM.	Paradise.	York.	19 Sept., 1762.
BERNARD SPENGLER.	York.	York.	19 Sept., 1762.
GEORGE ZIMERMAN.	Maxatawny.	Berks.	19 Sept., 1762.
JACOB DEBRE.	Alsace.	Berks.	16 Sept., 1762.
JOHN RESLER.	Earl.	Lancaster.	23 Aug., 1762.
BALTZER GAITZ.	Earl.	Lancaster.	23 Aug. 1762.
HENRY RYCLEDORFER.	Albany.	Berks.	2 Sept., 1762.
JOHN WEAVER.	Lebanan.	Lancaster.	12 Sept., 1762.
HENRICK NEHROOT.	Albany.	Berks.	2 Sept., 1762.
JOHN HIEN.	Albany.	Berks.	8 Sept., 1762.
DANIEL SMITH.	Albany.	Berks.	8 Sept., 1762.
BERNARD WANNEMAKER.	Lynn.	Northampton.	8 Sept., 1762.
MARX WANNEMAKER.	Lynn.	Northampton.	8 Sept., 1762.
JACOB GERHART.	Albany.	Berks.	8 Sept., 1762.
GEORGE DRUM.	Albany.	Berks.	8 Sept., 1762.
JOHN PHILIPS.	Alsace.	Berks.	13 Sept., 1762
JACOB SHURMAN.	Tulpehoccon.	Berks.	16 Sept., 1762.

Foreigners' Names.	Township.	County.	Sacrament when taken.
JOHN PHILIP BAKER.	Lancaster.	Lancaster.	12 Sept., 1762.
MARTIN LONG.	Heidleburg.	Berks.	12 Sept., 1762.
GEO. RODEBACK.	Tulpehoccon.	Berks.	12 Sept., 1762.
JACOB ARTZ.	Heidleburgh.	Berks.	12 Sept., 1762.
JACOB HEEK.	Manchester.	York.	20 Sept., 1762.
ANDREW SMITH.	Manchester.	York.	20 Sept., 1762.
PETER SCHRIBER.	Manchester.	York.	20 Sept., 1762.
NICHOLAS WILD.	Manchester.	York.	19 Sept., 1762.
JOHN JACOB POH.	Albany.	Berks.	2 Sept., 1762.
WEINER STONCK.	Reading.	Berks.	5 Sept., 1762.
JOHN MILLER.	Albany.	Berks.	2 Sept., 1762.
JACOB NAGLE.	Douglass.	Berks.	19 Sept., 1762.
PETER LEBENGUT.	Douglass.	Berks.	19 Sept., 1762.
LUDWICK BENDER.	Douglass.	Berks.	19 Sept., 1762.
ROWLAND YOUNG.	Douglass.	Berks.	19 Sept., 1762.
JOHN KEHL.	Douglass.	Berks.	19 Sept., 1762.
CONRAD REIFFSNEIDER.	Douglass.	Berks.	19 Sept., 1762.
ANDREW WEILER.	Douglass.	Berks.	19 Sept., 1762.
ADAM LUBENGUT.	Newhanover.	Philadelphia.	19 Sept., 1762.
ABRAHAM JORRIGG.	Lancaster.	Lancaster.	25 June, 1762.
JACOB KINSER.	Earl.	Lancaster.	23 Aug., 1762.
PETER RODEBACH.	Bern.	Berks.	16 Sept., 1762.
ANDW. AULENBACHER.	Tulpehoccon.	Berks.	16 Sept., 1762.
JACOB WHITNER.	Heidleburg.	Lancaster.	19 Sept., 1762.
HENRY LEINWÉBER.	Heidleburg.	Lancaster.	19 Sept., 1762.
STEPHEN HAUK.	near Oley Hills.	Berks.	19 Sept., 1762.
HENRY ANTHY. KŒNIG.	Albany.	Berks.	14 Sept., 1762.
PETER KLINGMAN.	Albany.	Berks.	2 Sept., 1762.
MARTIN PROBST.	Albany.	Berks.	2 Sept., 1762.
FRED. HESSE.	Albany.	Berks.	2 Sept., 1762.
MICH. ZIMERMAN.	Lebannon.	Lancaster.	18 July, 1762.
PHILIP ENSMINGER.	Cocolico.	Lancaster.	23 Aug., 1762.
WILLIAM HEFFER.	Cocolico.	Lancaster.	23 Aug., 1762.
MICHAEL NECK.	Philadelphia.	Philadelphia.	23 Sept., 1762.
HENRY PETER.	York.	York.	19 Sept., 1762.
FRANCIS KUNTZ.	Lancaster.	Lancaster.	12 Sept., 1762.
ADAM KOHN.	Manchester.	York.	19 Sept., 1762.
CASPAR EGLY.	Bern.	Berks.	5 Sept., 1762.
GEORGE SCHRAM.	Manchester.	York.	19 Sept., 1762.
PETER SAHLER.	Limerick.	York.	19 Sept., 1762.
JOHN PHILIP LEYDIG.	Frederick.	Philadelphia.	19 Sept., 1762.
HENRY KRAUS.	Frederick.	Philadelphia.	19 Sept., 1762.
JACOB KOPP.	Newhanover.	Philadelphia.	12 Sept., 1762.
JACOB WIST.	Reading.	Berks.	5 Sept., 1762.
ULRICK MOHN.	Reading.	Berks.	5 Sept., 1762.
MARY ELIZH. ENDRIS.	Newhanover.	Philadelphia.	12 Sept., 1762.
GEORGE BERNHARDUS.	Reading.	Berks.	12 Sept., 1762.
PETER DIEHM.	Reading.	Berks.	12 Sept., 1762.
NICHS. MATEERY.	Reading.	Berks.	12 Sept., 1762.
NICHOLAS GOTSCHALL.	Reading.	Berks.	12 Sept., 1762.
BERNARD MAUS.	Heidleburg.	Lancaster.	12 Sept., 1762.
JOHN GAERBER.	Colesbrookdale.	Berks.	19 Sept., 1762.
JACOB FRIES.	Lannon.	Northampton.	19 Sept., 1762.
PETER FRIES.	Lannon.	Northampton.	19 Sept., 1762.

PENNSYLVANIA.

Foreigners' Names.	Township.	County.	Sacrament when taken.
GEO : SHIESLER.	Albany.	Berks.	19 Sept., 1762.
JOHN NYER.	Lannon.	Northampton.	5 Sept., 1762.
LAWRENCE KERSHNER.	Windsor.	York.	19 Sept., 1762.
JOHN MILLER.	Lancaster.	Lancaster.	17 Sept., 1762.
DIETRICK SHOPF.	Lancaster.	Lancaster.	21 Sept., 1762.
VEIT PENNER.	York.	York.	19 Sept., 1762.
PHILIP KOHL.	Reading.	Berks.·	5 Sept., 1762.
JOHN NIESS.	Rockhill.	Bucks.	14 Sept., 1762.
MICHAEL SHAFFER.	Williams.	Northampton.	12 Sept., 1762.
HENRY BERGER.	Bethel.	Berks.	16 Sept., 1762.
NICHOLAS PONTIUS.	Bethel.	Berks.	16 Sept., 1762.
PHILIP RHODE.	Exeter.	Berks.	16 Sept., 1762.
HENRY SLEIGH.	Exeter.	Berks.	5 Sept., 1762.
FREDERICK HERNER.	Exeter.	Berks.	5 Sept., 1762.
BERNARD TWEITZER.	Rockland.	Berks.	24 Aug., 1762.
GEORGE ANGSTAT.	Rockland.	Berks.	24 Aug., 1762.
GEORGE BORN.	Reading.	Berks.	6 Sept., 1762.
EMBRICK NONEMAKER.	Cushhohoppen.	Philadelphia.	24 Sept., 1762.
PETER SCHILP.	Allen.	Northampton.	12 Sept., 1762.
CONRAD FUCKS.	Bethlehem.	Northampton.	12 Sept., 1762.
JOHN SHULTZ.	Helm.	York.	19 Sept., 1762.
JACOB SHULTZ.	Helm.	York.	19 Sept., 1762.
JACOB WELSH.	York.	York.	19 Sept., 1762.
NICHOLAS SCHAVER.	York.	York.	19 Sept., 1762.
ADAM SCHMAAL.	Germany.	York.	19 Sept., 1762.
MARTYN GRYDER.	Duck Creek.	Kent.	15 Aug., 1762.
JOHN EMIG.	Manchester.	York.	19 Sept., 1762.
GODFREY FRY.	York.	York.	19 Sept., 1762.
GEORGE BABBON.	Whitemarsh.	Philadelphia.	19 Sept., 1762.
CATHERINE MILLER.	Whitemarsh.	Philadelphia.	19 Sept., 1762.
LAWRENCE BEBER.	Greenwich.	Berks.	12 Sept., 1762.
GEORGE MILLER.	Greenwich.	Berks.	12 Sept., 1762.
HENRY MILLER.	Greenwich.	Berks.	12 Sept., 1762.
ADAM BOWER.	Greenwich.	Berks.	12 Sept., 1762.
ADAM BROSSE.	Maccungy.	Northampton.	9 Sept., 1762.
BERNARD SMITH.	Maccungv.	Northampton.	9 Sept., 1762.
JOHN RICKART.	Whitemarsh.	Philadelphia.	19 Sept., 1762.
JOHN NIEP.	Heidleburg.	Lancaster.	1 Aug., 1762.
JACOB GRIMM.	Maccungy.	Northampton.	19 Sept., 1762.
HENRY KOCKENBACH.	Weisenburg.	Northampton.	19 Sept., 1762.
LUDWICK HUKE.	Rockhill.	Bucks.	21 Sept., 1762.
LEONARD BURKHEIMER.	Marlborough.	Philadelphia.	1 Aug., 1762.
HENRY ROCKY.	Salisbury.	Lancaster.	1 Aug., 1762.
FEOLIX BACHMAN.	Salisbury.	Lancaster.	1 Aug., 1762.
NICHOLAS SEYDALL.	Amity.	Berks.	19 Sept., 1762.
JACOB ECKELL.	Frederick.	Philadelphia.	19 Sept., 1762.
FREDERICK HUMMELL.	Derry.	Lancaster.	5 Sept., 1762.
PETER SCHUG.	Upper Salford.	Philadelphia.	12 Sept., 1762.
JOHN GANTZ.	Upper Salford.	Philadelphia.	12 Sept., 1762.
THEOPHILUS ENGELAND.	Heidleburg.	Lancaster.	5 Sept., 1762.
PAUL SCHWANGER.	Marlborough.	Philadelphia.	12 Sept., 1762.
PHILIP SCHOENEBERGER.	Whitpain.	Philadelphia.	19 Sept., 1762.
VALENTINE UHLER.	Forks.	Northampton.	27 June, 1762.

Foreigners' Names.	Township.	County.	Sacrament when taken.
WILLIAM FULBRIGHT.	Forks.	Northampton.	27 June, 1762.
JOHN MICHAEL KOCK.	Forks.	Northampton.	27 June, 1762.
GEORGE KEEN.	Forks.	Northampton.	27 June, 1762.
JOHN WILLIAM KELL.	Forks.	Northampton.	27 June, 1762.
SABASTIAN KAYSER.	Smithfield.	Northampton.	27 June, 1762.
FREDERICK WEISS.	Strasburg.	Lancaster.	1 Aug., 1762.
PETER MARCH.	Longswamp.	Berks.	19 Sept., 1762.
JOHN DEAL.	Longswamp.	Berks.	29 Sept., 1762.
JACOB BECHLEL.	Robertsons.	Berks.	5 Sept., 1762.
MICH : GREYSHER.	Windsor.	Berks.	15 Aug., 1762.
GEO : MAY.	Windsor.	Berks.	15 Aug., 1762.
MICHAEL PLUTNER.	Richmond.	Berks.	1 Aug., 1762.
CHRISTR. MAURER.	Lower Merrion.	Philadelphia.	29 Aug., 1762.

Quakers and other Protestants who conscientiously scruple to take an Oath.

Foreigners' Names.	Township.	County.	Moravians' time of taking their Sacrament.
GEORGE STALEY.	Earl.	Lancaster.	
JOHN DEER.	Earl.	Lancaster.	
JACOB SEYLER.	Earl.	Lancaster.	
ULRICK BEIGHART.	Lancaster.	Lancaster.	
JACOB HENNING.	Lancaster.	Lancaster.	
HENRY WAGGONER.	Bethlehem.	Lancaster.	
ISAIAH WHITEHEAD.	Lancaster.	Lancaster.	
ADAM FALKLER.	Earl.	Lancaster.	
ERONIMUS MILLER.	Strasburgh.	Lancaster.	
JOHN LOWTHERMAN.	Tulpehoccon.	Lancaster.	
JACOB KITZ.	Lancaster.	Lancaster.	
BARBARA MESSERSMIDT.	Exeter.	Berks.	
HANS HOPPEKER.	Berwick.	Lancaster.	
CHARLES ULLENDORF.	Plainfield.	Northampton.	
JNO. GEORGE GEITNER.	Bethlehem.	Northampton.	13 Aug., 1762.
CHRISTR : FRED : OETER.	Bethlehem.	Northampton.	13 Aug., 1762.
BENEDICT SPITZFARDEN.	Lancaster.	Lancaster.	
PETER KINGRICK.	Lebannon.	Lancaster.	
JNO : WILHELM FOULKE.	Rockland.	Berks.	
MATTHIAS CULP.	Rockland.	Berks.	
ADAM HELM.	Philadelphia.	Philadelphia.	31 July, 1762.
BERNARD STRAUS.	Salisbury.	Northampton.	
SIBELD TETERN.	Springfield.	Bucks.	
MARCUS HAINES.	York.	York.	
JACOB HENRICK.	Codorus.	York.	
CHRISTIAN GAYMAN.	Hereford.	Berks.	
BERNARD RAPP.	Whitemarsh.	Philadelphia.	
JACOB FRICK.	Lower Milford.	Bucks.	
JACOB PETERMAN.	Newhanover.	Philadelphia.	
ADAM HOFF.	Codorus.	York.	18 Sept., 1762.
JACOB UHLUM.	Providence.	Philadelphia.	
JNO. MATTHEW OTTO.	Bethlehem.	Northampton.	13 Aug., 1762.
MATHEW SCHROPP.	Bethlehem.	Northampton.	8 Sept., 1762.
CASPAR DEVILSBIT.	Manacasy.	Frederick County, Maryland.	
HENRY MANN.	Northern Liberties.	Philadelphia.	

List certified by JOSEPH SHIPPEN, Jr., Secretary.
Philadelphia, 16 Nov., 1763.

X. 53.   PENNSYLVANIA.

Supreme Court held at Philadelphia, 11 April, 1763.

Jurors' Names.	Township.	County.	Sacrament, when taken.
MICHAEL SCHLATTER.	Springfield.	Philadelphia.	3 Aug., 1763.
GEORGE ADAM LEOPOLD.	City of Philadelphia.	Philadelphia.	3 Aug., 1763.
BALTHASAR STEINFURT.	City of Philadelphia.	Philadelphia.	3 Aug., 1763.
JOHN ANDREW MYER.	City of Philadelphia.	Philadelphia.	3 Aug., 1763.
JOHN MARTIN ROW.	City of Philadelphia.	Philadelphia.	3 Aug., 1763.
HENRY HENKEY.	City of Philadelphia.	Philadelphia.	3 Aug., 1763.
JOHN TRUCKENMILLER.	City of Philadelphia.	Philadelphia.	3 Aug., 1763.
ARND ROSE.	City of Philadelphia.	Philadelphia.	3 Aug., 1763.
JOHN YAHN.	Newhanover.	Philadelphia.	3 Aug., 1763.
BALTZER FILLER.	Frederick.	Philadelphia.	7 Apr., 1763.
JOHN LAMPARDER.	Northern Liberties.	Philadelphia.	3 Apr., 1763.
GREGORY RITCHEY.	Whitemarsh.	Philadelphia.	3 Apr., 1763.
JOHN KUHN.	City of Philadelphia.	Philadelphia.	3 Apr., 1763.
PETER DRAISS.	City of Philadelphia.	Philadelphia.	7 Apr., 1763.
LEONARD KESLER.	City of Philadelphia.	Philadelphia.	7 Apr., 1763.
JACOB ERANTZ.	City of Philadelphia.	Philadelphia.	3 Apr., 1763.
JOHN REILY.	City of Philadelphia.	Philadelphia.	3 Apr., 1763.
HENRY STIENMETZ.	City of Philadelphia.	Philadelphia.	3 Apr., 1763.
ANDREAS SHWARTZ.	Strasburgh.	York.	4 Apr., 1763.
HENRY WALDER.	Strasburgh.	York.	3 Apr., 1763.
CASPAR GLATTFELDER.	Codorus.	York.	3 Apr., 1763.
JACOB KERN.	York.	York.	3 Apr., 1763.
JOHN HENRY FISHER.	Frankford.	Philadelphia.	3 Apr., 1763.
RUDOLPH NEFF.	Northern Liberties.	Philadelphia.	3 Apr., 1763.
JACOB NEFF.	Oxford.	Philadelphia.	3 Apr., 1763.
MICHAEL KIRMAN.	Northern Liberties.	Philadelphia.	3 Apr., 1763.
JOHN ERNST MANGEN.	Northern Liberties.	Philadelphia.	3 Apr., 1763.
CONRAD LAUDENBOUGH.	York.	York.	3 Apr., 1763.
CHRISTR: LUDWIG.	Philadelphia.	Philadelphia.	3 Apr., 1763.
GEO: PHILIP WEISSMAN.	Philadelphia.	Philadelphia.	3 Apr., 1763.
JOHN DANIEL MAUTY.	Philadelphia.	Philadelphia.	3 Apr., 1763.
PHILIP NAGLE.	Reading.	Berks.	3 Apr., 1763.
ULRICK NODLE.	Reading.	Berks.	3 Apr., 1763.
MICHL: STECKTELL.	Reading.	Berks.	3 Apr., 1763.
JOHN JACOB RHEIN.	Strasburg.	York.	3 Apr., 1763.
JACOB WALTER.	Codorus.	York.	3 Apr., 1763.
MARTIN WALTER.	Northern Liberties.	Philadelphia.	8 Apr., 1763.
JACOB EHRARD.	Northern Liberties.	Philadelphia.	8 Apr., 1763.
ADAM HEISS.	Northern Liberties.	Philadelphia.	8 Apr., 1763.
EBERHARD SMITH.	Weisburg.	Northampton.	31 Mar., 1763.
PHILIP WEIDMAN.	Lynn.	Northampton.	31 Mar., 1763.
FREDERICK FISHELL.	Codorus.	York.	3 Apr., 1763.
PHILIP SHEERMAN.	Lynn.	Northampton.	5 Apr., 1763.
HENRY OSWALD.	Lynn.	Northampton.	5 Apr., 1763.
SIMON PETER SCHOOL.	Lynn.	Northampton.	31 Mar., 1763.
VALENTINE HAGENER.	City of Philadelphia.	Philadelphia.	3 Apr., 1763.
JOHN FREDERICK TEETZ.	City of Philadelphia.	Philadelphia.	3 Apr., 1763.
GEORGE PETER KOCKENDOFFER.	City of Philadelphia.	Philadelphia.	3 Apr., 1763.
LUDWICK SPAMAGLE.	Whitemarsh.	Philadelphia.	3 Apr., 1763.
PHILIP VENUS.	York.	York.	4 April 1763

Jurors' Names.	Township.	County.	Sacrament when taken.
HENRY MAURER.	Lancaster.	Lancaster.	3 Apr., 1763.
BALTHASAR FEDERFAAFF.	Manheim.	Lancaster.	3 Apr., 1763.
PHILIP WEBER.	York.	York.	3 Apr., 1763.
NICHOLAS TIK.	Reading.	Berks.	3 Apr., 1763.
ANDREAS FICKTHORN.	Reading.	Berks.	3 Apr., 1763.
JOHN MAHRIGEN.	Reading.	Berks.	3 Apr., 1763.
CATHRINA KENDEL.	Reading.	Berks.	3 Apr., 1763.
HENRY SPENGLER.	York.	York.	3 Apr., 1763.
PETER TRETT.	Windsor.	York.	3 Apr., 1763.
ADAM POWLUS.	Windsor.	York.	3 Apr., 1763.
JOHN CRONE.	Windsor.	York.	3 Apr., 1763.
MICHAEL POWLUS.	Windsor.	York.	3 Apr., 1763.
WILPERT CAMPER.	Lancaster.	Lancaster.	3 Apr., 1763.
CHRISTR : PECHIN.	City of Philadelphia.	Philadelphia.	3 Apr., 1763.
HENRY RUNG.	Lancaster.	Lancaster.	3 Apr., 1763.
PETER SMIDT.	Heidleburg.	Berks.	3 Apr., 1763.
BERNARD SHERER.	Whitpain.	Philadelphia.	4 Apr., 1763.
VALENTINE SHERER.	Whitpain.	Philadelphia.	4 Apr., 1763.
JACOB RENNER.	Worcester.	Philadelphia.	4 Apr., 1763.
LEONARD SPEAR.	Worcester.	Berks.	3 Apr., 1763.
PHILIP LEISTER.	Rockland.	Bucks.	3 Apr., 1763.
JACOB NONNEMAKER.	Hill Town.	Bucks.	3 Apr., 1763.
NICHOLAS SLIECKTING.	Reading.	Berks.	3 Apr., 1763.
JOHANNES KURTZ.	Reading.	Berks.	3 Apr., 1763.
HENRY HAEFFNER.	Richmond.	Berks.	3 Apr., 1763.
DAVID KAMP.	Richmond.	Berks.	3 Apr., 1763.
MELCHIOR FRITZ.	Richmond.	Berks.	3 Apr., 1763.
MICHL. REIFFSNIEDER.	Dublin.	Philadelphia.	3 Apr., 1763.
JOHN FRY.	Philadelphia.	Philadelphia.	3 Apr., 1763.
PHILIP FILMAN.	Upper Salford.	Philadelphia.	3 Apr., 1763.
LEONARD SHNEIDER.	Upper Salford.	Philadelphia.	3 Apr., 1763.
CHRISTR. GYSER.	Marlborough.	Philadelphia.	3 Apr., 1763.
LEONARD FRUTSHY.	Lower Saucon.	Northampton.	3 Apr., 1763.
HENRY BUMBARGER.	Upper Salford.	Philadelphia.	3 Apr., 1763.
CASPAR HINTERLIETER.	Marlborough.	Philadelphia.	3 Apr., 1763.
MATHIAS HINTERLIETER.	Marlborough.	Philadelphia.	3 Apr., 1763.
JOHN ALT.	Marlborough.	Philadelphia.	3 Apr., 1763.
JEREMIAH ZIMMER.	Brecknock.	Berks.	3 Apr., 1763.
MICHAEL FRANKHAUSER.	Brecknock.	Berks.	3 Apr., 1763.
DANIEL HOFFMAN.	Reading.	Berks.	3 Apr., 1763.
THOMAS DEEM.	Reading.	Berks.	3 Apr., 1763.
JNO. CHRISTR. LEHMAN.	Reading.	Berks.	3 Apr., 1763.
JOHN MICHL. BECKER.	Heidleburg.	Lancaster.	3 Apr., 1763.
WILHELM HOSTER.	Heidleburg.	Lancaster.	3 Apr., 1763.
BALTHASAR DERTER.	Heidleburg.	Lancaster.	3 Apr., 1763.
JACOB ROSSELL.	Tulpohoccon.	Berks.	3 Apr., 1763.
JACOB MILLER.	Tulpohoccon.	Berks.	3 Apr., 1763.
PETER LIESS.	Tulpohoccon.	Berks.	3 Apr., 1763.
JOHAN HESS.	Tulpohoccon.	Berks.	3 Apr., 1763.
HENRY KRIMLER.	Reading.	Berks.	3 Apr., 1763.
JOHANNES SASSAMANHAUSE.	Greenwich.	Berks.	3 Apr., 1763.
PETER GRIENWALD.	Richmond.	Berks.	3 Apr., 1763.
HENRY ARDELLE.	Richmond.	Berks.	3 Apr., 1763.
GEORGE KREEMER.	Greenwich.	Berks.	31 Mar., 1763.

PENNSYLVANIA.

Jurors' Names.	Township.	County.	Sacrament when taken.
JACOB LEWEGOOD.	Tulpohoccon.	Berks.	3 April 1763.
GODFRIED KIRKER.	Heidleburgh.	Berks.	3 Apr., 1763.
JOHN GEORGE OTT.	Bristol.	Bucks.	3 Apr., 1763.
JNO. PAUL BOOSSE.	Bristol.	Bucks.	3 Apr., 1763.
WILLIAM ALBERT.	Salisbury.	Northampton.	3 Apr., 1763.
HENRICK ECHARD.	Reading.	Berks.	3 Apr., 1763.
JACOB FISCHER.	Reading.	Berks.	3 Apr., 1763.
NICHS. FIERSTONE.	Paradice.	York.	3 Apr., 1763.
ANDREW FREDERICK.	Paradice.	York.	3 Apr., 1763.
PETER FLICK.	Heidleburg.	Berks.	13 Feb., 1763.
PAUL CRUSS.	Frederick.	Frederick County in Maryland.	3 Apr., 1763.
SEBASTIAN TRUCKENMILLER.	Upper Milford.	Northampton.	4 Apr., 1763.
MATHEW LANDENBERGER.	City of Philadelphia.	Philadelphia.	11 Apr., 1763.
JOHN NICHOLAS STRASSER.	Albany.	Berks.	11 Apr., 1763.
PETER KRUGER.	Tulpohoccon.	Berks.	3 Apr., 1763.
HILARIUS BEKER.	Germantown.	Philadelphia.	11 Apr., 1763.
MATTHIAS SMITH.	Upper Dublin.	Philadelphia.	11 Apr., 1763.
FREDERICK KNAPP.	Springfield.	Philadelphia.	11 Apr., 1763.
JOHN UNRUH.	Bristol.	Philadelphia.	3 Apr., 1763.
FREDERICK KAMMERER.	Maccungy.	Northampton.	27 Mar., 1763.
JACOB KUNS.	Springfield.	Philadelphia.	3 Apr., 1763.
FELIX DUTWYLER.	Springfield.	Philadelphia.	3 Apr., 1763.
ABRAHAM WAKERLEY.	Springfield.	Philadelphia.	3 Apr., 1763.
ANDREW HIGHBERGER.	Springfield.	Philadelphia.	3 Apr., 1763.
ADAM HOFFMAN.	North Wales.	Philadelphia.	10 Apr., 1763.
HENRY CRESS.	Germantown.	Philadelphia.	3 Apr., 1763.
JOHN GOTTFRIED TEELE.	Northern Liberties.	Philadelphia.	3 Apr., 1763.
CHARLES WITTERHOLD.	Germantown.	Philadelphia.	3 Apr., 1763.
FREDERICK BECKING.	Lower Merion.	Philadelphia.	3 Apr., 1763.
PETER STIREWALT.	Northern Liberties.	Philadelphia.	3 Apr., 1763.
ANDREW ERDMAN LEINAU.	Philadelphia.	Philadelphia.	3 Apr., 1763.
MEYER JOSEPHSON.	Reading.	Berks.	A Jew.
LYON NATHAN.	Reading.	Berks.	A Jew.
BARNARD GRATS.	Philadelphia.	Philadelphia.	A Jew.
ISAAC LEVY.	Philadelphia.	Philadelphia.	A Jew.

Quakers and other Protestants who scruple to take an Oath.

Affirmers' Names.	Township.	County.	If Moravians, their time of taking the Sacrament.
JACOB LONGACRE.	Coventry.	Chester.	
SUSANNAH LONGACRE.	Coventry.	Chester.	
ANNA ANDREWS.	Towamensing.	Philadelphia.	
SIMBRIGHT HELSELL.	Langenhose.	Frederick County in Maryland.	
FREDERICK SHOLEBERGER.	Greenwich.	Berks.	
GEORGE RICHWIND.	Upper Dublin.	Philadelphia.	
FREDERICK SALLADY.	Earl.	Lancaster.	
VALENTINE SHAMBACK.	New Providence.	Philadelphia.	
WILLIAM BUSLER.	Windsor.	Berks.	
PHILIP SURFACE.	Philadelphia.	Philadelphia.	
JOHN IZYLE.	Lancaster.	Lancaster.	
JOHN BAKER.	Plymouth.	Lancaster.	

Affirmers' Names.	Township.	County.	If Moravians, their time of taking the Sacrament
SIMON HELLER.	Lower Saucon.	Northampton.	
DANIEL HELLER.	Lower Saucon.	Northampton.	
LUDWICK HELLER.	Lower Saucon.	Northampton.	
HENRY MILLER.	Mount Bethel.	Northampton.	
ADAM EVEY.	Philadelphia.	Philadelphia.	
GEORGE MARTIN.	Charlestown.	Chester.	
JOHN ELLICK.	City of Philadelphia.	Philadelphia.	
STEPHEN GOODMAN.	Lower Merrion.	Philadelphia.	
CHRISTR. MASON.	Whitemarsh.	Philadelphia.	
CHARLES HAY.	Bristol.	Philadelphia.	
JOHN STYER.	Hunterdon.	In New Jersey.	
JOHN SPORE.	Lancaster.	Lancaster.	1 Apr., 1763.

Certified by JOSEPH SHIPPEN, Jr., Secretary.
Philadelphia, 16 Nov., 1763.

Y. 6.   C.O. 5. 1277.

(Supreme Court at Philadelphia, 24 September, 1763.)

Foreigners' Names.	Township.	County.	Sacrament, when taken.
PHILIP HALL.	Philadelphia.	Philadelphia.	18 Sept., 1763.
JACOB LOOSS.	Windsor.	Berks.	11 Sept., 1763.
CHRISTIAN STEAR.	Upper Milford.	Bucks.	18 Sept., 1763.
BALTHAZER KLEBER.	Reading.	Berks.	18 Sept., 1763.
JACOB FRY.	Brecknock.	Berks.	11 Sept., 1763.
JACOB CROWL.	Reading.	Berks.	18 Sept., 1763.
JNO. GEORGE WEENDER.	Reading.	Berks.	18 Sept., 1763.
JOHN GEETZ.	Philadelphia.	Philadelphia.	22 Sept., 1763.
DAVID SHAEFER.	Strewsbury.	York.	18 Sept., 1763.
CHARLES DEHL.	Strewsbury.	York.	18 Sept., 1763.
JOHN MEYER.	Strewsbury.	York.	18 Sept., 1763.
NICHOLAS SCHOUSTER.	Strewsbury.	York.	11 Sept., 1763.
HENRY EBERHARD.	Manchester.	York.	23 Sept., 1763.
ANTHONY WOLF.	Manchester.	York.	21 Aug., 1763.
JACOB RENO.	Philadelphia.	Philadelphia.	18 Sept., 1763.
ANDREW WEIDER.	Manchester.	York.	21 Aug., 1763.
MICHAEL ZEH.	Philadelphia.	Philadelphia.	18 Sept., 1763.
PHILIP GENTLER.	York.	York.	21 Aug., 1763.
ERASMUS HOTZAPFEL.	Manchester.	York.	21 Aug., 1763.
MARTIN HARRY.	Manchester.	York.	21 Aug., 1763.
GEORGE LIEWENSTIEN.	Manchester.	York.	21 Aug., 1763.
VALENTINE HAMME.	Paradise.	York.	21 Aug., 1763.
PHILIP LAU.	Manchester.	York.	4 Sept., 1763.
TOBIAS PLIGER.	Lancaster.	Lancaster.	4 Sept., 1763.
JOSEPH LONG.	Lancaster.	Lancaster.	4 Sept., 1763.
JOHN BROWN.	Lancaster.	Lancaster.	4 Sept., 1763.
PHILIP OHLEWEYLER.	Manor.	Lancaster.	4 Sept., 1763.
ANDREW HEIMS.	Philadelphia.	Philadelphia.	18 Sept., 1763.
JNO. GEORGE HEUSUNG.	Brecknock.	Berks.	22 Sept., 1763.
CONRAD STENGER.	Rockhill.	Bucks.	23 Sept., 1763.
LEONARD MILLER.	Marlborough.	Philadelphia.	20 Sept., 1763.
JOHN RUPP.	Philadelphia.	Philadelphia.	23 Sept., 1763.
JACOB BERNHARD.	Limerick.	Philadelphia.	22 Sept., 1763.
YODOCUS DOBELER.	Lancaster.	Lancaster.	4 Sept., 1763.

PENNSYLVANIA.

Foreigners' Names.	Township.	County.	Sacrament when taken.
MICHAEL FREDERICK.	Douglas.	Philadelphia.	21 Aug., 1763.
MICHAEL WEIDMAN.	Douglas.	Philadelphia.	21 Aug., 1763.
ARNDT KURTZ.	Limerick.	Philadelphia.	21 Aug., 1763.
THEOBALD SHALLUS.	Mountpleasant.	York.	4 Sept., 1763.
JOHN HOFFMAN.	Lancaster.	Lancaster.	28 Aug., 1763.
PETER ISH.	Lancaster.	Lancaster.	28 Aug., 1763.
ABRAHAM LE ROY.	Lancaster.	Lancaster.	28 Aug., 1763.
JOHN PETER LE ROY.	Lancaster.	Lancaster.	28 Aug., 1763.
JOHN SHRIET.	Cumru.	Berks.	11 Sept., 1763.
MICHAEL BELTZ.	Lebanon.	Lancaster.	14 Aug., 1763.
PHILIP WONSIDLER.	Lower Milford.	Bucks.	14 Aug., 1763.
NICHOLAS HAINE.	Cocolico.	Lancaster.	11 Sept., 1763.
PHILIP JACOB FOCSIG.	Reading.	Berks.	11 Sept., 1763.
CASPER PFISTER.	Lampeter.	Lancaster.	19 Aug., 1763.
MICHAEL KURTZ.	Newhanover.	Philadelphia.	21 Aug., 1763.
PETER GABEL.	Newhanover.	Philadelphia.	21 Aug., 1763.
JOHN MECKLIEN.	Newhanover.	Philadelphia.	21 Aug., 1763.
CHRISTIAN REYNER.	Upper Milford.	Northampton.	14 Aug., 1763.
JACOB SEECHER.	Upper Milford.	Northampton.	14 Aug., 1763.
JACOB WALTER.	Tulpehoccon.	Berks.	17 July, 1763.
PHILIP ZEIGLER.	Upper Salford.	Philadelphia.	18 Sept., 1763.
SOLOMON RUCKSTOOL.	Upper Salford.	Philadelphia.	11 Sept., 1763.
JOHN FAUST.	Upper Salford.	Philadelphia.	11 Sept., 1763.
ULRICK HERTZELL.	Upper Salford.	Philadelphia.	11 Sept., 1763.
PHILIP STAUG.	Lower Salford.	Philadelphia.	11 Sept., 1763.
GEORGE FREDERICK.	Earl.	Lancaster.	14 Sept., 1763.
FREDERICK LEESER.	Cocolico.	Lancaster.	21 Aug., 1763.
FREDERICK KOELER.	Worcester.	Philadelphia.	21 Aug., 1763.
PETER KROWT.	Worcester.	Philadelphia.	21 Aug., 1763.
PETER PECHIN.	Haverford.	Chester.	25 Aug., 1763.
NICHOLAS GODSCHALL.	Greenwich.	Berks.	4 Sept., 1763.
CONRAD FLECK.	Northern Liberties.	Philadelphia.	4 Sept., 1763.
FREDERICK GROH.	Lower Merion.	Philadelphia.	11 Sept., 1763.
HENRY SCHMIDT, Senr.	Frederick.	Philadelphia.	24 Sept., 1763.
HENRY SCHMIDT, Junr.	Upper Hanover.	Philadelphia.	24 Sept., 1763.
JACOB DUERR.	Upper Hanover.	Philadelphia.	24 Sept., 1763.
JOHN BELTZ.	Passyunk.	Philadelphia.	23 Sept., 1763.

Quakers and others who scruple to take an Oath.

Foreigners' Names.	Township.	County.	Moravians Sacrament when taken
JULIUS BROOKHART.	Helm.	York.	
GEORGE PEARSHLER.	Oley.	Berks.	
JACOB SALBACK.	Berwick.	York.	
HENRY WEALER.	Paradise.	York.	
HENRY FRANK.	Berwick.	Lancaster.	
PETER OVERSHIELD.	Kingwood.	West New Jersey.	
VALENTINE FRY.	Heidleberg.	Berks.	11 Sept., 1763.
CHRISTIAN STOVER.	Lampeter.	Lancaster.	
JACOB CUMERAH.	Maxatawny.	Berks.	
CONRAD VANDERWEIT.	Northern Liberties.	Philadelphia.	
ANDREW PAUL.	Limerick.	Philadelphia.	

Foreigners' Names.	Township.	County.	Moravian. Sacrament when taken.
JOSEPH PIFFER.	Springfield.	Philadelphia.	
JACOB CARTER.	Springfield.	Philadelphia.	
MARTIN BINDER.	York.	York.	
ANDREW WEIBERICK.	Lancaster.	Lancaster.	3 Sept., 1763.
JNO. ROADERMILL.	Richmond.	Berks.	
JACOB HOOBLER.	Blanfeild.	Northampton.	
PHILIP HELZELL.	Philadelphia.	Philadelphia.	

Certified by JOSEPH SHIPPEN, Jr., Secretary.
Philadelphia, 20 July, 1764.

Y. 6. (Supreme Court at Philadelphia, 10 and 23 April, 1764.)

Foreigners' Names.	Township.	County.	Sacrament, when taken.
CONRAD MAAG.	Philadelphia.	Philadelphia.	Apr. 6, 1764.
JACOB KEISER.	Philadelphia.	Philadelphia.	Apr. 6, 1764.
GEORGE DAVID SIEKEL.	Philadelphia.	Philadelphia.	Mar. 11, 1764.
JOHN GEORGE REES.	Philadelphia.	Philadelphia.	Mar. 11, 1764.
GEORGE WALKER.	Philadelphia.	Philadelphia.	Mar. 11, 1764.
JACOB LYDIE.	Codorus.	York.	Apr. 4, 1764.
ULRICK HESS.	Strasburg.	York.	Apr. 4, 1764.
MARTIN FRY.	Strasburg.	York.	Mar. 25, 1764.
GERRARD STEIGLER.	Strasburg.	York.	Mar. 25, 1764.
MATHIAS ALBER.	Cocolico.	York.	Mar. 25, 1764.
ABRAHAM STONE.	Cocolico.	York.	Mar. 25, 1764.
NICHOLAS HOFFMAN.	Dover.	York.	Apr. 1, 1764.
GEORGE STOWGH.	Dover.	York.	Apr. 1, 1764.
FREDERICK STOWGH.	Dover.	York.	Apr. 1, 1764.
ADAM DEEL.	Dover.	York.	Apr. 1, 1764.
GEORGE DEEL.	Dover.	York.	Apr. 1, 1764.
GEORGE HERHOLD.	Heidelberg.	Berks.	Apr. 6, 1764.
JACOB ERB.	Heidelberg.	Berks.	Apr. 6, 1764.
MARY ERB.	Heidelberg.	Berks.	Apr. 6, 1764.
CHRISTIAN VOGHT.	Lancaster.	Lancaster.	Apr. 1, 1764.
NICHS. TORSBERG.	Philadelphia.	Philadelphia.	Mar. 11, 1764.
FREDERICK KUHN.	York.	York.	Apr. 1, 1764.
MICHAEL BOWSMAN.	Lancaster.	Lancaster.	Apr. 5, 1764.
JACOB TASHT.	Marlborough.	Philadelphia.	Mar. 23, 1764.
JOHN ADAM HILLIGAS.	Upper Hanover.	Philadelphia.	Mar. 25, 1764.
KILLIAN DEBBINGER.	Roseborough.	York.	Apr. 4, 1764.
JOHN MICHL. PIPER.	Philadelphia.	Philadelphia.	Mar. 11, 1764.
JACOB FUCKEROOT.	Oxford.	Philadelphia.	Mar. 11, 1764.
BENEDICT KEBNER.	Bern.	Berks.	Feb. 26, 1764.
FREDERICK REEMER.	Codorus.	York.	Apr. 4, 1764.
JOHN JACOB VOGHT.	Paradice.	York.	Apr. 11, 1764
HENRY BOLLINGER.	Long Swamp.	Berks.	Apr. 8, 1764.
PETER SWARTZ.	Philadelphia.	Philadelphia.	Apr. 11, 1764.
ADAM ERBEN.	Philadelphia.	Philadelphia.	Apr. 8, 1764.
JACOB HUBER.	Rockhill.	Bucks.	Apr. 1, 1764.
CONRAD KOTHER.	Hilltown.	Bucks.	Apr. 8, 1764.
FELIX LEY.	Rockhill.	Bucks.	Apr. 1, 1764.
CASPAR NAGLEE.	Bedminster.	Bucks.	Apr. 1, 1764.
CHRISTR. RICKOTINE.	Maiden Creek.	Berks.	Mar. 29, 1764.
GEORGE DESCH.	Haycock.	Bucks.	Apr. 8, 1764.
MICHAEL YOST.	Bedminster.	Bucks.	Apr. 8, 1764.

PENNSYLVANIA.

Foreigners' Names.	Township.	County.	Sacrament when taken.
VALENTINE REINTZELL.	Tulpehoccon.	Berks.	Apr. 1, 1764.
CHARLES HEI.	Tulpehoccon.	Berks.	Apr. 1, 1764.
GEORGE BOLTZ.	Tulpehoccon.	Berks.	Apr. 1, 1764.
MICHAEL FAUCKS.	Philadelphia.	Philadelphia.	Mar. 11, 1764.
NICHOLAS JACOB.	Philadelphia.	Philadelphia.	Mar. 11, 1764.
JACOB MEENICH.	Bethel.	Berks.	Apr. 1, 1764.
PHILIP DRESCHER.	Maccungy.	Northampton.	Mar. 25, 1764.
JACOB WAGNER.	Maccungy.	Northampton.	Mar. 25, 1764.
DETRICK YOUMER.	Maccungy.	Northampton.	Mar. 25, 1764.
MATHEW LUDWICK.	Maccungy.	Northampton.	Mar. 25, 1764.
JOHN SCHAFFER.	Amwell Hunterdon.	West New Jersey.	Mar. 25, 1764.
PAUL MOSER.	New Hanover.	Philadelphia.	Apr. 8, 1764.
ANDREAS YEAGER.	New Hanover.	Philadelphia.	Apr. 8, 1764.
PHILIP ALBERT.	Hempfield.	Lancaster.	Mar. 4, 1764.
JOHN GEORGE LOWNESS.	Cusshahoppen.	Bucks.	Apr. 6, 1764.
LEONARD GENNEVINE.	Manheim.	York.	Apr. 10, 1764.
CONRAD KEEFABER.	Manheim.	York.	Apr. 10, 1764.
BASTIAN MOSER.	Hanover.	Philadelphia.	Apr. 10, 1764.
FREDERICK SHOEMAKER.	Upper Milford.	Northampton.	Apr. 2, 1764.
ADAM SHOEMAKER.	Upper Milford.	Northampton.	Apr. 2, 1764.
JOHN PETER MILLER.	Upper Milford.	Northampton.	Apr. 3, 1764.
JNO. RAUNFAUNER.	Rockland.	Berks.	Apr. 8, 1764.
GEO. FUCKRODT.	Oxford.	Philadelphia.	Mar. 11, 1764.
BENJ. LESLEY.	Brecknock.	Lancaster.	Mar. 18, 1764.
JNO. PHILIP DEHAAS.	Philadelphia.	Philadelphia.	Apr. 22, 1764.
MYER HART.	Easton.	Northampton.	A Jew.

Quakers and other Protestants who scruple to take an Oath.

Foreigners' Names.	Township.	County.	Sacrament, when taken by Moravians.
ISAAC STOHLER.	Manchester.	York.	
MARTIN MYER.	Strasburg.	York.	
GEORGE CONRAD.	Paradise.	York.	
JACOB STIGLIMAN.	Lancaster.	Lancaster.	Feb. 25, 1764.
JNO. CONRAD KNIGHT.	Canewaga.	York.	
GEORGE MEINTZER.	Robeson.	Berks.	
JOHN MUSCH.	Easton.	Northampton.	
MICHAEL BURKEY.	York.	York.	
JACOB HELM.	Providence.	Philadelphia.	
JNO. HARTMAN HAAS.	Providence.	Philadelphia.	
JOHN BEHM.	North Wales.	Philadelphia.	
HENRY SEITENBENDER.	Cumru.	Berks.	
DANIEL BUSSART.	Cumru.	Berks.	
DAVID ZEISBERGER.	Bethlehem.	Northampton.	Apr. 9, 1764.
JNO. JACOB SCHMICK.	Bethlehem.	Northampton.	Mar. 24, 1764.
ANDREW HORN.	Warwick.	Lancaster.	Mar. 17, 1764.
JOHN CLINE.	Warwick.	Lancaster.	
CASPAR STRAAB.	Alsase.	Berks.	
JACOB PLILER.	Alsase.	Berks.	
HERMAN MILLER.	York.	York.	
NICHOLAS HAZLEBACK.	Germantown.	Philadelphia.	
DANIEL KLIEST.	Bethlehem.	Northampton.	Mar. 10, 1764.

Foreigners' Names.	Township.	County.	Sacrament when taken by Moravian.
JNO. ADAM HORSFIELD.	Bethlehem.	Northampton.	
HERMAN TITIAR.	Reading.	Yorks.	
DANIEL PFEIFFER.	Amwell.	Hunterdon in West New Jersey.	
PETER MIERS.	Amwell.	Hunterdon in West New Jersey.	
PHILIP PETER SCHOLL.	Maxatawny.	Berks.	
CHRISTR. LOWBOUGHER.	Amwell.	Hunterdon in West New Jersey.	
BARNARD WINTRINGER.	Hilltown.	Bucks.	
DANIEL PRICE.	Darby.	Philadelphia.	
SAMUEL KOFFMAN.	Lower Milford.	Bucks.	
WILLIAM LONG.	New Providence.	Philadelphia.	
ANTHONY STEIMER.	Germantown.	Philadelphia.	
PHILIP SCHNEIDER.	Lower Saucon.	Northampton.	

Certified by JOSEPH SHIPPEN, Jr., Secretary.

Philadelphia, 20 July, 1764.

Y. 8.

Supreme Court at Philadelphia, 24 and 25 Sept., 1764.

Foreigners' Names.	Township.	County.	Sacrament, when taken
JOHN FRITZ.	Southwark.	Philadelphia.	Sept. 9, 1764.
MICHAEL HETZELL.	Northern Liberties.	Philadelphia.	Sept. 9, 1764.
CHRISTIAN BICK.	Philadelphia.	Philadelphia.	Sept. 9, 1764.
JACOB FRELICK.	Lancaster.	Lancaster.	Aug. 5, 1764.
JACOB BOYTHYMAN.	Northern Liberties.	Philadelphia.	Sept. 9, 1764.
JACOB WIRKING.	Philadelphia.	Philadelphia.	Sept. 9, 1764.
GEORGE KEMMELL.	Lancaster.	Lancaster.	Sept. 2, 1764.
FRANCIS PETER LOHRENS.	Lancaster.	Lancaster.	Aug. 5, 1764.
GEORGE GERLACH.	Lancaster.	Lancaster.	Aug. 5, 1764.
JOHN KEHLER.	Lancaster.	Lancaster.	Aug. 5, 1764.
ANDREW PERTSCH.	Philadelphia.	Philadelphia.	Sept. 9, 1764.
GEORGE KNAIRR.	Philadelphia.	Philadelphia.	Sept. 9, 1764.
JOHN NEXLEY.	Philadelphia.	Philadelphia.	Sept. 9, 1764.
GEORGE AACHE.	Cocolico.	Lancaster.	Sept. 20, 1764.
HENRY AACHE.	Cocolico.	Lancaster.	Sept. 15, 1764.
MICHAEL KISSINGER.	Cocolico.	Lancaster.	Sept. 9, 1764.
JACOB GREINER.	Philadelphia.	Philadelphia.	Sept. 9, 1764.
DAVID ETELIN.	Paxton.	Lancaster.	July 22, 1764.
MELCHIOR GYSERT.	Paxton.	Lancaster.	July 22, 1764.
JACOB FRANK.	Germantown.	Philadelphia.	Sept. 8, 1764.
FREDERICK SINSEL.	Oley.	Berks.	Aug. 23, 1764.
CHAS. FRED. WILDBAHNE.	Heidleberg.	York.	Sept. 18, 1764.
DANIEL SHNEYDER.	Bethel.	Berks.	Aug. 12, 1764.
ADAM KRIERCHBAUM.	Tulpehoccon.	Berks.	Aug. 12, 1764.
SEBASTIAN BROSIUS.	Tulpehoccon.	Berks.	Aug. 12, 1764.
ABRAHAM SCHNEIDER.	Tulpehoccon.	Berks.	Aug. 12, 1764.
PETER KRIETZER.	Tulpehoccon.	Berks.	Aug. 12, 1764.
NICHOLAS GIBHARD.	Bethel.	Berks.	Aug. 12, 1764.
FREDERICK HOFFMAN.	Tulpehocken.	Berks.	Aug. 12, 1764.
HENRY HOLTZMAN.	Tulpehocken.	Berks.	Aug. 12, 1764.
GEORGE WIEKHART.	Tulpehocken.	Berks.	Aug. 12, 1764.
PETER MENGE.	Heidleberg.	Lancaster.	Sept. 23, 1764.

PENNSYLVANIA.

Foreigners' Names.	Township.	County.	Sacrament when taken.
JOHN LAHN.	Heidleberg.	Lancaster.	Sept. 23, 1764.
ADAM MENGS.	Lebanon.	Lancaster.	Sept. 23, 1764.
FRANCIS SMITH.	Heidleberg.	Lancaster.	Sept. 23, 1764.
GEORGE ULRICH.	Heidleberg.	Lancaster.	Aug. 12, 1764.
JACOB FOTLER.	Heidleberg.	Lancaster.	Aug. 12, 1764.
JOHN MOYER.	Douglass.	Philadelphia.	Sept. 21, 1764.
JOHN TZOLLER.	Hanover.	Philadelphia.	Sept. 21, 1764.
GEORGE ADAM EGOLD.	Hanover.	Philadelphia.	Sept. 21, 1764.
MARTIN DOGGENBACK.	Hanover.	Philadelphia.	Sept. 23, 1764.
JOHN SCHAINER.	Douglass.	Philadelphia.	Sept. 23, 1764.
PHILIP WIRTH.	Union.	Berks.	Sept. 23, 1764.
JACOB BECK.	Cocolico.	Lancaster.	Sept. 2, 1764.
JACOB BYLESTINE.	Bart.	Lancaster.	Sept. 3, 1764.
PAUL FAIGER.	Plymouth.	Philadelphia.	Sept. 23, 1764.
WILHELM HILDNER.	Whitemarsh.	Philadelphia.	Sept. 23, 1764.
ANTHONY RITZ.	York.	York.	Aug. 27, 1764.
GEORGE EISENHARD.	York.	York.	Aug. 27, 1764.
PETER POPP.	Brecknock.	Lancaster.	Sept. 9, 1764.
CONRAD POPP.	Brecknock.	Lancaster.	Sept. 9, 1764.
CASPAR DEAL.	Carnarvon.	Lancaster.	Sept. 9, 1764.
HENRY SIECTNIST.	Rapho.	Lancaster.	Aug. 5, 1764.
ADAM PARTMESS.	Dover.	York.	Sept. 16, 1764.
JACOB WIEST.	Oley.	Berks.	Sept. 23, 1764.
JACOB NAGLE.	Oley.	Berks.	Aug. 29, 1764.
JOHN JORDAN.	Oley.	Berks.	Aug. 29, 1764.
HENRY KREYER.	Abington.	Philadelphia.	Sept. 23, 1764.
LUDWICK SPIES.	Dover.	York.	Aug. 12, 1764.
JACOB HOUK.	Frederick.	Philadelphia.	Sept. 23, 1764.
PETER HOLLEBUSH.	Frederick.	Philadelphia.	Sept. 23, 1764.
CHRISTIAN HOLLEBUSH.	Frederick.	Philadelphia.	Sept. 23, 1764.
FREDERICK MAY.	Upper Salford.	Philadelphia.	Sept. 23, 1764.
JOHN ZOLLER.	Upper Hanover.	Philadelphia.	Sept. 23, 1764.
PHILIP ROWK.	Upper Hanover.	Philadelphia.	Sept. 23, 1764.
GEORGE LETHER.	Passyunk.	Philadelphia.	Sept. 9, 1764.
GOTLIEB KRIESENGER.	Germantown.	Philadelphia.	Sept. 23, 1764.
CONRAD SCHUTZ.	Upper Hanover.	Philadelphia.	Sept. 16, 1764.
ADAM STAIGER.	Lebanon.	Lancaster.	Aug. 29, 1764.
MARTIN ELIE.	Lebanon.	Lancaster.	Aug. 26, 1764.
JOHN METZLER.	Germantown.	Philadelphia.	Sept. 9, 1764.
MARTIN OBERLIN.	Bethel.	Lancaster.	Aug. 26, 1764.
SEBASTIAN NAGLE.	Bethel.	Lancaster.	Aug. 26, 1764.
FREDERICK HUBLEY.	Lancaster.	Lancaster.	Sept. 2, 1764.
RHINEHART KAHMER.	Philadelphia.	Philadelphia.	Sept. 23, 1764.
MANUS WEBER.	Rockland.	Bucks.	Aug. 20, 1764.
JACOB DENTZELLER.	Rockland.	Bucks.	Aug. 2, 1764.
JOHN MANGEN.	Philadelphia.	Philadelphia.	Sept. 9, 1764.
CHRISTOPHER KNOWER.	East Nantmell.	Chester.	July 15, 1764.
BURKHARD BECKTEL.	East Nantmell.	Chester.	July 11, 1764.
FREDERICK SHENKEL.	Philadelphia.	Philadelphia.	Sept. 23, 1764.
MATTHIAS GEBLER.	Passyunk.	Philadelphia.	Sept. 23, 1764.
GEORGE WECK.	Philadelphia.	Philadelphia.	Sept. 23, 1764.
GODFRIED LEHR.	Passyunk.	Philadelphia.	Sept. 23, 1764.
JOHN ERNST HAYSER.	Philadelphia.	Philadelphia.	Sept. 23, 1764.

Foreigners' Names.	Township.	County.	Sacrament when taken.
GEORGE JUSTUS.	Philadelphia.	Philadelphia.	Sept. 23, 1764.
WILLIAM FOX.	Philadelphia.	Philadelphia.	Sept. 23, 1764.
HENRY RHINEHART.	Philadelphia.	Philadelphia.	Sept. 23, 1764.
HENRY GAMPER.	Blockley.	Philadelphia.	Sept. 23, 1764.
GEORGE PLUM.	Philadelphia.	Philadelphia.	Sept. 23, 1764.
WILLIAM MILLER.	Philadelphia.	Philadelphia.	Sept. 23, 1764.
MICHL. WIEN.	Philadelphia.	Philadelphia.	Sept. 23, 1764.
JOHN STROOP.	Philadelphia.	Philadelphia.	Sept. 23, 1764.
GEORGE MERKELL.	Richmond.	Berks.	Sept. 20, 1764.
GODFRIED TOWENHOWER.	Coventry.	Chester.	Sept. 23, 1764.
MICHL. MILDEBERGER.	Philadelphia.	Philadelphia.	Sept. 9, 1764.
JACOB KUTCH.	Passyunk.	Philadelphia.	Sept. 9, 1764.
DANL. DINCKLE.	York.	York.	Sept. 23, 1764.
JOHN GARDNER.	Germantown.	Philadelphia.	Sept. 23, 1764.
MATHIAS HEISS.	Cheltenham.	Philadelphia.	Sept. 23, 1764.
BALTHAZAR ERNST.	Cheltenham.	Philadelphia.	Sept. 23, 1764.
CHRISTR. WEIGLE.	Douglass.	Berks.	Sept. 24, 1764.
JACOB BARE.	Philadelphia.	Philadelphia.	Sept. 23, 1764.
BERNHARD ROOPE.	Philadelphia.	Philadelphia.	Sept. 23, 1764.
MATTHEW WALTER.	Marlborough.	Philadelphia.	Sept. 16, 1764.
WILLIAM BAUCCUS.	Northern Liberties.	Philadelphia.	Sept. 23, 1764.
JNO. RUDOLPH KOHLER.	Northern Liberties.	Philadelphia.	Sept. 23, 1764.
JNO. RITENAUER.	Tulpehocken.	Berks.	Sept. 12, 1764.
THOMAS MEYER.	Philadelphia.	Philadelphia.	Sept. 9, 1764.
CASPAR GLOCKNER.	Passyunk.	Philadelphia.	Sept. 23, 1764.
PHILIP KLUMBERG.	Philadelphia.	Philadelphia.	Sept. 23, 1764.
GEORGE LOSH.	Northern Liberties.	Philadelphia.	Sept. 24, 1764.
ADAM HAAS.	Germantown.	Philadelphia.	Sept. 24, 1764.
DAVID HEIM.	Northern Liberties.	Philadelphia.	Sept. 24, 1764.
JACOB MITSHED.	Northern Liberties.	Philadelphia.	Sept. 23, 1764.
NICHOLAS HAUER.	Lancaster.	Lancaster.	Aug. 5, 1764.
JACOB HILDEBRAND.	Lancaster.	Lancaster.	Aug. 20, 1764.
CHARLES KLUG.	Lancaster.	Lancaster.	Aug. 20, 1764.
GEORGE SCHEFFER.	Germantown.	Philadelphia.	Sept. 16, 1764.
NICHOLAS RITENAUER.	Lancaster.	Lancaster.	Aug. 5, 1764.
QUIRINUS MORNER.	Brecknock.	Lancaster.	Sept. 24, 1764.
DIETRICK REES.	Philadelphia.	Philadelphia.	Sept. 9, 1764.
JUSTUS DRIBER.	Lancaster.	Lancaster.	Aug. 5, 1764.
JOHN BECK.	Lancaster.	Lancaster.	Sept. 23, 1764.
CHRISTIAN RITZ.	Lancaster.	Lancaster.	Sept. 23, 1764.
JNO. HENRY SMITH.	Tulpehocken.	Berks.	Sept. 24, 1764.
LEWIS HESS.	Philadelphia.	Philadelphia.	Sept. 23, 1764.
HENRY SMITH.	Philadelphia.	Philadelphia.	Sent. 23, 1764.
JACOB DAUBENDISTEIL.	Philadelphia.	Philadelphia.	Sept. 23, 1764.
MARTIN WORN.	Philadelphia.	Philadelphia.	Sept. 23, 1764.
JOHN GERLACH.	Philadelphia.	Philadelphia.	Sept. 23, 1764.
MATTHEW KERN.	Cushehoppen.	Philadelphia.	Sept. 2? 1764.
BALTHAZAR SMIDT.	Philadelphia.	Philadelphia.	Sept. 23, 1764.
CHRISTIAN MINCKE.	Southwark.	Philadelphia.	Sept. 23, 1764.
GEORGE DOCTOR.	Upper Salford.	Philadelphia.	Sept. 23, 1764.
GEORGE SCHANCK.	Lancaster.	Lancaster.	Sept. 8, 1764.
PHILIP ULRICH.	Blockley.	Philadelphia.	Sept. 23, 1764.
CHRISTIAN DIETRICK.	Philadelphia.	Philadelphia.	Sept. 9, 1764.
ANDREW BOWSHARD.	Philadelphia.	Philadelphia.	Sept. 9, 1764.

PENNSYLVANIA.

Foreigners' Names.	Township.	County.	Sacrament when taken.
CASPER GYER.	Philadelphia.	Philadelphia.	Sept. 23, 1764.
FREDERICK SCHREYER.	Philadelphia.	Philadelphia.	Sept. 23, 1764.
EVA CATHERINA SCHLISHTERN.	Philadelphia.	Philadelphia.	Sept. 9, 1764.
CONRAD SCHNEIDER.	Philadelphia.	Philadelphia.	Sept. 23, 1764.
MOSES MORDECAI.	Philadelphia.	Philadelphia.	A Jew.

Quakers and other Protestants who scruple to take an Oath.

Foreigners' Names.	Township.	County.	Moravians Sacrament, when taken.
MATTHEW REEZER.	Lancaster.	Lancaster.	Sept. 8, 1764.
JACOB BROWN.	Philadelphia.	Philadelphia.	
GEORGE SHEPPARD.	Philadelphia.	Philadelphia.	
DAVID SULDRICK.	Lower Merrion.	Philadelphia.	
PETER MAY.	Upper Hanover.	Philadelphia.	
GEORGE ROUDERBUSH.	Upper Hanover.	Philadelphia.	
JESSE GREYGER.	Merrion.	Philadelphia.	
PHILIP KOUSE.	Oley.	Berks.	
JOHN TAYMOOT.	Lower Milford.	Bucks.	
MICHL. HOGBERR.	Upper Hanover.	Philadelphia.	
JOHN BUSSINBERGER.	Amwell.	Hunterdon in New Jersey.	
JACOB HOUSER.	Earl.	Lancaster.	
JOHN KROSSER.	Northern Liberties.	Philadelphia.	
ABRAHAM GROVE.	Earl.	Lancaster.	
JOSEPH SMITH.	Greenwich.	Sussex in New Jersey.	
MICHL. DOWDLE.	York.	York.	
LODWIC STONE.	Lancaster.	Lancaster.	
JACOB SNYDER.	Germantown.	Philadelphia.	
ABRAHAM KRYDER.	Allenstown.	Northampton.	
HENRY LEPPY.	Passyunk.	Philadelphia.	
WINDELL KINGFIELD.	Lower Merrion.	Philadelphia.	
PETER SMITH.	Germantown.	Philadelphia.	
HENRY KRAAFF.	Tulpehocken.	Berks.	
MICHL. MILLER.	Cocolico.	Lancaster.	
ADAM WEAVER.	Bensalem.	Berks.	
HENRY HOFFMAN.	Chestnut Hill.	Philadelphia.	
CHRISTIAN FRY.	Springfield.	Berks.	
JOHN LIGHT.	Piles Grove.	Salem West New Jersey.	
CHRISTR. RIGHART.	Lancaster.	Lancaster.	
MICHAEL MILLER.	Antrim.	Cumberland.	
JOHN GROFF.	Plymouth.	Philadelphia.	
JACOB STADLER.	Philadelphia.	Philadelphia.	Sept. 22, 1764.
JOHN ADOLPH GILMAN.	Germantown.	Philadelphia.	
LEONARD STONEBURNER.	Germantown.	Philadelphia.	
JACOB WEAVER.	Northern Liberties.	Philadelphia.	

Certified by JOSEPH SHIPPEN, Jr.,
Philadelphia, 18 June, 1765.

Supreme Court at Philadelphia, 10 April, 1765.

Foreigners' Names.	Township.	County.	Sacrament when taken.
GEORGE MELEON.	Moyamesink.	Philadelphia.	Apr. 7, 1765.
JOHN RIBONE.	City of Philadelphia.	Philadelphia.	Apr. 7, 1765.
GEORGE KEEFER.	City of Philadelphia.	Philadelphia.	Apr. 8, 1765.

Foreigners' Names.	Township.	County.	Sacrament when taken.
GEORGE SCHNECK.	City of Philadelphia.	Philadelphia.	Apr. 9, 1765.
WILHELM WAGNER.	of New Jersey.		Apr. 7, 1765.
JOSEPH SPITTAL.	Douglass.	Philadelphia.	Apr. 7, 1765.
WILHELM GOETLING.	Philadelphia.	Philadelphia.	Apr. 7, 1765.
JACOB BEENER.	Philadelphia.	Philadelphia.	Apr. 7, 1765.
GEORGE KIEHMLY.	Philadelphia.	Philadelphia.	Apr. 9, 1765.
HENRY FOX.	Douglass.	Philadelphia.	Apr. 7, 1765.
NICHOLAS WIRKING.	Connewago.	York.	Apr. 8, 1765.
PETER MANN.	Northern Liberties.	Philadelphia.	Apr. 7, 1765.
MICHL. WEAVER.	Northern Liberties.	Philadelphia.	Apr. 7, 1765.
JOHN WEEBER.	Philadelphia.	Philadelphia.	Apr. 7, 1765.
PHILIP SENSFELDER.	Philadelphia.	Philadelphia.	Apr. 7, 1765.
GEORGE STREYPER.	Philadelphia.	Philadelphia.	Apr. 7, 1765.
GEO. FREDERCK SCHEFFER.	Rockland.	Berks.	Apr. 1, 1765.
JNO. WILHELM ENGELFRIED.	Philadelphia.	Philadelphia.	Apr. 7, 1765.
MATTHIAS BASTIAN.	Hereford.	Berks.	Apr. 7, 1765.
JACOB ANDREW SPREGHER.	Lancaster.	Lancaster.	Mar. 3, 1765.
GODFRIED KLINE.	Lancaster.	Lancaster.	Apr. 8, 1765.
MATHEW BUFFENMEYER.	Hempfield.	Lancaster.	Apr. 7, 1765.
ABRAHAM KESLER.	Heidleberg.	Berks.	Apr. 7, 1765.
ANDREW HAMMER.	Brecknock.	Lancaster.	Apr. 7, 1765.
JOHN BECK.	Brecknock.	Lancaster.	Apr. 7, 1765.
PETER BECK.	Earl.	Lancaster.	Apr. 7, 1765.
MATTHEW GURNER.	Earl.	Lancaster.	Apr. 7, 1765.
CHRISTIAN SWARTSWELLER.	Earl.	Lancaster.	Apr. 7, 1765.
ADAM GERMAN.	Earl.	Lancaster.	Apr. 7, 1765.
LUDWICK KIEFFER.	Codorus.	York.	Apr. 7, 1765.
GEORGE JACOB SCHEFFER.	Codorus.	York.	Apr. 7, 1765.
MELCHIOR STRICKER.	Forks.	Northampton.	Apr. 7, 1765.
BARTHOLOMEW ZIEBACH.	Tulpehocken.	Berks.	Mar. 7, 1765.
JACOB SPEES.	Bethel.	Berks.	Mar. 7, 1765.
CHAS. BAUMBERGER.	Tulpehocken.	Berks.	Mar. 7, 1765.
JACOB AWLEM.	Haycock.	Bucks.	Apr. 8, 1765.
VALENTINE PHILIP.	Rockland.	Bucks.	Apr. 8, 1765.
NICHS. POPP.	Bedminster.	Bucks.	Apr. 5, 1765.
JACOB FISCHER.	Cheltenham.	Philadelphia.	Apr. 8, 1765.
JOSHUA LAMPARTER.	Philadelphia.	Philadelphia.	Apr. 7, 1765.
CASPAR BRUNNER.	Lancaster.	Lancaster.	Apr. 7, 1765.
GEORGE SHAAF.	Philadelphia.	Philadelphia.	Apr. 7, 1765.
PHILIP WALTER.	Maccungy.	Northampton.	Apr. 4, 1765.
JOHN PHILIP PENTZ.	York.	York.	Apr. 9, 1765.
BALTHAZAR GOLL.	York.	York.	Apr. 9, 1765.
PETER GASCHA.	York.	York.	Apr. 9, 1765.
MICHAEL WEIDER.	York.	York.	Apr. 9, 1765.
ZACHARY BATH.	Lampeter.	Lancaster.	Apr. 8, 1765.
MARTIN TOREWARD.	Lancaster.	Lancaster.	Apr. 7, 1765.
Revd. JOHN SIGFRED GEROCK.	Lancaster.	Lancaster.	Apr. 7, 1765.
JACOB METZER.	Lancaster.	Lancaster.	Apr. 7, 1765.
JACOB ROW.	Philadelphia.	Philadelphia.	Apr. 7, 1765.
PETER LEASH.	Passyunk.	Philadelphia.	Apr. 7, 1765.
LUDWICK SHITTLER.	Frederick.	Philadelphia.	Apr. 7, 1765.
STEPHEN STEESELMYER.	Frederick.	Philadelphia.	Apr. 9, 1765.
JACOB SELTZER.	Heidleberg.	Berks.	Apr. 7, 1765.
JOHN HIRT.	Whitemarsh.	Philadelphia.	Apr. 7, 1765.

h

PENNSYLVANIA.

Foreigners' Names.	Township.	County.	Sacrament when taken.
PHILIP YOUNG.	Philadelphia.	Philadelphia.	Apr. 7, 1765.
JACOB BOWER.	Philadelphia.	Philadelphia.	Apr. 7, 1765.
JACOB UNDERKOFFLER.	Frederick.	Philadelphia.	Mar. 17, 1765.
GEORGE GERSTER.	Oxford.	Philadelphia.	Apr. 7, 1765.
JACOB KING.	Lynn.	Northampton.	Apr. 7, 1765.
GEORGE SHREEDER.	Weisenberg.	Northampton.	Apr. 7, 1765.
MICHAEL WOOLPERT.	West New Jersey.		Apr. 9, 1765.
PHILIP FACKEROTH.	Oxford.	Philadelphia.	Apr. 7, 1765.
BALTZER STOWSS.	Philadelphia.	[blank]	[blank]
GEORGE CRESH.	Douglass.	Berks.	Apr. 7, 1765.
MICHL. STOFFLAT.	Douglass.	Philadelphia.	Apr. 7, 1765.
HENRY BOUQUET.	Colonel in the Royal American Regiment.		Mar. 3, 1765.
VALENTINE SAILER.	Providence.	Philadelphia.	Apr. 14, 1765.

Quakers and others who scruple taking an Oath.

Foreigners' Names.	Township.	County.	Moravians Sacrament, when taken.
ADAM SHELLICK.	Paradice.	York.	
JACOB KUNTZ.	Germany.	York.	
RUDOLPH HUBER.	City of Philadelphia.	Philadelphia.	
JOSEPH FUNK.	Northern Liberties.	Philadelphia.	
MICHAEL FEEDLEE.	New Hanover.	Philadelphia.	
PAUL ENGLE.	Germantown.	Philadelphia.	
PETER REPPART.	New Britain.	Bucks.	
JACOB BIESER.	Hatfield.	Philadelphia.	
ADAM SMITH.	Hatfield.	Philadelphia.	
MARTIN SHLATTER.	Upper Merrion.	Philadelphia.	
CASPER RAWN.	New Providence.	Philadelphia.	
CHRISTR. GIDEON MYRTETUS.	Philadelphia.	Philadelphia.	Mar. 23, 1765.
HENRY HOOBER.	Lower Milford.	Bucks.	Apr. 7, 1765.
ANTHY. LICHTEL.	Upper Salford.	Philadelphia.	Apr. 7, 1765.
JACOB CONRAD.	Lebanon.	Lancaster.	
VALENTINE KIME.	Maiden Creek.	Berks.	
MICHAEL BEARD.	Providence.	Philadelphia.	
PETER FREED.	York.	York.	
JOHN HORNECKER.	Rockland.	Bucks.	
HENRY KIRTZ.	Philadelphia.	Philadelphia.	
NICHOLAS WIRKHISER.	Worcester.	Philadelphia.	
ANTHONY OSSHYER.	Easton.	Northampton.	
ANDREW LANTZ.	Harrow.	York.	
ADAM RICHARDS.	East Caln.	Chester.	
GEORGE RYCHART.	Lower Saucon.	Northampton.	
WYRICK SELSER.	Tulpehocken.	Berks.	

Certified by JOSEPH SHIPPEN, Jr.,

Philadelphia, 18 June, 1765.

Y. 15.

Supreme Court at Philadelphia, 24—28 and 30 Sept., and 3—5, 7—9, 12, 14—19, 22—26 Oct., 1765.

Jurors' Names.	Township.	County.	Sacrament, when taken.
Michael Andreas.	Maxatawny.	Berks.	Sept. 8, 1765.
George Presler.	Tulpehoccon.	Berks.	Aug. 4, 1765.
John Christian Seiler.	Tulpehoccon.	Berks.	Aug. 4, 1765.
Peter Hoffman.	Tulpehoccon.	Berks.	Aug. 4, 1765.
George Berger.	Bethel.	Berks.	Sept. 17, 1765.
Adam Daniel.	Bethel.	Berks.	Sept. 17, 1765.
Jno. Samuel Swordfeger.	Frederick County.	Maryland.	June 23, 1765.
Frederick Hauer.	Albany.	Berks.	Sept. 8, 1765.
George Leli.	Albany.	Berks.	Sept. 8, 1765.
John Shartel.	Lancaster.	Lancaster.	Sept. 15, 1765.
Henry Waggoner.	Lancaster.	Lancaster.	Sent. 15, 1765.
Christopher Meyer.	Lancaster.	Lancaster.	Sept. 15, 1765.
George Odellwald.	Lancaster.	Lancaster.	Sept. 15, 1765.
Jonas Metzger.	Lancaster.	Lancaster.	Sept. 15, 1765.
Michael Kearn.	Lancaster.	Lancaster.	Sept. 15, 1765.
Henry Gross.	Lancaster.	Lancaster.	Sept. 15, 1765.
Colman Gryner.	Lancaster.	Lancaster.	Sept. 15, 1765.
Anthony Zeyner.	Lancaster.	Lancaster.	Sept. 15, 1765.
John Adam Edelman.	Lancaster.	Lancaster.	Sept. 15, 1765.
Conrad Raber.	Tulpehoccon.	Berks.	Sept. 17, 1765.
George Weber.	Tulpehoccon.	Berks.	Sept. 17, 1765.
Jacob Kantner.	Tulpehoccon.	Berks.	Sept. 17, 1765.
John Meyer.	Tulpehoccon.	Berks.	Sept. 17, 1765.
Marks Brinig.	Tulpehoccon.	Berks.	Sept. 17, 1765.
Philip Klaar.	Tulpehoccon.	Berks.	Sept. 17, 1765.
Jacob Mulheisen.	Tulpehoccon.	Berks.	Sept. 17, 1765.
Michael Bretzius.	Tulpehoccon.	Berks.	Sept. 17, 1765.
Caspar Long.	Tulpehoccon.	Berks.	Sept. 17, 1765.
John Michl. Weidmeyer.	Frederick.	Maryland.	Sept. 23, 1765.
Michael Hummell.	Tulpehoccon.	Berks.	Sept. 22, 1765.
Charles Smith.	Bern.	Berks.	July 28, 1765.
George Gottschalt.	Bern.	Berks.	July 28, 1765.
George Smith.	Heidleberg.	Lancaster.	Sept. 15, 1765.
Martin Trester.	Bethel.	Berks.	Aug. 4, 1765.
George Sherman.	Tulpehoccon.	Berks.	Aug. 4, 1765.
Dietrick Six.	Bethel.	Berks.	Sept. 15, 1765.
Nicholas Brosius.	Bethel.	Berks.	Sept. 15, 1765.
John Stein.	Bethel.	Berks.	Sept. 15, 1765.
Michael Kuntz.	Tulpehoccon.	Berks.	Sept. 15, 1765.
Nicholas Schlisman.	Tulpehoccon.	Berks.	Sept. 15, 1765.
Harman Miller.	Tulpehoccon.	Berks.	Sept. 15, 1765.
Michl. Kock.	Lancaster.	Lancaster.	Sept. 15, 1765.
George Reitzel.	Lancaster.	Lancaster.	Sept. 15, 1765.
Henry Staut.	Lancaster.	Lancaster.	Sept. 15, 1765.
George Ludwig.	Tulpehoccon.	Berks.	Sept. 15, 1765.
Christr. Hauer.	Warwick.	Lancaster.	Sept. 15, 1765.
Michael Long.	Woodbridgy.	New Jersey.	Sept. 22, 1765.
Jno. Geo. Bernard.	Easton.	Northampton.	Sept. 23, 1765.
John Gethert.	Easton.	Northampton.	Sept. 23, 1765.
Philip Muth.	Marlborough.	Philadelphia.	Aug. 25, 1765.
Peter Darand.	Haycock.	Bucks.	Sept. 8, 1765.

NATURALIZATIONS

PENNSYLVANIA.

Jurors' Names.	Township.	County.	Sacrament when taken.
JOHN RISS.	Easton.	Northampton.	Sept. 8, 1765.
CONRAD BAAR.	Colebrookdale.	Berks.	Sept 21, 1765.
JOHN ECHEL.	Philadelphia.	Philadelphia.	Sept. 22, 1765.
ERHART DIERWACHTER.	Heidleberg.	Lancaster.	Sept. 15, 1765.
ANTHONY SHALLER.	Albany.	Berks.	Sept. 15, 1765.
GEORGE BETZ.	Lancaster.	Lancaster.	Sept. 15, 1765.
GEORGE HAYDE.	Lancaster.	Lancaster.	Sept. 15, 1765.
CHRISTOPHER GRAAF.	Lancaster.	Lancaster.	Sept. 15, 1765.
HENRY HELLZELL.	Lancaster.	Lancaster.	Sept. 15, 1765.
GEO. LUDWIG MEIDINGER.	Lancaster.	Lancaster.	Sept. 15, 1765.
JACOB RAINDOLLAR.	Philadelphia.	Philadelphia.	Sept. 22, 1765.
JOHN NICHOLAS SMITH.	Albany.	Berks.	Sept. 8, 1765.
CHRISTIAN KEEPER.	Lancaster.	Lancaster.	Sept. 15, 1765.
JOHN FRY.	Lancaster.	Lancaster.	Sept. 15, 1765.
MICHL. EIDEMILLER.	New Cushahoppen.	Philadelphia.	Aug. 25, 1765.
GEORGE FREISS.	White Marsh.	Philadelphia.	Sept. 22, 1765.
RUDOLPH WEISS.	Upper Milford.	Northampton.	Sept. 20, 1765.
JOHN MARBURGER.	Upper Milford.	Northampton.	Sept. 20, 1765.
ANDREAS WEISS.	Earl.	Lancaster.	Sept. 15, 1765.
HENRY SHULTZ.	Earl.	Lancaster.	Sept. 15, 1765.
HENRY HUBER.	Upper Milford.	Northampton.	Sept. 20, 1765.
DIETRICK BIEBER.	Maxatawny.	Berks.	Sept. 8, 1765.
HENRY STERNER.	Maxatawny.	Berks.	Sept. 8, 1765.
GEO. LEIBELSPERGER.	Weisenberg.	Northampton.	Sept. 8, 1765.
NICHS. SMITH.	Warwick.	Lancaster.	Sept. 1, 1765.
JNO. JACOB SNEILBERGER.	Heidleberg.	Lancaster.	Aug. 4, 1765.
EMANUEL SEISS.	Warwick.	Lancaster.	Sept. 1, 1765.
HERMAN NEIMAN.	Limerick.	Philadelphia.	Sept. 20, 1765.
GEORGE BRYNIG.	Weisenberg.	Northampton.	Sept. 8, 1765.
STEPHEN BERHEINEZER.	Warwick.	Lancaster.	Sept. 1, 1765.
JACOB BARGER.	Long Swamp.	Berks.	Sept. 22, 1765.
WILLIAM FINSTERMAKER.	Long Swamp.	Berks.	Sept. 22, 1765.
MICHAEL DIEHL.	Long Swamp.	Berks.	Sept. 22, 1765.
NICHOLAS MILLER.	Hanover.	Philadelphia.	Aug. 25, 1765.
PETER MILLER.	Lower Milford.	Bucks.	Aug. 25, 1765.
MICHAEL BAUERMAN.	Weisenberg.	Northampton.	Sept. 22, 1765.
GODFREY SEIDELL.	Windsor.	Berks.	July 24, 1765.
JNO. BREIDENBACH.	Lancaster.	Lancaster.	Sept. 15, 1765.
JACOB DANEY.	Bethel.	Berks.	Sept. 18, 1765.
MICHAEL LANG.	Long Swamp.	Berks.	Sept. 21, 1765.
GEORGE HAUER.	Windsor.	Berks.	July 14, 1765.
THOMAS PHILBERT.	Bern.	Berks.	Sept. 15, 1765.
NICHOLAS MEYER.	Rockland.	Berks.	Sept. 4, 1765.
NICHOLAS LANG.	Rockland.	Berks.	Sept. 4, 1765.
JACOB ELINGER.	Rockland.	Berks.	Sept. 4, 1765.
DANIEL NEIDIG.	Rockland.	Berks.	Aug. 25, 1765.
MATHIAS SHEIFFELE.	Cushahoppen.	Philadelphia.	Aug. 25, 1765.
GEORGE HENRY BAUER.	Heidleberg.	Berks.	Sept. 15, 1765.
JUSTUS FISHBACH.	Heidleberg.	Berks.	Sept. 15, 1765.
ERHART CHAPPELL.	Windsor.	Berks.	Sept. 15, 1765.
CLEMENS DUNKLEBERGER.	Windsor.	Berks.	Sept. 15, 1765.
NICHOLAS WEINNINGER.	Windsor.	Berks.	Sept. 15, 1765.

Jurors' Names.	Township.	County.	Sacrament when taken.
Andrew Schadt.	Tulpehoccon.	Berks.	Sept. 15, 1765.
Conrad Wierth.	Tulpehoccon.	Berks.	Sept. 15, 1765.
Peter Ahman.	Tulpehoccon.	Berks.	Sept. 15, 1765.
John Nichs. Philip.	Bern.	Berks.	July 28, 1765.
Henry Frieman.	Bern.	Berks.	Sept. 17, 1765.
George Ludwig.	Bern.	Berks.	Sept. 17, 1765.
Jacob Kreisenger.	New Cushahoppen.	Philadelphia.	Aug. 25, 1765.
David Wildemuth.	Bern.	Berks.	July 28, 1765.
Benedict Nydlinger.	New Cushahoppen.	Philadelphia.	Sept. 21, 1765.
Valentine Kayser.	New Cushahoppen.	Philadelphia.	Aug. 21, 1765.
Jacob Pfiefer.	Heidleberg.	Berks.	Aug. 4, 1765.
Adam Pfatticher.	Tulpehoccon.	Berks.	Sept. 15, 1765.
Nicholas Blatter.	Reading.	Berks.	Sept. 15, 1765.
Frederick Yerde.	Reading.	Berks.	Sept. 15, 1765.
John Conrad Koch.	Reading.	Berks.	Sept. 1, 1765.
Wm. Kreitchbaum.	Bethel.	Berks.	Sept. 1, 1765.
Melchior Dietzler.	Bethel.	Berks.	Sept. 1, 1765.
George Wolf, Senr.	Bethlehem.	Northampton.	Sept. 22, 1765.
George Deerhamer.	Bethlehem.	Northampton.	Sept. 22, 1765.
Mathias Ley.	Greenwich.	Berks.	Sept. 18, 1765.
Jacob Rodt.	Rockhill.	Bucks.	Sept. 18, 1765.
George Weldonger.	Haycock.	Bucks.	Sept. 18, 1765.
John Fry.	Haycock.	Bucks.	Sept. 18, 1765.
Jacob Hossbenner.	Rockhill.	Bucks.	Sept. 18, 1765.
Peter Henry.	Rockhill.	Bucks.	Sept. 18, 1765.
Lawrence Mayer.	Rockhill.	Bucks.	Sept. 18, 1765.
Michael Schull.	Rockhill.	Bucks.	Aug. 25, 1765.
Henry Weiber.	Heidleberg.	Berks.	Aug. 4, 1765.
Valentine Hoffman.	Maiden Creek.	Berks.	Aug. 4, 1765.
Andrew Day.	Philadelphia.	Philadelphia.	Sept. 23, 1765.
Martin Camp.	Albany.	Berks.	Sept. 8, 1765.
Adam Weider.	Salsbury.	Northampton.	Sept. 15, 1765.
Frederick Kearn.	Rockhill.	Bucks.	Sept. 8, 1765.
Valentine Petri.	Albany.	Berks.	Sept. 8, 1765.
Thomas Smith.	New Hanover.	Philadelphia.	Sept. 22, 1765.
Jacob Hummell.	Windsor.	Berks.	Sept. 20, 1765.
Joseph Stump.	Franconia.	Philadelphia.	Sept. 15, 1765.
Adam Bossert.	Marlborough.	Philadelphia.	Sept. 15, 1765.
David Levy.	Upper Hanover.	Philadelphia.	Sept. 15, 1765.
Philip Smith.	Richland.	Bucks.	Sept. 15, 1765.
Nicholas Faust.	Lower Milford.	Bucks.	Sept. 15, 1765.
Philip Hager.	Lower Milford.	Bucks.	Sept. 15, 1765.
Jacob Waggoner.	Rockhill.	Bucks.	Sept. 15, 1765.
John Buchler.	Heidleberg.	Lancaster.	Aug. 4, 1765.
George Fegele.	Colebrookdale.	Philadelphia.	Aug. 4, 1765.
George Fegele.	Maiden Creek.	Berks.	Sept. 20, 1765.
Adam Lautenschleger.	Upper Hanover	Philadelphia.	Aug. 25, 1765.
John Unrou.	Manheim.	Lancaster.	Aug. 25, 1765.
Peter Ribtell.	Lancaster.	Lancaster.	Sept. 15, 1765.
Henry Eisenmenger.	Heidelberg.	Berks.	Sept. 15, 1765.
Peter Kuhl.	Heidelberg.	Berks.	Sept. 8, 1765.
Jno. Christian Bentz.	Bern.	Berks.	Sept. 17, 1765.
Ludwick Uber.	Philadelphia.	Philadelphia.	Sept. 22, 1765.
Daniel Conrad.	Exeter.	Berks.	Sept. 22, 1765.

PENNSYLVANIA.

Jurors' Names.	Township.	County.	Sacrament when taken.
JOHN MERTZ.	Oley.	Berks.	Sept. 8, 1765.
CHRISTIAN BOLLINGER.	Berwick.	Lancaster.	Sept. 15, 1765.
MARTIN GROSS.	Warwick.	Lancaster.	Sept. 1. 1765.
CASPER WERNER.	Berwick.	Lancaster.	Sept. 15, 1765.
HENRY LEINER.	Manheim.	York.	Sept. 15, 1765.
HENRY LEINER, Junr.	Manheim.	York.	Sept. 15, 1765.
PETER LANG.	Abington.	Philadelphia.	Sept. 22, 1765.
JACOB BRETZIUS.	Tulpehoccon.	Berks.	Aug. 4, 1765.
BENJ. FRED. WILBERT.	Philadelphia.	Philadelphia.	Sept. 22, 1765.
GEO. GODFREIDT WILBERT.	Philadelphia.	Philadelphia.	Sept. 22, 1765.
JNO. GEORGE ZACHARIUS.	Manheim.	York.	Sept. 15, 1765.
JOHN JACOB WOLF.	Berwick.	York.	Sept. 15, 1765.
JNO. NICHS. FISHER.	Manheim.	York.	Sept. 15, 1765.
ABRAHAM HOLLE.	Berwick.	York.	Sept. 15, 1765.
ALEXANDER STAMM.	Paradice.	York.	Sept. 15, 1765.
JOHN SEITZ.	Bern.	Berks.	Sept. 1, 1765.
JOHN CHRISTR. KREPTS.	Philadelphia.	Philadelphia.	Sept. 22, 1765.
GEORGE MAYER.	Cumry.	Berks.	Sept. 1, 1765.
BALTZER NEIFANG.	Windsor.	Berks.	Sept. 1, 1765.
SEBASTIAN WILDFANG.	Blockley.	Philadelphia.	Sept. 24, 1765.
ADAM SMELL.	Ruscomb Manor.	Berks.	Sept. 1, 1765.
VALENTINE HUN.	Manheim.	Lancaster.	Sept. 21, 1765.
JNO. CHRISTIAN KREBS.	Northern Liberties.	Philadelphia.	Sept. 22, 1765.
HENRY NAGLE.	Philadelphia.	Philadelphia.	Sept. 22, 1765.
HENRY BAUCHMAN.	Cushahoppen.	Philadelphia.	Sept. 22, 1765.
FERDINAND FACUNDUS.	Philadelphia.	Philadelphia.	Sept. 22, 1765.
JOHN GOETZ.	Lancaster.	Lancaster.	Sept. 15, 1765.
PETER KEIFER.	Rockland.	Berks.	Sept. 22, 1765.
RICHARD HOFFMAN.	Rockland.	Berks.	Sept. 17, 1765.
GEORGE FOULKE.	Rockland.	Berks.	Sept. 22, 1765.
ADAM BETTINGER.	Berwick.	York.	Sept. 23, 1765.
MICHL. KEIFFER.	Richmond.	Berks.	Sept. 22, 1765.
JOHN BACH.	Philadelphia.	Philadelphia.	Sept. 22, 1765.
CHRISTIAN CHRESS.	Germant[own].	Philadelphia.	Sept. 22, 1765.
JOHN BILLMAN.	Cocolico.	Lancaster.	Sept. 15, 1765.
CHRISTOR. WEIBRIGHT.	Philadelphia.	Philadelphia.	Sept. 22, 1765.
NICHS. LUCHMAN.	Philadelphia.	Philadelphia.	Sept. 22, 1765.
BASTIAN GERHAUDT.	Greenwich.	Berks.	Sept. 20, 1765.
MATHIAS KOCH.	Windsor.	Berks.	July 14, 1765.
MICHL. HOTZ.	Philadelphia.	Philadelphia.	Sept. 22, 1765.
HENRY HAFFA.	Greenwich.	Berks.	Sept. 8, 1765.
CONRAD ROSCH.	Kingsington.	Philadelphia.	Sept. 22, 1765.
NICHS. BACHER.	Albany.	Berks.	Sept. 8, 1765.
JOHN WEBER.	Philadelphia.	Philadelphia.	Sept. 22, 1765.
CHAS. SHOEMAKER.	Windsor .	Berks.	Sept. 20, 1765.
JOHN MARTIN RAYSER.	Philadelphia.	Philadelphia.	Sept. 22, 1765.
VINCENT KIEFFER.	York.	York.	Sept. 22, 1765.
THOMAS BUHL.	Philadelphia.	Philadelphia.	Sept. 22, 1765.
MATHIAS FOX.	Douglass.	Philadelphia.	Sept. 22, 1765.
MARTIN AUPITCH.	Philadelphia.	Philadelphia.	Sept. 22, 1765.
JACOB GODSCHALT.	Philadelphia.	Philadelphia.	Sept. 22, 1765.
GEORGE FRED. STIEFF.	Reading.	Berks.	Sept. 20, 1765.

Jurors' Names.	Township.	County.	Sacrament when taken.
GEORGE MILLER.	Windsor.	Berks.	July 14, 1765.
FREDERICK DAUBER.	Northern Liberties.	Philadelphia.	Sept. 22, 1765.
MICHAEL HUBER.	Derry.	Lancaster.	Sept. 22, 1765.
JACOB LANTZ.	Albany.	Berks.	Sept. 22, 1765.
FREDERICK RUHL.	York.	York.	Sept. 15, 1765.
MICHAEL MILLER.	Philadelphia.	Philadelphia.	Sept. 22, 1765.
JOHN ADAM GIST.	Weisenberg.	Northampton.	Sept. 18, 1765.
JACOB ERNST.	Heidleberg.	Berks.	Sept. 15, 1765.
BERNHARD POPP.	Heidleberg.	Berks.	Sept. 15, 1765.
FREDERICK BROWN.	Windsor.	Berks.	July 14, 1765.
JOHN ERHLEY.	Derry.	Lancaster.	Sept. 28, 1765.
JACOB SMITH.	Derry.	Lancaster.	Sept. 28, 1765.
FREDERICK FORSTER.	Derry.	Lancaster.	Sept. 28, 1765.
GEORGE ITZANGMISTER.	Lower Milford.	Bucks.	Sept. 22, 1765.
MELCHIOR SHEWRER.	Philadelphia.	Philadelphia.	Sept. 22, 1765.
GEORGE HAAL.	Albany.	Berks.	Sept. 8, 1765.
GEORGE WELTER.	Lower Milford.	Bucks.	Sept. 22, 1765.
GEORGE STAHL.	Lower Milford.	Bucks.	Sept. 22, 1765.
JACOB HUBER.	Lower Milford.	Bucks.	Sept. 22, 1765.
JONAS ECKERT.	Tulpehoccon.	Berks.	Sept. 17, 1765.
PHILIP STAMBACH.	Linn.	Northampton.	Sept. 8, 1765.
MELCHIOR STOK.	Tulpehoccon.	Berks.	Sept. 17, 1765.
MICHAEL DRION.	Heidleberg.	Lancaster.	Sept. 21, 1765.
REGINA OTTMAN.	Philadelphia.	Philadelphia.	Sept. 22, 1765.
GEORGE SMITH.	Philadelphia.	Philadelphia.	Sept. 22, 1807.
JOHN HARTMAN.	Reading.	Berks.	Sept. 1, 1765.
JACOB FOX.	Ruscomb Manor.	Berks.	Sept. 22, 1765.
CHRISTIAN LENTZ.	Warwick.	Lancaster.	Sept. 15, 1765.
ANDREAS BURGHART.	Philadelphia.	Philadelphia.	Sept. 22, 1765.
JOHN ERRET.	Philadelphia.	Philadelphia.	Sept. 22, 1765.
MICHAEL BUSCH.	Heidleberg.	Berks.	Sept. 15, 1765.
LUDWICK SWERENTZ.	Cumru.	Berks.	Sept. 21, 1765.
BERNARD GILBERT.	Cushahoppen.	Philadelphia.	July 25, 1765.
JOHN ADAM FUCKS.	Heidleberg.	Berks.	Sept. 21, 1765.
DAVID MECHEL.	Lower Milford.	Bucks.	Sept. 8, 1765.
CHRISTR. GOEBRECHT.	Germantown.	Philadelphia.	Sept. 22, 1765.
PETER ERMAN.	Warwick.	Lancaster.	Sept. 13, 1765.
DAVID FORTENY.	Warwick.	Lancaster.	July 14, 1765.
SEBASTIAN STIEHLER.	Brecknock.	Lancaster.	Sept. 8, 1765.
MICHAEL LOWREY.	White Hall.	Northampton.	Sept. 23, 1765.
NICHOLAS GERRINGER.	Weisenberg.	Northampton.	Sept. 18, 1765.
RUDOLPH BOLLINGER.	Heidleberg.	Lancaster.	June 30, 1765.
JOHN WIEBER.	Heidleberg.	Lancaster.	June 30, 1765.
URBAN FRIEBELE.	Philadelphia.	Philadelphia.	Sept. 22, 1765.
JACOB SIXT.	Lancaster.	Lancaster.	Sept. 15, 1765.
MATHIAS ROST.	Lancaster.	Lancaster.	Sept. 15, 1765.
LEONARD FLOHR.	Dover.	York.	Sept. 8, 1765.
GEORGE DIETERLE.	Earle.	York.	Sept. 17, 1765.
HENRY SWENCKE.	Albany.	Berks.	Sept. 8, 1765.
HIERONIMUS DRAUTMAN.	Heidleberg.	Lancaster.	Sept. 15, 1765.
LUDWICK HASPELHORN.	Greenwich.	Berks.	Sept. 20, 1765.
CHRISTIAN SCHIEB.	Weisenberg.	Northampton.	Sept. 15, 1765.
VALENTINE GRAMLICH.	Weisenberg.	Northampton.	Sept. 8, 1765.
MICHAEL BRAUCHER.	Weisenberg.	Northampton.	Sept. 8, 1765.

PENNSYLVANIA.

Jurors' Names.	Township.	County.	Sacrament when taken.
Henry Grub.	Bristol.	Philadelphia.	Sept. 22, 1765.
Philip Alberti.	Philadelphia.	Philadelphia.	Sept. 22, 1765.
John George Derr.	Richmond .	Berks.	Sept. 20, 1765.
Conrad Gensely.	Philadelphia.	Philadelphia.	Sept. 22, 1765.
Nichs. Gress.	Bethlehem.	Northampton.	Sept. 22, 1765.
Christian Freymayer.	Bethlehem.	Northampton.	Sept. 22, 1765.
Caspar Lutz.	Cocolico.	Lancaster.	Sept. 8, 1765.
Michael Red.	Cocolico.	Lancaster.	Sept. 8, 1765.
John Dubs.	Hanover.	Lancaster.	Sept. 20, 1765.
John Roodt.	Tulpehoccon.	Lancaster.	Sept. 15, 1765.
Lawrence Brundle.	Derry.	Lancaster.	Sept. 15, 1765.
Henry Ensmenger.	Newberg.	York.	Sept. 1, 1765.
Jno. Mich. Snyder.	Philadelphia.	Philadelphia.	Sept. 22, 1765.
George Kamp.	Greenwich.	Berks.	Sept. 20, 1765.
Philip Poger.	Weisenberg.	Northampton.	Sept. 18, 1765.
Philip Odenswelder.	Forks.	Northampton.	Sept. 22, 1765.
Jacob Xander.	Lebanon.	Lancaster.	Sept. 15, 1765.
Jno. George Snyder.	Reading.	Berks.	Sept. 1, 1765.
Christian Ungerer.	Greenwich.	Berks.	Sept. 20, 1765.
Nicholas Pox.	Haycock.	Bucks.	Sept. 12, 1765.
Philip Herple.	Bedminster.	Bucks.	Sept. 8, 1765.
Anna Barbara Redmanner.	Cushahoppen.	Philadelphia.	July 25, 1765.
Henry Briel.	Lower Milford.	Bucks.	Sept. 8, 1765.
Michael Swenck.	Lower Milford.	Bucks.	Sept. 8, 1765.
John Arbegast.	Bern.	Berks.	July 28, 1765.
Thomas Lennich.	Tulpehoccon.	Berks.	Sept. 1, 1765.
Christian Frantz.	Heidleberg.	Berks.	Sept. 8, 1765.
Jacob Kemmerling.	Heidleberg.	Berks.	Sept. 20, 1765.
Peter Brua.	Tulpehoccon.	Berks.	Sept. 20, 1765.
Henry Geiss.	Maccungy.	Northampton.	Sept. 22, 1765.
Henry Friely.	Germantown.	Philadelphia.	Sept. 22, 1765.
Nichs. Weigand.	Tulpehoccon.	Berks.	Sept. 15, 1765.
Michael Dichert.	Tulpehoccon.	Berks.	Aug. 4, 1765.
George Kline.	Philadelphia.	Philadelphia.	Sept. 22, 1765.
Jacob Greenwalt.	Weisenberg.	Northampton.	Sept. 15, 1765.
Anthony Kelker.	Bethel.	Lancaster.	Sept. 20, 1765.
Michael Scheaffer.	Rockland.	Berks.	Sept. 8, 1765.
Michael Blocker.	Philadelphia.	Philadelphia.	Sept. 22, 1765.
Michael Goodman.	Philadelphia.	Philadelphia.	Sept. 22. 1765.
Philip Klingersmith.	Sadsbury.	Northampton.	Sept. 22. 1765.
Lawrence Bahman.	Lynn.	Northampton.	Sept. 15, 1765.
Nicholas Bibble.	Willingstown.	Northampton.	Aug. 15, 1765.
John Shuch.	Willingstown.	Northampton.	Aug. 15, 1765.
Nicholas Wolf.	Bethel.	Lancaster.	Sept. 4, 1765.
Jacob Huber.	Upper Milford.	Northampton.	Sept. 12, 1765.
Simon Aspect.	Lebanon.	Lancaster.	Aug. 11, 1765.
Daniel Behtely.	Whitpain.	Philadelphia.	Sept. 22, 1765.
Martin Hauser.	Germant[own].	Philadelphia.	Sept. 20, 1765.
Michael Friedly.	Chesnut Hill.	Philadelphia.	Sept. 20, 1765.
Philip Straus.	Tulpehoccon.	Berks.	July 22, 1765.
Bernard Siegman.	Tinicum.	Bucks.	Sept. 15, 1765.
Baltzer Kohler.	Tinicum.	Bucks.	Sept. 15, 1765.

Jurors' Names.	Township.	County.	Sacrament when taken.
CHRISTIAN KAUB.	Sadsbury.	Northampton.	Sept. 22, 1765.
FREDERICK KAYSER.	Tulpehoccon.	Berks.	Sept. 22, 1765.
SEBASTIAN SMITH.	Haycock.	Bucks.	July 7, 1765.
JOHN KNIGHT.	Lower Saucon.	Northampton.	Sept. 12, 1765.
BERNARD NEITZER.	Cocolico.	Lancaster.	Aug. 13, 1765.
MATTHIAS SOMMER.	Roxboro.	Philadelphia.	Sept. 22, 1765.
GEORGE MAISHE.	Creesham.	Philadelphia.	Sept. 22, 1765.
JOHN GEORGE WEISS.	Salisbury.	Northampton.	Sept. 22, 1765.
PETER STECKELL.	Whitehall.	Northampton.	Sept. 22, 1765.
FREDERICK FLEAGER.	Creesham.	Philadelphia.	Sept. 22, 1765.
ANDREW KRYNER.	White Marsh.	Philadelphia.	Sept. 22, 1765.
PETER GRUBER.	Haycock.	Bucks.	Sept. 22, 1765.
ANDREW KREPS.	Philadelphia.	Philadelphia.	Sept. 22, 1765.
HENRY FEGER.	Plymouth.	Philadelphia.	Sept. 22, 1765.
HENRY MINICH.	Tulpehoccon.	Berks.	Sept. 22, 1765.
HENRY NICHODEMUS.	Warwick.	Lancaster.	Sept. 15, 1765.
LAWRENCE BUMBERGER.	Northern Liberties.	Philadelphia.	Sept. 20, 1765.
JOHN FISHER.	Creesham.	Philadelphia.	Sept. 23 1765.
ADAM SHISSLER.	Germantown.	Philadelphia.	Sept. 23, 1765.
HENRY KNOTH.	Exeter.	Berks.	Sept. 23, 1765.
FREDERICK WENTZ.	Upper Salford.	Berks.	Sept. 23, 1765.
GEORGE ADAM GROH.	Linn.	Northampton.	Sept. 23, 1765.
GEORGE RUHL.	Tulpehoccon.	Berks.	Sept. 23, 1765.
MICHL. CHRISTMAN.	Maxatawny.	Berks.	Sept. 23, 1765.
JOHN SCHNEE.	Tulpehoccon.	Berks.	Sept. 23, 1765.
PETER KERN.	Rockhill.	Bucks.	Sept. 23, 1765.
MATHIAS KNOLL.	Heidleberg.	Lancaster.	Sept. 23, 1765.
JACOB BACKER.	Albany.	Berks.	Sept. 18, 1765.
PHILIP SHERER.	Upper Saucon.	Northampton.	Sept. 22, 1765.
GOTLIEP STROHOCKER.	Reading.	Berks.	Sept. 1, 1765.
GEORGE MARTIN ERNST.	Bern.	Berks.	Sept. 1, 1765.
CHRISTIAN RICHARD.	Cumru.	Berks.	Sept. 9, 1765.
JOHN WEAVER.	Hanover.	Lancaster.	Aug. 24, 1765.
JOHN SHNEIDO.	Warwick.	Lancaster.	Sept. 15, 1765.
THOMAS HANSUCKER.	Allen.	Northampton.	Sept. 15, 1765.
JOHN SHOUT.	Upper Saucon.	Northampton.	Sept. 15, 1765.
MARTIN SENFENDORFER.	New Hanover.	Philadelphia.	Sept. 15, 1765.
JOHN GEORGE MECKLINE.	New Hanover.	Philadelphia.	Sept. 15, 1765.
GEORGE BECK.	Bethlehem.	Northampton.	July 14, 1765.
JACOB SHREINER.	Philadelphia.	Philadelphia.	Sept. 22, 1765.
ANDREW HERTZHOG.	Philadelphia.	Philadelphia.	Sept. 22, 1765.
GEORGE COOPER.	Philadelphia.	Philadelphia.	Sept. 22, 1765.
LUDWICK PFIFER.	Bern.	Berks.	July 28, 1765.
HENRY HARTMAN.	Northern Liberties.	Philadelphia.	Sept. 23, 1765.
CONRAD LAMBARGAR.	Northern Liberties.	Philadelphia.	Sept. 23, 1765.
HENRY HERTZHELL.	Upper Milford.	Northampton.	Sept. 23, 1765.
GEORGE MUSTELLER.	Hartford.	Berks.	Sept. 24, 1765.
HENRY SHEFFER.	Rockland.	Berks.	Sept. 24, 1765.
JOHN RODE.	Heidleberg.	Lancaster.	Sept. 20, 1765.
GEORGE ETZLER.	Heidleberg.	York.	Sept. 20, 1765.
JOHN BAKER.	Philadelphia.	Philadelphia.	Sept. 22, 1765.
PHILIP STEIN.	Northern Liberties.	Philadelphia.	Sept. 22, 1765.
MELCHIOR MYER.	Oley.	Berks.	Sept. 10, 1765.
FREDK. DOUBLEBAUER.	Passyunk.	Philadelphia.	Sept. 22, 1765.

PENNSYLVANIA.

Persons' Names.	Township.	County.	Sacrament when taken.
JACOB KAYSER.	Reading.	Berks.	Sept. 1, 1765.
JOHN PHILIP FISHER.	Philadelphia.	Philadelphia.	Sept. 22, 1765.
GEORGE METZGER.	Philadelphia.	Philadelphia.	Sept. 22, 1765.
JACOB ESCH.	Philadelphia.	Philadelphia.	Sept. 22, 1765.
STEPHEN BIEGLER.	Germantown.	Philadelphia.	Sept. 24, 1765.
PHILIP FOX.	Cheltenham.	Philadelphia.	Sept. 1, 1765.
PHILIP SEIDLEMAN.	Philadelphia.	Philadelphiā.	Sept. 22, 1765.
JOHN LEIM.	Philadelphia.	Philadelphia.	Sept. 22, 1765.
CHAS. WILLIAMS NUSHACK.	Philadelphia.	Philadelphia.	Sept. 22, 1765.
PAUL BECK.	Philadelphia.	Philadelphia.	Sept. 22, 1765.
DAVID SEYFERHELD.	Germantown.	Philadelphia.	Sept. 22, 1765.
GEORGE STEES.	Northern Liberties.	Philadelphia.	Sept. 22, 1765.
GEORGE KUNTZELMAN.	Plymouth.	Philadelphia.	Sept. 24, 1765.
JACOB BUCH.	Philadelphia.	Philadelphia.	Sept. 24, 1765.
TIETMAN SCHMOLL.	Creesham.	Philadelphia.	Sept. 15, 1765.
JOHN GEISELL.	Northern Liberties.	Philadelphia.	Sept. 15, 1765.
LEWIS BERNHARD.	Creesham.	Philadelphia.	Sept. 15, 1765.
GEORGE FREY.	Pextang.	Lancaster.	Sept. 23, 1765.
HENRY WOOLF.	Bethleham.	Northampton.	Sept. 22, 1765.
ADAM SMITH.	Maccungy.	Northampton.	Sept. 24, 1765.
JNO. BALTHAS SMITH.	Maccungy.	Northampton.	Sept. 24, 1765.
JOHN THOMAS.	Philadelphia.	Philadelphia.	Sept. 25, 1765.
CASPAR WINDISCH.	Germantown.	Philadelphia.	Sept. 22, 1765.
JACOB SWITZER.	Horsham.	Philadelphia.	Sept. 22, 1765.
HENRY KUNTZ.	Germantown.	Philadelphia.	Sept. 22, 1765.
JOHN ADOLPH.	Germantown.	Philadelphia.	Sept. 22, 1765.
PETER SMITH.	Northern Liberties.	Philadelphia.	Sept. 22, 1765.
HENRY FANS.	Northern Liberties.	Philadelphia.	Sept. 22, 1765.
JACOB KNODEL.	Philadelphia.	Philadelphia.	Sept. 23, 1765.
GEORGE BECHTELL.	Philadelphia.	Philadelphia.	Sept. 23, 1765.
CONRAD YOU.	Tulpehoccon.	Berks.	Sept. 23, 1765.
SAML. NEYSHEVANDER.	Germantown.	Philadelphia.	Sept. 22, 1765.
CONRAD CRAMER.	Germantown.	Philadelphia.	Sept. 22, 1765.
CHRISTIAN GIESLER.	Germantown.	Philadelphia.	Sept. 22, 1765.
JOHN BENNER.	Germantown.	Philadelphia.	Sept. 22, 1765.
GEORGE BENNER.	Germantown.	Philadelphia.	Sept. 22, 1765.
JOHN KERBACK.	Germantown.	Philadelphia.	Sept. 22, 1765.
GODFREY HENRY.	Oxford.	Philadelphia.	Sept. 22, 1765.
JACOB WIDEMAN.	Germantown.	Philadelphia.	Sept. 22, 1765.
HENRY OBERLANDER.	Springfield.	Philadelphia.	Sept. 23, 1765.
THEOBALD DIEHL.	Germantown.	Philadelphia.	Sept. 22, 1765.
GEORGE NICHS. UNRUH.	Germantown.	Philadelphia.	Sept. 22, 1765.
GEORGE SEBASTIAN UNRUH.	Germantown.	Philadelphia.	Sept. 22, 1765.
JACOB HORDER.	Germantown.	Philadelphia.	Sept. 22, 1765.
ABRAHAM HENRY.	Germantown.	Philadelphia.	Sept. 22, 1765.
PETER KAMPMAN.	Germantown.	Philadelphia.	Sept. 22, 1765.
CHRISTOPHER WILL.	Germantown.	Philadelphia.	Sept. 22, 1765.
MICHAEL LUTZ.	Roxborough.	Philadelphia.	Sept. 22, 1765.
NICHOLAS PENTER.	Northern Liberties.	Philadelphia.	Sept. 22, 1765.
GEORGE KRAUSCOP.	Northern Liberties.	Philadelphia.	Sept. 22, 1765.
ADAM HOLD.	Oxford.	Philadelphia.	Sept. 23, 1765.
ADAM BEILINGER.	Germantown.	Philadelphia.	Sept. 22, 1765.

Jurors' Names.	Township.	County.	Sacrament when taken.
MICHAEL SMITH.	Germantown.	Philadelphia.	Sept. 24, 1765.
JACOB AMOS.	Roxborough.	Philadelphia.	Sept. 24, 1765.
HENRY SCHAFFER.	Northern Liberties.	Philadelphia.	Sept. 24, 1765.
MICHAEL DEITHER.	Northern Liberties.	Philadelphia.	Sept. 24, 1765.
MICHAEL WALTER.	New Hanover.	Philadelphia.	Sept. 22, 1765.
PETER STEINMETZ.	Germant[own].	Philadelphia.	Sept. 22, 1765.
NICHS. HOUSEGGER.	Heidleberg.	Lancaster.	Sept. 25, 1765.
JOHN PHILE.	Philadelphia.	Philadelphia.	Sept. 25, 1765.
JOHN YETTER.	Philadelphia.	Philadelphia.	Sept. 25, 1765.
JOHN GREISS.	Philadelphia.	Philadelphia.	Sept. 25, 1765.
BALTZER FETTERMAN.	Upper Milford.	Northampton.	Sept. 23, 1765.
JACOB WETZEL.	Hartford.	Berks.	Sept. 23, 1765.
GEORGE BADER.	Upper Milford.	Northampton.	Sept. 23, 1765.
GEORGE FLUFT.	Maccungy.	Northampton.	Sept. 23, 1765.
MATHIAS GARRETT.	Philadelphia.	Philadelphia.	Sept. 23, 1765.
WILLIAM GARRETT.	Philadelphia.	Philadelphia.	Sept. 23, 1765.
FREDERICK STUBER.	Philadelphia.	Philadelphia.	Sept. 23, 1765.
MORDECAI M. MORDECAI.	Philadelphia.	Philadelphia.	[A Jew].
PETER KEYSER.	Maccungy.	Northampton.	Sept. 26, 1765.
PHILIP HEN.	Hertford.	Berks.	Sept. 26, 1765.
SIMON HEN.	Maccungy.	Northampton.	Sept. 26, 1765.
PHIL. JACOB MICHAEL.	Rockland.	Berks.	Sept. 22, 1765.
MATHIAS BOOR.	Hanover.	Lancaster.	Aug. 11, 1765.
ADAM BART.	Lebanon.	Lancaster.	Aug. 11, 1765.
CHRISTIAN HEISSLER.	Maccungy.	Northampton.	Sept. 24, 1765.
FRANCIS BROWNHALT.	Northern Liberties.	Philadelphia.	Sept. 22, 1765.
PHILIP GREUSE.	Lower Milford.	Bucks.	Sept. 8, 1765.
HERMAN STUMP.	Bristol.	Philadelphia.	Sept. 22, 1765.
CHRISTR. RACK.	Philadelphia.	Philadelphia.	Sept. 22, 1765.
JNO. SCHWEITZER.	Philadelphia.	Philadelphia.	Sept. 22, 1765.
SIMON HEYDELL.	Philadelphia.	Philadelphia.	Sept. 22, 1765.
SYLVESTER FRED. GRUBER.	Elizabeth.	Northampton.	Sept. 23, 1765.
TEWALD BECK.	Maccungy.	Northampton.	Sept. 23, 1765.
PETER KEYNER.	Maccungy.	Northampton.	Sept. 23, 1765.
JACOB KLINE.	Amity.	Berks.	Sept. 25, 1765.
JOHN MARCUS BECK.	Philadelphia.	Philadelphia.	Sept. 22, 1765.
PETER HARTMAN.	Philadelphia.	Philadelphia.	Sept. 25, 1765.
GEO. LAUTZENSLEGHER.	Heidleberg.	Lancaster.	Sept. 1, 1765.
PETER BOHRER.	Heidleberg.	Lancaster.	Sept. 1, 1765.
FRED. MILLER.	Heidleberg.	Lancaster.	Sept. 1, 1765.
TEWALD MILLER.	Heidleberg.	Lancaster.	Sept. 1, 1765.
JACOB MILLER.	Heidleberg.	Lancaster.	Sept. 1, 1765.
LEONARD LEIDICH.	Elizabeth.	Lancaster.	Sept. 1, 1765.
JOHN LOUSER.	Heidleberg.	Lancaster.	Sept. 1, 1765.
GEORGE MATTER.	Earl.	Lancaster.	Sept. 26, 1765.
JOHN MATTER.	Earl.	Lancaster.	Sept. 26, 1765.
GEORGE WIKE.	Earl.	Lancaster.	Sept. 26, 1765.
THEOBALD FIRFROCK.	Earl.	Lancaster.	Sept. 26, 1765.
JACOB KEYSER.	Earl.	Lancaster.	Sept. 26, 1765.
ADOLPH REIHL.	Northern Liberties.	Philadelphia.	Sept. 27, 1765.
FRED. KAIGHNLEY.	Northern Liberties.	Philadelphia.	Sept. 22, 1765.
CONRAD RIES.	Northern Liberties.	Philadelphia.	Sept. 22, 1765.
JNO. SIGMUND HAGELGAUS.	Philadelphia.	Philadelphia.	Sept. 27, 1765.
PHILIP MAUS.	Philadelphia.	Philadelphia.	Sept. 27, 1765.

PENNSYLVANIA.

Jurors' Names.	Township.	County.	Sacrament when taken.
DANIEL HECK.	Philadelphia.	Philadelphia.	Sept. 27, 1765.
GEORGE FEADEL.	Philadelphia.	Philadelphia.	Sept. 27, 1765.
ABRAHAM FRIOTH.	Philadelphia.	Philadelphia.	Sept. 27, 1765.
MARTIN WAAL.	Philadelphia.	Philadelphia.	Sept. 27, 1765.
HENRY RORMAN.	Philadelphia.	Philadelphia.	Sept. 22, 1765.
LUDWIC YETTER.	Philadelphia.	Philadelphia.	Sept. 22, 1765.
FREDERICK KERN.	White Marsh.	Philadelphia.	Sept. 22, 1765.
JOHN HANCKER.	Philadelphia.	Philadelphia.	Sept. 22, 1765.
HENRY ZIMMERMAN.	Albany.	Berks.	Sept. 8, 1765.
NICHOLAS SMITH.	Linnon.	Northampton.	Sept. 26, 1765.
PETER LUTZ.	Linnon.	Northampton.	Sept. 26, 1765.
JOHN FRIESS.	Linnon.	Northampton.	Sept. 26, 1765.
GEORGE HERMANY.	Linnon.	Northampton.	Sept. 26, 1765.
GEORGE BLENSIG.[1]	Philadelphia.	Philadelphia.	Sept. 22, 1765.
CONRAD RORMAN.	Philadelphia.	Philadelphia.	Sept. 22, 1765.
JACOB MILLER.	Rockland.	Berks.	Sept. 27, 1765.
GEORGE DERR.	Rockland.	Berks.	Sept. 27, 1765.
NICHS. BERLINGER.	Rockland.	Berks.	Sept. 27, 1765.
CASPAR WIEZER.	Rockland.	Berks.	Sept. 27, 1765.
ADAM RAUENTSANER.	Ruscomb Manor.	Berks.	Sept. 27, 1765.
JOHN KINELY.	Maccungy.	Northampton.	Sept. 24, 1765.
MARTIN MARQUART.	Amity.	Berks.	Sept. 7, 1765.
JACOB PLESSING.	Upper Milford.	Northampton.	Sept. 24, 1765.
JACOB MEYER.	Oxford.	Philadelphia.	Sept. 24, 1765.
JACOB STUMPH.	Albany.	Berks.	Sept. 26, 1765.
JOHN CORRELL.	Albany.	Berks.	Sept. 26, 1765.
JOHN KREITZ.	Albany.	Berks.	Sept. 26, 1765.
JACOB DONAT.	Albany.	Berks.	Sept. 26, 1765.
JOHN BECKER.	Rockland.	Berks.	Sept. 27, 1765.
LUDWICK RAUHENZANER.	Rockland.	Berks.	Sept. 27, 1765.
CASPAR RUPPARD.	Rockland.	Berks.	Sept. 27, 1765.
PETER FOLIK.	Rockland.	Berks.	Sept. 27, 1765.
MICHL. FISHER.	Long Swamp.	Berks.	Sept. 27, 1765.
GEORGE SYNG.	Springfield.	Philadelphia.	Sept. 22, 1765.
BERNARD KUTER.	Springfield.	Philadelphia.	Sept. 22, 1765.
CHRISTR. WIDEMAN.	Creesham.	Philadelphia.	Sept. 22, 1765.
JACOB MEYER.	Lower Dublin.	Philadelphia.	Sept. 22, 1765.
GEORGE KERMAN.	Lower Dublin.	Philadelphia.	Sept. 22, 1765.
JACOB BROWN.	Lower Dublin.	Philadelphia.	Sept. 22, 1765.
GEORGE SOMMER.	Lower Dublin.	Philadelphia.	Sept. 22, 1765.
GEORGE MILDEBERGER.	Northern Liberties.	Philadelphia.	Sept. 22, 1765.
BERNARD CRICT.	Blockley.	Philadelphia.	Sept. 22, 1765.
GEORGE FAGER.	New Hanover.	Philadelphia.	Sept. 22, 1765.
MARTIN WORTH.	Philadelphia.	Philadelphia.	Sept. 22, 1765.
JOHN DALCHER.	Philadelphia.	Philadelphia.	Sept. 24, 1765.
JACOB HERMAN.	Maccungy.	Northampton.	Sept. 25, 1765.
JACOB DANNER.	Maccungy.	Northampton.	Sept. 25, 1765.
GEORGE DELCHER.	Cheltenham.	Philadelphia.	Sept. 22, 1765.
HENRY GILBERT.	Cheltenham.	Philadelphia.	Sept. 22, 1765.
PAUL GIMBERLING.	Heidleberg.	Lancaster.	Sept. 22, 1765.

1. From a marginal note in the MS. it appears that this and the following entry should have immediately followed that of HENRY RORMAN above.

Jurors' Names.	Township.	County.	Sacrament when taken.
HENRY PETERS.	Lebanon.	Lancaster.	July 21, 1765.
CHRISTOPHER BECK.	Philadelphia.	Philadelphia.	Sept. 22, 1765.
ANDREW GRUBEL.	Philadelphia.	Philadelphia.	Sept. 22, 1765.
ELIJAH ETTING.	York.	York.	[A Jew].
ERHART GRIM.	Philadelphia.	Philadelphia.	Sept. 22, 1765.
FREDERICK WOLBER.	Northern Liberties.	Philadelphia.	Oct. 3, 1765.
PHILIP SOMMER.	Northern Liberties.	Philadelphia.	Oct. 3, 1765.
ANDREW BECK, Junr.	Philadelphia.	Philadelphia.	Oct. 3, 1765.
MICHAEL GITTS.	Philadelphia.	Philadelphia.	Oct. 3, 1765.
AND. BECK, Senr.	Philadelphia.	Philadelphia.	Sept. 22, 1765.
JOHN SLYERWALD.	Albany.	Berks.	Oct. 3, 1765.
GEORGE BREINER.	Albany.	Berks.	Oct. 3, 1765.
JACOB GORTNER.	Albany.	Berks.	Oct. 3, 1765.
CHRISTR. BRAUCKER.	Albany.	Berks.	Oct. 3, 1765.
GEORGE SAUSELE.	Linon.	Northampton.	Oct. 3, 1765.
LEWIS GRAAS.	Northern Liberties.	Philadelphia.	Oct. 3, 1765.
LUDWICK SNYDER.	Northern Liberties.	Philadelphia.	Oct. 3, 1765.
JOHN STROHM.	Northern Liberties.	Philadelphia.	Oct. 3, 1765.
CHRISTR. WHITNER.	Northern Liberties.	Philadelphia.	Oct. 3, 1765.
NICHS. KLEIN.	Northern Liberties.	Philadelphia.	Oct. 3, 1765.
GEORGE TERNIS.	Northern Liberties.	Philadelphia.	Oct. 3, 1765.
ADAM FRITCHMAN.	Bethlehem.	Northampton.	Sept. 22, 1765.
LUDWICK LYNBERGER.	Bethlehem.	Northampton.	Sept. 26, 1765.
PHILIP FOX.	Bethlehem.	Northampton.	Sept. 28, 1765.
CHRISTOPHER DAVID COTZ.	Bethlehem.	Northampton.	Sept. 26, 1765.
JACOB FREY.	District in	Berks.	Oct. 1, 1765.
FRANTZ MOSER.	Oley.	Berks.	Aug. 4, 1765.
JOHN ALBRECHT.	Rachlin.	Berks.	Sept. 8, 1765.
NICHOLAS KUNTZ.	Oley.	Berks.	Sept. 27, 1765.
GOTLEP DORNBLASER.	Bethlehem.	Northampton.	Sept. 22, 1765.
JOHN HUMMEL.	Greenwich.	Berks.	Oct. 1, 1765.
JACOB WIBLE.	Lebanon.	Lancaster.	July 21, 1765.
NICHOLAS WEISS.	Lebanon.	Lancaster.	July 21, 1765.
GEORGE HAERING.	Greenwich.	Berks.	Sept. 28, 1765.
JOHN HAERING.	Greenwich.	Berks.	Sept. 28, 1765.
HENRY MINICH.	Greenwich.	Berks.	Oct. 3, 1765.
ANDREAS BOLCH.	Greenwich.	Berks.	Oct. 2 1765.
JOHN WITT.	Greenwich.	Berks.	Oct. 3, 1765.
PETER HAAL.	Greenwich.	Berks.	Oct. 3, 1765.
MARTIN IMHOOF.	Lebanon.	Lancaster.	July 21, 1765.
CONRAD SEINMAN.	Lebanon.	Lancaster.	Sept. 22, 1765.
MICHAEL FISHER.	Ruscom Manor.	Berks.	Sept. 8, 1765.
GEO. MICHAEL STERN.	Greenwich.	Berks.	Sept. 28, 1765.
PHILIP MEYER.	Maxatawny.	Berks.	Sept. 28, 1765.
LEONARD SAUL.	Weisenberg.	Northampton.	Sept. 28, 1765.
ANTHONY ALTMAN.	Maxatawny.	Berks.	Sept. 28, 1765.
SEBASTIAN GERINGER.	Weisenberg.	Northampton.	Sept. 18, 1765.
PETER GARTNER.	Albany.	Berks.	Aug. 25, 1765.
LEWIS WINCKLER.	Bethlehem.	Northampton.	Sept. 22, 1765.
CHRISTIAN CONRAD.	Rockland.	Berks.	Sept. 22, 1765.
MELCHIOR WEBER.	Hartford.	Berks.	Oct. 1, 1765.
ADAM HUTTER.	Hartford.	Berks.	Oct. 1, 1765.
PETER MILLER.	Maxatawny.	Berks.	Sept. 2, 1765.
PHILIP HEN.	Maxatawny.	Berks.	Sept. 2, 1765.

PENNSYLVANIA.

Jurors' Names.	Township.	County.	Sacrament when taken.
JACOB KRIEY.	Maxatawny.	Berks.	Sept. 2, 1765.
YOST LATIGH.	Maxatawny.	Berks.	Sept. 2, 1765.
SIMON HIRSH.	Maxatawny.	Berks.	Sept. 2, 1765.
JACOB HOFFMAN.	Rachlin.	Berks.	Sept. 22, 1765.
PETER BECHTEL.	Rachlin.	Berks.	Sept. 22, 1765.
JACOB BARREL.	Rachlin.	Berks.	Sept. 22, 1765.
MICHAEL LANG.	Rachlin.	Berks.	Sept. 22, 1765.
JOHN RUDRAFF.	Weisenberg.	Northampton.	Sept. 22, 1765.
THEOBALD DRUMHELLER.	Weisenberg.	Northampton.	Sept. 22, 1765.
JOHN LUTZ.	Philadelphia.	Philadelphia.	Sept. 22, 1765.
SIMON ZIENRICH.	Philadelphia.	Philadelphia.	Sept. 22, 1765.
JACOB BRAND.	Philadelphia.	Philadelphia.	Sept. 22, 1765.
HENRY GROB.	Philadelphia.	Philadelphia.	Oct. 3, 1765.
CONRAD MENGES.	District in	Berks.	Sept. 8, 1765.
FREDERICK WEISS.	Philadelphia.	Philadelphia.	Oct. 4, 1765.
JOHN WEBER.	Philadelphia.	Philadelphia.	Oct. 4, 1765.
FREDERICK MARTIN.	Providence.	Philadelphia.	Oct. 3, 1765.
NICHOLAS SNYDER.	Providence.	Philadelphia.	Oct. 3, 1765.
GEORGE WISSNER.	Douglass.	Philadelphia.	Sept. 3, 1765.
ADAM SHIB.	Northern Liberties.	Philadelphia.	Sept. 3, 1765.
JOHN SHLOTHIRE.	Philadelphia.	Philadelphia.	Sept. 3, 1765.
JNO. LEWIS DIETTERLE.	Northern Liberties.	Philadelphia.	Sept. 22, 1765.
STEPHEN KNEISLER.	Northern Liberties.	Philadelphia	Sept. 22, 1765.
JOHN GRAUB.	Northern Liberties.	Philadelphia.	Sept. 22, 1765.
PHILIP LAUTER.	Northern Liberties.	Philadelphia.	Oct. 3, 1765.
JNO. MARTIN KEILER.	Northern Liberties.	Philadelphia.	Oct. 3, 1765.
PETER GABEL.	Philadelphia.	Philadelphia.	Oct. 3, 1765.
STEPHEN RYBOLD.	Linn.	Northampton.	Oct. 3, 1765.
CONRAD. SNYDER.	Linn.	Northampton.	Oct. 3, 1765.
JNO. GRIEFFENSTEIN.	Northern Liberties.	Philadelphia.	Oct. 3, 1765.
GEORGE STRAUS.	Frederick.	Philadelphia.	Oct. 4, 1765.
PETER HEYGES.	Philadelphia.	Philadelphia.	Oct. 4, 1765.
NICHOLAS FINCK.[1]	Hartford.	Berks.	Sept. 28, 1765.
LEONARD WISSNER.	Douglass.	Philadelphia.	Sept. 3, 1765.
CONRAD MAESSER.	Springfield.	Philadelphia.	Oct. 4, 1765.
MICHAEL PALMER.	Elizabeth.	Lancaster.	Oct. 1, 1765.
PETER HERTZELL.	Elizabeth.	Lancaster.	Oct. 1, 1765.
MICHAEL WISELER.	Pikeland.	Chester.	Oct. 5, 1765.
JOHN ROTH.	Philadelphia.	Philadelphia.	Oct. 5, 1765.
HENRY ROAN.	Bethlehem.	Northampton.	Oct. 5, 1765.
JOHN GERMAN.	Elizabeth.	Lancaster.	Oct. 5, 1765.
LUDWICK MICHAEL.	Elizabeth.	Lancaster.	Oct. 5, 1765.
ALEXR. ZARTMAN.	Warwick.	Lancaster.	Oct. 5, 1765.
MARTIN GEETZ.	Elizabeth.	Lancaster.	Oct. 5, 1765.
CONRAD REINHARD.	Elizabeth.	Lancaster.	Oct. 5, 1765.
MICHAEL DIETRICK.	Philadelphia.	Philadelphia.	Oct. 4, 1765.
JACOB WALTER.	Warwick.	Lancaster.	Sept. 1, 1765.
MICHL. WENTZ.	Philadelphia.	Philadelphia.	Sept. 1, 1765.
LAWRENCE SPATZ.	Philadelphia.	Philadelphia.	Sept. 1, 1765.
JOHN KLINE.	Passyunk.	Philadelphia.	Oct. 3, 1765.

1. From a marginal note it appears that this and the following entry should have immediately followed that of GEORGE WISSNER above.

Jurors Names.	Township.	County.	Sacrament when taken.
GEORGE FOX.	Oxford.	Philadelphia.	Oct. 3, 1765.
HENRY MITSHETT.	Northern Liberties.	Philadelphia.	Oct. 3, 1765.
WILLIAM SHAUT.	Cocolico.	Lancaster.	Oct. 1, 1765.
JACOB STAISS.	Northern Liberties.	Philadelphia.	Oct. 3, 1765.
ADAM REESER.	Cumberland in	Jersey.	Sept. 29, 1765.
JOHN SHIMP.	Cumberland in	Jersey.	Sept. 29, 1765.
ADAM MINSH.	Cumberland in	Jersey.	Sept. 29, 1765.
GEORGE FISHER.	Cumberland in	Jersey.	Sept. 29, 1765.
PHILIP SHIMP.	Cumberland in	Jersey.	Sept. 29, 1765.
ANDREW HAEGY.	Northern Liberties.	Philadelphia.	Oct. 3, 1765.
GEORGE KRAIK.	Northern Liberties.	Philadelphia.	Oct. 3, 1765.
GEORGE MEBOLD.	Lower Dublin.	Philadelphia.	Oct. 6, 1765.
ADAM GRAAF.	Haycock.	Bucks.	Oct. 6, 1765.
FRED, SMITH.	Haycock.	Bucks.	Oct. 6, 1765.
JACOB AMEN.	Philadelphia.	Philadelphia.	Oct. 6, 1765.
CHRISTOPHER FRINK.	Philadelphia.	Philadelphia.	Oct. 6, 1765.
GEORGE PENTER.	Northern Liberties.	Philadelphia.	Oct. 3, 1765.
ANTHY. BERBENBILE.	Passyunk.	Philadelphia.	Oct. 3, 1765.
CHRISTOPHER TULL.	Conegecheeg.	Cumberland.	Sept. 22, 1765.
NICHOLAS DIEHL.	York.	York.	Sept. 22, 1765.
GEORGE ADAMS.	Eastown.	Chester.	Sept. 22, 1765.
ANTHY. SNYDER.	Springfield.	Philadelphia.	Sept. 23, 1765.
HENRY SLOTTER.	Oxford.	Philadelphia.	Sept. 23, 1765.
GEORGE UNUNGST.	Oxford.	Philadelphia.	Sept. 23, 1765.
PETER TEATTS.	Oxford.	Philadelphia.	Sept. 23, 1765.
MARTIN KEEMERLIN.	Bethel.	Lancaster.	Aug. 4, 1765.
GEORGE LOOSER.	Bethel.	Lancaster.	Aug. 4, 1765.
WENDEL WOLF.	Bethel.	Lancaster.	Aug. 4, 1765.
VALENTINE NICHOLAS.	Haycock.	Bucks.	July 7, 1765.
JNO. ANTHY. SIMON.	Bedminster.	Bucks.	Oct. 8, 1765.
HENRY ERNIG.	Haycock.	Bucks.	July 7, 1765.
HENRY EAGLE.	Bedminster.	Bucks.	Sept. 8, 1765.
GEORGE SPRINGHER.	Richmond.	Berks.	Sept. 22, 1765.
MICHAEL PAGE.	Northern Liberties.	Philadelphia.	Sept. 22, 1765.
NICHOLAS SINGER.	Worcester.	Philadelphia.	Sept. 22, 1765.
ANDREAS KRAMER.	Bethel.	Berks.	Sept. 17, 1765.
BALTZER SMITH.	Bethel.	Berks.	Sept. 17, 1765.
GEORGE GANTZEL.	Bern.	Berks.	Aug. 28, 1765.
LUDWICK GANTZEL.	Bern.	Berks.	Aug. 28, 1765.
JOHN NICHOLAS MILDENBERGER.	Albany.	Berks.	Sept. 8, 1765.
LAWRENCE KURTZ.	Lancaster.	Lancaster.	Sept. 15 1765.
CHRISTIAN SMITH.	Lancaster.	Lancaster.	Sept. 15, 1765.
STEPHEN SWITZER.	Lancaster.	Lancaster.	Sept. 15, 1765.
MICHAEL STEINDEL.	Lancaster.	Lancaster.	Sept. 15, 1765.
FELIX BUCH.	Lancaster.	Lancaster.	Sept. 15, 1765.
JOHN HELD.	Lancaster.	Lancaster.	Sept. 15, 1765.
PETER BON.	Lancaster.	Lancaster.	Sept. 15, 1765.
CHRISTIAN WERTZ.	Lancaster.	Lancaster.	Sept. 15, 1765.
HENRY STOUTER.	Lancaster.	Lancaster.	Sept. 15, 1765.
JACOB FRANTZ.	Lancaster.	Lancaster.	Sept. 15, 1765.
JACOB LOOS.	Tulpehoccon.	Berks.	Sept. 17, 1765.
ADAM JACOBY.	Tulpehoccon.	Berks.	Sept. 17, 1765.
WILHELM WIBER.	Tulpehoccon.	Berks.	Sept. 17, 1765.

PENNSYLVANIA.

Jurors' Names.	Township.	County.	Sacrament when taken.
JOHN HERBERBERGER.	Tulpehoccon.	Berks.	Sept. 17, 1765.
SIMON GROH.	Tulpehoccon.	Berks.	Sept. 17, 1765.
EPHRAIM BENEDICT GARBLE.	Lancaster.	Lancaster.	Sept. 15, 1765.
MICHAEL HAMBERGHER.	Tulpehoccon.	Berks.	Sept. 17, 1765.
PETER DIEMIGH.	Marlboro.	Philadelphia.	Aug. 25, 1765.
DAVID KRIMM.	Bern.	Berks.	July 28, 1765.
FREDERICK GOTTSHALT.	Bern.	Berks.	July 28, 1765.
HENRY SEIDELL.	Bern.	Berks.	July 28, 1765.
ADAM HEISER.	Bern.	Berks.	July 28, 1765.
HENRY STRACK.	Heidleberg.	Lancaster.	Sept. 15, 1765.
JACOB GASSER.	Tulpehoccon.	Berks.	Aug. 4, 1765.
ULRICK FISHER.	Tulpehoccon.	Berks.	Aug. 4, 1765.
WILLIAM STEIN.	Bethel.	Berks.	Sept. 17, 1765.
JACOB METZ.	Bethel.	Berks.	Sept. 17, 1765.
LAWRENCE SAMPLE.	Bethel.	Berks.	Sept. 17, 1765.
STOPHEL WOOLFART.	Tulpehoccon.	Berks.	Sept. 17, 1765.
PETER RITZMAN.	Tulpehoccon.	Berks.	Sept. 17, 1765.
JOHN HENRY SIESS.	Tulpehoccon.	Berks.	Aug. 4, 1765.
JACOB WEAVER.	Lancaster.	Lancaster.	Sept. 15, 1765.
MARTIN TOREWARD.	Lancaster.	Lancaster.	Sept. 15, 1765.
JOHN SHRIEBER.	Lancaster.	Lancaster.	Sept. 15, 1765.
PHILIP CRAEFERT.	Lancaster.	Lancaster.	Sept. 15, 1765.
BERNARD HOWER.	Cocolico.	Lancaster.	Sept. 15, 1765.
PHILIP PASTERS.	Eastown.	Northampton.	Sept. 23, 1765.
JOHN SIMON.	Eastown.	Northampton.	Sept. 23, 1765.
CHRISTIAN PFIFER.	Forks.	Northampton.	Sept. 23, 1765.
JACOB BECK.	Tulpehoccon.	Berks.	Aug. 31, 1765.
JACOB SCHNOR.	Whitehall.	Northampton.	Sept. 24, 1765.
MICHAEL KURTZ.	Tulpehoccon.	Berks.	Sept. 21, 1765.
PETER STEIN.	Heidleberg.	Lancaster.	Sept. 15, 1765.
JACOB DANNER.	Long Swamp.	Berks.	Sept. 20, 1765.
ABRAHAM DAUBER.	Worcester.	Philadelphia.	Sept. 22, 1765.
MARTIN LOWMAN.	Lancaster.	Lancaster.	Sept. 15, 1765.
MICHAEL GUNTAKER.	Lancaster.	Lancaster.	Sept. 15, 1765.
GEORGE HAYDE.	Lancaster.	Lancaster.	Sept. 15, 1765.
JACOB FEESELL.	Lancaster.	Lancaster.	Sept. 15, 1765.
STEPHEN MANN.	Lancaster.	Lancaster.	Sept. 15, 1765.
PETER SNYDER.	Conestogo.	Lancaster.	Sept. 15, 1765.
MATHIAS STREEHER.	Conestogo.	Lancaster.	Sept. 15, 1765.
ANDREAS WENNER.	Albany.	Berks.	Sept. 15, 1765.
BERNARD BECKER.	Lancaster.	Lancaster.	Sept. 15, 1765.
HENRY SCHLESMAN.	Philadelphia.	Philadelphia.	Sept. 22, 1765.
RUDOLPH BIGGY.	Bristol.	Philadelphia.	Sept. 22, 1765.
PHILIP HERTEG.	Upper Milford.	Northampton.	Sept. 20, 1765.
JACOB FUNK.	Upper Milford.	Northampton.	Sept. 20, 1765.
MARTIN NEHR.	Earl.	Lancaster.	Sept. 15, 1765.
CASPAR GINTHER.	Earl.	Lancaster.	Sept. 15, 1765.
BERNARD FRANK.	Earl.	Lancaster.	Sept. 15, 1765.
SEBASTIAN HOWER.	Earl.	Lancaster.	Sept. 15, 1765.
FREDERICK NEEMYER.	Upper Hanover.	Philadelphia.	Aug. 25, 1765.
JACOB BIEBER.	Maxatawny.	Berks.	Sept. 8, 1765.
CHARLES BERNARD.	Long Swamp.	Berks.	Sept. 8, 1765.

Jurors' Names.	Township.	County.	Sacrament when taken.
ULRICK MICHAEL.	Heidleberg.	Berks.	Sept. 8, 1765.
ADAM AARES.	Heidleberg.	Berks.	Sept. 15, 1765.
MARTIN HARSH.	Heidleberg.	Berks.	Sept. 15, 1765.
MICHAEL HAAS.	Pikeland.	Chester.	Sept. 23, 1765.
GEO. REIGNER.	Limerick.	Philadelphia.	Sept. 20, 1765.
HENRY BRILL.	Heidleberg.	Lancaster.	Sept. 15, 1765.
JACOB SALTZER.	Heidleberg.	Lancaster.	Sept. 15, 1765.
ADAM EDLEMAN.	Saucon.	Northampton.	Sept. 22, 1765.
FREDERICK DYSS.	Long Swamp.	Berks.	Sept. 22, 1765.
JACOB WYMER.	Long Swamp.	Berks.	Sept. 22, 1765.
THEOBALD KEPPELE.	Long Swamp.	Berks.	Sept. 22, 1765.
LUDWICK RICART.	Weisenberg.	Northampton.	Sept. 22, 1765.
JACOB BEGT.	Oley.	Northampton.	Sept. 22, 1765.
ANDREAS SEIDELL.	Windsor.	Berks.	July 14, 1765.
MICHAEL JACOBY.	Long Swamp.	Berks.	Sept. 22, 1765.
GEORGE HAAMER.	Upper Milford.	Northampton.	Sept 8, 1765.
JACOB LONG.	Long Swamp.	Berks.	Sept. 22, 1765.
MICHAEL HIDDLE.	Salsbury.	Northampton.	Sept 8, 1765.
MICHAEL OTH.	Salsbury.	Northampton.	Sept 8, 1765.
WENDAL HAUER.	Windsor.	Berks.	July 14, 1765.
NICHOLAS BLADER.	Rockland.	Berks.	Sept. 4, 1765.
NICHOLAS JACOBY.	Rockland.	Berks.	Sept. 4, 1765.
JOHN CAUFMAN.	Tulpehoccon.	Berks.	Sept. 1, 1765.
ADAM NEIDIG.	Newhanover.	Berks.	Aug. 24, 1765.
DANIEL SHUMACKER.	Weisenberg.	Northampton.	Sept. 12, 1765.
PHILIP WAGNER.	Heidleberg.	Berks.	Sept. 15, 1765.
JOHN GEO. YAKLE.	Heidleberg.	Berks.	Sept. 15, 1765.
JEREMIAH SCHAPPELL.	Windsor.	Berks.	Sept. 15, 1765.
CASPAR HENTSELL.	Windsor.	Berks.	Sept. 15, 1765.
GEORGE SNYDER.	Windsor.	Berks.	Sept. 15, 1765.
NICHOLAS WINGERT.	Windsor.	Berks.	Sept. 15, 1765.
VALENTINE NEU.	Tulpehoccon.	Berks.	Sept. 15, 1765.
FRED. DEGLER.	Tulpehoccon.	Berks.	Sept. 15, 1765.
PHILIP HINCKELL.	Windsor.	Berks.	July 14, 1765.
CASPAR PHILIP.	Bern.	Berks.	Sept. 28, 1765.
LUDWICK MARSTELLER.	Bern.	Berks.	Sept. 28, 1765.
PHILIP BAYER.	Bern.	Berks.	Sept. 28, 1765.
PHILIP BOBBEMIRE.	Windsor.	Berks.	July 14, 1765.
JOHN ACHE.	Tulpehoccon.	Berks.	Aug. 20, 1765.
LUDWIC LAROS.	Maccungy.	Northampton.	Sept. 20, 1765.
ANTHONY PETRI.	Lancaster.	Lancaster.	Sept. 15, 1765.
JOHN KLUCK.	Albany.	Berks.	Sept. 8, 1765.
PETER FOGT.	Windsor.	Berks.	July 14, 1765.
GEORGE RIGEL.	Greenwich.	Berks.	Sept. 15, 1765.
PETER LIPPO.	Heidleberg.	Berks.	Aug. 4, 1765.
PETER MILLER.	Reading.	Berks.	Sept. 15, 1765.
BASTIAN LENTZ.	Rockland.	Berks.	Sept. 8, 1765.
STOPHEL HERRALD.	Rockland.	Berks.	Sept. 8, 1765.
ADAM SNYDER.	Cusshahoppon.	Bucks.	Aug. 24, 1765.
GEO. WOLF, Junr.	Bethlehem.	Northampton.	Sept. 22, 1765.
JACOB TURNER.	Bethlehem.	Northampton.	Sept. 22, 1765.
MICHAEL OTT.	Bedminster.	Bucks.	Sept. 22, 1765.
ULRICK STOLLER.	Bedminster.	Bucks.	Sept. 22, 1765.
VALENTINE RENNER.	Bedminster.	Bucks.	Sept. 22, 1765.

i

PENNSYLVANIA.

Jurors' Names.	Township.	County.	Sacrament when taken.
PHILIP FLUCK.	Hilltown.	Bucks.	Sept. 22, 1765.
PHILIP PERSON.	Hilltown.	Bucks.	Sept. 22, 1765.
JOHN BOWS.	Hilltown.	Bucks.	Sept. 22, 1765.
FRED. SOLLITE.	Rockhill.	Bucks.	Sept. 22, 1765.
GEORGE ERNIG.	Rockhill.	Bucks.	Sept. 22, 1765.
HERWART LEER.	Rockhill.	Bucks.	Sept. 22, 1765.
LUDWIC NOSBITTLE.	Rockhill.	Bucks.	Sept. 22, 1765.
JACOB LEIBY.	Greenwich.	Berks.	Sept. 15, 1765.
GEORGE MICHL. LEIBY.	Greenwich.	Berks.	Sept. 15, 1765.
MICHAEL DUNCKELL.	Douglass.	Philadelphia.	Sept. 22, 1765.
JOHN DAMPMAN.	Douglass.	Philadelphia.	Sept. 22, 1765.
MICHAEL SINGER.	Bethel.	Lancaster.	Aug. 4, 1765.
FREDERICK DORFLINGER.	Rockhill.	Bucks.	Sept. 8, 1765.
JNO. ADAM STIEN.	Heidleberg.	Berks.	Aug. 4, 1765.
GEORGE PRENSH.	Lynn.	Northampton.	Sept. 8, 1765.
FREDERICK GIETZ.	Lower Salford.	Philadelphia.	Sept. 15, 1765.
JOHN MUCK.	Marlborough.	Philadelphia.	Sept. 15, 1765.
FREDERICK MILLER.	Marlborough.	Philadelphia.	Sept. 15, 1765.
JNO. ECHART WEISS.	Upper Hanover.	Philadelphia.	Sept. 15, 1765.
PETER WERNER.	Frederick.	Philadelphia.	Sept. 15, 1765.
NICHOLAS MUMBOWER.	Lower Milford.	Bucks.	Sept. 15, 1765.
RUDOLPH HUBER.	Lower Milford.	Bucks.	Sept. 15, 1765.
STOPHEL SHABER.	Heidleberg.	Berks.	Sept. 8, 1765.
JOHN BECKER.	Weisenberg.	Northampton.	Sept. 18, 1765.
ADAM SMITH.	Tulpehoccon.	Berks.	Sept. 20, 1765.
FREDERICK HAUSMAN.	Maxatawny.	Berks.	Sept. 22, 1765.
JOHN BACHMAN.	Marlborough.	Philadelphia.	Sept. 21, 1765.
MICHAEL BOWER.	Philadelphia.	Philadelphia.	Sept. 22, 1765.
WILLIAM LERCH.	Heidelberg.	Berks.	Sept. 8, 1765.
PHILIP SPAET.	Bern.	Berks.	Sept. 21, 1765.
NICHOLAS LERCH.	Heidleberg.	Berks.	Sept. 8, 1765.
JACOB BACKENSTOS.	Lancaster.	Lancaster.	Sept. 15, 1765.
HENRY SPAET.[1]	Bern.	Berks.	Sept. 21, 1765.
DANIEL SWARTZ.	Oley.	Berks.	Sept. 4, 1765.
JOHN CONRAD.	Exeter.	Berks.	Sept. 22, 1765.
HERMAMES LORCHBACK.	Lancaster.	Lancaster.	Sept. 15, 1765.
JOHN ENK.	Warwick.	Lancaster.	Sept. 15, 1765.
CHRISTIAN LAMBACK.	Warwick.	Lancaster.	Sept. 15, 1765.
JOHN BENDER.	Warwick.	Lancaster.	Sept. 15, 1765.
PETER SHARMAN.	Cumru.	Berks.	Sept. 8, 1765.
ANDREAS WINTER.	Bern.	Berks.	Sept. 28, 1765.
MATTHIAS WAIGELL.	Philadelphia.	Philadelphia	Sept. 22, 1765.
NICHOLAS MILLER.	Heidleberg.	Berks.	Sept. 8, 1765.
LUDWIC MOUSE.	Cocolico.	Lancaster.	Sept. 15, 1765.
JOHN BITTLE.	Manheim.	York.	Sept. 23, 1765.
NICHOLAS RUPP.	Blockley.	Philadelphia.	Sept. 24, 1765.
GEO. WILL. KERBACH.	Berwick.	York.	Sept. 15, 1765.
CONRAD FELTE.	Manheim.	York.	Sept. 15, 1765.
JNO. FRED. WOLF.	Berwick.	York.	Sept. 15, 1765.
ADAM DEGOMOY.	Berwick.	York.	Sept. 15, 1765.

1. From a marginal note it appears that this name should have been entered immediately after that of PHILIP SPAET above,

Jurors' Names.	Township.	County.	Sacrament when taken.
STEPHEN POPPENMYER.	Upper Milford.	Northampton.	Sept. 15, 1765.
JOHN MECKLIN.	Cheltenham.	Philadelphia.	Sept. 13, 1765.
JACOB ZANGER.	Ruscom. Manor.	Berks.	Sept. 1, 1765.
HENRY KLOSS.	Bern.	Berks.	Sept. 1, 1765.
PETER HICKMAN.	Alsace.	Berks.	Sept. 1, 1765.
JOHN KLOSS.	Alsace.	Berks.	Sent. 1, 1765.
JOHN RIEGELL.	Ruscom Manor.	Berks.	Sept. 1, 1765.
PHILIP KEESICKER.	Heidleberg.	Lancaster.	Sept. 15, 1765.
KILLIAN RUPP.	Blockley.	Philadelphia.	Sept. 24, 1765.
GEO. SEIGENTHALER.	Cocolico.	Lancaster.	Sept. 8, 1765.
HENRY HAIN.	Philadelphia.	Philadelphia.	Sept. 22, 1765.
JACOB PENNINGHOFF.	Philadelphia.	Philadelphia.	Sept. 22, 1765.
ANTHONY NAGLE.	Philadelphia.	Philadelphia.	Sept. 22, 1765.
JOHN HAAGER.	Richmond.	Berks.	Sept. 20, 1765.
HENRY WELLFLING.	Philadelphia.	Philadelphia.	Sept. 22, 1765.
HENRY HOOFMAN.	Rockland.	Berks.	Sept. 22, 1765.
ABRAHAM HAAS.	Bern.	Berks.	Sept. 17, 1765.
MOSES BENTER.	New Hanover.	Philadelphia.	Sept. 22, 1765.
HENRY MENCH.	Philadelphia.	Philadelphia.	Sept. 22, 1765.
NICHOLAS NEWMAN.	Manheim.	York.	Sept. 22, 1765.
THEOBALD KEEFER.	Richmond.	Berks.	Sept. 22, 1765.
HENRY STILLER.	Philadelphia.	Philadelphia.	Sept. 22, 1765.
PETER CLEIN.	Philadelphia.	Philadelphia.	Sept. 22, 1765.
GEO. MICHL. BRENNER.	Cocolico.	Lancaster.	Sept. 15, 1765.
GEORGE SHALL.	Oley.	Berks.	Sept. 22, 1765.
GEORGE RUSE.	Philadelphia.	Philadelphia.	Sept. 22, 1765.
JOHN GODFRY HALL.	Philadelphia.	Philadelphia.	Sept. 22, 1765.
MICHAEL HOLLEBACH.	Linn.	Northampton.	Sept. 18, 1765.
GEORGE HELLER.	Philadelphia.	Philadelphia.	Sept. 8, 1765.
SIMON SNYDER.	Upper Milford.	Northampton.	Sept. 15, 1765.
PETER EDLEMAN.	Upper Milford.	Northampton.	Sept. 15, 1765.
HENRY SHOEMAKER.	Windsor.	Berks.	Sept. 20, 1765.
JOHN FRED. BASH.	Philadelphia.	Philadelphia.	Sept. 22, 1765.
ERNST LUDWICK BASH.	Philadelphia.	Philadelphia.	Sept. 22, 1765.
JOHN JACOB RAYSER.	Philadelphia.	Philadelphia.	Sept. 22, 1765.
PHILIP PRINKENMILLER.	Philadelphia.	Philadelphia.	Sept. 22, 1765.
GEORGE KINSINGER.	Philadelphia.	Philadelphia.	Sept. 22, 1765.
GEORGE STO.	Philadelphia.	Philadelphia.	Sept. 22, 1765.
ANDREW GETTER.	Philadelphia.	Philadelphia.	Sept. 22, 1765.
JOHN KOSER.	Greenwich.	Berks.	Sept. 20, 1765.
CHRISTOPHER SHUM.	Tulpehoccon.	Berks.	Sept. 15, 1765.
JOHN KANN.	Tulpehoccon.	Berks.	Aug. 4, 1765.
ANTHONY EGGY.	Northern Liberties.	Philadelphia.	Sept. 22, 1765.
GEORGE SEETZ.	Philadelphia.	Philadelphia.	Sept. 22, 1765.
DANIEL BENDER.	Philadelphia.	Philadelphia.	Sept. 22, 1765.
GEORGE GASSINGER.	Gwinedth.	Philadelphia.	Aug. 25, 1765.
JACOB YENSER.	Weisenburg.	Northampton.	Sept. 22, 1765.
JACOB KOCH.	York.	York.	Sept. 15, 1765.
JOHN KOCHENBACH.	Weisenberg.	Northampton.	Sept. 18, 1765.
MELCHIOR WEISINGER.	Philadelphia.	Philadelphia.	Sept. 22, 1765.
FREDERICK MEYERLY.	Reading.	Berks.	Sept. 1, 1765.
PETER ZIMMERMAN.	Reading.	Berks.	Sept. 1, 1765.
FREDERICK KOST.	Reading.	Berks.	Sept. 1, 1765.
GEORGE MEYER.	Tulpehoccon.	Berks.	Aug. 22, 1765.

PENNSYLVANIA.

Jurors' Names.	Township.	County.	Sacrament when taken.
Albright Sickly.	Paxton.	Lancaster.	July 28, 1765.
Christr. Kisterer.	Elizabeth .	Lancaster.	Sept. 15, 1765.
Adam Lotz.	Northern Liberties.	Philadelphia.	Sept. 22, 1765.
John Brundle.	Derry.	Lancaster.	Sept. 15, 1765.
Melchior Ram.	Hanover.	Philadelphia.	Aug. 21, 1765.
Andrew Engleman.	Lower Milford.	Bucks.	Sept. 22, 1765.
Peter Schlosser.	Lower Milford.	Bucks.	Sept. 22, 1765.
Christian Fisher.	Lower Milford.	Bucks.	Sept. 22, 1765.
Henry Olt.	Lower Milford.	Bucks.	Sept. 22, 1765.
Theobald Browkler.	Lower Milford.	Bucks.	Sept. 22, 1765.
Conrad Eckert.	Heidleberg.	Berks.	Sept. 9, 1765.
Andreas Scholl.	Heidleberg.	Lancaster.	Sept. 20, 1765.
John Kurtz.	Heidleberg.	Lancaster.	Sept. 20, 1765.
John Thuddy.	Reading.	Berks.	Sept. 8, 1765.
Henry Swallbach.	Philadelphia.	Philadelphia.	Sept. 22, 1765.
John Keller.	Philadelphia.	Philadelphia.	Sept. 22, 1765.
Henry Mertz.	Rockland.	Berks.	Sept. 8, 1765.
Andreas Mishslegel.	Richmond.	Berks.	Sept. 20, 1765.
Conrad Abel.	Philadelphia.	Philadelphia.	Sept. 20, 1765.
Ludwick Benner.	Rockhill.	Bucks.	Aug. 8, 1765.
George Grot.	Philadelphia.	Philadelphia.	Sept. 22, 1765.
Chas. Chamberlain.	Philadelphia.	Philadelphia.	Sept. 22, 1765.
Jacob Albert.	Bethel.	Lancaster.	Sept. 22, 1765.
Henry Werheim.	Heidleberg.	Berks.	Sept. 9, 1765.
Jacob Snyder.	Marlboro.	Philadelphia.	July 25, 1765.
John Frantz.	Heidleberg.	Berks.	Sept. 9, 1765.
Christian Maurer.	Reading.	Berks.	Sept. 9, 1765.
Caspar Reinecker.	Warwick.	York.	Sept. 23, 1765.
Michael Mattinger.	Upper Milford.	Northampton.	Sept. 8, 1765.
Valentine Kryner.	Warwick.	Lancaster.	July 14, 1765.
Peter Armishon.	Warwick.	Lancaster.	July 14, 1765.
Philip Knappenberger.	Whitehall.	Northampton.	Sept. 23, 1765.
Wendal Waitman.	Plymouth.	Philadelphia.	Sept. 22, 1765.
Conrad Gertenger.	Plymouth.	Philadelphia.	Sept. 22, 1765.
Wendall Martzall.	Rappho.	Lancaster.	Sept. 23, 1765.
Andreas Wittemire.	Heidleberg.	Lancaster.	Sept. 20, 1765.
Nichs. Kuntz.	Tulpehoccon.	Berks.	Aug. 4, 1765.
Henry Rathflag.	Philadelphia	Philadelphia.	Sept .22, 1765.
Peter Heist.	Marlboro.	Philadelphia.	July 25, 1765.
Jno. Philip Sprecker.	Earl.	Lancaster.	Sept. 17, 1765.
Jacob Glaser.	Earl.	Lancaster.	Sept. 17, 1765.
Frederick Deim.	Earl.	Lancaster.	Sept. 17, 1765.
Leonard Acre.	Earl.	Lancaster.	Sept. 17, 1765.
Caspar Grubb.	Warwick.	Lancaster.	Sept. 25, 1765.
Nicholas Shoemaker.	Greenwich.	Berks.	Sept. 20, 1765.
Godfrey Krœmer.	Greenwich.	Berks.	Sept. 20, 1765.
Jacob Holbe.	Weisenberg.	Northampton.	Sept. 15, 1765.
George Shoemaker.	Weisenberg.	Northampton.	Sept. 8, 1765.
George Bender.	Bern.	Berks.	Sept. 1, 1765.
Adam Gebhart.	Upper Milford.	Northampton.	Sept. 15, 1765.
George Merkell.	Windsor.	Berks.	Sept. 20, 1765.
Conrad Beetis,	Philadelphia.	Philadelphia.	Sept. 22, 1765.

Jurors' Names.	Township.	County.	Sacrament when taken.
PHILIP EGER.	Philadelphia.	Philadelphia.	Sept. 22, 1765.
PETER SHLOSSER.	Lebanon.	Lancaster.	Sept. 22, 1765.
PETER EIT.	Bethlehem.	Northampton.	Sept. 22, 1765.
ADAM GORRINGER.	Bethlehem.	Northampton.	Sept. 22, 1765.
PETER SEIP.	Forks.	Northampton.	Sept. 22, 1765.
JOHN FASSNIGHT.	Cocolico.	Lancaster.	Sept. 8, 1765.
HENRY LEED.	Cocolico.	Lancaster.	Sept. 8, 1765.
JACOB WEST.	Cocolico.	Lancaster.	Sept. 8, 1765.
HENRY JACOBY.	Whitehall.	Northampton.	Sept. 15, 1765.
ERHARD FOSSELMAN.	Linn.	Northampton.	Sept. 14, 1765.
JOHN MEASE.	Lebanon.	Lancaster.	Sept. 18, 1765.
JOHN PERRET.	Whitehall.	Northampton.	Sept. 22, 1765.
STEPHEN MARTIN.	Lancaster.	Lancaster.	Sept. 22, 1765.
GEORGE SHOEMAKER.	Reading.	Berks.	Sept. 1, 1765.
CONRAD SHESER.	Reading.	Berks.	Sept. 1, 1765.
HENRY GERLACH.	Strasburg.	York.	Sept. 22, 1765.
JOHN BACKASTOES.	Lebanon.	Lancaster.	Sept. 20, 1765.
PETER DRUNKENMILLER.	Warwick.	Lancaster.	Sept. 14, 1765.
ANDREAS DRESSLER.	Greenwich.	Berks.	Sept. 20, 1765.
MATTHIAS KAMMERER.	Reading.	Berks.	Sept. 1, 1765.
JACOB YERLING.	Tinicum.	Bucks.	July 28, 1765.
JACOB LOOS.	Bern.	Berks.	Sept. 21, 1765.
HENRY HOOVER.	Lower Milford.	Bucks.	Sept. 8, 1765.
VALENTINE KREES.	Richmond.	Berks.	Sept. 20, 1765.
CONRAD KRAFT.	Reading.	Berks.	Sept. 1, 1765.
JOSHUA SEASE.	Maiden Creek.	Berks.	Sept. 4, 1765.
CHRISTIAN HENDRICK.	Rockland.	Berks.	Sept. 8, 1765.
JACOB STRUNK.	Heidleberg.	Berks.	Sept. 21, 1765.
MICHAEL KELI.	Plymouth.	Philadelphia.	Sept. 23, 1765
JNO. GEO. KUNKELL.	Albany.	Berks.	Sept. 18, 1765.
THEOBALD STORK.	Moyamens.	Philadelphia.	Sept. 22, 1765.
CHRISTIAN PHILIPPI.	Cocolico.	Lancaster.	Sept. 15, 1765.
JACOB STOUGH.	Maccungy.	Northampton.	Sept. 22, 1765.
JACOB SARBER.	Germantown.	Philadelphia.	Sept. 22, 1765.
FREDERICK WINTER.	Tulpehoccon.	Berks.	Sept. 15, 1765.
JOHN BICKELL.	Bethel.	Lancaster.	Sept. 20, 1765.
JACOB PHILLIPPI.	Heidleberg.	Berks.	Sept. 21, 1765.
LUDWICK SHEETZ.	Lower Milford.	Bucks.	Sept. 8, 1765.
GEORGE RHINEHART.	Philadelphia.	Philadelphia.	Sept. 22, 1765.
CHRISTR. RATZ.	Philadelphia.	Philadelphia.	Sept. 22, 1765.
PETER MILLER.	Sadsbury.	Northampton.	Sept. 15, 1765.
CHRISTIAN MILLER.	Linn.	Northampton.	Sept. 11, 1765.
PETER TAYLER.	Willingstown.	Northampton.	Sept. 1, 1765.
MICHL. SHOEMAKER.	Willingstown.	Northampton.	Aug. 15, 1765.
MICHAEL STEINLER.	Philadelphia.	Philadelphia.	Sept. 22, 1765.
HERMAN BRILL.	Lower Milford.	Bucks.	Sept. 22, 1765.
PETER TAESTER.	Bethel.	Lancaster.	Sept. 20, 1765.
MARTIN RUDY.	Bethel.	Lancaster.	Sept. 20, 1765.
JOHN MISH.	Bethel.	Lancaster.	Sept. 20, 1765.
PETER HAY.	Germantown.	Philadelphia.	Sept. 22, 1765.
PAUL BOWER.	White Marsh.	Philadelphia.	Sept. 20, 1765.
JACOB SHERATEEN.	Maxatawny.	Berks.	Sept. 22, 1765.
JACOB PHILIP GEES.	Tulpehoccon.	Berks.	July 22, 1765.
JOSEPH FOLTZ.	Heidleberg.	Lancaster.	Sept. 20, 1765.

PENNSYLVANIA,

Jurors' Names.	Township.	County.	Sacrament when taken.
GODFREY HEBBERLIN.	Heidleberg.	Lancaster.	Sept. 20, 1765.
JOHN 'KELLER.	Haycock.	Bucks.	July 7, 1765.
GEORGE LABACH.	Lower Saucon.	Northampton.	Sept. 12, 1765.
REINARD LABACH.	Lower Saucon.	Northampton.	Sept. 12, 1765.
PETER LABACH.	Lower Saucon.	Northampton.	Sept. 12, 1765.
CHARLES BOWER.	Roxborough.	Philadelphia.	Sept. 15, 1765.
HENRY STIEF.	Roxborough.	Philadelphia.	Sept. 22, 1765.
JOHN BOWER.	Whitpain.	Philadelphia.	Sept. 22, 1765.
JOHN FISHER.	Whitpain.	Philadelphia.	Sept. 22, 1765.
PETER PANCAKE.	Paxton.	Lancaster.	Sept. 8, 1765.
CASPAR SESLER.	Creesham.	Philadelphia.	Sept. 22, 1765.
WILLIAM RUFF.	Creesham.	Philadelphia.	Sept. 22, 1765.
JACOB FEINER.	Whitemarsh.	Philadelphia.	Sept. 22, 1765.
JOHN STUBER.	Whitemarsh.	Philadelphia.	Sept. 22, 1765.
PETER BAADER.	Hilltown.	Bucks.	Sept. 23, 1765.
MICHL. HELDER.	Hilltown.	Bucks.	Sept. 23, 1765.
FREDERICK DULL.	Plymouth.	Philadelphia.	Sept. 22, 1765.
HENRY MILLER.	Philadelphia.	Philadelphia.	Sept. 22, 1765.
JOHN SHREIVER.	Philadelphia.	Philadelphia.	Sept. 22, 1765.
FREDERICK ZIMMERMAN.	Elizabeth.	Lancaster.	Sept. 1, 1765.
JOHN SHEE.	Northern Liberties.	Philadelphia.	Sept. 20, 1765.
JOHN KNIPE.	Guinedth.	Philadelphia.	Sept. 22, 1765.
CHRISTIAN FOTH.	Philadelphia.	Philadelphia.	Sept. 22, 1765.
MARIA MAGDALENA HANNEKAN.	Philadelphia.	Philadelphia.	Sept. 22, 1765.
JOHN GRABER.	Northern Liberties.	Philadelphia.	Sept. 22, 1765.
PHILIP CLONINGER.	Maiden Creek.	Berks.	Sept. 22, 1765.
BARTHOLOMEW SHEITZLIN.	Philadelphia.	Philadelphia.	Sept. 22, 1765.
JOHN BENDER.	Passyunk.	Philadelphia.	Sept. 30, 1765.
FREDERICK RICHENACRE.	Passyunk.	Philadelphia.	Sept. 30, 1765.
LEWIS KOCH.	Passyunk.	Philadelphia.	Sept. 30, 1765.
GEORGE STAYLEY.	Passyunk.	Philadelphia.	Sept. 30, 1765.
DANIEL RUYTER.	Roxborough.	Philadelphia.	Sept. 22, 1765.
JOST FEIDT.	Northern Liberties.	Philadelphia.	Sept. 22, 1765.
FREDERICK HAMMON.	Greenwich.	Berks.	Sept. 22, 1765.
HENRY ROSHONG.	Germantown.	Philadelphia.	Sept. 22, 1765.
JOHN SHLESSMAN.	Philadelphia.	Philadelphia.	Sept. 22, 1765.
JACOB KARL.	Bedminster.	Bucks.	Sept. 22, 1765.
HENRY SNYDER.	Philadelphia.	Philadelphia.	Sept. 22, 1765.
JACOB YOUNG.	Philadelphia.	Philadelphia.	Sept. 22, 1765.
MICHL. MILTEBERGER.	Creesham.	Philadelphia.	Sept. 22, 1765.
JACOB FISHER.	Germantown.	Philadelphia.	Sept. 22, 1765.
ADAM STEIN.	Northern Liberties.	Philadelphia.	Sept. 22, 1765.
FRED. GASSLER.	Northern Liberties.	Philadelphia.	Sept. 22, 1765.
FRED. ENTSMINGER.	Philadelphia.	Philadelphia.	Sept. 22, 1765.
WENDAL FETTER.	North Wales.	Philadelphia.	Sept. 22, 1765.
JOHN VANDERLIND.	Roxborough.	Philadelphia.	Sept. 22, 1765.
ULRICK FREIAUR.	Lower Dublin.	Philadelphia.	Sept. 22, 1765.
JACOB GREES.	Lower Merrion.	Philadelphia.	Sept. 22, 1765.
VALENTINE CLAGES.	Germantown.	Philadelphia.	Sept. 22, 1765.
MICHL. HINTZ.	Germantown.	Philadelphia.	Sept. 22, 1765.
CONRAD MACH.	Germantown.	Philadelphia.	Sept. 22, 1765.
FREDERICK MAUSE.	Philadelphia.	Philadelphia.	Sept. 22, 1765.

Jurors' Names.	Township.	County.	Sacrament when taken.
DANIEL MAUSE.	Philadelphia.	Philadelphia.	Sept. 22, 1765.
YOST MEYER.	Whitehall.	Northampton.	Sept. 23, 1765.
FRED. ERMENDROUT.	Germantown.	Philadelphia.	Sept. 24, 1765.
JNO. ADAM SWAAB.	Northern Liberties.	Philadelphia.	Sept. 24, 1765.
BALTHAZER GEYER.	Northern Liberties.	Philadelphia.	Sept. 24, 1765.
JOHN NICHS. HERTZHOGG.	Whitehall.	Northampton.	Sept. 24, 1765.
JNO. GEO. RINGER.	Whitehall.	Northampton.	Sept. 24, 1765.
ABRAHAM YOUNG.	Whitehall.	Northampton.	Sept. 24, 1765.
JACOB MEYER.	Cheltenham.	Philadelphia.	Sept. 22, 1765.
JNO. MICHL. MEYER.	Williams.	Northampton.	Sept. 22, 1765.
HENRY KRISE.	Bethlehem.	Northampton.	Sept. 22, 1765.
JACOB LUPFER.	Richmond.	Berks.	Aug. 4, 1765.
JOHN ANDREW REY.	Maiden Creek.	Berks.	Sept. 20, 1765.
JOHN DIETER FALL.	Ruscomb Manor.	Berks.	Sept. 22, 1765.
MICHAEL BROWN.	Lebanon.	Lancaster.	Aug. 18, 1765.
MICHAEL BOLTZ, Junr.	Lebanon.	Lancaster.	July 28, 1765.
GEORGE MEYER.	Germantown.	Philadelphia.	Sept. 29, 1765.
JOHN NISE.	Frederick.	Philadelphia.	Sept. 19, 1765.
ADAM HOLLBUCH.	Frederick.	Philadelphia.	Sept. 19, 1765.
ANDREW YOUNG.	Upper Hanover.	Philadelphia.	Sept. 19, 1765.
PHILIP KRESSLER.	Frederick.	Philadelphia.	Sept. 29, 1765.
JACOB SHWEIGER.	Maxatawny.	Berks.	Sept. 8, 1765.
GEORGE SHWEIGER.	Maxatawny.	Berks.	Sept. 8, 1765.
BERNARD EYTEL.	Frederick.	Philadelphia.	Aug. 25, 1765.
VALENTINE WOOLRIGH.	Hatfield.	Philadelphia.	Sept. 29, 1765.
VALENTINE STRITCHER.	Douglass.	Philadelphia.	Sept. 29, 1765.
JACOB SEYFRIED.	Douglass.	Philadelphia.	Sept. 29, 1765.
CASPAR LAY.	Douglass.	Philadelphia.	Sept. 29, 1765.
PETER STOUT.	Northern Liberties.	Philadelphia.	Sept. 30, 1765.
JOHN MUTSHITLER.	Philadelphia.	Philadelphia.	Sept. 22, 1765.
JACOB SEYFRED.	White Marsh.	Philadelphia.	Sept. 22, 1765.
WILLIAM STEIN.	Passyunk.	Philadelphia.	Sept. 29, 1765.
MICHL. HELLMAN.	Vincent.	Chester.	Oct. 4, 1765.
JNO. ADAM FRITZENBAGH.	Philadelphia.	Philadelphia.	Sept. 30, 1765.
JNO. ANDREAS FORSTER.	Philadelphia.	Philadelphia.	Sept. 30, 1765.
CMRISTIAN SHIDE.	Marlboro.	Philadelphia.	Sept. 22, 1765.
GEORGE RAPP.	Marlboro.	Philadelphia.	Sept. 22, 1765.
MARTIN KISTNER.	Marlboro.	Philadelphia.	Sept. 22, 1765.
GEORGE MARTIN.	Upper Salford.	Philadelphia.	Sept. 22nd, 1765.
GEORGE WYANDT.	Upper Salford.	Philadelphia.	Sept. 22nd, 1765.
HENRY KIPPELL.	Upper Salford.	Philadelphia.	Sept. 22nd, 1765.
GEORGE BEYER.	Frederick.	Philadelphia.	Sept. 22nd, 1765.
JACOB SHEFFER.	Upper Hanover.	Philadelphia.	Sept. 22nd, 1765.
JACOB KRESS.	Worcester.	Philadelphia.	Sept. 30th, 1765.
JNO. MARTIN FORSTER.	Northern Liberties.	Philadelphia.	Aug. 25th, 1765.
HENRY BEYER.	Frederick.	Philadelphia.	Aug. 25th, 1765.
GEORGE DERR.	Upper Salford.	Philadelphia.	Oct. 2nd, 1765.
JNO. PHILIP KREBS.	Northern Liberties.	Philadelphia.	Oct. 2nd, 1765.
MICHAEL SHARP.	Northern Liberties.	Philadelphia.	Oct. 2nd, 1765.
PANCRATIUS NIZEL.	Northern Liberties.	Philadelphia.	Oct. 3rd, 1765.
MICHAEL LABOURER.	Warwick.	Lancaster.	Oct. 4th, 1765.
SAMUEL SPAET.	Oley.	Berks.	Oct. 4th, 1765.
CHRISTIAN SHIEK.	Richmond.	Berks.	Oct. 3rd, 1765.
CHRISTIAN GUTNECHT.	Germantown.	Philadelphia.	

PENNSYLVANIA.

Jurors' Names.	Township.	County.	Sacrament when taken.
John Mankell.	Frederick.	Philadelphia.	Oct. 4th, 1765.
Mary Hasselwanger.	Northern Liberties.	Philadelphia.	Sept. 22nd, 1765.
Henry Gessner.	Moyamens :	Philadelphia.	Oct. 3rd, 1765.
Fred. Renn.	Moyamens :	Philadelphia.	Oct. 3rd, 1765.
George Michl. Craft.	Northern Liberties.	Philadelphia.	Oct. 3rd, 1765.
Conrad Smith.	Horsham.	Philadelphia.	Oct. 3rd, 1765.
Michl. Rapp.	Germantown.	Philadelphia.	Oct. 3rd, 1765.
Jacob Kneedler.	M. Moreland.	Philadelphia.	Oct. 3rd, 1765.
Lawrence Sandman.	M. Moreland.	Philadelphia.	Oct. 3rd, 1765.
Adam Gerich.	Passyunk.	Philadelphia.	Sept. 30th, 1765.
George Kneedler.	Philadelphia.	Philadelphia.	Oct. 4th, 1765.
Jacob Shuster.	Bristol.	Philadelphia.	Oct. 4th, 1765.
John Pless.	Philadelphia.	Philadelphia.	Oct. 4th, 1765.
Wm. Eckert.	Philadelphia.	Philadelphia.	Oct. 4th, 1765.
Nichs. Linderman.	Cheltenham.	Philadelphia.	Sept. 22nd, 1765.
Conrad Cott.	Northern Liberties.	Philadelphia.	Oct. 4th, 1765.
Philip Waggoner.	Northern Liberties.	Philadelphia.	Oct. 4th, 1765.
Jno. Philip Rœrich.	Northern Liberties.	Philadelphia.	Oct. 4th, 1765.
George Smith.	Northern Liberties.	Philadelphia.	Oct. 4th, 1765.
Anthony Kern.	Northern Liberties.	Philadelphia.	Oct. 3rd, 1765.
George Adam Bortz.	Maccungy.	Northampton.	Sept. 29th, 1766.
Fred. Wertz.	Upper Milford.	Northampton.	Sept. 15th, 1765.
Stephen Wunder.	Maccungy.	Northampton.	Sept. 29th, 1765.
John Mitchell.	Whitemarsh.	Philadelphia.	Oct. 4th, 1765.
George Fisher.	Whitemarsh.	Philadelphia.	Oct. 4th, 1765.
Michael Teiss.	Tredryffrin.	Chester.	Oct. 4th, 1765.
George Hanselman.	Douglass.	Berks.	Oct. 4th, 1765.
Christofr. Bittle.	Douglass.	Berks.	Oct. 4th, 1765.
Jacob Debertshauser.	Douglass.	Berks.	Oct. 4th, 1765.
Conrad Smith.	Douglass.	Berks.	Oct. 4th, 1765.
John Ebener.	Rachlin.	Berks.	Sept. 8th, 1765.
John Romicht.	Douglass.	Berks.	Oct. 4th, 1765.
Christr. Bearman.	Skippack.	Philadelphia.	Oct. 2nd 1765.
Bernard Gartner.	Cocolico.	Lancaster.	Sept. 15th, 1765.
Hartman Cook.	Lebanon.	Lancaster.	Sept. 15th, 1765.
Jonas Rubb.	Lebanon.	Lancaster.	Sept. 22nd, 1765.
Benedict Storney.	New Hanover.	Philadelphia.	Oct. 4th, 1765.
John Kamerling.	Lebanon.	Lancaster.	Sept. 22nd, 1765.
Christopher Mayer.	Philadelphia.	Philadelphia.	Oct. 4th, 1765.
Baltzer Kientzler.	Philadelphia.	Philadelphia.	Oct. 4th, 1765.
Jonas Metzger.	Upper Salford.	Philadelphia.	Oct. 4th, 1765.
Theodore Kiehl.	Greenwich.	Berks.	Sept. 15th, 1765.
Jno. Jacob Faust.	Greenwich.	Berks.	Sept. 15th, 1765.
Eberhard Michael.	Philadelphia.	Philadelphia.	Sept. 15th, 1765.
John Vogel.	Bethlehem.	Northampton.	Sept. 22nd, 1765.
John Nydich.	Frederick.	Philadelphia.	Oct. 3rd, 1765.
Leonard Nydich.	Frederick.	Philadelphia.	Oct. 3rd, 1765.
Jacob Dantfelzer.	Pikes.	Chester.	Oct. 4th, 1765.
Wendal Hendrich.	Pikes.	Chester.	Oct. 4th, 1765.
Conrad Miller.	Pikes.	Chester.	Oct. 4th, 1765.
Jacob Eppele.	Vincent.	Chester.	Oct. 4th, 1765.
Martin Gloss.	Douglass.	Philadelphia.	Oct. 4th, 1765.

Jurors' Names.	Township.	County.	Sacrament when taken.
EBERHARD DIEHL.	Northern Liberties.	Philadelphia.	Oct. 4th, 1765.
ADAM CUMPAR.	Bethlehem.	Northampton.	Sept. 30th, 1765.
HENRY HINTZ.	Germantown.	Philadelphia.	Sept. 22nd, 1765.
NICHS. HOOFMAN.	Worcester.	Philadelphia.	Sept. 29th, 1765.
JOHN JUNT.	Upper Salford.	Northampton.	Sept. 15th, 1765.
CHRISTR. WEAVER.	Plymouth.	Philadelphia.	Oct. 4th, 1765.
GEORGE WOLKEMAR.	White Marsh.	Philadelphia.	Oct. 3rd, 1765.
MICHL. TEISS.	Plymouth.	Philadelphia.	Oct. 3rd, 1765.
JOHN NESSLY.	Germantown.	Philadelphia.	Sept. 22nd, 1765.
JACOB LŒSHER.	Lower Dublin.	Philadelphia.	Oct. 4th, 1765.
MICHL. HARMAN.	Lower Dublin.	Philadelphia.	Oct. 4th, 1765.
MICHL. BROTHEARS.	Philadelphia.	Philadelphia.	Oct. 4th, 1765.
JOHN OGENBACH.	Lebanon.	Lancaster.	Sept. 28th, 1765.
CONRAD LOUBSHER.	Lebanon.	Lancaster.	Sept. 28th, 1765.
CONRAD MESSINGER.	Lebanon.	Lancaster.	Sept. 28th, 1765.
MATHIAS BOGER.	Lebanon.	Lancaster.	Sept. 28th, 1765.
BERNARD KETZ.	Lower Salford.	Philadelphia.	Sept. 28th, 1765.
PETER HEYLMAN.	Lebanon.	Lancaster.	Sept. 28th, 1765.
DANIEL STROH.	Lebanon.	Lancaster.	Sept. 28th, 1765.
NICHS. ENTSMINGER.	Lebanon.	Lancaster.	Sept. 28th, 1765.
GEORGE STERR.	Northern Liberties.	Philadelphia.	Oct. 3rd, 1765.
JOHN JACOB GLOSS.	Northern Liberties.	Philadelphia.	Oct. 4th, 1765.
JACOB RILL.	Northern Liberties.	Philadelphia.	Oct. 4th, 1765.
JACOB BAUM.	Northern Liberties.	Philadelphia.	Oct. 4th, 1765.
GEORGE SNYDER.	Northern Liberties.	Philadelphia.	Oct. 4th, 1765.
LEONARD UMBERGER.	Lebanon.	Lancaster.	Oct. 3rd, 1765.
SEBASTIAN SONLEIGHTNER.	Northern Liberties.	Philadelphia.	Oct. 4th, 1765.
RUDOLPH MEYER.	Philadelphia.	Philadelphia.	Oct. 4th, 1765.
NICHOLAS BALTEWIN.	Movamens :	Philadelphia.	Oct. 3rd, 1765.
MICHL. SEYFRIED.	Whitpain.	Philadelphia.	Oct. 3rd, 1765.
GOLLIP ZINCH.	Northern Liberties.	Philadelphia.	Oct. 3rd, 1765.
CONRAD ZELLNER.	Pikeland.	Chester.	Oct. 3rd, 1765.
FELIX FENNER.	Philadelphia.	Philadelphia.	Oct. 3rd, 1765.
WILLIAM GRISCUM.	Philadelphia.	Philadelphia.	Oct. 3rd, 1765.
JOHN BRAININGER.	Windsor.	Berks.	Sept. 20th, 1765.
CHRISTR. BOL.	Northern Liberties.	Philadelphia.	Oct. 3rd, 1765.
HENRY UMBERGER.	Lebanon.	Lancaster.	Oct. 3rd, 1765.
CONRAD WAGNER.	Northern Liberties.	Philadelphia.	Oct. 3rd, 1765.
JOHN GEORGE KREISS.	Northern Liberties.	Philadelphia.	Oct. 3rd, 1765.
PAUL DULLMAN.	Philadelphia.	Philadelphia.	Oct. 3rd, 1765.
ANDREW STOLLBERGER.	Philadelphia.	Philadelphia.	Oct. 3rd, 1765.
JOHN JOSEPH GRAFF.	Philadelphia.	Philadelphia.	Oct. 3rd, 1765.
GEORGE BAKEOVEN.	Philadelphia.	Philadelphia.	Oct. 3rd, 1765.
CONRAD GRIM.	Upper Salford.	Philadelphia.	Oct. 4th, 1765.
JOHN GEORGE GRIM.	Upper Salford.	Philadelphia.	Oct. 4th, 1765.
JOHN SHLOTTER.	Philadelphia.	Philadelphia.	Oct. 4th, 1765.
FRED. HOBBAKER.	Germantown.	Philadelphia.	Oct. 3rd, 1765.
JOHN FEHR.	Tinnicum.	Bucks.	Oct. 4th, 1765.
CHRISTR. NOTZ.	Lower Dublin.	Philadelphia.	Sept. 15th, 1765.
GEORGE FECK.	Philadelphia.	Philadelphia.	Sept. 22nd, 1765.
MARTIN FARRINGER.	Philadelphia.	Philadelphia.	Sept. 22nd, 1765.
ANTHONY HEIGHT.	Philadelphia.	Philadelphia.	Sept. 22nd, 1765.
MARTIN SNYDER.	Philadelphia.	Philadelphia.	Sept. 22nd, 1765.
CHRISTIAN HUNTZIKER.	Allen.	Northampton.	Oct. 6th, 1765.

PENNSYLVANIA.

Jurors' Names.	Township.	County.	Sacrament when taken.
PETER KLEIN.	Maccungy.	Northampton.	Sept. 29th, 1765.
JOHN GEO. EHRENHART.	Lowhill.	Northampton.	Sept. 29th, 1765.
ANDREW ERSHBACH.	Lowhill.	Northampton.	Sept. 29th, 1765.
GEORGE KIND.	Lowhill.	Northampton.	Sept. 29th, 1765.
LORENTZ KLEIN.	Lowhill.	Northampton.	Sept. 29th, 1765.
JACOB BACHMAN.	Lowhill.	Northampton.	Oct. 10th, 1765.
YOST GEORGE.	Lowhill.	Northampton.	Oct. 10th, 1765.
MARTIN BUCHMAN.	Lowhill.	Northampton.	Oct. 10th, 1765.
GEORGE SEIGER.	Weisenberg.	Northampton.	Sept. 22nd, 1765.
BARTHOLOMEW MILLER.	Maccungy.	Northampton.	Oct. 7th, 1765.
HENRY GRIGELL.	Lowhill.	Northampton.	Oct. 7th, 1765.
NICHS. MANNABACH.	Weisenburg.	Northampton.	Oct. 7th, 1765.
MARTIN SHOB.	Weisenburg.	Northampton.	Oct. 7th, 1765.
DANIEL STETLER.	Weisenburg.	Northampton.	Oct. 7th, 1765.
ADAM KLEIN.	Weisenburg.	Northampton.	Oct. 7th, 1765.
FREDERICK MOYER.	Heidleberg.	Northampton.	22nd Sept., 1765.
SIMON WEHR.	Heidleberg.	Northampton.	Oct. 6th, 1765.
FREDERICK SNYDER.	Heidleberg.	Northampton.	Oct. 6th, 1765.
JOHN REINSHMIT.	Heidleberg.	Northampton.	Oct. 6th, 1765.
ADOLPH PETER.	Richmond.	Berks.	Sept. 8th, 1765.
JOHN PETER.	Richmond.	Berks.	Sept. 8th, 1765.
HENRY SHEFFER.	Weisenberg.	Northampton.	Sept. 8th, 1765.
JNO. MARTIN WUCHTER.	Heidleberg.	Northampton.	Sept. 22nd, 1765.
HENRY SHIMPFER.	Lowhill.	Northampton.	Oct. 10th, 1765.
GEORGE GEORGE.	Lowhill.	Northampton.	Oct. 10th, 1765.
ENGLE THOMAS.	Lowhill.	Northampton.	Oct. 10th, 1765.
MICHL. BIEBER.	Weisenberg.	Northampton.	Oct. 8th, 1765.
FRANCIS GILDENER.	Heidleberg.	Northampton.	Sept. 22nd, 1765.
CHARLES RUPPERT.	Heidleberg.	Northampton.	Sept. 22nd, 1765.
DANIEL BURGER.	Heidleberg.	Northampton	Oct. 6th, 1765.
ADAM THOMAS.	Heidleberg.	Northampton.	Oct. 6th, 1765.
JACOB TAUBENSPECK.	Heidleberg.	Northampton.	Oct. 6th, 1765.
JACOB SNYDER.	Lowhill.	Northampton.	Oct. 10th, 1765.
FREDERICK POPPEMYER.	Long Swamp.	Berks.	Oct. 6th, 1765.
MARTIN EILERT.	Lowhill.	Northampton.	Oct. 10th. 1765.
PETER KROH.	Weisenburg.	Northampton.	Oct. 8th, 1765.
PETER CONFER.	Weisenburg.	Northampton.	Oct. 8th. 1765.
JACOB KLEIN.	Weisenburg.	Northampton.	Sept. 22nd, 1765.
PETER SELT.	Heidleberg.	Northampton.	Sept. 22nd, 1765.
JACOB ARNDT.	Heidleberg.	Northampton.	Sept. 22nd, 1765.
MELCHIOR SEIP.	Maccungy.	Northampton.	Sept. 29th, 1765.
CHRISTOPR. OBLE.	Lowhill.	Northampton.	Oct. 10th, 1765.
HENRY BECKLEE.	Northern Liberties.	Philadelphia.	Oct. 9th, 1765.
JOHN CASPAR SNERR.	Heidleberg.	Northampton.	Oct. 6th, 1765.
GEORGE SPARR.	Heidleberg.	Northampton.	Oct. 6th, 1765.
LEONARD FUHR.	Heidleberg.	Northampton.	Oct. 6th, 1765.
JOHN WARNER.	Philadelphia.	Philadelphia.	Oct. 7th, 1765.
WIGAND DIEHL.	Frederick.	Philadelphia.	Oct. 10th, 1765.
CONRAD BLOTZ.	Heidleberg.	Northampton.	Oct. 6th, 1765.
CASPAR PETER.	Heidleberg.	Northampton.	Oct. 6th, 1765.
JACOB BEEREN.	Maccungy.	Northampton.	Sept. 24th, 1765.
JOHN MILLER.	Heidleberg.	Northampton.	Sept. 22nd, 1765.

Jurors' Names.	Township.	County.	Sacrament when taken.
John Fœller,	Heidleberg.	Northampton.	Oct. 6th, 1765.
Rudolph Peter.	Heidleberg.	Northampton.	Oct. 8th, 1765.
John Keck.	Heidleberg.	Northampton.	Sept. 22nd, 1765.
Jacob Fœrber.	Heidleberg.	Northampton.	Oct. 8th, 1765.
George Stern.	Lowhill.	Northampton.	Oct. 10th, 1765.
Jacob Klotz.	Lowhill.	Northampton.	Oct. 10th, 1765.
Michl. Dieber.	Lowhill.	Northampton.	Oct. 10th, 1765.
Samuel Mehl.	Heidleberg.	Northampton.	Oct. 8th, 1765.
Jacob Guiger.	Heidleberg.	Northampton.	Sept. 22nd, 1765.
Leonard Wassum.	Heidleberg.	Northampton.	Sept. 22nd, 1765.
Henry Shlebach.	Heidleberg.	Northampton.	Sept. 22nd, 1765.
Jacob Shankweiler.	Maccungy.	Northampton.	Oct. 9th, 1765.
Peter Rethler.	Maccungy.	Northampton.	Oct. 9th, 1765.
Christian Trefensted.	Maccungy.	Northampton.	Oct. 9th, 1765.
Bernard Fegele.	Long Swamp.	Berks.	Oct 6th, 1765.
Conrad Yeger.	Long Swamp.	Berks.	Oct 6th, 1765.
Matthias Eigner.	Maccungy.	Northampton.	Oct. 9th, 1765.
George Hauser.	Whitehall.	Northampton.	Oct. 8th, 1765.
John Siegell.	Whitehall.	Northampton.	Oct. 8th, 1765.
Martin Semell.	Whitehall.	Northampton.	Oct. 8th, 1765.
Melchior Ziegler,	Maccungy.	Northampton.	Oct. 9th, 1765.
Christian Reys.	Linn.	Northampton.	Oct. 11th, 1765.
Henry Witerstien.	Linn.	Northampton.	Oct. 11th, 1765.
Peter Hatterick,	Richland.	Bucks.	Aug. 8th, 1765.
Nichs. Hatterick.	Bedminster.	Bucks.	Aug. 8th, 1765.
Leonard Hinckell.	Richland.	Bucks.	Aug. 8th, 1765.
Philip Hœring.	Richland.	Bucks.	Aug. 8th, 1765.
John Mann.	Springfield.	Bucks.	Oct. 10th, 1765.
Peter Hefft.	Haycock.	Bucks.	Oct. 10th, 1765.
Simon Peter Geres.	Springfield.	Bucks.	Oct. 10th, 1765.
Peter Shuk.	Springfield.	Bucks.	Oct. 10th, 1765.
Philip Correll.	Springfield.	Bucks.	Oct. 10th, 1765.
Isaac Wyerbach.	Springfield.	Bucks.	Oct. 10th, 1765.
Michl. Diehl.	Springfield.	Bucks.	Oct. 10th, 1765.
Daniel Diehl.	Springfield.	Bucks.	Oct. 10th, 1765.
George Hammond.	Haycock.	Bucks.	Oct. 10th, 1765.
Joseph Gerber.	Linn.	Northampton.	Oct. 11th, 1765.
Jacob Weitzell.	Linn.	Northampton.	Oct. 11th, 1765.
Michl. Weitzell.	Linn.	Northampton.	Oct. 11th, 1765.
Peter Gift.	Linn.	Northampton.	Oct. 11th, 1765.
Dewald Myer.	Weisenburg.	Northampton.	Aug. 4th, 1765.
John Henningher.	Rockhill.	Bucks.	Aug. 4th, 1765.
Dietrick Batteauf.	Linn.	Northampton.	Oct. 11th, 1765.
Valentine Durr.	Linn.	Northampton.	Oct. 11th, 1765.
George Breyner.	Linn.	Northampton.	Oct. 11th, 1765.
Philip Anthony.	Linn.	Northampton.	Oct. 11th, 1765.
Melchior Durr.	Linn.	Northampton.	Oct. 11th, 1765.
Andreas Wilt.	Weisenburg.	Northampton.	Oct. 8th, 1765.
Sebastian Werlein.	Weisenburg.	Northampton.	Oct. 8th, 1765.
Adam Klauss.	Linn.	Northampton.	Oct. 8th, 1765.
Jacob Snyder.	Linn.	Northampton.	Oct. 8th, 1765.
Ludwick Hantz.	Linn.	Northampton.	Oct. 8th, 1765.
Sylvester Holloe.	Linn.	Northampton.	Oct. 8th, 1765.
George Binkes.	Linn.	Northampton.	Oct. 8th, 1765.

NATURALIZATIONS

PENNSYLVANIA.

Jurors' Names.	Township.	County.	Sacrament when taken.
GEORGE NYDIG.	Linn.	Northampton.	Oct. 8th, 1765.
PETER MARTIN.	Upper Milford.	Northampton..	Oct. 9th, 1765.
MICHAEL RINGER.	Upper Milford.	Northampton.	Oct. 9th, 1765.
GEORGE STEINROC.	Douglass.	Philadelphia.	Oct. 11th, 1765.
PHILIP KISTNER.	Weisenburg.	Northampton.	Oct. 11th, 1765.
JACOB BOGER.	Lowhill.	Northampton.	Oct. 11th, 1765.
MARTIN SHUCK.	Linn.	Northampton.	Oct. 11th, 1765.
MICHAEL HEDINGER.	Linn.	Northampton.	Oct. 11th, 1765.
BALTZER SMITH.	Long Swamp.	Berks.	Oct. 9th, 1765.
GEORGE EDLEMAN.	Maccungy.	Northampton.	Oct. 9th, 1765.
CONRAD KLEIN.	Upper Milford.	Northampton.	Sept. 9th, 1765.
HONNES KRAUS.	Heidleberg.	Northampton.	Sept. 22nd, 1765.
ANDREAS HOOTZ.	Heidleberg.	Northampton.	Sept. 22nd, 1765.
HENRY NELICH.	Whitehall.	Northampton.	Sept. 22nd, 1765.
JOSEPH KENDELL.	Whitehall.	Northampton.	Sept. 22nd, 1765.
THEOBALD KENDELL.	Whitehall.	Northampton.	Sept. 22nd, 1765.
JOHN MARTIN EYRE.	Bedminster.	Bucks.	Sept. 8th, 1765.
JOHN PHILIP SHRIER.	Bedminster.	Bucks.	Sept. 8th, 1765.
HARTMAN LEIBENGUT.	Upper Milford.	Northampton.	July 15th, 1765.
JACOB DIEHL.	Upper Milford.	Northampton.	July 15th, 1765.
BERNARD DORR.	Upper Milford.	Northampton.	July 15th, 1765.
MICHL. WARMKESSELL.	Maccungy.	Northampton.	Oct. 9th, 1765.
JOHN WEIBAR.	Maccungy.	Northampton.	Oct. 9th, 1765.
CHRISTIAN SEITER.	Maccungy.	Northampton.	Oct. 9th, 1765.
MICHL. BASLER.	Maccungy.	Northampton.	Oct. 9th, 1765.
ANDREAS FETZER.	Maccungy.	Northampton.	Oct. 9th, 1765.
JACOB FINSTERMAKER.	Long Swamp.	Berks.	Sept. 22nd, 1765.
ENGLE BINCKES.	Upper Hanover.	Philadelphia.	Sept. 22nd, 1765.
SAMUEL DORMEYER.	Longswamp.	Berks.	Sept. 13th, 1765.
THEOBALD KLINE.	Longswamp.	Berks.	Sept. 13th, 1765.
GEORGE KLINE.	Longswamp.	Berks.	Sept. 13th, 1765.
PETER WEISS.	Weisenburg.	Northampton.	Oct. 11th, 1765.
JOHN MERCKLE.	Maccungy.	Northampton.	Oct. 11th, 1765.
CHRISTIAN SEIBERLING.	Weisenburg.	Northampton.	Oct. 11th, 1765.
PHILIP KRIG.	Warwick.	Lancaster.	Oct. 13th, 1765.
JACOB LEHMAN.	Cocolico.	Lancaster.	Sept. 1st, 1765.
JOHN FLAMMER.	Longswamp.	Berks.	Sept. 22nd, 1765.
CONRAD DREES.	Longswamp.	Berks.	Sept. 22nd, 1765.
ANDREAS SAAM.	Longswamp.	Berks.	Sept. 22nd, 1765.
JACOB BLESING.	Cocolico.	Lancaster.	Oct. 14th, 1765.
JACOB THOMAS.	Elizabeth.	Lancaster.	Oct. 14th, 1765.
GEO. HETZLER.	Warwick.	Lancaster.	Sept. 1st, 1765.
BALTZER HETZLER.	Elizabeth.	Lancaster.	Sept. 1st, 1765.
CASPAR AUGISLIN.	Elizabeth.	Lancaster.	Sept. 1st, 1765.
NICHS. MARX.	Whitehall.	Northampton.	Sept. 22nd, 1765
GEORGE MYER.	Whitehall.	Northampton.	Sept. 22nd, 1765.
DANIEL SNYDER.	Whitehall.	Northampton.	Sept. 22nd, 1765.
FELIX ARNER.	Whitehall.	Northampton.	Sept. 22nd, 1765.
CHRISTOPHER MILLER.	Maccungay.	Northampton.	Sept. 22nd, 1765.
PHILIP ARNOLD.	Weisenburg.	Northampton.	Sept. 22nd, 1765
GEORGE KNŒDLER.	Lowhill.	Northampton.	Sept. 24th, 1765.
ANDREAS LEISER.	Lowhill.	Northampton.	Sept. 24th, 1765

Jurors' Names.	Township.	County.	Sacrament when taken.
GEORGE HARTMAN.	Lowhill.	Northampton.	Sept. 24th, 1765.
LEONARD WELKER.	Maccungy.	Northampton.	Sept. 24th, 1765.
JOHN TSERFASS.	Lowhill.	Northampton.	Sept. 24th, 1765.
GEORGE SINN.	Lowhill.	Northampton.	Sept. 24th, 1765.
PHILIP STEIN.	Bedminster.	Bucks.	July 15th, 1765.
GEORGE GOOTEKUNTZ.	Weisenburg.	Northampton.	Oct. 12th, 1765.
PAUL SHUMAKER.	Lowhill.	Northampton.	Sept. 24th, 1765.
GODFREY BECKER.	Exeter.	Berks.	Oct. 14th, 1765.
FREDERICK BECK.	Weisenberg.	Northampton.	Oct. 12th, 1765.
JACOB WINTER.	Lowhill.	Northampton.	Sept. 24th, 1765.
CASPAR BANER.	Maccungy.	Northampton.	Sept. 18th, 1765.
CONRAD MAINTZER.	Warwick.	Lancaster.	Sept. 1st, 1765.
MICH. MAINTZER.	Warwick.	Lancaster.	Sept. 1st, 1765.
NICHS. KIENDT.	Weisenberg.	Northampton.	Oct. 12th, 1765.
MARTIN KARCH.	Weisenberg.	Northampton.	Oct. 12th, 1765.
ADAM DIEDERICK.	Lowhill.	Northampton.	Sept. 30th, 1765.
SIMON MOSER.	Linn.	Northampton.	Sept. 30th, 1765.
ADAM MAURER.	Whitehall.	Northampton.	Sept. 22nd, 1765.
ADAM SHNECK.	Whitehall.	Northampton.	Sept. 22nd, 1765.
CONRAD LUDWICK.	Hertford.	Berks.	Oct. 13th, 1765.
PHILIP LEYTENTECKER.	Hertford.	Berks.	Oct. 13th, 1765.
CASPAR BERICH.	Upper Hanover.	Philadelphia.	Oct. 13th, 1765.
ABRAHAM GERRARD.	Douglass.	Philadelphia.	Oct. 13th, 1765.
JOHN GEORGE STERRY.	Whitehall.	Northampton.	Sept. 30th, 1765.
SAMUEL MUSE.	Whitehall.	Northampton.	Sept. 30th, 1765.
JOHN MARTIN HERTER.	Whitehall.	Northampton.	Sept. 30th, 1765.
JACOB HENRICK.	Whitehall.	Northampton.	Sept. 30th, 1765.
JACOB WIRT.	Whitehall.	Northampton.	Sept. 30th, 1765.
YOST DIEHL	Lowhill.	Northampton.	Sept. 12th, 1765.
GEORGE RUPPERT.	Heidleberg.	Northampton.	Sept. 30th, 1765.
JOHN FREY.	Heidleberg.	Northampton.	Oct. 6th, 1765.
NICHS. STŒRNER.	Allen.	Northampton.	Oct. 13th, 1765.
DAVID HAUSMAN.	Allen.	Northampton.	Oct. 13th, 1765.
BARTHOLOMEW RIBELET.	Allen.	Northampton.	Oct. 15th, 1765.
YOST SHLIGER.	Upper Hanover.	Philadelphia.	Oct. 13th, 1765.
HENRY RESS.	Hatfield.	Philadelphia.	Oct. 13th, 1765.
FREDERICK KARN.	Heidleberg.	Northampton.	Sept. 30th, 1765.
JACOB GUTNER.	Heidleberg.	Northampton.	Sept. 30th, 1765.
JOHN KUNKLE.	Heidleberg.	Northampton.	Sept. 30th, 1765.
JACOB HAUSMAN.	Heidleberg.	Northampton.	Sept. 30th, 1765.
PETER GUTH.	Whitehall.	Northampton.	Oct. 11th, 1765.
PETER BECKLER.	Whitehall.	Northampton.	Oct. 11th, 1765.
HENRY TURNET.	Whitehall.	Northampton.	Oct. 11th, 1765.
PAUL GROSS.	Whitehall.	Northampton.	Oct. 11th, 1765.
ABRA'M KNERR.	Lowhill.	Northampton.	Oct. 11th, 1765.
JOHN WASEM.	Heidleberg.	Northampton.	Oct. 11th, 1765.
JACOB HORNER.	Lowhill.	Northampton.	Oct. 11th, 1765.
CASPAR KOCH.	Warwick.	Lancaster.	Sept. 1st, 1765.
CATHERINE KOPPIN.	Weisenberg.	Northampton.	Sept. 30th, 1765.
PETER ELSER.	Warwick.	Lancaster.	Oct. 15th, 1765.
BALTZER WIRTZ.[1]	Whitehall.	Northampton.	Sept. 30th, 1765.
GEORGE STOBER.	Cocolico.	Lancaster.	Oct. 15th, 1765.

1. According to a marginal note this entry should have followed immediately that of JACOB WIRT above.

NATURALIZATIONS

PENNSYLVANIA.

Jurors' Names.	Township.	County.	Sacrament, when taken
BERNARD KUHNS.	Lehi.	Northampton.	Oct. 6th, 1765.
JOHN SOLD.	Lehi.	Northampton.	Oct. 6th, 1765.
JOHN SHAEFFER.	Maccungy.	Northampton.	Oct. 9th, 1765.
WILLIAM KREITZ.	Whitehall.	Northampton.	Oct. 13th, 1765.
GEORGE HEITZELMAN.	Lowhill.	Northampton.	Sept. 30th, 1765.
CHRISTIAN HOFFMAN.	Heidleberg.	Northampton.	Oct. 12th, 1765.
PETER BEHR.	Heidleberg.	Northampton.	Oct. 12th, 1765.
HENRY REINHARD.	Heidleberg.	Northampton.	Oct. 12th, 1765.
CONRAD KOLB.	Richmond.	Berks.	Oct. 15th, 1765.
ADAM GERRMAN.	Bern.	Berks.	July 22nd, 1765.
CHARLES GUSS.	Upper Hanover.	Philadelphia.	Sept. 30th, 1765.
JOHN MILLER.	Tredeffrin.	Chester.	Sept. 14th, 1765.
JACOB HAUSER.	Tredeffrin.	Chester.	Sept. 14th, 1765.
PAUL GERHARDING.	Tredeffrin.	Chester.	Sept. 14th, 1765.
SEBASTIAN RINK.	Tredeffrin.	Chester.	Sept. 14th, 1765.
JOHN KECK.	Tredeffrin.	Chester.	Sept. 14th, 1765.
PETER SMITH.	Weisenburg.	Northampton.	Sept. 30th, 1765.
CHRISTR. TRESHER.	Weisenburg.	Northampton.	Sept. 30th, 1765.
JACOB VOGEL.	Maccungy.	Northampton.	Oct. 9th, 1765.
PETER GEISS.	Maccungy.	Northampton.	Oct. 9th, 1765.
PETER HAFF.	Maccungy.	Northampton.	Oct. 9th, 1765.
ANDREW SUSANG.	Longswamp.	Berks.	Oct. 15th, 1765.
GEORGE PARALL.	Longswamp.	Berks.	Oct. 15th, 1765.
MICHAEL KERN.	Linn.	Northampton.	Oct. 13th, 1765.
JOHN YEAGER.	Heidleberg.	Northampton.	Oct. 6th, 1765.
CHRISTIAN SMITH.	Heidleberg.	Northampton.	Oct. 6th, 1765.
ULRICK NEFF.	Heidleberg.	Northampton.	Oct. 6th, 1765.
HENRY SMITH.	Heidleberg.	Northampton.	Oct. 6th, 1765.
JOHN REBER.	Heidleberg.	Northampton.	Oct. 6th, 1765.
PHILIP FITLER.	Heidleberg.	Northampton.	Oct. 6th, 1765.
HENRY HOFFMAN.	Heidleberg.	Northampton.	Oct. 6th, 1765.
JOHN NOMAN.	Bedminster.	Bucks.	Sept. 15th, 1765.
CONRAD MITTMAN.	Bedminster.	Bucks.	Sept. 15th, 1765.
ANNA BARBARA BENSHERIN.	Bedminster.	Bucks.	Sept. 15th, 1765.
JNO. DIEHL HERMAN.	Weisenburg.	Northampton.	Sept. 30th, 1765.
FREDERICK HIRSH.	Weisenburg.	Northampton.	Sept. 30th, 1765.
ADAM WEBER.	Weisenburg.	Northampton.	Sept. 30th, 1765.
JACOB BARRALL.	Weisenburg.	Northampton.	Sept. 30th, 1765.
JOHN RUMPELL.	Heidleberg.	Northampton.	Sept. 30th, 1765.
PETER HEYMBACH.	Weisenburg.	Northampton.	Sept. 30th, 1765.
JNO. NICH. GIFT.	Weisenburg.	Northampton.	Sept. 30th, 1765.
MATTHIAS GIFT.	Weisenburg.	Northampton.	Sept. 30th, 1765.
FRED. DOUEY.	Providence.	Philadelphia.	Sept. 15th, 1765.
SEBASTIAN WERNER.	Heidleberg.	Northampton.	Oct. 15th, 1765.
JACOB PETER.	Heidleberg.	Northampton.	Oct. 15th, 1765.
PETER FELLER.	Heidleberg.	Northampton.	Oct. 15th, 1765.
ANDREAS FELLER.	Heidleberg.	Northampton.	Oct. 15th, 1765.
GEORGE ARNOLD.	Albany.	Berks.	Oct. 15th, 1765.
HENRY FRY.	Albany.	Berks.	Oct. 15th, 1765.
GEORGE BAUMAN.	Greenwich.	Berks.	Oct. 15th, 1765.
RUDOLPH ZIEMER.	Greenwich.	Berks.	Oct. 15th, 1765.
MATHIAS RŒMER,	Greenwich.	Berks,	Oct. 15th, 1765.

Jurors' Names.	Township.	County.	Sacrament, when taken
MARTIN UNUNGST.	Greenwich.	Berks.	Oct. 15th, 1765.
JACOB FOST.	Bedminster.	Bucks.	Oct. 15th, 1765.
PHILIP HAMMELL.	Maccungy.	Northampton.	Oct. 9th, 1765.
JNO. ADAM DELL.	Greenwich.	Berks.	Oct. 15th, 1765.
ANTHY. SHRETER.	Richmond.	Berks.	Oct. 15th, 1765.
PHILIP SHUUNS.	Richmond.	Berks.	Oct. 15th, 1765.
JOHN KOHLER.	Greenwich.	Berks.	Oct. 15th, 1765.
ADAM MEYER.	Greenwich.	Berks.	Oct. 15th, 1765.
JACOB WILLDRAUT.	Greenwich.	Berks.	Oct. 15th, 1765.
NICHOLAS BARON.	Richmond.	Berks.	Oct. 15th, 1765.
LUDWICK OTTERMAN.	Richmond.	Berks.	Oct. 15th, 1765.
NICHS. QUIERIN.	Maxatawny.	Berks.	Oct. 13th, 1765.
GEO. OLINGER.	Richmond.	Berks.	Oct. 15th, 1765.
GODFRY STIRN.	Greenwich.	Berks.	Oct. 13th, 1765.
MICH. MAUSER.	Greenwich.	Berks.	Oct. 13th, 1765.
ANTHY. WALTER.	Greenwich.	Berks.	Oct. 13th, 1765.
JACOB HARTMAN.	Maxatawny.	Berks.	Oct. 13th, 1765.
JUSTUS TRESHBACH.	Lehi.	Northampton.	July 16th, 1765.
ADAM TRESHBACH.	Lehi.	Northampton.	July 16th, 1765.
SIMON DREISHBACH.	Lehi.	Northampton.	July 16th, 1765.
JOHN TRESBACH.	Lehi.	Northampton.	July 16th, 1765.
HENRY ULRICK.	Lehi.	Northampton.	July 16th, 1765.
CONRAD BAUER.	Greenwich.	Berks.	Oct. 13th, 1765.
JACOB ALMAND.	Lehi.	Northampton.	Oct. 6th, 1765.
JACOB BUCKMAN.	Lehi.	Northampton.	Oct. 6th, 1765.
NICHS. ALMAND.	Lehi.	Northampton.	Oct. 6th, 1765.
CHRISTR. HOWER.	Cocolico.	Lancaster.	Sept. 29th, 1765.
HENRY RATEMAKER.	Bern.	Berks.	Sept. 22nd, 1765.
BERNARD SNYDER.	Linn.	Northampton.	Oct. 6th, 1765.
GEORGE OBERDORF.	Maxatawny.	Berks.	Oct. 13th, 1765.
GEORGE ADAM KOBER.	Rockhill.	Bucks.	Oct. 15th, 1765.
SAMUEL WEISS.	Long Swamp.	Berks.	Oct. 6th, 1765.
JACOB BERNER.	Weisenberg.	Northampton.	Oct. 6th, 1765.
SOLOMON BAKER.	Albany.	Northampton.	Oct. 6th, 1765.
BERNARD REISS.	Lehi.	Northampton.	Oct. 6th, 1765.
ANDREW PETRI.	Providence.	Philadelphia.	Oct. 6th, 1765.
GEORGE WACHTER.	Cocolico.	Lancaster.	Sept. 1st, 1765.
JOHN PHILLIPPI.	Elizabeth.	Lancaster.	Oct. 13th. 1765.
HARTMAN KUNTZ.	Linn.	Northampton.	Oct. 14th, 1765.
CHRISTR. EILENBERGER.	Eastown.	Northampton.	Aug. 18th, 1765.
JOHN SHREIBER.	Whitehall.	Northampton.	Oct. 6th, 1765.
NICHS. CARKER.	Pikes.	Chester.	Oct. 12th, 1765.
PETER HARDMAN.	Pikes.	Chester.	Oct. 12th, 1765.
MICHL. PETZ.	Warwick.	Lancaster.	Oct. 14th, 1765.
MICHL. KING.	Pikes.	Chester.	Oct. 17th, 1765.
GEORGE EMIG.	Pikes.	Chester.	Oct. 17th, 1765.
JOHN KLINGER.	Pikes.	Chester.	Oct. 17th, 1765.
JOHN MILLAR.	Colebrookdale.	Berks.	Oct. 16th, 1765.
JACOB SMITH.	Colebrookdale.	Berks.	Oct. 16th, 1765.
JACOB BIEL.	Linn.	Northampton.	Oct. 14th, 1765.
PETER BERNARD HINKEN.	Pikes.	Chester.	Oct. 6th, 1765.
THEOBALD LONG.	Colebrookdale.	Berks.	Oct. 17th, 1765.
JOHN HILBERT.	Oley.	Berks.	Oct. 17th, 1765.
JACOB KEPPLER.	Upper Milford.	Northampton.	Sept. 29th, 1765.

PENNSYLVANIA.

Jurors' Names.	Township.	County.	Sacrament, when taken
ADAM MOSES.	Pikes.	Chester.	Oct. 12th, 1765.
JACOB SLEER.	Pikes.	Chester.	Oct. 12th, 1765.
GEORGE FISLAR.	Pikes.	Chester.	Oct. 12th, 1765.
PETER DEMLER.	Pikes.	Chester.	Oct. 12th, 1765.
PHILIP MENTZ.	Pikes.	Chester.	Oct. 12th, 1765.
GEORGE SHEETZ.	Lower Milford.	Bucks.	Oct. 6th, 1765.
GEORGE ZIGENFOOS.	Lower Milford.	Bucks.	Oct. 6th, 1765.
JOHN HARTMAN.	Pikes.	Chester.	Oct. 12th, 1765.
FRANCIS OBERKIRSH.	Maccungy.	Northampton.	Oct. 14th, 1765.
GEORGE BRAIDBECK.	Maccungy.	Northampton.	Oct. 14th, 1765.
MICHL. OBERKIRSH.	Maccungy.	Northampton.	Oct. 14th, 1765.
WILLIAM DEILE.	Springfield.	Bucks.	Oct. 15th, 1765.
JACOB BACHMAN.	Weisenberg.	Northampton.	Oct. 15th, 1765.
CHRISTOPHER ROUCH.	Lower Saucon.	Northampton.	Oct. 14th, 1765.
PETER DIEHL.	Lower Saucon.	Northampton.	Oct. 14th, 1765.
PHILIP ENNES.	Linn.	Northampton.	Oct. 15th, 1765.
JACOB BERR.	Linn.	Northampton.	Oct. 15th, 1765.
JACOB LIESER.	Linn.	Northampton.	Oct. 15th, 1765.
VALENTINE YAGER.	Lower Saucon.	Northampton.	Oct. 15th, 1765.
CONRAD DITHART.	Springfield.	Bucks.	Oct. 14th, 1765.
PAUL EBERHARD.	Whitehall.	Northampton.	Oct. 16th, 1765.
ADAM KNAPPENBERGER.	Whitehall.	Northampton.	Oct. 16th, 1765.
ADAM KEHL.	Upper Milford.	Northampton.	Sept. 29th, 1765.
MATHIAS KERN.	Upper Milford.	Northampton.	Sept. 29th, 1765.
JOHN GEO. KERN.	Upper Milford.	Northampton.	Sept. 29th, 1765.
STEPHEN ACKERMAN.	Haycock.	Bucks.	Oct. 13th, 1765
DANIEL NAREGANY.	Lower Saucon.	Northampton.	Oct. 13th, 1765
HENRY WEITZELL.	Springfield.	Bucks.	Oct. 14th, 1765.
JOHN GEO. WIMMAR.	Haycock.	Bucks.	Oct. 13th, 1765
JACOB SHOCK.	Haycock.	Bucks.	Oct. 13th, 1765.
PAUL FRANTZ.	Lower Saucon.	Northampton.	Oct. 14th, 1765.
MICHL. HELLER.	Lower Saucon.	Northampton.	Oct. 14th, 1765.
HENRY CRATZER.	Lower Saucon.	Northampton.	Oct. 14th, 1765.
GEO. REIGELL.	Lower Saucon.	Northampton.	Oct. 14th, 1765.
PHILIP REIFFSNIDER.	Lower Saucon.	Northampton.	Oct. 14th, 1765.
YOST SMITH.	Springfield.	Bucks.	Sept. 15th, 1765.
EIE FRANKENFIELD.	Springfield.	Bucks.	Oct. 14th, 1765.
BALTZER LOTZ.	Long Swamp.	Berks.	Sept. 16th, 1765.
JOHN KEISTNER.	Long Swamp.	Berks.	Sept. 16th, 1765.
PETER ANTHONY.	Lehi.	Northampton.	Oct. 18th, 1765.
JOHN PETER ALTMAN.	Lehi.	Northampton.	Oct. 18th, 1765.
JACOB STROH.	Lehi.	Northampton.	Oct. 18th, 1765.
CASPAR ALTMAN.	Lehi.	Northampton.	Oct. 18th, 1765.
MICHL. BOCH.	Linn.	Northampton.	Oct. 14th, 1765.
CHRISTR. FEHR.	Heidleberg.	Northampton.	Oct. 18th, 1765.
PETER HEIMBACH.	Lindaw.	Northampton.	Oct. 18th, 1765.
HENRY SANDER.	Lindaw.	Northampton.	Oct. 18th, 1765.
JACOB SHENK.	Longswamp.	Berks.	Sept. 8th, 1765.
WENDEL RENNINGER.	Upper Hanover.	Philadelphia.	Oct. 17th, 1765.
FRED. GWINNER.	Lower Saucon.	Northampton.	Oct. 14th, 1765.
CASPAR KIENTZ.	Philadelphia.	Philadelphia.	Oct. 14th, 1765.
WILLIAM DETER.	Lehi.	Northampton.	Oct. 14th, 1765.

Jurors' Names.	Township.	County.	Sacrament, when taken
JOHN KUNKELL.	Franconia.	Philadelphia.	Sept. 15th, 1765.
JOHN LADEMACHER.	Lower Saucon.	Northampton.	Oct. 14th, 1765.
HENRY CAPPES.	Lower Saucon.	Northampton.	Oct. 14th, 1765.
JACOB HUBER.	Weisenburg.	Northampton.	Oct. 14th, 1765.
JOHN KLEIN.	Maccungy.	Northampton.	Sept. 20th, 1765.
ANDREAS SINTEL.	Lowhill.	Northampton.	Sept. 16th, 1765.
CHRISTR. RENTSBERGER.	Albany.	Berks.	Oct. 19th, 1765.
JACOB SHANTZ.	Lehi.	Northampton.	Oct. 18th, 1765.
JOHN KROOM.	Heidleberg.	Northampton.	Oct. 6th, 1765.
FRANCIS KRUM.	Heidleberg.	Northampton.	Oct. 6th, 1765.
CHRISTIAN KRUM.	Heidleberg.	Northampton.	Oct. 6th, 1765.
WILLIAM MEYER.	Lowhill.	Northampton.	Oct. 16th, 1765.
MICH. KICHLEIN.	Maccungy.	Northampton.	Oct. 17th, 1765.
JOSEPH STEIDELL.	Linn.	Northampton.	Oct. 14th, 1765.
DAVID BEILMAN.	Linn.	Northampton.	Oct. 14th, 1765.
DEWALD KUNTZ.	Maccungy.	Northampton.	Oct. 17th, 1765.
ANDREW SHEIBLING.	Lower Saucon.	Bucks.	Oct. 13th, 1765.
JACOB SHEIBLING.	Lower Saucon.	Bucks.	Oct. 13th, 1765.
JACOB WITMAN.	Hartford.	Berks.	Oct. 13th, 1765.
JOHN WEIN.	Upper Hanover.	Philadelphia.	Oct. 13th, 1765.
JACOB TOMMAYER.	Maccungy.	Northampton.	Oct. 17th, 1765.
MATHIAS SHUTZ.	Linn.	Northampton.	Oct. 19th, 1765.
MARTIN HOE.	Cocolico.	Lancaster.	Sept. 29th, 1765.
GEORGE HOE.	Cocolico.	Lancaster.	Sept. 29th, 1765.
GEORGE SHAEFFER.	Springfield.	Bucks.	Oct. 13th, 1765.
MICHAEL WERNER.	Springfield.	Bucks.	Oct. 13th, 1765.
HENRY YOUNG.	Passyunk.	Philadelphia.	Sept. 21st, 1765.
GEORGE WANNEMACHER.	Lechaw.	Northampton.	Sept. 21st, 1765.
LUDWICK KŒSTER.	Lechaw.	Northampton.	Sept. 21st, 1765.
ANDREW SHETTERLY.	Lechaw.	Northampton.	Sept. 21st, 1765.
NICHS. SHYER.	Lechaw.	Northampton.	Sept. 21st, 1765.
NICHS. GEISSEL.	Lechaw.	Northampton.	Sept. 21st, 1765.
WILLIAM BEST.	Lechaw.	Northampton.	Sept. 21st, 1765.
HENRY BEST.	Lechaw.	Northampton.	Sept. 21st, 1765.
JOHN GEO. WEBER.	Upper Saucon.	Northampton.	Sept. 13th, 1765.
ADAM KURTZ.	Upper Saucon.	Northampton.	Sept. 13th, 1765.
JOHN GODFRY. STEIBERITZ.	Chestnut Hill.	Philadelphia.	Sept. 13th, 1765.
GEO. STEIBESAND.	Oley.	Berks.	Sept. 13th, 1765.
NICHS. GRUBER.	Tinicum.	Bucks.	Sept. 15th, 1765.
GEORGE MICHAEL.	Maccongy.	Northampton.	Oct. 20th, 1765.
FRED. BACHMAN.	Ruscomb Manor.	Berks.	Oct. 20th, 1765.
CHRISTN. BACHMAN.	Ruscomb Manor.	Berks.	Oct. 20th, 1765.
GEORGE BRAUN.	Ruscomb Manor.	Berks.	Oct. 20th, 1765.
HENRY KALBACH.	Windsor.	Berks.	Oct. 21st, 1765.
MICHAEL CONFER.	Windsor.	Berks.	Oct. 21st, 1765.
ADAM KLEIN.	Windsor.	Berks.	Oct. 21st, 1765.
JOHN BACK.	Windsor.	Berks.	Oct. 21st, 1765.
MARTIN NYFANG.	Windsor.	Berks.	Oct. 21st, 1765.
PETER NEFANG.	Windsor.	Berks.	Oct. 21st, 1765.
PETER STETSTER.	Windsor.	Berks.	Oct. 21st, 1765.
VAL. EMRICH.	Windsor.	Berks.	Oct. 21st, 1765.
JNO. WENDAL ERNST.	Windsor.	Berks.	Oct. 21st, 1765.
MARTIN HUMMELL.	Windsor.	Berks.	Oct. 21st, 1765.
JNO. MICHL. KARBER.	Rockland.	Berks.	Oct. 21st, 1765.

j

PENNSYLVANIA.

Jurors' Names.	Township.	County.	Sacrament, when taken
CONRAD WINKLER.	Windsor.	Berks.	Oct. 21st, 1765.
FRED. BAYER.	Ruscomb Manor.	Berks.	Oct. 20th, 1765.
CONRAD BACHMAN.	Lehi.	Northampton.	Oct. 21st, 1765.
HENRY BARTHOLOMEW.	More.	Northampton.	Sept. 2nd, 1765.
NICHS. SHALL.	Lower Saucon.	Northampton.	Sept. 14th, 1765.
PHIL. HENRY SHOLL.	Lower Saucon.	Northampton.	Sept. 14th, 1765.
TOBIAS SHOLL.	Lower Saucon.	Northampton.	Sept. 14th, 1765.
JNO. PHILIP HALL.	Upper Saucon.	Northampton.	Sept. 14th, 1765.
HENRY EGLE.	Amity.	Berks.	Sept. 21st, 1765.
MICH. HOFFMAN.	Douglass.	Berks.	Sept. 21st, 1765.
GEO. FRITZ.	Amity.	Berks.	Sept. 21st, 1765.
JOHN MAYER.	Amity.	Berks.	Sept. 21st, 1765.
GEORGE RUPP.	Maccungy.	Northampton.	Sept. 20th, 1765.
MELCHR. DANNER.	Maccungy.	Northampton.	Sept. 20th, 1765.
CONRAD KUHL.	Brecknock.	Lancaster.	Sept. 20th, 1765.
JNO. JACOB STICKLER.	Brecknock.	Lancaster.	Sept. 20th, 1765.
PHILIP MATHIAS.	District.	Berks.	Sept. 20th, 1765.
JOSEPH LEHMAN.	Oley.	Berks.	Sept. 22nd, 1765.
JOHN HAUSER.	Windsor.	Berks.	Oct. 21st, 1765.
JACOB ROTH.	Lehi.	Northampton.	Oct. 21st, 1765.
ANDREW MYER.	Lehi.	Northampton.	Oct. 21st, 1765.
DIETRICK MATTHEW.	Oley.	Berks.	Oct. 21st, 1765.
JACOB BARR.	Maccungy.	Northampton.	Oct. 20th, 1765.
JOHN DORR.	Lehi.	Northampton.	Oct. 20th, 1765.
MICH. KROLMAN.	Rockhill.	Bucks.	Oct. 20th, 1765.
JACOB HILL.	Windsor.	Berks.	Oct. 6th, 1765.
MICH. KATZ.	Philadelphia.	Philadelphia.	Oct. 22nd, 1765.
GEO. KRISTEIN.	Philadelphia.	Philadelphia.	Oct. 22nd, 1765.
GEO. WAGNER.	Lower Milford.	Bucks.	July 28th, 1765.
SEBASTIAN STEIN.	Bedminster.	Bucks.	Oct. 15th, 1765.
LUDWICK LINDENSHMITT.	Haycock.	Bucks.	Oct. 20th, 1765.
GODFREY GRUBER.	Germant[own].	Philadelphia.	Oct. 22nd, 1765.
WILLIAM SHAFFER.	Upper Milford.	Northampton.	Oct. 8th, 1765.
GEO. MILLAR.	Upper Milford.	Northampton.	Oct. 8th, 1765.
JOHN GEO. KRAUS.	Heidleberg.	Northampton.	Oct. 14th, 1765.
ADAM BLATT.	Bern.	Berks.	Oct. 6th, 1765.
STEPH. KREITTER.	Bern.	Berks.	Oct. 6th, 1765.
JNO. ADAM KREITZ.	Albany.	Berks.	Oct. 6th, 1765.
CHRISTIAN LAUFFER.	Lehi.	Northampton.	Oct. 20th, 1765.
ADAM MARITS.	More.	Northampton.	Oct. 20th, 1765.
CHRISTIAN MILLAR.	Lehi.	Northampton.	Oct. 22nd, 1765.
PETER EVSENMAN.	Lehi.	Northampton.	Oct. 19th, 1765.
CONRAD HOUSMAN.	Windsor.	Berks.	Oct. 21st, 1765.
MICH. SHLYER.	Windsor.	Berks.	Oct. 21st, 1765.
ANDREW MAY.	Windsor.	Berks.	Oct. 21st, 1765.
CONRAD ZORA.	Windsor.	Berks.	Oct. 21st, 1765.
MATHIAS SHAPPELE.	Windsor.	Berks.	Oct. 21st, 1765.
AUDS. WEYMAGER.	Windsor.	Berks.	Oct. 21st, 1765.
JACOB SHAPPELE.	Windsor.	Berks.	Oct. 21st, 1765.
GEORGE HAND.	Albany.	Berks.	Oct. 20th, 1765.
MICHL. WERLEIN.	Albany.	Berks.	Oct. 20th, 1765.
MICHL. GALINGER,	Richmond.	Berks,	Oct. 20th, 1765.

Jurors' Names.	Township.	County.	Sacrament, when taken
WM. BECK.	Lehi.	Northampton.	Oct. 20th, 1765.
JACOB YOLMAN.	Ruscom Manor.	Berks.	Oct. 20th, 1765.
JNO. HEINTZICKER.	Heidleberg.	Northampton.	Oct. 20th, 1765.
MICHL. WENDERRIGHT.	Bedminster.	Bucks.	Sept. 22nd, 1765.
CASPAR PEISHLEIN.	Bedminster.	Bucks.	Sept. 22nd, 1765.
PETER STAWERWALD.	Greenwich.	Berks.	Sept. 22nd, 1765.
JNO. ANGSTET.	Rockland.	Berks.	Sept. 22nd, 1765.
GEO. SNYDER.	Lowhill.	Northampton.	Sept. 22nd, 1765.
GEO. ALSBACH.	Windsor.	Berks.	Sept. 22nd, 1765.
PHIL. ALSBACH.	Windsor.	Berks.	Sept. 22nd, 1765.
FRED. SEITZ.	Maccungy.	Northampton.	Sept. 22nd, 1765.
HENRY GROSS.	Windsor.	Berks.	Sept. 22nd, 1765.
JOHN HOEFER.	Windsor.	Berks.	Oct. 22nd, 1765.
JACOB MILLER.	Windsor.	Berks.	Oct. 22nd, 1765.
MARTIN RAUST.	Windsor.	Berks.	Oct. 22nd, 1765.
GEO. GORDNER.	Windsor.	Berks.	Oct. 22nd, 1765.
JACOB HILL.	Windsor.	Berks.	Oct. 22nd, 1765.
YOST SHALM.	Maccungy.	Northampton.	Oct. 20th, 1765.
MICHL. FEEGER.	Lower Saucon.	Northampton.	Oct. 14th, 1765.
HENRY DIEHL.	More.	Northampton.	Oct. 20th, 1765.
JACOB BATSH.	Northern Liberties.	Philadelphia.	Oct. 22nd, 1765.
BARENTZ JACOB.	Heidleberg.	Lancaster.	[A Jew.]
JACOB OB.	Dover.	York.	Sept. 29th, 1765.
PHILIP JACOB JULIUS.	Dover.	York.	Sept. 29th, 1765.
CATHA. DORITHEA MATTHESEN.	Greenw.	Berks.	Sept. 21st, 1765.
ABRAHAM FREY.	Linn.	Northampton.	Sept. 20th, 1765.
GEORGE MILLER.	Weisenberg.	Northampton.	Sept. 20th, 1765.
CHRISTIAN METZGER.	Upper Milford.	Northampton.	Sept. 29th, 1765.
MICHL. SEIBLY.	Upper Milford.	Northampton.	Sept. 29th, 1765.
JACOB BERGER.	Richland.	Bucks.	Oct. 20th, 1765.
JNO. PHIL. TUTSH.	York.	York.	Oct. 22nd, 1765.
JACOB GRAIBER.	York.	York.	Oct. 22nd, 1765.
FRED. STEITINGER.	York.	York.	Oct. 22nd, 1765.
PHIL. CONRAD WOLF.	Dover.	York.	Oct. 22nd, 1765.
MARGT. TAWNEY.	Upper Milford.	Northampton.	Sept. 29th, 1765.
FEIGHT HEERD.	Windsor.	Berks.	Sept. 22nd, 1765.
THOMAS MAY.	Windsor.	Berks.	Sept. 22nd, 1765.
JACOB LIEHTNER.	Windsor.	Berks.	Sept. 22nd, 1765.
JOHN EMMELL.	Whitpain.	Philadelphia.	14th Sunday post Trinity, 1765.
HENRY KOENICH.	York.	York.	Oct. 24th, 1765.
GEO. ADAM GOSLER.	York.	York.	Oct. 24th, 1765.
JACOB FREY.	Linn.	Northampton.	Sept. 20th, 1765.
CONRAD BEISER.	York.	York.	Oct. 24th, 1765.
SEBASTIAN WEIGELL.	York.	York.	Oct. 24th, 1765.
PHILIP OPP.	Williams.	Northampton.	Oct. 24th, 1765.
JNO. RHINEHART.	Albany.	Berks.	Oct. 24th, 1765.
JOHN MANTZ.	Albany.	Berks.	Oct. 24th, 1765.
JOHN HANDWERK, Senr.	Heidleberg.	Northampton.	Oct. 24th, 1765.
JOHN HANDWERK, Jr.	Heidleberg.	Northampton.	Oct. 24th, 1765.
LUDWICK WALTIMYER.	York.	York.	Oct. 24th, 1765.
WILLIAM SNYDER.	Upper Douglass.	Berks.	Oct. 24th, 1765.
MICHL. SPATZ.	Upper Douglass.	Berks.	Oct. 24th, 1765.
PHILIP LAUNCE.	Windsor.	York.	Oct. 24th, 1765.

PENNSYLVANIA.

Jurors' Names.	Township.	County.	Sacrament, when taken.
PHILIP MELLEHOOF.	Windsor.	York.	Oct. 24th, 1765.
NICHS. BRAND.	York.	York.	Oct. 24th, 1765.
ADAM HUNDEL.	Windsor.	York.	Oct. 24th, 1765.
GEORGE MEYER.	Windsor.	York.	Oct. 24th, 1765.
GEORGE MYERS.	Fairfield.	Cumberland in Jersey.	Oct. 24th, 1765.
WILL. LOHMAN.	Passyunk.	Philadelphia.	Oct. 26th, 1765.
PHILIP GAUFF.	Codorus.	York.	Oct. 29th, 1765.
TOBIAS ZIMMERMAN.	Northern Liberties.	Philadelphia.	Oct. 22nd, 1765.

Mordecai M. Mordecai, Barentz Jacob, and Elijah Etting within mentioned, being Jews, were qualified and subscribed the Declarations, &c., according to the directions of the Act of the thirteenth of King George the Second.

Quakers and other Protestants who scruple to take an Oath.

Affirmers' Names.	Township.	County	Sacrament, when taken by Moravians.
JACOB DESTER.	Bern.	Berks.	
CHRISTR. SHOCKEE.	Antrim.	Cumberland.	
PETER BOOS.	Cocolico.	Lancaster.	
JACOB KELLER.	Cocolico.	Lancaster.	
GODLIP SENER.	Lancaster.	Lancaster.	
HENRY SHLYFER.	Upper Milford.	Northampton.	
JACOB SHLYFER.	Upper Milford.	Northampton.	
GEORGE BODEROH.	Allen.	Northampton.	
PETER HEFFLY.	Lancaster.	Lancaster.	
GEO. ACKERMAN.	Lancaster.	Lancaster.	
BALTZER ACKERMAN.	Lancaster.	Lancaster.	
ANTHY. SERICH.	Frederick in	Maryland.	
FRANCIS THOMAS.	Lancaster.	Lancaster.	
FRED. ALDER.	Exeter.	Berks.	
LAWRENTZ ERBACH.	Lower Milford	Bucks.	
NICHS. BARTOLEMOW.	Lancaster.	Lancaster.	
HENRY BERGER.	Richmond.	Berks.	
NICHS. KEESEL.	Warwick.	Lancaster.	
JACOB HOWETT.	Exeter.	Berks.	
GEORGE BOOCH.	Manheim.	Lancaster.	
JACOB SMOCK.	Warwick.	Lancaster.	
LUDWICK RIEHL.	Alsace.	Berks.	
WILLIAM YANS.	Heidleberg.	Berks.	
JOHN HOOVE.	Oley.	Berks.	
GIDEON CHRISTIAN.	Lower Saucon.	Northampton.	
PETER KRINE.	Saucon.	Northampton.	
MARTIN CLEVER.	Hereford.	Berks.	
DANIEL GRUB.	Philadelphia.	Philadelphia.	
FREDERICK LEESER.	Lancaster.	Lancaster.	
MICHL. FOLTZ.	Lancaster.	Lancaster.	
PHILIP KLIES.	Lancaster.	Lancaster.	
JACOB MILLER.	Lancaster.	Lancaster.	
CONRAD SHOUP.	Hereford.	Berks.	
THOMAS DERRINGER.	Providence.	Philadelphia.	
JOHN STITZEL.	Oley.	Berks.	
BALTZER BOOCHACRE.	Saucon.	Northampton.	

Affirmers' Names.	County.	Township.	Sacrament, when taken by Moravians.
JOHN STONER.	Hempfield.	Lancaster.	
PETER KNAPPLEY.	Upper Saucon.	Northampton.	
ABRAHAM STUMP.	Heidleberg.	Lancaster.	
JACOB SHITZ.	Whitpain.	Philadelphia.	
CASPAR SNEVELY.	Lebanon.	Lancaster.	
GEORGE HOKE.	Lebanon.	Lancaster.	
JOHN MILLER.	Philadelphia.	Philadelphia.	
DANIEL HENDRICKSON.	Germantown.	Philadelphia.	
CHRISTR. ANGNEY.	Bedminster.	Bucks.	
PHILIP SELLER.	Upper Saucon.	Northampton.	
JACOB HOSER.	White Marsh.	Philadelphia.	
JNO. HERMAN NIESS.	Upper Milford.	Northampton.	
HENRY HOLLER.	Reading.	Berks.	
GEORGE GEESMAN.	Lebanon.	Lancaster.	
JACOB LEBBERT.	Ruscomb Mannor.	Berks.	
HENRY BOOCHACRE.	Upper Saucon.	Northampton.	
JOHN GROSH [a Moravian].	Hempfield.	Lancaster.	Aug. 24th, 1765.
NICHS. SALLADY.	Tulpehoccon.	Berks.	
HENRY GESSLER.	Lancaster.	Lancaster.	
JACOB RADGAY.	Union.	Berks.	
CHRISTN. FREDERICK.	Warwick.	Lancaster.	
LUDWICK WITTEMYER.	Heidleberg.	Lancaster.	
ROBERT HALLAFEL.	Lancaster.	Lancaster.	
JOHN LUSH.	Heidleberg.	Berks.	
JACOB SHITZ.	Strasburg.	Lancaster.	
YOST RYDLE.	Warwick.	Lancaster.	
JACOB NEEDHOCK.	Reading.	Berks.	
JACOB DRAWER.	Heidleberg.	Lancaster.	
HENRY PENNER.	Coventry.	Chester.	
HENRY WINTERBERGER.	Robeson.	Berks.	
JOHN PEETLER.	Union.	Berks.	
BERNARD WUNSH.	Salisbury.	Northampton.	
PHILIP RUPERT.	Reading.	Berks.	
LUDWICK BRAIHL.	Philadelphia.	Philadelphia.	
HENRY KROUT.	Bedminster.	Bucks.	
PETER LAWKS.	Bedminster.	Bucks.	
GEORGE BOSSELL.	Haverford.	Chester.	
SIMON LITZENBERGER.	Haverford.	Chester.	
JUSTUS FOX.	Germantown.	Philadelphia.	
JOHN RIGHTS.	Philadelphia.	Philadelphia.	
GEORGE GARTNER.	Heidleberg.	Lancaster.	
MICHL. BRANSON.	Germantown.	Philadelphia.	
GEORGE MENGES.	Bern.	Berks.	
GEORGE GARTNER.	Plainfield.	Northampton.	
HENRY SHOISTER.	Lower Morrion.	Philadelphia.	
JOHN KOLER.	Upper Dublin.	Philadelphia.	
FRANCIS DIEHL.	Northern Liberties.	Philadelphia.	
PETER LOWREY.	Philadelphia.	Philadelphia.	
CHRISTIAN ALBERGER.	Northern Liberties.	Philadelphia.	
PHILIP ALBERGER.	Northern Liberties.	Philadelphia.	
ADAM ALBERGER.	Northern Liberties.	Philadelphia.	
SIMON WALTER.	Upper Milford.	Northampton.	
JOHN WIKART.	Tulpehoccon.	Berks.	
JACOB SEISS.	Easton.	Northampton.	

PENNSYLVANIA.

Affirmers' Names.	Township.	County.	Sacrament, when taken by Moravians.
John Shlessman.	Cheltenham.	Philadelphia.	
Caspar White.	Cheltenham.	Philadelphia.	
John Adam.	Germantown.	Philadelphia.	
Godlip Leffler.	Heidleberg.	Berks.	
Frederick Umpert.	Maxatawny.	Berks.	
Joseph Browne.	Philadelphia.	Philadelphia.	
Jno. Wm. Troutwine	Northern Liberties.	Philadelphia.	
John Conrad Young.	Philadelphia.	Philadelphia.	
Conrad Good.	Germantown.	Philadelphia.	
Jacob Rabsom.	Philadelphia.	Philadelphia.	
Casemir Massemir.	New Hanover.	Philadelphia.	
Conrad Jacobi.	New Hanover.	Philadelphia.	
Fred. Strousnider.	Springfield.	Bucks.	
Henry Sharpkneck.	Germantown.	Philadelphia.	
John Strousnider.	Springfield.	Bucks.	
Martin Housman.	Springfield.	Bucks.	
Philip Kreighbaum.	Lower Merrion.	Philadelphia.	
Jacob Ries.	Germantown.	Philadelphia.	
Augustine Nessor.	Germantown.	Philadelphia.	
Andrew Shirl.	Upper Merrion.	Philadelphia.	
Martin Beck.	Germantown.	Philadelphia.	
John Tripler.	Germantown.	Philadelphia.	
John Switzer.	Bethlehem.	Northampton.	
Jacob Hersberger.	Cocolico.	Lancaster.	
George Zinn.	Cocolico.	Lancaster.	
Adam Beckele.	Reading.	Berks.	
Thomas Bissert.	Philadelphia.	Philadelphia.	
Henry Snyder.	Plymouth.	Philadelphia.	
Henry Goodman.	Plymouth.	Philadelphia.	
George Fetterman.	Upper Merrion.	Philadelphia.	
Peter Shouster.	Germantown.	Philadelphia.	
Charles Sowder.	Philadelphia.	Philadelphia.	
John Herman.	Montgomery.	Philadelphia.	
Frederick Haas.	Windsor.	Berks.	
Jno. Martin Shiebly.	Upper Milford.	Northampton.	
Philip Hertzhog.	Upper Milford.	Northampton.	
Andrew Shetler.	York.	York.	
Nichs. Wondsidler.	Rockhill.	Bucks.	
Adam Kable.	Rockhill.	Bucks.	
John Wellar.	Conestogo.	Lancaster.	
George Heck.	Philadelphia.	Philadelphia.	
Fred. Kuhn.	Forks.	Northampton.	
Michl. Stadleman.	Radnor.	Chester.	
Rudolph Latchy.	Blockley.	Philadelphia.	
Rudolph Siebly.	Lower Merrion.	Philadelphia.	
Jno. Nichs. Billman.	Northern Liberties.	Philadelphia.	
John Whitmer.	Northern Liberties.	Philadelphia.	
Christr. Effreky.	Northern Liberties.	Philadelphia.	
Henry Stoffel.	Upper Merrion.	Philadelphia.	
Henry Boyle.	Germantown.	Philadelphia.	
Ulrick Buttman.	Germantown.	Philadelphia.	
Geo. Barkman.	Germantown.	Philadelphia.	

Affirmers' Names.	Township.	County.	Sacrament, when taken by Moravians.
MICHL. FOLTZ.	Springfield.	Bucks.	
JACOB BARE.	Lancaster.	Lancaster.	
PHILIP SEEBOLT.	Upper Milford.	Northampton.	
JOHN STEER.	Germantown.	Philadelphia.	
JACOB GILBERT.	Germantown.	Philadelphia.	
PHILIP LUDWIE.	Pikeland.	Chester.	
NICHOLAS RIFFET.	Charlestown.	Chester.	
CASPAR WHITEMAN.	Blockley.	Philadelphia.	
CHRISTIAN HEPLER.	Frederick.	Philadelphia.	
JOHN OMELER.	Heidleberg.	Berks.	
WENDAL BRETZIUS.	Northern Liberties.	Philadelphia.	
SEBASTIAN MYER.	Philadelphia.	Philadelphia.	
WILLIAM SMALL.	Northern Liberties.	Philadelphia.	
JACOB LUSH.	Germantown.	Philadelphia.	
JACOB BOWMAN.	Germantown.	Philadelphia.	
NICHS. HARTZBACH.	Philadelphia.	Philadelphia.	
JNO. HALVEIRSTADT.	Philadelphia.	Philadelphia.	
HENRY SOMMERS.	Northern Liberties.	Philadelphia.	
EZEKIEL SANGMASTER.	Cocolico.	Lancaster.	
JOHN MARTIN.	Cocolico.	Lancaster.	
JNO. ADAM KELP.	Cocolico.	Lancaster.	
CHRISTIAN LUTHER.	Cocolico.	Lancaster.	
GEORGE KOHN.	Germant[own].	Philadelphia.	
JOHN FRY.	Germant[own].	Philadelphia.	
JNO. CREIGHTBAUM.	Maxatawny.	Berks.	
JOHN HAAS.	Germantown.	Philadelphia.	
CHRISTR. GREEN.	Germantown.	Philadelphia.	
PETER LONG.	Upper Milford.	Northampton.	
PHILIP BECK.	Hertford.	Berks.	
JOHN ABLE.	Bristol.	Philadelphia.	
CHRISTR. HOOFMAN.	Maccungy.	Northampton.	
WM. LESHER.	Germantown.	Philadelphia.	
PETER CARE.	Bristol.	Philadelphia.	
PHIL. EDDIBURNE.	Creesham.	Philadelphia.	
CONRAD SWITZER.	Northern Liberties.	Philadelphia.	
JOSEPH SHAANK.	York.	York.	Sept. 14th, 1765.
PETER BUCCHIUS.	Germantown.	Philadelphia.	
PETER BENEDICT.	Lebanon.	Lancaster.	
JACOB BRENNISER.	Lebanon.	Lancaster.	
CHRISTR. GARRETT.	New Hanover.	Philadelphia.	
GEORGE WUNDERLIN.	Creesam.	Philadelphia.	
ANDREW HANS.	Dover.	York.	
PHILIP ALTLAND.	Paradise.	York.	
JOHN SERBER.	Springfield.	Philadelphia.	
PETER GOOCHER.	Frederick.	Philadelphia.	
FRANCIS LEYDITCH.	Frederick.	Philadelphia.	
JASPAR ACKABACH.	Frederick.	Philadelphia.	
JACOB MILLER.	White Marsh.	Philadelphia.	
BARNABY FRANCIS.	Springfield.	Philadelphia.	
CHAS. BOWMER.	Northern Liberties.	Philadelphia.	
NICHS. BERMINGER.	Douglass.	Philadelphia.	
MICHL. KLINE.	Merion.	Philadelphia.	
BARTHOLOMEW LAMB.	Germantown.	Philadelphia.	
JOHN LAMB.	Germantown.	Philadelphia.	

NATURALIZATIONS

PENNSYLVANIA.

Affirmers' Names.	Township.	County.	Sacrament, when taken by Moravians.
JOHN SHEARER.	Whitpain.	Philadelphia.	
LAWRENCE SHEARER.	Whitpain.	Philadelphia.	
ADAM RENNER.	Worcester.	Philadelphia.	
CASPAR ZELLING.	Whitpain.	Philadelphia.	
ADAM TRUMP.	Upper Milford.	Northampton.	
ANTHY. HONE.	Springfield.	Philadelphia.	
BALTZER SHELLING.	Manheim.	Lancaster.	
JOHN MOYSTER.	Manheim.	Lancaster.	
CHRISTIAN KELLER.	Lower Salford.	Philadelphia.	
JACOB RENNER.	Worcester.	Philadelphia.	
GARRET BORNHÜTTER.	Creesham.	Philadelphia.	
GEO. KEITEL.	Creesham.	Philadelphia.	
MARTIN HUBACKER.	Worcester.	Philadelphia.	
PETER YOH.	Hatfield.	Philadelphia.	
JOHN BEIDLER.	Richland.	Bucks.	
LUDWICK SHEARER.	Norrington.	Bucks.	
FREDERICK SURFACE.	Worcester.	Philadelphia.	
JACOB RENGER.	Roxborough.	Philadelphia.	
PETER MEFFERT.	Douglass.	Berks.	
CONRAD ECHER.	Limerick.	Philadelphia.	
JOHN FERTICH.	Limerick.	Philadelphia.	
JACOB LINN.	Richland.	Bucks.	
CONRAD ISONN.	Creesham.	Philadelphia.	
CHRISTIAN BOOS.	Haycock.	Bucks.	
CHRISTIAN SNYDER.	Haycock.	Bucks.	
HENRY BROWER.	Coventry.	Chester.	
JACOB SENOR.	Worcester.	Philadelphia.	
GEORGE ROH.	Vincent.	Chester.	
JACOB DETWIDER.	Upper Hanover.	Philadelphia.	
JOHN SWANER.	Coventry.	Chester.	
JOHN HANGEY.	Pikeland.	Chester.	
MARTIN KILLER.	Limerick.	Philadelphia.	
PHILIP LEESE.	Vincent.	Chester.	
ANDREW HERSTER.	Providence.	Philadelphia.	
MICHL. SINK.	Coventry.	Chester.	
GEORGE SHIMMEL.	Springfield.	Bucks.	
JACOB SIGFRID.	North Wales.	Philadelphia.	
JACOB SERBER.	Hatfield.	Philadelphia.	
WM. SPRINGHER.	Towamensing.	Philadelphia.	
JACOB RESTER.	White Marsh.	Philadelphia.	
JOHN SPRINGHER.	Towamensing.	Philadelphia.	
JOHN CLOWES.	Allen.	Northampton.	
GEORGE LAWRENCE.	Allen.	Northampton.	Aug. 17th, 1765.
MATHIAS DIEHL.	Germantown.	Philadelphia.	
JOHN SHEPHARD.	Lower Dublin.	Philadelphia.	
HENRY CASSELL.	Lower Salford.	Philadelphia.	
MELCHIOR YODER.	Perquioming.	Philadelphia.	
PETER DEFRAIN.	Vincent.	Chester.	
PETER SHOEMAN.	Pikeland.	Chester.	
JOHN WAGGONER.	Pikeland.	Chester.	
PHILIP WAGGONER.	Pikeland.	Chester.	
WILLIAM WALTER.	Pikeland.	Chester.	

Affirmers' Names.	Township.	County.	Sacrament, when taken by Moravians.
ISAIAS CARL.	Pikeland.	Chester.	
SIMON SHUNK.	Vincent.	Chester.	
CONRAD SHEIMER.	Vincent.	Chester.	
NICHS. MENSH.	Springfield.	Bucks.	
HENRY YONERS.	Northern Liberties.	Philadelphia.	
MATHIAS FORKER.	Northern Liberties.	Philadelphia.	
HENRY DEBAREAR.	Philadelphia.	Philadelphia.	
HENRY LENINGER.	Lower Merrion.	Philadelphia.	
JUSTUS LINDERMAN.	Coventry.	Chester.	
JACOB ERIEN.	Philadelphia.	Philadelphia.	
MICHL. REICHART.	White Marsh.	Philadelphia.	
JOHN HARTMAN.	White Marsh.	Philadelphia.	
HENRY BERGER.	Bristol.	Philadelphia.	
HENRY MARKLAN.	Cheltenham.	Philadelphia.	
GEORGE YEAGER.	Vincent.	Chester.	
CHRISTOPHER WOLTZ.	Pikes.	Chester.	
VALENTINE OPP.	Easton.	Northampton.	
JNO. WM. WYNANDT.	Linnen.	Northampton.	
FRED. SWARTZ.	Kensington.	Philadelphia.	
ADAM WALTER.	Forks.	Northampton.	
JACOB KECKLER.	Blockley.	Philadelphia.	
JOHN PLANKENHORN.	Whitpain.	Philadelphia.	
PETER CLINE.	Philadelphia.	Philadelphia.	
MICHAEL WOOLER.	Oxford.	Philadelphia.	
ADAM SITER.	Radnor.	Chester.	
HENRY SNYDER.	Gwenidth.	Philadelphia.	
CASPAR PURBOWER.	Pikeland.	Chester.	
SAMUEL ROYER.	Warwick.	Lancaster.	
ISAAC BOUDEMAN.	Germantown.	Philadelphia.	
HENRY KEPHART.	Bedminster.	Bucks.	
JOHN ROM.	Philadelphia.	Philadelphia.	
CASPAR SOUDER.	Philadelphia.	Philadelphia.	
PETER DISHONG.	Roxborough.	Philadelphia.	
FREDERICK DISHONG.	Roxborough.	Philadelphia.	
HENRY RICH.	Lower Dublin.	Philadelphia.	
JNO. ADAM HOE, Senr.	Lower Dublin.	Philadelphia.	
JNO. ADAM HOE, Junr.	Lower Dublin.	Philadelphia.	
DAVID JUVENAH.	Bristol.	Philadelphia.	
MICHL. OBERLE.	Darby.	Chester.	
HENRY LONG.	Paradise.	York.	
CHRISTR. ERNST.	Philadelphia.	Philadelphia.	
WILLIAM WOLF.	Philadelphia.	Philadelphia.	
HENRY SHARER.	Allen.	Northampton.	
MATHIAS CRAWL.	Heidleberg.	Lancaster.	
GEORGE STROHM.	Lebanon.	Lancaster.	
MICHL. DIDDERLIE.	Rockhill.	Bucks.	
JEREMIAH HERPLE.	Hanover.	Philadelphia.	
SOLOMON NONOMECKER.	Rockhill.	Bucks.	
FREDERICK WOLF.	Tulpehoccon.	Berks.	
CASPAR GROSS.	Richland.	Bucks.	
ANDREW KNŒDLER.	Heidleberg.	Northampton.	
PHILIP HARDING.	Philadelphia.	Philadelphia.	
MICHL. BARRENSTONE.	Creesham.	Philadelphia.	
CHRISTR. SOWER.	Germantown.	Philadelphia.	

NATURALIZATIONS

PENNSYLVANIA.

Affirmers' Names.	Township.	County.	Sacrament, when taken by Moravians.
LEONARD TUTWEILER.	Easton.	Northampton.	
JOHN SLYFER.	Springfield.	Bucks.	
GEORGE LOOSH.	Bern.	Berks.	
JOHN KEELY.	Plymouth.	Philadelphia.	
WILLIAM MYER.	Springfield.	Bucks.	
CHRISTIAN GAYMAN.	Springfield.	Bucks.	
JOHN ULEY RINKER.	Saucon.	Northampton.	
HENRY SEAWITZ.	Saucon.	Northampton.	
PETER KLINE.	Haycock.	Bucks.	
MARIA JACOBI.	Haycock.	Bucks.	
JACOB WEISELL.	Bedminster.	Bucks.	
JOHN CHRISTN. BECK.	East Nantmell.	Chester.	
VALENTINE KROEMER.	Hilltown.	Bucks.	
ADAM STOCK.	Limerick.	Philadelphia.	
JACOB BUMM.	Northern Liberties.	Philadelphia.	
SYRACH JUDY.	Oxford.	Philadelphia.	
JACOB SEBELY.	Northern Liberties.	Philadelphia.	
HENRY BOOSER.	Frankfort.	Philadelphia.	
WILLIAM GROH.	Haycock.	Bucks.	
PHILIP JACOB WOLF.	Haycock.	Bucks.	
DAVID AND. GEBHART.	New Briton.	Bucks.	
HENRY EFFINGER.	Ridley.	Philadelphia.	
JOHN HUPPNY LEER.	Tinicum.	Bucks.	
ARNOLD SHUMAN.	Tinicum.	Bucks.	
PETER KUNKLE.	Hartford.	Berks.	
PHILIP BURRIER.	Longswamp.	Berks.	
JACOB LONG.	Long Swamp.	Berks.	
PETER BAHL.	Lowhill.	Northampton.	
WILLIAM TURF.	Cushahoppen.	Philadelphia.	
WILLIAM SILVIUS.	Heidleberg.	Northampton.	
PETER SHWENCK.	Salisbury.	Northampton.	
JACOB SHNOLL.	Germantown.	Philadelphia.	
NICHS. SMITH.	Elizabeth.	Lancaster.	
FRANCIS FEWER.	Cocolico.	Lancaster.	
JACOB JUDY.	Lehi.	Northampton.	
ADAM SNYDER.	Douglass.	Philadelphia.	
JOHN SILVIUS.	Weisenberg.	Northampton.	
LORENTZ MILLER.	Linnen.	Northampton.	
HANS ZIMMERMAN.	Earl.	Lancaster.	
PHILIP HECK.	Bern.	Berks.	
PHILIP BAUM.	Rappho.	Lancaster.	
CONRAD MONS.	Linn.	Northampton.	
PETER DIEHL.	Haycock.	Bucks.	
MICHAEL FOUK.	New Briton.	Bucks.	
JOSEPH BASLER.	Vincent.	Chester.	
CONRAD SILVIUS.	Lehi.	Northampton.	
LORENTZ KIBLE.	Vincent.	Chester.	
GEORGE KEYSER.	Douglass.	Philadelphia.	
JOHN SMITH.	Douglass.	Philadelphia.	
JACOB GOTTSHALT.	Cole Brookdale.	Berks.	
LORENTZ SHALER.	District.	Berks.	
NICHS. MUFFLEY.	Maxatawny.	Berks.	

Affirmers' Names.	Township.	County.
VALENTINE HEVINS.	Pikeland.	Chester.
FRANCIS KEHL.	Maccungy.	Northampton.
JOHN MERTZ.	Pikes.	Chester.
JACOB GINTHER.	Pikes.	Chester.
JOHN SNYDER.	Pikes.	Chester.
VALENTINE SMITH.	Pikes.	Chester.
HENRY KIPPELL.	Pikes.	Chester.
GEORGE EMRICH.	Pikes.	Chester.
CONRAD WOLFKEEL.	Earl.	Lancaster.
JACOB RAUGH.	Rockhill.	Bucks.
GEORGE RAUGH.	Rockhill.	Bucks.
ALEXANDER NEGLEE.	Rockhill.	Bucks.
LUDWICK SHRYER.	Haycock.	Bucks.
ANNA MARIA SHRYER.	Haycock.	Bucks.
ABRAHAM HARP.	Hertford.	Berks.
JOHN SHAUMAN.	Hertford.	Berks.
ULRICK KOOLEY.	Hertford.	Berks.
MICHL. EVERHEITER.	Haycock.	Bucks.
PHILIP MENN.	Springfield.	Bucks.
PETER MENN.	Springfield.	Bucks.
GEORGE KOHL.	Springfield.	Bucks.
MICHL. WUMPLER.	Lebanon.	Lancaster.
PETER DIEHL.	Springfield.	Bucks.
KILLIAN HAWKER.	Springfield.	Bucks.
SEBASTIAN HORN.	Springfield.	Bucks.
ANDREAS TREBICH.	Springfield.	Bucks.
NICHS. FISHER.	Rockhill.	Bucks.
JACOB KLEIN.	Franconia.	Philadelphia.
HENRY FRITZ.	New Cushahoppen.	Philadelphia.
GEO. SHLOTTERER.	Lower Salford.	Philadelphia.
ULRICK BRENNER.	Maxatawny.	Berks.
HENRY DIETSH.	Antrim.	Cumberland.
BARTH WHITE.	Bedminster.	Bucks.
ADAM FOULKE.	Blockley.	Philadelphia.
SEBASTIAN SHALLUS.	Reading.	York.
ANTHY. KLICKNER.	Lower Saucon.	Northampton.
PETER HEEDER.	Rockland.	Berks.
LEBOLT YOST.	Brennock.	Lancaster.
GEORGE STINGAR.	Windsor.	Berks.
PHILIP SHOCK.	Plainfield.	Northampton.
JOHN BECKLEY.	Oley.	Berks.
TOBIAS FIES.	Oley.	Berks.
DIETRICK METZNER.	Philadelphia.	Philadelphia.
VALENTINE KAHN.	Robeson.	Berks.
VALENTINE AMES.	Robeson.	Berks.
CHRISTIAN SWARTZ.	New Briton.	Bucks.
NICHOLAS CLEMENS.	Rockland.	Bucks.
GALLUS GULEDY.	Skippack.	Philadelphia.
JACOB HOOFHANS.	Bern.	Berks.
JACOB RODE.	Bern.	Berks.
PHILIP HEHN.	Bern.	Berks.
PHILIP WAGGONER.	Bern.	Berks.
DANIEL SLOPPICK.	Bern.	Berks.
YOST SLOPPICK.	Bern.	Berks.

PENNSYLVANIA.

Affirmers' Names.	Township.	County.	Sacrament, when taken by Moravians.
WM. LEIMASTER.	Bern.	Berks.	
LUDWICK RIMEL.	Brecknock.	Lancaster.	
LORENTZ SHOLLBERGER.	Greenwich.	Berks.	
HENRY SHOLLBERGER.	Greenwich.	Berks.	
GARRET SHOLLBERGER.	Greenwich.	Berks.	
HENRY BARK.	Greenwich.	Berks.	
ELIZABETH REISIN.	Oley.	Berks.	
GEORGE FOHLER.	Carnarvon.	Lancaster.	
GEORGE REDDICH.	Cocolico.	Lancaster.	
HENRY PLUMSHINE.	Cocolico.	Lancaster.	
LEONARD REESH.	Cocolico.	Lancaster.	
MICHL. SHICK.	Nockamixon.	Bucks.	
JOHN PYLE.	Nockamixon.	Bucks.	
MICHL. SNOWPER.	Robeson.	Berks.	
FRED. PERSHING.	Hamiltons Bann.	York.	
JACOB SHORP.	Nockamixon.	Bucks.	
GEORGE MENTZER.	Earl.	Lancaster.	
JOHN FEHR.	Carnarvon.	Berks.	
MATHIAS BRIGHTSWORTH.	Carnarvon.	Berks.	
JACOB HOFFMAN.	Carnarvon.	Berks.	
FRED. HEIL.	Lancaster.	Lancaster.	
HENRY CHRISHNAN.	Greenwich.	Berks.	
RUDY BUSSART.	Greenwich.	Berks.	
NICHS. LINN.	Greenwich.	Berks.	
MARTIN KEEFER.	Bethel.	Lancaster.	
ADAM RAMSOWER.	Radnor.	Chester.	
WILLIAM OTTERBEIN.	York.	York.	
JOHN SPITLER.	York.	York.	
JACOB MILLER.	York.	York.	
HENRY BOOSER.	York.	York.	
JOHN BUSH.	York.	York.	July 20th, 1765.
MICHL. FIRHELL.	York.	York.	
PETER PFAFF.	Manchester.	York.	
PHILIP HANS.	Manchester.	York.	
ADAM FISHEL.	York.	York.	
PETER FEISER.	York.	York.	
HENRY FRANTZ.	Chesnut Hill.	Northampton.	
JEAN HUGON.	Nockamixon.	Bucks.	
FRED. EVERHART.	Nockamixon.	Bucks.	
JACOB WAGGONER.	Bern.	Berks.	
PETER GASHAU, Junr.	York.	York.	
ANTHY. GOSSLER.	York.	York.	
HENRY SHAEFFER.	Leacock.	Lancaster.	
ENGLEHART BROWN.	Leacock.	Lancaster.	
JACOB CREISHER.	Leacock.	Lancaster.	
MICHL. LONG.	York.	York.	
HENRY BENTZELL.	Dover.	York.	
PHILIP BENTZELL.	Dover.	York.	
JOHN BENTZELL.	Dover.	York.	
JOHN SHUMAN.	York.	York.	
JOHN WONNEMACKER.	Plumsted.	Bucks.	
MELCHIOR FISHER.	York.	York.	

Affirmers' Names.	Township.	County.
Christian Zimmerman.	Earl.	Lancaster.
Henry Rust.	Tulpehoccon.	Berks.
Henry Hasher.	Heidleberg.	Berks.
Andreas Gilbert.	Conestogo.	Lancaster.
Christr. Hatterick.	Tulpehoccon.	Berks.
Simon Pressler.	Tulpehoccon.	Berks.
Mathias Kemp.	Tulpehoccon.	Berks.
George Neiman.	Douglass.	Philadelphia.
Peter Moser.	Douglass.	Philadelphia.
Henry Meelhaan.	Douglass.	Philadelphia.
Henry Shuert.	Horsham.	Philadelphia.
Killian Small.	York.	York.
George Hassebecker.	York.	York.
George Stak.	York.	York.
Christr. Weider.	York.	York.
George Landzer.	Windsor.	Berks.
Nichs. Reisinger.	Windsor.	York.
Peter Reisinger.	Windsor.	York.
Wendal Reisinger.	Windsor.	York.
William Backer.	Springfield.	Bucks.
Paul Delcork.	Hatfield.	Philadelphia.
Solomon Weshley.	Douglass.	Philadelphia.
Christian Moser.	Douglass.	Berks.
Jerome Heinzelman.	Manheim.	Lancaster.
Philip Gimmell.	Pequea.	Lancaster.
Zacharias Nordein.	Lancaster.	Lancaster.
John Boochamer.	Hatfield.	Philadelphia.
George Garber.	York.	York.
Michl. Stacklick.	Lebanon.	Lancaster.
John Marks.	York.	York.
Dewald Sampson.	Lower Milford.	Bucks.
Arnold Eberhart.	Lower Saucon.	Northampton.
Michl. Rapp.	Oley.	Berks.
Christr. Rapp.	Oley.	Berks.
Daniel Peterman.	Windsor.	York.
Christian Lehnhart.	York.	York.
Christr. Zigenfoos.	Springfield.	Bucks.
Caspar Rubi.	Windsor.	York.
Peter Peterman.	Windsor.	York.
Michl. Peterman.	Windsor.	York.
Baltzer Stahley.	Bethlehem.	Northampton.
Henry Custabather.	Plainfield.	Northampton.
Peter Stout.	Plainfield.	Northampton.
Geo. Claywell.	Plainfield.	Northampton.
Leonard Obitz.	Plainfield.	Northampton.
Graff Goss.	Hempfield.	Lancaster.
Conrad Hayflich.	Lancaster.	Lancaster.
Tobias Reihm.	Lancaster.	Lancaster.
Andreas Mannykinger.	Lower Milford.	Bucks.
John Trickler.	Richland.	Bucks.
John Klaas.	Richmond.	Berks.
Godfry Krips.	Lancaster.	Lancaster.
Geo. Diffebiss.	Frederick in	Maryland.
Nichs. Miller.	Lancaster.	Lancaster.

NATURALIZATIONS

PENNSYLVANIA.

Affirmers' Names.	Township.	County.	Sacrament, when taken by Moravians.
PHILIP HART.	Lancaster.	Lancaster.	
JACOB DIKERT.	Lancaster.	Lancaster.	
DANIEL WENTZELL.	Oley.	Berks.	
JOHN EISENHAWER.	Bethel.	Lancaster.	
ARNOLD BECKER.	Lancaster.	Lancaster.	
MICHL. KLINGMAN.	Northern Liberties.	Philadelphia.	
DAVID HARMAN.	Exeter.	Berks.	
MARTIN WALTZ.	Exeter.	Berks.	
JOHN MESSENCOPE.	Lancaster.	Lancaster.	
BALTZER FUNCANNON.	Leacock.	Lancaster.	
ADAM GLOVER.	Warwick.	Lancaster.	
JOHN IBELING.	Alsace.	Berks.	
JOHN SMITH.	Hanover.	Philadelphia.	
JOHN MOSER.	Cocolico.	Lancaster.	
NICHS. LUSH.	Easton.	Northampton.	
LUDWICK CHRISTIAN.	Lower Saucon.	Northampton.	
TOBIAS MILLER.	Cocolico.	Lancaster.	
CHRISTIAN ISUN.	Lancaster.	Lancaster.	
STEPHEN HORNBERGER.	Lancaster.	Lancaster.	
PHILIP DIETRICK.	Conestogo.	Lancaster.	
JACOB ENGLE.	Bristol.	Philadelphia.	
LAWRENCE BAUSMAN.	Paradice.	York.	
PHILIP SNYDER.	Hempfield.	Lancaster.	
CHRISTIAN HOOFNAGLE.	Ruscom Manor.	Berks.	
JOHN TIES KLAAS.	Richmond.	Berks.	
HENRY WALD.	Upper Salford.	Philadelphia.	
JOHN GRAYBILL.	Heidleberg.	Lancaster.	
JOHN KINGERY.*	Warwick.	Lancaster.	
CHRISTIAN KINGERY.	Warwick.	Lancaster.	
ADAM LUTZ.	Whitpain.	Philadelphia.	
CONRAD DEEMER.	Whitpain.	Philadelphia.	
JNO. ULRICK SNIVELY.	Lebanon.	Lancaster.	
MARTIN ERTMAN.	Chesnut Hill.	Philadelphia.	
JACOB STAHL.	Upper Milford.	Northampton.	
HENRY STOFER.	Bedminster.	Bucks.	
HENRY BERRINGER.	Bedminster.	Bucks.	
LEONARD CARMAN.	Earl.	Lancaster.	
WILLM. TOUVER.	Northern Liberties.	Philadelphia.	
JOHN YAUNCE.	Upper Milford.	Northampton.	
CONRAD RYKLEY.	Upper Saucon.	Northampton.	
NICHS. WEAVER.	Northern Liberties.	Philadelphia.	
PHILIP BOOHOTAR.	Upper Saucon.	Northampton.	
JOHN KOCH.	Warwick.	Lancaster.	
PETER KASTER.	Tulpehoccon.	Berks.	
GODFREY LAUDERMILK.	Heidleberg.	Lancaster.	
HENRY LAYER.	Amity.	Berks.	
ULRICK HORNECKER.	Rockhill.	Bucks.	
JOHN BLATTINGER.	Warwick.	Lancaster.	
ADAM STAHLER.	Albany.	Berks.	
PHILIP THOMAS.	Lancaster.	Lancaster.	

* *Originally written Klingery but the l has been erased.*

Affirmers' Names.	Township.	County.	Sacrament, when taken by Moravians.
GEORGE NEISSER.	Philadelphia.	Philadelphia.	
HENRY MATTHIAS.	Strasburg.	Lancaster.	
ADAM HOOKE.	Strasburg.	Lancaster.	
JACOB MEYER.	Warwick.	Lancaster.	
MICHAEL GLOSS.	Bethlehem.	Northampton.	
DANIEL PENNER.	Coventry.	Chester.	
CHRISTIAN PENNER.	Coventry.	Chester.	
ADAM EAFF.	Upper Merion.	Philadelphia.	
HENRY ROADEBUSH.	Berwick.	York.	
ANDREW CAMPBLE.	Germantown.	Philadelphia.	
JOHN BAKER.	New Hanover.	Philadelphia.	
MATTHIAS WESNER.	Sadsbury.	Northampton.	
JACOB LETHERMAN.	Bedminster.	Bucks.	
CHRISTIAN FRETZ.	Tinicum.	Bucks.	
CHRISTR. GATSELMAN.	Haverford.	Chester.	
JACOB GROSS.	Philadelphia.	Philadelphia.	
JACOB HOFNER.	Philadelphia.	Philadelphia.	
ANDREAS BERTRAFF.	Rapho.	Lancaster.	
JOHN LEECH.	Kingcess.	Philadelphia.	
JOHN PETER YOUNG.	Northern Liberties.	Philadelphia.	
PHILIP RAPP.	Upper Merion.	Philadelphia.	
JACOB WEISS.	Lower Saucon.	Philadelphia.	
JOHN DOULOUSANT.	Germantown.	Philadelphia.	
PETER BOKE.	Norriton.	Philadelphia.	
JOHN HARTMAN.	New Hanover.	Philadelphia.	
ANDREAS PFY.	Springfield.	Philadelphia.	
JOHN HAAS.	Bethlehem.	Northampton.	
ADAM BOLE.	Upper Darby.	Chester.	
GEORGE STEPHEN.	Germantown.	Philadelphia.	
MICHL. HOSLER.	Lower Merrion.	Philadelphia.	
CHAS. MAUS.	Philadelphia.	Philadelphia.	
JACOB ULRICH.	Whitpaine.	Philadelphia.	
JACOB BURRELL.	Germantown.	Philadelphia.	
LAWRENCE ZIMMERLY.	Germantown.	Philadelphia.	
JOHN ZELL.	Lower Merrion.	Philadelphia.	
GEORGE KLINGELL.	Germantown.	Philadelphia.	
DAVID SMITH.	Plumsted.	Bucks.	
ANDREAS ALBRECHT.	Bethlehem.	Northampton.	Sept. 21st, 1765.
CARL SIGMOND WEINICKE.	Bethlehem.	Northampton.	Sept. 21st, 1765.
THOMAS FISHER.	Bethlehem.	Northampton.	Sept. 21st, 1765.
JNO. JACOB WEISINGER.	Bethlehem.	Northampton.	Sept. 21st, 1765.
ERNST WALTER.	Bethlehem.	Northampton.	Sept. 21st, 1765.
FRANCIS CLEWALDT.	Plainfield.	Northampton.	
JOHN GROVES.	Philadelphia.	Philadelphia.	
PETER KURTZ.	Philadelphia.	Philadelphia.	
CONRAD HOOVER.	Blockley.	Philadelphia.	
JACOB LAUB.	Blockley.	Philadelphia.	
JACOB RIDEBACHER.	Warwick.	Lancaster.	
CONRAD KILE.	Lower Milford.	Bucks.	
PETER SAIGER.	Richland.	Bucks.	
PHILIP HALL.	Upper Saucon.	Northampton.	
GABRIEL SAIGER.	Rockhill.	Bucks.	
JOHN HANKEY.	Upper Milford.	Northampton.	
JOHN GANN,	Upper Saucon.	Northampton.	

PENNSYLVANIA.

Affirmers' Names.	Township.	County.	Sacrament, when taken by Moravians.
Elias Jordan.	Warwick.	Lancaster.	
Peter Kammer.	Philadelphia.	Philadelphia.	
Urbanus Long.	Bethel.	Lancaster.	
Henry Haitz.*	Rockhill.	Bucks.	
Peter Sampson.	Lower Milford.	Bucks.	
Philip Wilheimer.	Radnor.	Chester.	
John Danl. Frailey.	Amity.	Berks.	
Fred. Stillwaggon.	Merion.	Philadelphia.	
Simon Sweitzer.	Germantown.	Philadelphia.	
John Baker.	Philadelphia.	Philadelphia.	
Jacob Kibler.	Germantown.	Philadelphia.	
Rosina Pfinstag.	Passyunk.	Philadelphia.	Aug. 24th, 1765.
Henry Beck.	Germantown.	Philadelphia.	
John Lender.	Earl.	Lancaster.	
George Bogart.	Earl.	Lancaster.	
John Grous.	Earl.	Lancaster.	
Andrew Keyser.	Earl.	Lancaster.	
Henry Valentine.	Earl.	Lancaster.	
Ernst Keesicker.	Earl.	Lancaster.	
Daniel Maurer.	Germantown.	Philadelphia.	
Christian Diehl.	Germantown.	Philadelphia.	
Conrad Meyer.	Earl.	Lancaster.	
Lawrence Smith.	Roxborough.	Philadelphia.	
Peter Hinkle.	Germantown.	Philadelphia.	
Nichs. Yisely.	Maccungy.	Northampton.	
Jacob Barger.	Upper Milford.	Northampton.	
Ludwick Sweitzer.	Germantown.	Philadelphia.	
Caspar Nill.	Horsham.	Philadelphia.	
Jacob Hauser.	Linn.	Northampton.	
Dewald Grim.	Weisenburg.	Northampton.	
Ulrick Waggoner.	Albany.	Berks.	
Jacob Staam.	Albany.	Berks.	
Jno. Laubach.	Pikes.	Chester.	
Conrad Shierer.	Pikes.	Chester.	
William Bercart.	Philadelphia.	Philadelphia.	
Adam Shirly.	Lebanon.	Lancaster.	
Christian Shirly.	Lebanon.	Lancaster.	
Michl. Albright.	Linn.	Northampton.	
Jacob Spainhower	Warwick.	Lancaster.	
Michl. Pitzer.	Leacock.	Lancaster.	
Mathias Pitzer.	Leacock.	Lancaster.	
Christr. Johnson.	Upper Saucon.	Northampton.	
Jacob Lehrey.	Philadelphia.	Philadelphia.	
Baltzer Stann.	Hatfield.	Philadelphia.	
Christr. Shubart.	White Marsh.	Philadelphia.	
George Wambolt.	White Marsh.	Philadelphia.	
Martin Walter.	Upper Merrion.	Philadelphia.	
Henry Noblo.	Maccungy.	Northampton.	
John Foulke.	Maccungy.	Northampton.	
Peter Piper.	White Marsh.	Philadelphia.	
Henry Desh.	Upper Milford.	Northampton.	

The a has been struck through.

Affirmers' Names.	Township.	County.	Sacrament, when taken by Moravians.
PHILIP SHARER.	Maccungy.	Northampton.	
ERASMUS ALSHOUSE.	Richland.	Berks.	
JOHN PENNER.	Windsor.	Chester.	
DANL. TSER.	Philadelphia.	Philadelphia.	
MICHL. MALVIER.	Lebanon.	Lancaster.	
JOHN HAYFER.	Cocolico.	Lancaster.	
PETER BRIGHTBILL.	Lebanon.	Lancaster.	
CASPAR SHRIGHT.	Cocolico.	Lancaster.	
DEWALD MAIDER.	Cocolico.	Lancaster.	
PETER CRUMBACKER.	Coventry.	Chester.	
JACOB FAUTZ.	Warwick.	Lancaster.	
CHRISTIAN MILLER.	New Britain.	Bucks.	
HENRY WUNNERLY.	Bristol.	Philadelphia.	
MICHL. KEESELMAN.	Hertford.	Chester.	
JACOB KNOLL.	Lower Merrion.	Philadelphia.	
PETER KNIPPER.	Albany.	Berks.	
JACOB LEHRE.	Albany.	Berks.	
DAVID HANSELL.	Upper Darby.	Chester.	
JACOB MAURER.	Northern Liberties.	Philadelphia.	
CASPAR SERBER.	Germantown.	Philadelphia.	
DAVID GILBERT.	Germantown.	Philadelphia.	
JOHN RITZLE.	Hempfield.	Lancaster.	
ADAM WILLIAM.	Northern Liberties.	Philadelphia.	
FRED. ROUSHENBERGER.	Upper Milford.	Northampton.	
PHILIP ETTER.	Germantown.	Philadelphia.	
GEORGE GREAGER.	Worcester.	Philadelphia.	
PHILIP TUSH.	Springfield.	Bucks.	
JOHN EVERLY.	Passyunk.	Philadelphia.	
JOHN BROWN.	Lebanon.	Lancaster.	
LEONARD GERRARD.	Norrington.	Philadelphia.	
PETER GERRARD.	Norrington.	Philadelphia.	
JEREMIAH RUNKELL.	Norrington.	Philadelphia.	
SAMUEL RUNKLE.	Norrington.	Philadelphia.	
JOHN YOUNGBLUT.	Charles.	Chester.	
GEORGE RUSH.	Whitpain.	Philadelphia.	
FREDERICK RECOPE.	Providence.	Philadelphia.	
JNO. NICHS. GERRARD.	Whitpain.	Philadelphia.	
MICHL. LENTZ.	Whitpain.	Philadelphia.	
MATTHEW LENTZ.	Whitemarsh.	Philadelphia.	
BENEDICT GARBER.	Providence.	Philadelphia.	
FRANCIS HUBER.	Springfield.	Bucks.	
MICHL. SHMELL.	Haycock.	Bucks.	
FRED. FLECKENSTEIN.	Germantown.	Philadelphia.	
FRED. SHIENLIN.	Upper Hanover.	Philadelphia.	
JACOB SMITH.	Upper Hanover.	Philadelphia.	
MELCHR. COLP.	Upper Hanover.	Philadelphia.	
HENRY WEBER.	Heidleberg.	Berks.	
MICHL. WEIRMAN.	Hatfield.	Philadelphia.	
GEORGE REINHEIMER.	Upper Hanover.	Philadelphia.	
GEORGE HOLTZSCHUCH.	Oley.	Berks.	
MATHIAS ABEL.	Philadelphia.	Philadelphia.	
ANDREAS SCHAFFER.	Philadelphia.	Philadelphia.	
PETER HERBLE.	Providence.	Philadelphia.	
JACOB HILL.	Kensington.	Philadelphia.	

k

PENNSYLVANIA.

Affirmers' Names.	Township.	County.	Sacrament, when taken by Moravians.
JOHN CRAMP.	Kensington.	Philadelphia.	
JOHN SNYDER.	Kensington.	Philadelphia.	
MARTIN SHNIEB.	Kensington.	Philadelphia.	
JOHN SMITH.	Upper Hanover.	Philadelphia.	
CONRAD LEONARD.	Lancaster.	Lancaster.	
JACOB RIES.	Germantown.	Philadelphia.	
PHILIP HIRSH.	Whitemarsh.	Philadelphia.	
RUDOLPH WHITE.	Germant[own].	Philadelphia.	
FRED. SHWARTZ.	Frankford.	Philadelphia.	
PETER MUTH.	Oxford.	Philadelphia.	
CASPAR SHISLER.	Oxford.	Philadelphia.	
JACOB CONRAD.	Lower Merrion.	Philadelphia.	
NICHS. SHULTZ.	Lower Merrion.	Philadelphia.	
PETER CONRAD.	Lower Merrion.	Philadelphia.	
HENRY HEYMAN.	Springfield.	Philadelphia.	
PETER OTT.	Blockley.	Philadelphia.	
HENRY SWEITZER.	Skippack.	Philadelphia.	
PETER PEPPEL.	Manheim.	Lancaster.	
CHRISTR. BYERLY.	Philadelphia.	Philadelphia.	
GEORGE GEORGE, Jr.	Abington.	Philadelphia.	
GEORGE GEORGE, Senr.	Abington.	Philadelphia.	
GEORGE HELTENBACH.	Upper Dublin.	Philadelphia.	
JACOB WAGNER.	Philadelphia.	Philadelphia.	
CHRISTIAN VAN ERDEN.	Philadelphia.	Philadelphia.	
PHILIP PETER WALTER.	Philadelphia.	Philadelphia.	
CHRISTIAN SMITH.	Northern Liberties.	Philadelphia.	
GEORGE GEYLER.	Northern Liberties.	Philadelphia.	
GEORGE SHUTZ.	Northern Liberties.	Philadelphia.	
ADAM FARBER.	Upper Salford.	Philadelphia.	
NICHOLAS LEISTER.	Franconia.	Philadelphia.	
PETER FRICK.	Hatfield.	Philadelphia.	
CONRAD SHAUECKER.	Northern Liberties.	Philadelphia.	
JACOB WAGGONER.	Gwenidth.	Philadelphia.	
MICHL. ETZEL.	Gwenidth.	Philadelphia.	
JNO. NICHS. WAGNER.	Northern Liberties.	Philadelphia.	
PETER HAAN.	Northern Liberties.	Philadelphia.	
GEORGE SHRYER.	Northern Liberties.	Philadelphia.	
JACOB NICHOLAS.	Northern Liberties.	Philadelphia.	
PHILIP STAIBER.	Northern Liberties.	Philadelphia.	
CHARLES JONES.	Roxborough.	Philadelphia.	
CHRISTIAN CONVER.	North Wales.	Philadelphia.	
JOHN FLIMAN.	Pikeland.	Chester.	
JACOB KEHR.	Pikeland.	Chester.	
JASPAR HORN.	Rockhill.	Bucks.	
PETER YOST.	Philadelphia.	Philadelphia.	
BALTIS KLEIMER.	Philadelphia.	Philadelphia.	
PHILIP MEREVIEN (?).*	Roxborough.	Philadelphia.	
JOHN PFEIL.	Roxborough.	Philadelphia.	
GEORGE FREY.	Roxborough.	Philadelphia.	
ANDREW CLOSS.	Northern Liberties.	Philadelphia.	

The name has been corrected. The first e has a line over it, the v is a correction and the last e has been inserted above the line.

Affirmers' Names.	Township.	County.	Sacrament, when taken by Moravians.
HENRY LEWIS.	Roxborough.	Philadelphia.	
PETER WAGGONER.	Philadelphia.	Philadelphia.	
MICHL. GEBHARD.	Northern Liberties.	Philadelphia.	
THEOBALD SHEIB.	Philadelphia.	Philadelphia.	
HENRY RUSH.	Philadelphia.	Philadelphia.	
JNO. FRED. LEYDICH.	Philadelphia.	Philadelphia.	
HENRY ENGLE.	Douglass.	Philadelphia.	
JACOB DENGLER.	Douglass.	Philadelphia.	
ANTHY. SPIES.	Douglass.	Philadelphia.	
CONRAD RICHER.	York.	York.	
GEORGE LUDWICK.	Philadelphia.	Philadelphia.	
JOHN MYER.	White Marsh.	Philadelphia.	
GEORGE HUBER.	Bethlehem.	Northampton.	Sept. 26th, 1765.
MICHL. SMITH.	Germant[own].	Philadelphia.	
JNO. NICHOLAS FOOKS.	Bethlehem.	Northampton.	
MARTIN KRATZ.	Philadelphia.	Philadelphia.	Sept. 26th, 1765.
JOHN GUCKUS.	Manchester.	York.	
GEORGE SHWENKER.	Upper Saucon.	Northampton.	
THOMAS BALTZER.	Greenwich.	Berks.	
GEORGE BAUERMAN.	Weisenberg.	Northampton.	
YOST EBERT.	Pikeland.	Chester.	
PETER BROWN.	Maxatawny.	Berks.	
FRED. BROWN.	Long Swamp.	Berks.	
ARNOLD KRAMER.	Northern Liberties.	Philadelphia.	
NICHS. REHRIG.	Salford.	Philadelphia.	
ABRAHAM PETER.	Philadelphia.	Philadelphia.	
CONRAD HOFF.	Philadelphia.	Philadelphia.	
JOHN MESSEMIR.	Passyunk.	Philadelphia.	
JNO. FRED. MULENFELD.	Passyunk.	Philadelphia.	
PETER KNIPPER.	Albany.	Berks.	
VALENTINE PETRI.	Weisenburg.	Northampton.	
MATHIAS BRUKERT.	Weisenburg.	Northampton.	
ANDREW STAHL.	Germantown.	Philadelphia.	
CHRISTIAN YENTZER.	Northern Liberties.	Philadelphia.	
PAUL BENNER.	Vincent.	Chester.	
CONRAD YOST.	Germantown.	Philadelphia.	
CHRISTOPHER LENTZ.	Springfield.	Bucks.	
JOHN STAR.	Germantown.	Philadelphia.	
BERNARD FEDER.	Cocolico.	Lancaster.	
JOHN HOFEMAN.	Germantown.	Philadelphia.	
CHARLES COTY.	Germantown.	Philadelphia.	
GEORGE MEYER.	Bristol.	Philadelphia.	
JACOB HOFFMAN.	Germantown.	Philadelphia.	
JACOB FRICK.	Hanover.	Philadelphia.	
RUDOLPH KITTINGER.	Cheltenham.	Philadelphia.	
ANDREW SMITH.	Germantown.	Philadelphia.	
PHILIP CULP.	Lower Milford.	Philadelphia.	
JACOB NERACHER.	Springfield.	Philadelphia.	
FREDERICK BANTLION.	Philadelphia.	Philadelphia.	
CHRISTR. ROHRBACH.	Vincent.	Chester.	
JOHN ROHNER.	Philadelphia.	Philadelphia.	
HENRY KUNTZ.	Springfield.	Philadelphia.	
JOHN STOUT.	North Liberties.	Philadelphia.	
HENRY KNERR.	Vincent.	Chester.	

PENNSYLVANIA.

Affirmers' Names.	Township.	County.	Sacrament, when taken by Moravians.
LAWRENCE PEARSON.	Nockamixon.	Bucks.	
PETER YOUNG.	Nockamixon.	Bucks.	
PETER EDENBORN.	Germantown.	Philadelphia.	
HENRY MILLER.	Vincent.	Chester.	
CONRAD MILLER.	Manchester.	York.	
GEORGE BROWNISH.	Waterford.	Gloucester in West New Jersey.	
PETER BRINTLE.	Cheltenham.	Philadelphia.	
MARK TOMI.*	Philadelphia.	Philadelphia.	
JACOB BUCK.	Philadelphia.	Philadelphia.	
CHAS. GARTZ.	Philadelphia.	Philadelphia.	
SIMON VOGELGESANG.	Germantown.	Philadelphia.	
JOHN ENGLE.	Germantown.	Philadelphia.	
CHRISTR. KUHN.	Bristol.	Philadelphia.	
JOHN KOMER.	Springfield.	Philadelphia.	
PETER STROUB.	Germantown.	Philadelphia.	
CASKAR WIRSHURN.	Northern Liberties.	Philadelphia.	
ULRICK RUHNER.	Northern Liberties.	Philadelphia.	
PETER ALT.	Springfield.	Bucks.	
PHILIP WENTZELL.	Northern Liberties.	Philadelphia.	
JOHN RUSH.	Leacock.	Lancaster.	
JACOB PLANKENHORN.	Whitpaine.	Philadelphia.	
PETER STEGES.	Vincent.	Chester.	
CASPAR SNYDER.	Vincent.	Chester.	
PIERRE ROUSHON.	Roxborough.	Philadelphia.	
PETER FAUST.	Roxborough.	Philadelphia.	
PETER LAUB.	Springfield.	Philadelphia.	
WENDAL HORST.	Springfield.	Philadelphia.	
SEBASTIAN EIGELBERGER.	Springfield.	Philadelphia.	
JNO. MICHL. NEWHAUSER.	Springfield.	Philadelphia.	
JACOB STRAUS.	Springfield.	Philadelphia.	
CHARLES CRAMP.	Springfield.	Philadelphia.	
PETER SHUG.	Worcester.	Philadelphia.	
CHRISTR. HERTZELL.	Worcester.	Philadelphia.	
JNO. MICH FREY.	Worcester.	Philadelphia.	
LEONARD ROST.	Worcester.	Philadelphia.	
JOHN WALTER.	Pikeland.	Chester.	
THOMAS SNYDER.	Pikeland.	Chester.	
PETER WAGNER.	Pikeland.	Chester.	
HENRY SMITH.	Pikeland.	Chester.	
PHILIP STEFFAN.	Pikeland.	Chester.	
GEORGE PENTER.	Providence.	Philadelphia.	
PETER PUTHA.	Cheltenham.	Philadelphia.	
HENRY SHLVER.	Pikeland.	Chester.	
PHILIP WEIAND.	Pikeland.	Chester.	
CONRAD RAUCH.	Vincent.	Chester.	
JOHN YOUNG.	Cheltenham.	Philadelphia.	
HENRY MECHLIN.	Cheltenham.	Philadelphia.	
JOHN GRAFF.	Philadelphia.	Philadelphia.	
MELCHIOR KNORR.	White Marsh.	Philadelphia.	

There is a line over the m.

Affirmers' Names.	Township.	County.	Sacrament, when taken by Moravians.
SEBASTIAN SEIFERT.	Northern Liberties.	Philadelphia.	
JOHN KERBACH.	White Marsh.	Philadelphia.	
ABRAHAM FORRE.	Mountjoy.	Lancaster.	
MICHL. SNYDER.	Mountjoy.	Lancaster.	
JACOB KLOTI.	Mountjoy.	Lancaster.	
GEORGE SHUSS.	Warwick.	Lancaster.	
JACOB KATZ.	Philadelphia.	Philadelphia.	
JACOB KIMMELL.	Philadelphia.	Philadelphia.	
GEORGE MERKER.	Philadelphia.	Philadelphia.	
HENRY SHAIT.	Frankfort.	Philadelphia.	
GEORGE WEISBACH.	Northern Liberties.	Philadelphia.	
ERNST MILLER.	Radnor.	Chester.	
JOHN UNGER.	Warwick.	Lancaster.	
GEORGE INGLE.	Warwick.	Lancaster.	
CASPAR UPPERMAN.	Elizabeth.	Lancaster.	
WILLIAM INGERSBACH.	Northern Liberties.	Philadelphia.	
JACOB ERING.	Northern Liberties.	Philadelphia.	
CONRAD SEIPELL.	Hilltown.	Bucks.	
RICHD. REILL.	Kensington.	Philadelphia.	
JOHN SAILER.	Passyunk.	Philadelphia.	
JOHN WESTBARGER.	Passyunk.	Philadelphia.	
HENRY STUBER.	Philadelphia.	Philadelphia.	
ALBRIGHT STIMMELL.	Philadelphia.	Philadelphia.	
MATHIAS STIMMELL.	Philadelphia.	Philadelphia.	
CHRISTR. PLICKENSTERFER.	Warwick.	Lancaster.	
CASPAR SHEARER.	Lower Dublin.	Philadelphia.	
PHILIP HAY.	Bristol.	Philadelphia.	
MICHL. CANER.	Philadelphia.	Philadelphia.	
ADAM GUIER.	Kingcess.	Philadelphia.	
JOHN PETERS.	Kingcess.	Philadelphia.	
STOPHEL GRASS.	Northern Liberties.	Philadelphia.	
CASPAR FETTER.	Manor Moreland.	Philadelphia.	
WILLIAM BISHOP.	Mountjoy.	Lancaster.	
PETER MEYER.	Springfield.	Bucks.	
HENRY RUMAN.	Upper Dublin.	Philadelphia.	
PETER FRANK.	Upper Saucon.	Northampton.	
ABRAHAM ELEY.	Richmond.	Berks.	

The Persons before named having entituled themselves to the Benefit of the Act of Parliament aforesaid, A perfect List is to be transmitted to the Lords Commissioners for Trade and Plantations; To which end in pursuance of said Act I have caused their names to be made known.   WILL. ALLEN, Chief Justice.

To Joseph Shippen, Junr., Esquire,   ⎫
Secretary of the Province of Pennsylvania ⎭

I do hereby certify that the foregoing is a true and perfect List taken from the Original Certificate under the Hand of William Allen, Esquire, Chief Justice of the Province of Pennsylvania, remaining in my office.   [*Signed* :] JOSEPH SHIPPEN, Jr.,

Secretary.

Philadelphia, 10th November, 1766.

PENNSYLVANIA.

Y. 16.

Supreme Court held at Philadelphia, 10 April, 1766.

Jurors' Names.	Township.	County.	Sacrament when taken.
PETER HUETT.	Exeter.	Berks.	April 10th, 1766.
PETER HEIMS.	Philadelphia.	Philadelphia.	Mar. 30th, 1766.
NICHS. LANTZ.	Williams.	Northampton.	Mar. 29th, 1766.
LEONARD WERNTZ.	Northern Liberties.	Philadelphia.	Mar. 30th, 1766.

Quakers, &c.

Affirmers' Names.	County.	Province.
PETER HAPPA.	Hunterdon.	New Jersey.
PETER YOUNG.	Hunterdon.	New Jersey.
YOST SHEFFER.	Hunterdon.	New Jersey.
PETER CLOVER.	Hunterdon.	New Jersey.
JOHN SMITH.	Hunterdon.	New Jersey.

Certified by JOSEPH SHIPPEN, Jr., Secretary.
Philadelphia, 10 Nov., 1766.

Y. 26.

Supreme Court held at Philadelphia, 24 September, 1766.

Jurors' Names.	Township.	County,	Sacrament when taken.
TOBIAS DITTIS.	Salisbury.	Lancaster.	Sept. 7th, 1766.
CASPAR SHIEBELE.	Lancaster.	Lancaster.	July 21st, 1766.
PHILIP KRAMER.*	Reading.	Berks.	Sept. 21st, 1766.
FRED. ULRICK.	Raclin.	Berks.	Sept. 18th, 1766.
LEONARD KEPLINGER.	Cumry.	Berks.	Sept. 22nd, 1766.
JACOB KEISLING.	Bern.	Berks.	Sept. 22nd, 1766.
GEORGE KEISLING.	Bern.	Berks.	Sept. 22nd, 1766.
YOST ERDMAN.	Lower Milford.	Bucks.	Sept. 14th, 1766.
GEO. DANNAHOWER.†	Robinson.	Berks.	Sept. 21st, 1766.
JOHN MILLER.	Earl.	Lancaster.	Sept. 23rd, 1766.
CHRISTR. HANLY.	Earl.	Lancaster.	Sept. 23rd, 1766.
JOHN CARR.	Whiteland.	Chester.	Sept. 24th, 1766.
DIETRICK MARCKY.	Heidleberg.	Lancaster.	Sept. 21st, 1766.
MICHL. GRATZ.	Philadelphia.	Philadelphia.	[a Jew].
PHILIP SUPER.	Haverford.	Chester.	Oct. 5th, 1766.

Quakers, &c.

Affirmers' Name .		
MARTIN REYLY.		
SAMUEL HARNISH.		
NICHS. HARVICK.		
JACOB GEEZY.		
JACOB ALBRECHT.		
DANL. TAYLOR.		
LUDWICK HIBNER.	Bethlehem . in	Northampton County.

Certified by JOSEPH SHIPPEN, Jr., Secretary.

* Krœmer in Y. 34.   † Dannahover in Y. 34.

Supreme Court held at Philadelphia, 10 April, 1767.

Jurors' Names.	Township.	County.	Sacrament when taken.
DAVID EPLER.	Earl.	Lancaster.	Apr. 5th, 1767.
CHRISTR.* LERCK.	Heidleberg.	Berks.	Apr. 5th, 1767.
PETER SOHL.	Heidleberg.	Berks.	Apr. 6th, 1767.
ABRAHAM BOLLMAN.	Heidleberg.	Lancaster.	Apr. 5th, 1767.
ELIAS LEWIS TREICHEL.	Philadelphia.	Philadelphia.	Apr. 9th, 1767.
ADAM BACH.	Lebanon.	Lancaster.	Apr. 5th, 1767.
JACOB MOREHARD.	Earl.	Lancaster.	Apr. 10th, 1767.
PETER KABLE.†	Marlborough.	Philadelphia.	Apr. 7th, 1767.
GEORGE POTTS.	Bethel.	Lancaster.	Apr. 5th, 1767.
GEORGE TRESSLY.	Lower Dublin.	Philadelphia.	Apr. 8th, 1767.
PAUL GEIGER.	Robinson.	Berks.	Mar. 29th, 1767.
STEPHEN FRANCISCUS WALCK.	Robinson.	Berks.	Mar. 29th, 1767.

* Cristopr. in Y. 35.   † Kabel in Y. 35.

Quakers, &c.

Affirmers' Names.	Township.	County.
AUGUSTUS SHUBART.	Philadelphia.	Philadelphia.
CASPAR SHELL.	Donegal.	Lancaster.
PHIL. HAMMERSMITH.	Douglass.	Philadelphia.
MICHL. BOWER.	Amity.	Berks.
ADAM SHYER.	Exeter.	Berks.
HENRY WACKS.	Alsace.	Berks.
PETER WACKS.	Bern.	Berks.
PETER WINGLEBLEGH.	Bethel.	Lancaster.
MICHL. SIGHTS.	Bedminster.	Chester.
JOHN PETER RUNYOE.	Bedminster.	Bucks.
STEPHEN ULRICK.	Frederick County in	Maryland.
JACOB STUTSMAN.	Cumberland County.	
MICHAEL MILLER.	Frederick County in	Maryland.
CONRAD FOX.	Frederick County in	Maryland.
JACOB SNYDER.	Frederick County in	Maryland.
SIMON STUCKY.	Frederick County in	Maryland.
PHILIP JACOB MILLER.	Frederick County in	Maryland.

Certified by JOSEPH SHIPPEN, Jr., Secretary.

[NOTE: Y. 34 and Y. 35 are duplicates of the preceding two lists (Y. 26). The variations in the two have been noted.]

Y. 36.

Supreme Court held at Philadelphia, 24 and 25 Sept., and 5 Oct., 1767.

Foreigners' Names.	Township.	County.	Sacrament when taken.
WILLIAM KURTZ.	Earl.	Lancaster.	Sept. 23rd, 1767.
DAVID FOOKES.	Reading.	Berks.	Aug. 30th, 1767.
JACOB MICHEL.	York.	York.	Aug. 2nd, 1767.
JNO. GEORGE WOOLF.	Tulpehockon.	Berks.	Sept. 16th, 1767.
JOHN ADAM MILLER.	Plainfield.	Northampton.	July 5th, 1767.
JNO. NICHS. MILLER.	Plainfield.	Northampton.	July 5th, 1767.
FRED. LIMBACH.	Upper Milford.	Northampton.	Sept. 21st, 1767.
JNO. GREESEMAN.	Whitehall.	Northampton.	Sept. 13th, 1767.

PENNSYLVANIA.

Foreigners' Names.	Township.	County.	Sacrament when taken.
JOHN PAUL.	Vincent.	Chester.	Sept. 20th, 1767.
HENY. SHENCKELL.	Coventry.	Chester.	Sept. 20th, 1767.
JACOB SCHUSTER.	Nantmile.	Chester.	Sept. 20th, 1767.
HENRY SHAVER.	Charlestown.	Chester.	Sept. 6th, 1767.
CONRAD MOORE.	Robeson.	Berks.	Sept. 24th, 1767.
JOHN GROWAR.	Lower Merrion.	Philadelphia.	Sept. 22nd, 1767.
LEOND. HEIDLEY.	Lower Merrion.	Philadelphia.	Sept. 22nd, 1767.
GIDEON MOORE.	Upper Hanover.	Philadelphia.	Sept. 10th, 1767.
PETER FOOKES.	Maccungy.	Northampton.	Sept. 19th, 1767.
ANDW. ZEIGERFOOS.	Springfield.	Bucks.	Sept. 23rd, 1767.
JOHN MILLER.	Northampton.	Northampton.	Sept. 13th, 1767.
JOHN WOOLMAN.	Horsham.	Philadelphia.	Sept. 24th, 1767.
CONRAD WANNEMACHER.	New Hanover.	Philadelphia.	July [sic].
LEONARD WEBER.	Gwinedth.	Philadelphia.	July 12th, 1767.
ANDREW LOYMAN.	New Castle County.		Sept. 24th, 1767.
MARTIN MILLER.	Merrion.	Philadelphia.	Sept. 30th, 1767.

Quakers, &c.

Foreigners' Names.	Township.	County.	
HENRY MILLER.	City of Philadelphia.	Philadelphia.	
DEWALD HUSHAA.	Brecknock.	Lancaster.	
ADAM HYNICKY.	York.	York.	
WENDAL SEIBERT.	Bethel.	Berks.	
CHRISTR. STEEL.	Manheim.	York.	
PETER GERRARD.	Upper Milford.	Northampton.	
MICHL. HIRSH.	Lebanon.	Lancaster.	
PETER SMITH.	Bethel.	Lancaster.	
STOPHEL KNEBBELL.	Bethel.	Berks.	
STOPHEL REYER.	Bethel.	Berks.	
JACOB WERRYFIELDS.	Frederick County in	Maryland.	
JACOB BOWMAN.	Frederick County in	Maryland.	
CHRISTIAN WHITMORE.	Frederick County in	Maryland.	
JOHN YEAGER.	Frederick County in	Maryland.	
HENRY INKLE.	Frederick County in	Maryland.	
SAML. WOLEGAMODE.	Frederick County in	Maryland.	
PAUL WESTERBERGER.	Frederick County in	Maryland.	
CHRISTR. ZIMMERMAN.	City of Philadelphia.	Philadelphia.	
WILLIAM CLAUS.	Upper Dublin.	Philadelphia.	
JOHN CORNMAN (Moravian).	City of Philadelphia.	Philadelphia.	took Sacrament Aug. 8th, 1767.

List certified by JOSEPH SHIPPEN, Jr., Secretary.

Y. 37.

Supreme Court held at Philadelphia, 11 April, 1768.

Foreigners' Names.	Township.	County.	Sacrament when taken.
CONRAD BROTZMAN.	Providence.	Philadelphia.	Apr. 1st, 1768.
ERHARD KLISS.	Earl.	Lancaster.	Apr. 11th, 1768.

List certified by JOSEPH SHIPPEN, Jr., Secretary.

Y. 38.

Nisi Prius Court held at Reading for the County of Berks., 13 May, 1768.

Foreigners' Names.	Township.	County.	Sacrament when taken.
LAWRENCE COOPER.	Amity.	Berks.	Apr. 24th, 1768.
JOHN REBER.	Heidleberg.	Berks.	Apr. 10th, 1768.
JOHN WOHLHEBER.	Tolpohocken.	Berks.	May 8th, 1768.
JOHN JACOB.	Bern.	Berks.	in Easter. 1768.
GEORGE MICHAEL KETTNER.	Tolpohocken.	Berks.	May 11th, 1768.

Nisi Prius Court held at York for the County of York, 20 May, 1768.

Foreigners' Names.	Township.	County.	Sacrament, when taken.
CHRISTOPHER SLIEGLE senior.	Berwick.	York.	May 20th, 1768.
LEWIS RUDISILLY,	Codorus.	York.	May 20th, 1768.
CHRISTIAN LOUGH.	Manchester.	York.	Apr. 17th, 1768.
PETER LOUGH.	Manchester.	York.	Apr. 17th, 1768.
FREDERICK MEYER.	Dover.	York.	Mar. 27th, 1768.
GEORGE MITCHELL.	Dover.	York.	Mar. 27th, 1768.
ABRAHAM BLEIMYER.	York.	York.	May 20th, 1768.

Nisi Prius Court at Reading in Berks. County, 13 May, 1768.

Affirmers' Name.	Township.	County.
JACOB KURTZ (' a foreign Pro-testant who conscientiously scruples to take an oath ').	Cumru.	Berks.

List certified by JOSEPH SHIPPEN, Jr., Secretary.

PENNSYLVANIA.

C.O. 5. 1278.

Z. 28.

A true and perfect List of the Names of all and every Person and Persons who have from the 1st day of June 1768 to the 1st day of June 1769 intituled themselves to the Benefit of being admitted to be His Majesty's natural born Subjects of the Kingdom of Great Britain before one or more of the Judges of the Supream Court of the Province of Pennsylvania according to the Directions of an Act of Parliament made in the thirteenth Year of the Reign of his late Majesty George the second intituled "An Act for naturalizing such foreign Protestants and others therein mentioned as are settled or shall settle in any of His Majesty's Colonies in America," and according to an Act of General Assembly of the said Province of Pennsylvania made in the sixteenth year of the Reign of his said late Majesty entituled "An Act for naturalizing such foreign Protestants as are settled or shall settle within this Province who, not being of the People called Quakers, do conscientiously scruple and refuse the taking of an Oath"; Vizt.

Jurors.	Foreigners' Names. Affirmers.	Places of Residence.	Sacrament, when taken.	When Naturalized.	In what County Naturalized.
Charles Ebersohl.		Berks County.	Sept. 23rd, 1768.	Sept. 24th, 1768.	Philadelphia.
Jacob Neff.		Berks County.	Sept. 23rd, 1768.	Sept. 24th, 1768.	Philadelphia.
William Croft.		New Jersey.	Sept. 24th, 1768.	Sept. 24th, 1768.	Philadelphia.
Nicholas Smidt.		Berks County.	Sept. 24th, 1768.	Sept. 24th, 1768.	Philadelphia.
Michael Swartz.		Philadelphia Cnty.	Sept. 29th, 1768.	Sept. 29th, 1768.	Philadelphia.
	John Edwin.	Northampton.	Aug. 13th, 1768.	Sept. 29th, 1768.	Philadelphia.
	Ferdinand Jacob Detmers.	Northampton.	Sept. 10th, 1768.	Sept. 29th, 1768.	Philadelphia.
John Francis Oberlin.		Northampton.	Sept. 10th, 1768.	Sept. 29th, 1768.	Philadelphia.
John Arbo.		Chester.	Sept. 10th, 1768.	Sept. 29th, 1768.	Philadelphia.
Jacob Stork.		Maryland.		Sept. 29th, 1768.	Philadelphia.
George Pooderbach.		Maryland.		Sept. 29th, 1768.	Philadelphia.
Catherine Toms.		York County.	Sept. 18th, 1768.	Nov. 18th, 1768.	York.
Nicholas Bittinger.		York County.	Sept. 4th, 1768.	Nov. 18th, 1768.	York.
George Swoab.		York County.	Sept. 4th, 1768.	Nov. 18th, 1768.	York.
Philip Christ.		York County.	Oct. 9th, 1768.	Nov. 18th, 1768.	York.
Daniel Amma.		York County.	Oct. 23rd, 1768.	Nov. 18th, 1768.	York.
Adam Kreemer.			Oct. 9th, 1768.	Nov. 18th, 1768.	York.
Peter Wolf.				Nov. 18th, 1768.	York.
	Jacob Lambert.			Nov. 18th, 1768.	York.
	Christian Ratfoun.				
	Adam Dick.				
	Nicholas Yoser.				
Henry Ruetlinger.		Bucks County.	Mar. 26th, 1769.	Apr. 10th, 1769.	Philadelphia.
John Philip Hazelbecher.		Berks County.	Apr. 7th, 1769.	Apr. 10th, 1769.	Philadelphia.
	Ann Mary Dorin.	Philadelphia.	Mar. 6th, 1769.	Apr. 10th, 1769.	Philadelphia.
George Dosch.		Lancaster Cnty.	Apr. 16th, 1769.	May 16th, 1769.	Lancaster.

Foreigners' Names. Jurors.	Affirmers	Places of Residence.	Sacrament, when taken	When Naturalized,	In what County Naturalized.
Jacob Wolf.	——	Lancaster Cnty.	Mar. 23rd, 1769.	May 16th, 1769.	Lancaster.
Peter Deihl.	——	Lancaster Cnty.	Mar. 23rd, 1769.	May 16th, 1769.	Lancaster.
Loidwick Lindenmuth.	——	Lancaster Cnty.	Mar. 23rd, 1769.	May 16th, 1769.	Lancaster.
Philip Brenner.	——	Lancaster Cnty.	Mar. 23rd, 1769.	May 16th, 1769.	Lancaster.
	Philip Grosh.	Lancaster Cnty.	Apr. 22nd, 1769.	May 16th, 1769.	Lancaster.
	Martin Meixell.	Lancaster Cnty.	——	May 16th, 1769.	Lancaster.
Michael Schneider.	——	Berks County.	Apr. 23rd, 1769.	May 30th, 1769.	Berks.
George Geret.	——	Berks County.	Mar. 26th, 1769.	May 30th, 1769.	Berks.
	Michael Hallem.	Cumberland.	——	May 22nd, 1769.	Cumberland.
Henry Bittinger.	——	Virginia.	May 15th, 1769.	May 20th, 1769.	York.
Michael Spaar.	——	York.	Apr. 2nd, 1769.	May 20th, 1769.	York.
	Henry Shadron.	York.	——	May 20th, 1769.	York.
	Christian Kare.	York.	——	May 20th, 1769.	York.

List certified by JOSEPH SHIPPEN, Jr., Secretary. Philadelphia, 13 Oct., 1772.

List [similar heading to foregoing] from 1 June 1769 to 1 June 1770.

Foreigners' Names. Jurors.	Affirmers	Places of Residence.	Sacrament, when taken	When Naturalized,	In what County Naturalized.
Michael Masser.		Bucks County.	Sept. 17th, 1769.	Sept. 25th, 1769.	Philadelphia.
John Phister.		Bucks County.	Aug. 13th, 1769.	Sept. 25th, 1769.	Philadelphia.
	Jacob Kieber.	Philadelphia Cnty.	——	Sept. 25th, 1769.	Philadelphia.
	John Koke.	Berks County.	——	Sept. 25th, 1769.	Philadelphia.
	Ludwick Nichola.	Philadelphia Cnty.	Oct. 15th, 1769.	Nov. 18th, 1769.	Berks.
Ludwick Lehman.		Berks County.	——	Nov. 18th, 1769.	Berks.
Peter Kochler.		Lancaster Cnty.	Nov. 1st, 1769.	Nov. 22nd, 1769.	Lancaster.
	John Stouffer.	Lancaster Cnty.	——	Nov. 21st, 1769.	Lancaster.
	John Rohrer.	Lancaster Cnty.	——	Nov. 21st, 1769.	Lancaster.
Tobias Heyer, Senior.		York County.	Oct. 19th, 1769.	Nov. 24th 1769.	York.
Matthias Hartman.		York County.	Sept. 3rd, 1769.	Nov. 24th 1769.	York.
	John Hagner.	York County.	——	Nov. 24th 1769.	York.
Andrew Dihm.		Berks County.	Apr. 10th, 1770.	Apr. 10th, 1770.	Philadelphia.
Zacharias Haller.		Northampton Cnty.	——	Apr. 10th, 1770.	Philadelphia.
Henry Leimbacker.		Bucks County.	——	Apr. 10th, 1770.	Philadelphia.
John Ludwig.		Lancaster Cnty.	Apr. 29th, 1770.	May 17th, 1770.	Lancaster.
Lawrence Shook.		Maryland.	——	May 25th, 1770.	Lancaster.
Conrod Stuck.		York County.	Apr. 29th, 1770.	May 21st, 1770.	York.
Adam Syfert.		York County.	May 13th, 1770.	May 21st, 1770.	York.
Conrod Witham.		York County.	Apr. 12th, 1770.	May 21st, 1770.	York.
	Matthias Detter.	York County.	——	May 21st, 1770.	York.
	Johannes Ermel.	York County.	——	May 21st, 1770.	York.

List certified by JOSEPH SHIPPEN, Jr., Secretary. Philadelphia, 13 Oct., 1772.

PENNSYLVANIA.

List [similar heading to foregoing] from 1 June 1770 to 1 June 1771.

Jurors.	Foreigners' Names.	Affirmers.	Names of Residence.	Sacrament when taken.	When Naturalized.	In what County Naturalized.
	WILLIAM CLAVER.		Philadelphia.	Mar. 31st, 1771.	Apr. 11th, 1771.	Philadelphia.
	PHILIPPINA WAGGONER.		Philadelphia.	Mar. 31st, 1771.	Apr. 11th, 1771.	Philadelphia.
	PETER LOBER.		Berks County.	Apr. 7th, 1771.	Apr. 11th, 1771.	Philadelphia.
	JOHN FRITZ.		Philadelphia Cnty.	Apr. 10th, 1771.	Apr. 11th, 1771.	Philadelphia.
	LEWIS STANNERT.		Philadelphia Cnty.	Apr. 7th, 1771.	Apr. 11th, 1771.	Philadelphia.
	CHARLES LEOPOLD.		Philadelphia Cnty.	Apr. 10th, 1771.	Apr. 11th, 1771.	Philadelphia.
	ANDREAS MAURER.		City of Philadelphia.	Mar. 31st, 1771.	Apr. 11th, 1771.	Philadelphia.
	LEWIS FARMER.		Northampton Cnty.	Mar. 31st, 1771.	Apr. 11th, 1771.	Philadelphia.
	JOHN HOPFF.	CATHARINE IKKEN.	Berks County.	May 7th, 1771.	May 17th, 1771.	Berks.
		ANDREAS YOST.	Berks County.		May 20th, 1771.	Berks.
	NICHOLAS LONG.		Lancaster Cnty.	May 19th, 1771.	May 24th, 1771.	Lancaster.
	JACOB BRUCKER.		Lancaster Cnty.	Mar. 31st, 1771.	May 24th, 1771.	Lancaster.
	MAURICE DUPPEL.		Lancaster Cnty.	May 21st, 1771.	May 24th, 1771.	Lancaster.
	FREDERICK HOUSMAN.	PETER SHOEMAKER.	York County.	May 19th, 1771.	May 30th, 1771.	York.
	MICHAEL HEMICKER.		York County.	May 19th, 1771.	May 30th, 1771.	York.
	JACOB PROBST.		York County.	Apr. 31 [sic] 1771.	May 30th, 1771.	York.
		GEORGE YERKARDT.	Maryland.		May 30th, 1771.	York.
		PETER NAFFREGER.	Maryland.		May 30th, 1771.	York.
		JOHN GEORGE STORM.	Maryland.		May 30th, 1771.	York.
	JACOB HEISLER.		Philadelphia.	Sept. 2nd, 1770.	Sept. 24th, 1770.	Philadelphia.
	GEORGE BARGE.		Philadelphia.	Sept. 24th, 1770.	Sept. 24th, 1770.	Philadelphia.
	JACOB MILLER.		New Jersey.	Sept. 24th, 1770.	Sept. 24th, 1770.	Philadelphia.
	LEVY MARKS.		City of Philadephia.	a Jew.	Sept. 24th, 1770.	Philadelphia.
	JOHN CONRAD GRAGG.		New Castle.	Sept. 1st, 1770.	Sept. 24th, 1770.	Philadelphia.
		WELDER DANTFELTZER.	Chester County.		Sept. 24th, 1770.	Philadelphia.
		PETER WENGER.	Chester County.		Sept. 24th, 1770.	Philadelphia.
		JOHN MINGLE.	New Jersey.		Sept. 24th, 1770.	Philadelphia.
		PETER KING.	Philadelphia Cnty.		Sept. 24th, 1770.	Philadelphia.
		JACOB DIEMER.	Lancaster Cnty.		Sept. 24th, 1770.	Philadelphia.
		JACOB FRITCH.	Bucks County.		Sept. 24th, 1770.	Philadelphia.
		GEORGE GRAUSS.	Chester County.		Sept. 24th, 1770.	Philadelphia.
	ANDREAS KACHEL.		Berks County.	Sept. 30th, 1770.	Nov. 19th, 1770.	Berks.
	JACOB HOLLINGER.		Lancaster Cnty.	Nov. 18th, 1770.	Nov. 21st, 1770.	Lancaster.
	MICHAEL KREHL.		Lancaster Cnty.	Oct. 14th, 1770.	Nov. 21st, 1770.	Lancaster.

Jurors. / Foreigners' Names. / Affirmers.	Places of Residence.	Sacrament, when taken.	When Naturalized.	In what County Naturalized.
ARNOLD SHERVITZ.	Lancaster Cnty.	Oct. 14th, 1770.	Nov. 21st, 1770.	Lancaster.
HENRY SCHMIDT.	Lancaster Cnty.	Nov. 18th, 1770.	Nov. 21st, 1770.	Lancaster.
SIMON SCHNEIDER.	Lancaster Cnty.		Nov. 21st, 1770.	Lancaster.

List certified by JOSEPH SHIPPEN, Jr., Secretary. Philadelphia, 13 Oct., 1772.

List [similar heading to foregoing] from 1 June 1771 to 1 June 1772.

Jurors. / Foreigners' Names. / Affirmers.	Places of Residence.	Sacrament, when taken.	When Naturalized.	In what County Naturalized.
NICHOLAS CARL.	Philadelphia Cnty.	Aug. 25th, 1771.	Sept. 24th, 1771.	Philadelphia.
CHRISTOPHER RICK.	Chester County.		Sept. 24th, 1771.	Philadelphia.
FREDERICK FREES.	Virginia.		Sept. 24th, 1771.	Philadelphia.
ADAM BEHM.	Berks County.	Oct. 13th, 1771.	Nov. 16th, 1771.	Berks.
PETER BUYFOGEL.	Berks County.		Nov. 16th, 1771.	Berks.
JACOB DECKER.	Boro' of Lancaster.	Sept. 1st, 1771.	Nov. 23rd, 1771.	Lancaster.
CHRISTIAN ILGNER.	Boro' of Lancaster.	Oct. 13th, 1771.	Nov. 23rd, 1771.	Lancaster.
WILLIAM SMITH.	City of Philadelphia.	Apr. 5th, 1772.	Apr. 10th, 1772.	Philadelphia.
JOHN WEBER.	Philadelphia Cnty.	Apr. 3rd, 1772.	Apr. 10th, 1772.	Philadelphia.
GEORGE RENNER.	Philadelphia Cnty.	Apr. 3rd, 1772.	Apr. 10th, 1772.	Ph. adelphia.
JOHN PETER EMRICK.	Philadelphia Cnty.	Mar. 30th, 1772.	Apr. 10th, 1772.	Philadelphia.
GODFREY RHEINHARD.	New Jersey.	Apr. 10th, 1772.	Apr. 10th, 1772.	Philadelphia.
GERARD HULSEKAMP.	City of Philadelphia.	Apr. 19th, 1772.	Apr. 10th, 1772.	Philadelphia.
JOHN SCHOTT.	Philadelphia Cnty.		Apr. 10th, 1772.	Philadelphia.
JOHN ERDMAN DONTG.	Maryland.		Apr. 10th, 1772.	Philadelphia.
HENRY SCHRAFFLER.	Berks County.	Apr. 19th, 1772.	May 18th, 1772.	Berks.
NICHOLAS KELLER.	Berks County.	Apr. 19th, 1772.	May 18th, 1772.	Berks.
ADAM CALBACK.	Berks County.	Apr. 19th, 1772.	May 20th, 1772.	Berks.
PHILIP FISHBOURN.	Maryland.	May 29th, 1772.	May 30th, 1772.	York.
MICHAEL HUBER.	Maryland.	May 29th, 1772.	May 30th, 1772.	York.
CHRISTOPHER MILLER.	Maryland.	May 30th, 1772.	May 30th, 1772.	York.
CHRISTIAN BOWER.	Maryland.		May 29th, 1772.	York.
JOHN HENRY DAVID.	Maryland.		May 29th, 1772.	York.
PHILIP HOMBOGH.	Maryland.		May 29th, 1772.	York.
MICHAEL BEALER.	York County.		May 29th, 1772.	York.
NICHOLAS FORNEY.	York County.		May 29th, 1772.	York.
MATTHIAS HEHR.	York County.		May 29th, 1772.	York.
HENRY WORMAN.	Maryland.		May 30th, 1772.	York.

List certified by JOSEPH SHIPPEN, Jr., Secretary. Philadelphia, 13 Oct., 1772.

Index

Index of Persons.

1

m

Index of Places.

Index of Subjects.

www.ingramcontent.com/pod-product-compliance
Lightning Source LLC
Chambersburg PA
CBHW020458030426
42337CB00011B/146